Childr

ILLUSTRATE

THESAURUS

Children's ILLUSTRATED THESAURUS

ARMADILLO

This edition published in 2007

ISBN 978-1-84322-464-8

3 5 7 9 10 8 6 4 2

Paperback edition first published in 2005 by
Armadillo Books
An imprint of Bookmart Ltd
Registered Number 2372865
Blaby Road, Wigston,
Leicestershire, LE18 4SE
United Kingdom

Production by Omnipress, Eastbourne

Printed in Thailand

YOUR THESAURUS AND HOW TO USE IT

FINDING A WORD

Entries are listed in alphabetical order. Make a guess at the first few letters of your word, for example, for 'satellite' find 'sat', then try different ways of spelling the next part.

LOOKING AT PAGES

Guide words help you to find the right page.

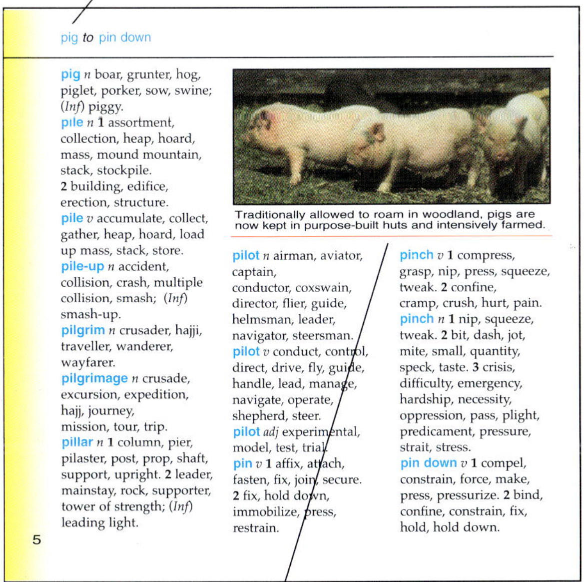
pig *to* pin down

pig *n* boar, grunter, hog, piglet, porker, sow, swine; (*Inf*) piggy.
pile *n* **1** assortment, collection, heap, hoard, mass, mound mountain, stack, stockpile. **2** building, edifice, erection, structure.
pile *v* accumulate, collect, gather, heap, hoard, load up mass, stack, store.
pile-up *n* accident, collision, crash, multiple collision, smash; (*Inf*) smash-up.
pilgrim *n* crusader, hajji, traveller, wanderer, wayfarer.
pilgrimage *n* crusade, excursion, expedition, hajj, journey, mission, tour, trip.
pillar *n* **1** column, pier, pilaster, post, prop, shaft, support, upright. **2** leader, mainstay, rock, supporter, tower of strength; (*Inf*) leading light.

Traditionally allowed to roam in woodland, pigs are now kept in purpose-built huts and intensively farmed.

pilot *n* airman, aviator, captain, conductor, coxswain, director, flier, guide, helmsman, leader, navigator, steersman.
pilot *v* conduct, control, direct, drive, fly, guide, handle, lead, manage, navigate, operate, shepherd, steer.
pilot *adj* experimental, model, test, trial.
pin *v* **1** affix, attach, fasten, fix, join, secure. **2** fix, hold down, immobilize, press, restrain.
pinch *v* **1** compress, grasp, nip, press, squeeze, tweak. **2** confine, cramp, crush, hurt, pain.
pinch *n* **1** nip, squeeze, tweak. **2** bit, dash, jot, mite, small, quantity, speck, taste. **3** crisis, difficulty, emergency, hardship, necessity, oppression, pass, plight, predicament, pressure, strait, stress.
pin down *v* **1** compel, constrain, force, make, press, pressurize. **2** bind, confine, constrain, fix, hold, hold down.

5

Illustrations with captions for certain words.

LOOKING AT ENTRIES

Headwords show how a word is spelt.

Parts of speech identify what a word does in a sentence (see p.6).

pan *v* **1** censure, criticize, knock, roast; (*Inf*) knock, rubbish, slag off, slam, slate. **2** search for, sift for. **3** follow, scan, sweep, track.

Informal words are used in everyday speech, but not in formal or official writing.

Numbers indicate a separate sense of the word.

Definitions explain what a word means and **related words** introduce words from the same family.

THE PARTS THAT WORDS PLAY IN SPEECH

Each word plays a different part in a sentence, depending on its part of speech. If you know a word's part of speech, you can work out how to use it.

noun (*n*) Nouns give the name of a person, animal or thing. They tell you who or what a sentence is about.

Jack is jumping.
Training is essential.

pronoun (*pronoun*) Pronouns refer to a person or thing without naming it. They act like nouns.

(John is very good at judo.)
He is very good at judo.

adjective (*adj*) Adjectives are descriptive words which tell you more about a person or thing. They are used with nouns and pronouns.

This round bowl is very colourful

verb (*v*) Verbs are action words. They say what someone or something does, thinks, or feels. All sentences need verbs to tell you what is happening.

Alan loves his motorbike, it goes really fast.

adverb (*adv*) Adverbs tell you how, when, where or why something happens. They are used with verbs.

Sue is skiing wildly, she may soon fall over.

conjunction (*conj*) Conjunctions are linking words. They join parts of sentences.

Penguins have wings, but cannot fly.

preposition (*prep*) Prepositions show where people or things are, or what relation they have to each other.

Amy is jumping over the skipping rope.

interjection (*interject*) Interjections are used to show surprise, delight or pain, or to get attention. They are sometimes known as exclamations and often have an exclamation mark.

"Wow!" cried the crowd as the basketball player put the ball in the net.

Aa

abandon *v* **1** desert, leave behind, quit. **2** depart from, evacuate, vacate. **3** abdicate, resign, surrender. **4** forfeit, forgo, give up, relinquish, resign, surrender.
abbey *n* cloister, convent, friary, monastery, nunnery, priory.
abdicate *v* abandon, give up, quit, relinquish, renounce, retire, surrender, vacate.
abduct *v* hold to ransom, kidnap, run away with, seize, snatch.

Westminster Abbey is one of the most famous abbeys in the world and the venue for many royal weddings.

abhorrent *adj* disgusting, horrible, obnoxious, offensive, repulsive, revolting.
abide *v* accept, bear, endure, put up with, suffer, tolerate.
ability *n* **1** aptitude, cleverness, ingenuity, knack, know-how, skill, talent. **2** competency, qualification. **3** calibre, faculty.
ablaze *adj* alight, blazing, burning, fiery, lit up, raging.
able *adj* accomplished, competent, expert, proficient, qualified, skilled, talented.
abnormal *adj* bizarre, eccentric, erratic, odd, peculiar, strange, unusual, weird.
abolish *v* axe, cancel, end, quash, revoke, stamp out, stop, terminate, wipe out.
abomination *n* aversion, disgust, hatred, horror, loathing, revulsion.
abortive *adj* futile, fruitless, incomplete, unsuccessful, useless, vain, worthless.
abound *v* be alive with, be full of, crowd, flourish, increase, overflow, swarm, swell, teem, thrive.
about *prep* **1** around, encircling, surrounding. **2** concerning, near, regarding. **3** all over, over, through.
about-turn *n* change of direction, reversal, U-turn.
aboveboard *adj* candid, frank, honest, open, straightforward, truthful, upright.
abrasive *adj* caustic, cutting, harsh, hurtful, irritating, nasty, rough, sharp, unpleasant.
abrasive *n* emery, glass paper, sandpaper.
abridge *v* abbreviate, condense, cut, lessen, précis, reduce, shorten, summarize.
abridgement *n* abbreviation, condensation, digest, summary, synopsis.
abrupt *adj* **1** hasty, hurried, quick, rapid, sudden, swift, unexpected. **2** sharp, sheer, steep. **3** blunt, direct, impolite, rude, short, terse, uncivil. **4** brisk, disconnected, jerky, snappy, terse.
absent *adj* **1** missing, playing truant. **2** blank, day-dreaming, dreamy, far-away, inattentive, oblivious, unaware, vacant, vague.
absent-minded *adj* careless, forgetful, heedless, scatter-brained, thoughtless, vague.
absolute *adj* **1** certain, complete, definite, entire, full, genuine, perfect, pure, sheer, total. **2** dictatorial, tyrannical. **3** exact, precise.
absolve *v* acquit, clear, exempt, excuse, forgive, free, liberate, let off, pardon, reprieve, set free, vindicate.
absorb *v* **1** consume, devour, digest, hold, retain, soak up, take in. **2** cushion, deaden, reduce, soften. **3** engage, engross, fascinate, involve, occupy.
absorbent *adj* porous, spongy.
absorbing *adj* captivating, gripping, intriguing, rivetting, spellbinding.
abstain *v* avoid, cease, decline, deny yourself, give up, go without, refrain, refuse, stop, withhold.

A sprinter accelerates from zero velocity by pushing against the blocks. This propels her forward and she will continue to accelerate for several more metres.

abundant *adj* ample, flourishing, full, generous, great, huge, overflowing, plentiful, profuse, rich, teeming.
abuse *v* **1** betray, deceive, dishonour, misuse, pervert, violate. **2** harm, hurt, ill-treat, injure. **3** curse, malign, swear, slander.
abuse *n* **1** dishonour, ill-use, mis-use. **2** cruelty, exploitation, ill-treatment, maltreatment. **3** defamation, disparagement, insult, rudeness, vilification.
academic *adj* collegiate, educational, instructional, lettered, scholastic.
academic *n* academician, classicist, doctor, don, fellow, pundit, scholar, student, teacher, thinker, tutor.
acceleration *n* advancement, expedition, forwarding, hastening, quickening, stepping up, stimulation.
accent *n* **1** acute, cedilla, circumflex, diacritic, grave, mark, sign, tilde, umlaut. **2** beat, emphasis, force, pitch, rhythm. stress. **3** enunciation, pronunciation, tone. **4** accentuate, emphasize, stress, underline, underscore.
accentuate *v* **1** accent, emphasize, mark, point up, punctuate, stress. **2** highlight, underline, underscore.
accept *v* **1** receive, take, welcome. **2** admit, assume, bear, undetake. **3** agree to, approve, believe in, consent to, take in, tolerate.
acceptable *adj* **1** agreeable, worthwhile. **2** adequate, appropriate, satisfactory, suitable, tolerable.
acceptance *n* agreement, approval, consent, willingness.
accepted *adj* agreed, approved, recognized, standard.
accessible *adj* **1** achievable, at hand, attainable, handy. **2** approachable, available, friendly, informal. **3** exposed, liable, open, subject, susceptible, vulnerable, wide open.
accessory *n* addition, attachment, extension, extra, fitting.
accident *n* **1** catastrophe, collision, crash, disaster, mishap, wreck. **2** chance, coincidence, fortune, luck.
accidental *adj* casual, chance, fortunate, lucky, random, unforeseen, unintended, unintended.
acclimatize *v* accustom, adapt, adjust, condition, familiarize, habituate, season.
accommodate *v* **1** contain, furnish, hold, oblige, serve, supply. **2** adapt, fit, suit. **3** adjust, compose, harmonize, reconcile, settle.
accomplice *n* accessory, ally, assistant, associate, collaborator, colleague, helper, mate, right-handman, sidekick, partner.

accomplished *adj* able, adept, cultivated, expert, gifted, skillful, skilled, talented.
account *n* **1** description, detail, explanation, history, narrative, portrayal, recital, record, report, statement, story, tale, version. **2** balance, balance sheets, bill, book, books, charge, computation, inventory, invoice, ledger, reckoning, register, score, statement, tally. **3** basis, cause, consideration, grounds, interest, motive, reason, score.
account *v* assess, calculate, compute, estimate, explain, judge, think, value, weigh.
accustom *v* acclimatize, acquaint, adapt, discipline, exercise, familiarize, season, train.
ache *n* discomfort, hurt, pain, soreness, throb, twinge.
acid *adj* **1** acrid, biting, bitter, pungent, sharp, sour, tangy, tart, vinegary. **2** caustic, cutting, sarcastic, sharp.
acidity *n* bitterness, sharpness, sourness, tartness.
acknowledgement *n* **1** acceptance, admission, confession, declaration, realization, yielding. **2** answer, appreciation, credit, gratitude, reaction, recognition, reply, response, return, thanks.
acquire *v* buy, collect, earn, gain, obtain, pick up, receive, secure, win.
act *n* **1** action, deed, exploit, move, operation, performance, step. **2** bill, decree, law, ruling, statute. **3** performance, routine, show, sketch, turn.
act *v* **1** behave, conduct yourself, seem to be. **2** function, have effect, operate, serve, take effect, work. **3** mime, perform, play, portray, represent.
act for *v* cover for, fill in for, replace, represent.
actor, actress *n* artist, artiste, leading man, leading lady, performer, play-actor, player, star, starlet, supporting actor.
acute *adj* **1** astute, clever, discerning, discriminating, incisive, ingenious, insightful, penetrating, perceptive, quick, sensitive, sharp, smart, subtle. **2** peaked, pointed, sharp, sharpened. **3** discerning, keen.
adapt *v* accommodate, adjust, alter, apply, change, comply, conform, familiarize, fashion, fit, habituate, harmonize, make, match; modify, prepare, qualify, remodel, shape, suit, tailor.
adaptation *n* adjustment, alteration, change, conversion, modification, refitting, remodelling, reworking, shift, transformation, variation, version.
addict *n* **1** abuser, junkie, user. **2** enthusiast, fan, follower.
addicted *adj* **1** absorbed, accustomed, dedicated,

The juice of citrus fruits, such as lemons and oranges, contains a weak acid called citric acid.

dependent, devoted, fond, obsessed, prone. **2** hooked.
adhere *v* attach, bind, bond, cement, cleave, cling, cohere, fasten, fix, glue, hold, fast, paste, stick, unite.
adhesive *adj* attaching, clinging, gluey, gummy, holding, sticking, sticky, tacky.
adhesive *n* glue, gum, paste.
adjudicate *v* arbitrate, decide, determine, give a ruling, judge, referee, settle, umpire.
adjustment *n* adaptation, alteration, fitting, fixing, modification, ordering, redress, remodelling, setting, tuning.
ad-lib *v* improvise, make up, speak off the cuff.
admit *v* **1** accept, let in, receive, take in. **2** acknowledge, confess, declare, profess, reveal. **3** agree, allow, grant, let, permit.
adolescent *adj* boyish, girlish, growing, immature, juvenile, teenage, young, youthful.
adolescent *n* juvenile, minor, teenager, youngster, youth.
adoption *n* **1** acceptance, choice, following, maintenance, support, taking on, taking over, taking up. **2** adopting, fostering, taking in.
advantageous *adj* **1** favourable, superior. **2** beneficial, convenient, helpful, of service, profitable, useful, valuable, worthwhile.
advertisement *n* advert, announcement, classified, commercial, poster, promotion.
adversity *n* bad luck, catastrophe, disaster, trouble.
advise *v* caution, counsel, recommend, suggest, urge.
aerodrome *n* airfield, airport, airstrip, landing-strip.
affair *n* **1** business, concern, subject, topic. **2** episode, event, incident, occasion. **3** love affair, relationship, romance.
affect *v* **1** act on, change, modify, transform. **2** assume, imitate, pretend, simulate.
affiliate *v* associate with, combine with, incorporate into, join with, unite with.
affirm *v* confirm, declare, pronounce, state, swear, testify.
afloat *adj* adrift, at sea, floating, on board ship.
afraid *adj* **1** alarmed, anxious, fearful, frightened, intimidated, nervous, scared. **2** regretful, sorry, unhappy. **3** dread, fear, tremble, quake.
alight *adj* burning, ignited, on fire.
alight *v* **1** descend, get down, get off. **2** land, perch, settler.
allotment *n* **1** amount, portion. **2** small piece of rented land for

Air travel has exploded in recent times which has meant that most cities and large towns now have their own airport or aerodrome.

cultivation, often of fruit and vegatables.
alone *adj* abandoned, apart, by itself, by oneself, deserted, desolate, detached, forlorn, forsaken, isolated, lonely, lonesome, only, separate, single, single-handed, sole, solitary, unaccompanied, unaided, unassisted, unattended, uncombined, unconnected, unescorted.
aloof *adj* chilly, cold, cool, indifferent, remote, unfriendly.
amalgamate *v* combine, fuse, join together, merge.
amaze *v* astonish, bewilder, confuse.
ambush *v* attack, surprise, trap.
amplify *v* **1** develop, enlarge, expand, fill out. **2** boost, increase, make louder, magnify.
analogy *n* comparison, likeness, resemblance, similarity.
analyze *v* examine, interpret, investigate, study.
anarchy *n* chaos, disorder, mutiny, riot.
ancestry *n* descent, family, genealogy, parentage, pedigree, roots, stock.
anchorage *n* harbour, marina, moorings, port, shelter.
angle *n* **1** bend, corner. **2** approach, point of view, position, viewpoint.
anguish *n* anxiety, distress, misery, pain, torment, torture.
animated *n* **1** cartoon. **2** alive, bright. excited, lively, vibrant.
animosity *n* bad blood, dislike, hatred, malice, resentment.

Antique engraved glass vases from the end of the nineteenth century.

annihilate *v* abolish, destroy, exterminate, slaughter, wipe out.
announce *v* **1** advertise, broadcast, declare, proclaim, publish, reveal. **2** introduce, present.
announcer *n* broadcaster, commentator, newscaster, reporter, town crier.
annoy *v* bother, irritate, try, upset, worry.
anonymous *adj* **1** incognito, nameless, unkown. **2** unsigned. **3** charcterless, nondescript.
answer *n* **1** reply, response. **2** explanation, outcome, solution. **3** countercharge, defence, plea.
antagonize *v* anger, annoy, irritate, offend, provoke, upset.
anthology *n* collection, compilation, digest, selection, treasury.
anticlimax *n* disappointment, let-down.
antidote *n* antitoxin, cure, remedy.
antiquarian *n* collector, dealer.
antique *n* curio, curiosity.
antique *adj* ancient, historic, veteran, vintage.
antiseptic *adj* clean, disinfected, germ-free, hygenic, sterile.
antisocial *adj* disorderly, nasty, offensive, rebellious, rude, unruly, unsociable.
anxiety *n* concern, distress, fear, stress, tension, worry.
anxious *adj* afraid, agitated, distressed, jittery, nervous, tense,

Saliva begins to flow when we see or even think about food. Making food look appetizing is a first step toward good digestion.

troubled, upset, worried.
apathetic *adj* cool, emotionless, unconcerned, unfeeling.
apex *n* crest, crown, peak, pinnacle, point, summit, top.
apiary *n* bee hive, hive.
apostle *n* crusader, missionary, preacher, teacher.
appal *v* alarm, disgust, horrify, outrage, shock, sicken, terrify.
apparatus *n* contraption, device, equipment, gadget, machine, tool.
apparent *adj clear*, evident, noticeable, visible.
apparition *n* ghost, illusion, presence, spirit.
appease *v* calm, pacify, quiet, soothe, win over.
appendix *n* addendum, addition, supplement.
appetite *n* desire, greed, longing, taste, thirst, wish, yearning.
appetizing *adj* delicious, tasty, tempting.
applaud *v* cheer, clap, congratulate, praise.
apply *v* **1** lay on, spread. **2** refer, relate. **3** employ, implement, use. **4** ask for, request.
appoint *v* **1** arrange, decide on, fix, settle. **2** choose, elect, name, select, vote for.
appointment *n* **1** arrangement, date, engagement, interview, meeting. **2** choice, election, selection. **3** job, place, position, post, situation.
appreciate *v* **1** admire, approve, enjoy, like, prize, value. **2** know, realize, understand. **3** gain, grow, increase, mount, rise, soar.
apprentice *n* beginner, learner, novice, pupil, trainee.
approach *n* **1** advance, arrival, nearing. **2** access, doorway, entrance, road, way in. **3** attitude, manner, method, style, technique, way. **4** appeal, application, invitation, offer, proposal.
appropriate *adj* apt, correct, deserved, fitting, proper, relevant, suitable, well-suited.
appropriate *v* confiscate, hijack, seize, steal, take over.
approve *v* **1** accept, agree to, bless, endorse, sanction, support. **2** admire, like, love, respect, value, welcome.
approximate *adj* close, estimated, near, rough.
approximately *adv* about, circa, just about, nearly, roughly.
arbitrary *adj* casual, random, unplanned.
arbitrate *v* judge, mediate, negotiate, referee, settle, umpire.
arbitrator *n* go-between, intermediary, judge, middleman, referee, troubleshooter, umpire.

An arch bridge uses the strength of an arch to support itself, although the roadway itself is usually straight.

arch *n* arc, archway, bridge.
archetype *n* example, model, original, pattern, prototype, standard.
archives *n* documents, history, libraries, museums, papers.
archivist *n* curator, historian, researcher.
arduous *adj* backbreaking, demanding, difficult, hard, harsh, severe, tough, uphill.
area *n* **1** extent, patch, sector, space, surface, width. **2** district, locality, neighbourhood, region, sector, territory, vicinity, zone. **3** field, subject.
arena *v* amphitheatre, field, ground, park, pitch, playing area, ring, rink, stadium.
argue *v* **1** bicker, differ, disagree, dispute, fall out, feud, fight, object, protest, quarrel, squabble, wrangle. **2** bargain, haggle. **3** claim, demonstrate, maintain, prove, reason, suggest. **4** debate, deliberate, discuss.
argument *n* clash, difference, dispute, feud, fight, quarrel, row, squabble, wrangle.
arid *adj* barren, dry, lifeless, parched.
arise *v* **1** appear, begin, come up, crop up emerge, happen, occur. **2** be caused by, be the result of, come out of, follow, result, stem from. **3** get out of bed, get to your feet, get up, stand up.
aristocrat *n* elite, lady, lord, noble, peer, priviledged, titled person, upper-class, well-born.
aristocratic *adj* courtly, lordly, princely, royal, thoroughbred, titled, upper-class.
arm *n* branch, extension, limb, offshoot, upper limb.
arm *v* equip, provide, supply.

Plants like cacti store water in their fleshy stems to survive in times of little rain in the arid conditions of deserts.

armada *n* convoy, fleet, flotilla, navy, squadron, task-force.
armistice *n* agreement, cease-fire, moratorium, peace, treaty, truce, understanding.
armoury *n* arsenal, depot, magazine, ordnance depot, stockpile.
aroma *n* bouquet, fragrance, odour, perfume, scent, smell.
arrange *v* **1** adjust, align, classify, collate, display, distribute, group, line-up, order, organize, sort. **2** coordinate, devise, fix manage, plan, prepare, settle, set up. **3** adapt, harmonize, orchestrate, score.
arrangement *n* alignment, design, display, grouping, layout, setting out, spacing.
array *n* arrangement, display, formation, muster, parade, show, spectacle.
array *v* attire, deck, dress, equip, rig out, robe.
arrears *n* backlog, overdue payment.

arrest *v* **1** block, check, delay, halt, impede, obstruct, stem, stop. **2** apprehend, capture, catch, detain, seize, take into custody, take prisoner.
arrival *n* **1** appearance, entrance, homecoming, landing, return, touchdown. **2** caller, newcomer, visitor.
arrive *v* **1** appear, disembark, enter, land, touch down, turn up. **2** get to the top, make good, succeed.
arrogant *adj* boastful, cocky, conceited, high and mighty, insolent, pompous, proud, scornful, superior, vain.
arsonist *n* fire-raiser, pyromaniac.
artful *adj* astute, clever, cunning, devious, ingenious, shrewd, skilful, smart, wily.
articulate *adj* clear, distinct, expressive, fluent, lucid, understandable, vocal.
articulated *adj* banding, flexible, hinged, jointed.
artificial *adj* assumed, bogus, counterfeit, fake, false, imitation, pseudo, sham, simulated, spurious, unreal.
artist *n* craftsman, craftswomen, designer.
artistic *adj* attractive, beautiful, creative, decorative, imaginative, ornamental, tasteful.
ascend *v* **1** climb, come up, go up, mount, move up, scale. **2** fly up, lift off, rise, soar, take off. **3** slope up.
ascent *n* climb, elevation, gradient, hill, incline, rise, slope.
ascertain *v* confirm, determine, discover, establish, find out, learn, settle, verify.
ascetic *adj* austere, frugal, harsh, plain, puritanical, rigorous, spartan, strict.
ash *n* burnt remains, cinders, embers.

The combination of physical effort, sense of achievement and staggering views from an improved elevation has meant that people have enjoyed the ascent of mountains since time began.

ashamed *adj* **1** aplogetic, distressed, guilty, humiliated, remorseful, sorry, upset. **2** bashful, embarrassed, modest, self-conscious, sheepish, shy.
ask *v* **1** appeal, badger, beg, crave, demand, enquire, inquire, plead, pose a question, request, seek. **2** bid, invite.
asleep *adj* dormant, hibernating, resting, sedated, sleeping, snoozing, unconscious.
aspect *n* **1** angle, detail, feature, side. **2** air, appearance, expression, look, manner. **3** direction, outlook, position, situation, view.
asperity *n* bitterness, crossness, harshness, hostility, irritability, roughness, severity, sourness, venom.
aspire *v* aim for, crave, dream of, long for, want, wish for.
aspiring *adj* intending, potential, would-be.
assail *v* bombard, pelt, set on.
assemble *v* **1** collect, come together, converge, gather, group, herd, rally round, swarm. **2** bring together, get together, marshal, muster, round up. **3** build, construct, erect, fabricate, manufacture, produce, put together.
assembly *n* conclave, congregation, convention, council, gathering, parliament, rally, synod.
assent *n* acceptance, agreement, approval, consent, permission, willingness.
assent *v* accept, agree, comply, concede, submit.
assert *v* allege, argue, claim, declare, insist, protest, state. swear, testify.
assertive *adj* aggressive, bold,

confident, decided, firm, forceful, pushy, strong, stubborn.
assess *v* calculate, consider, estimate, evaluate, judge, reckon, value, weigh up, work out.
asset *n* advantage, aid, benefit, help, support.
assign *v* **1** allocate, apportion, consign, distribute, hand over, share out. **2** appoint, choose, delegate, nominate, select, specify, stipulate. **3** accredit, ascribe, attribute, credit.
assignment *n* duty, errand, job, mission, post, project, responsibility, task, work.
assist *v* aid, back, collaborate, co-operate, further, rally round, relieve, serve, support.
assistant *n* accomplice, aide, ally, associate, colleague, deputy, helper, partner, second-in-command, supporter.
assortment *n* array, collection, mixture, selection, variety.
assumption *n* belief, expectation, guess, theory.
astonish *v* amaze, baffle, confound, flabbergast, startle, stun, surprise.
astute *adj* canny, clever, craft, cunning, ingenious, intelligent, sharp, shrewd, sly, subtle, wily.
asymmetrical *adj* crooked, distorted, irregular, uneven.
athletic *adj* active, energetic, fit, powerful, strong, sturdy.
atmosphere *n* **1** air, heavens, sky, stratosphere. **2** character, feeling, mood, spirit, tone, vibes.
atom *n* bit, crumb, grain, molecule, particle, spot, trace.
atone *v* compensate for, make up for, pay for, pay the price for.
atrocious *adj* barbaric, brutal, cruel, grim, hideous, savage, terrible, vicious, vile, wicked.

The Earth's atmosphere has layers of cooler and warmer air. In the diagram above, warm air is shown as pale blue, becoming darker as it gets colder.

atrophy *v* decay, decline, diminish, dwindle, fade, shrink, shrivel, wither.
attach *v* ad, affix, anchor, combine, connect, couple, fix, join, link, secure, stick, unite, weld.
attack *n* **1** ambush, assault, charge, counter-attack, invasion, offensive, raid, strike. **2** abuse, censure, critisism, tirade. **3** bout, convulsion, seizure, spasm, stroke.
attack *v* **1** ambush, bombard, invade, jump on, lash out at, pounce on, rush, storm, strike at, wade into. **2** abuse, libel, slander, snipe at.
attain *v* accomplish, achieve, acquire, complete, earn, fulfil, grasp, procure, reach, realize, secure, touch, win.
attend *v* **1** concentrate on, follow carefully, listen, notice, observe, pay attention, watch. **2** bicker, consideration, concern, recognition, thought, vigilance.
attic *n* loft, roof-space.
attire *v* apparel, clothes, costume, dress, garments, outfit.
attitude *n* **1** approach, behaviour, manner, mood. **2** belief, feeling, opinion, outlook, position, standpoint, thought, view.
attract *v* appeal to, captivate, charm, fascinate, interest, tempt.
attribute *v* assign, blame, credit, trace back.

attrition *n* erosion, friction, grinding down, wearing away, wearing down.
audible *adj* distinct, high, loud, noisy.
auditorium *n* assembly room, concert-hall, theatre.
augment *v* add to, boost, enlarge, expand, grow, increase, magnify, multiply, raise, swell.
augure *v* forewarn, predict, promise, signal.
austere *adj* **1** cold, hard, severe, stern, strict. **2** economical, frugal, spartan, thrifty. **3** modest, plain, simple, unfussy.
authentic *adj* **1** actual, bona fide, certain, genuine, original, real, true, valid. **2** accurate, factual, honest. reliable, truthful.
author *n* **1** composer, creator, novelist, playwright, poet, scriptwriter. **2** architect, designer, founder, inventor, maker, parent, producer.
authority *n* **1** approval, consent, licence, permission, permit, sanction, warrant. **2** command, control, force, influence, power. **3** boffin, expert, specialist.
authorize *v* agree to, allow, approve, consent to, endorse, entitle, permit, rubber-stamp, sanction, warrant.
autobiography *n* memoirs.
automated *adj* computerized, electronic, robotic.
automatic *adj* **1** habitual, natural, reflex, spontaneous, unconscious, unintentional. **2** automated, mechanical, robotic, unmanned.
autonomous *adj* free, independant, self-governing.

The monuments at Abu Simbel, Egypt are an awe-inspiring reminder of the powers of the ancient world.

autopsy *n* post-mortem.
auxiliary *adj* additional, emergency, extra, reserve, spare, substitute.
available *adj* accessible, convenient, disposable, free, handy, ready, usable.
average *adj* common, everyday, mediocre, normal, ordinary, run of the mill, typical, usual.
average *v* even out, normalize, standardize.
avert *v* change the course of, deflect, prevent, turn aside, turn away.
aviator *n* airman, pilot.
avoid *v* bypass, dodge, elude, escape, evade, shun, side-step.
await *v* be ready for, expect, hope for, look out for, wait for.
awake *adj* alert, attentive, aware, observant, ready, vigilant.
awaken *v* alert, arouse, awake, call, excite, rouse, stir up, waken.
award *v* asign, confer, give, grant, hand over, present.
aware *adj* conscious of, familiar, with, knowledge-able about, versed in.
awe *n* admiration, dread, fear, respect, terror, wonder.
awe-inspiring *adj* amazing, awful, breath-taking, dramatic, grand, impressive, overwhelming, solemn, stupendous.
awkward *adj* **1** bulky, cumbersome, unmanageable. **2** clumsy, inept, unskilful. **3** annoying, difficult, perplexing, throny, troublesome, trying, vexing. **4** embarrassing, uncomfortable, uneasy. **5** rude, stubborn, touchy, uncooperative. **6** defiant, disobedient, naughty, rebellious, unruly, wayward.
awning *n* canopy, fly-sheet, screen, shelter, tarpaulin.
awry *adj* crooked, off-centre, twisted, uneven.
axe *n* battleaxe, chopper, cleaver, hatchet, tomahawk.
axe *v* cut, dismiss, eliminate, get rid of, make redundant, remove, sack, terminate.
axis *n* centre-line, pivot.
axle *n* rod, shaft, spindle.

Bb

baby *n* babe, bairn, child, infant, papoose.
baby *v* cosset, indulge, molly-coddle, pamper, spoil.
baby *adj* dwarf, little, midget, miniature, minute, pygmy, small, tiny, wee.
back *v* **1** assist, endorse, favour, sponsor, support. **2** back away, backtrack, go back, retreat, withdraw.
back *n* backside, far end, hindpart, hindquarters, posterior, rear, reverse, stern, tail end.
back *adj* end, hind, hindmost, last, posterior, rear, tail.
backer *n* benefactor, patron, promoter, sponsor, supporter, underwriter, well-wisher.
backfire *v* fail, flop, miscarry, rebound, recoil.
background *n* **1** context, setting, surroundings. **2** history, preparation, tradition. **3** breeding, culture, education, experience, upbringing.
backing *n* **1** accompaniment, orchestration, scoring. **2** aid, assistance, endorsement, funds, help, loan, sponsorship, subsidy, support.
backlog *n* accumulation, build-up, excess, reserves, stock, supply.
back out *v* abandon, cancel, chicken out, give up, go back on, retreat, withdraw.
back up *v* aid, assist, bolster, confirm, reinforce, support.
back up *n* reinforcement, reserve, second, stand by, stand in for, substitute.
backward *adj* **1** reluctant, shy, unwilling. **2** dense, retarded, slow, stupid, under-developed.
backward *adv* in reverse, rearward.
bacon *n* gammon, ham, rashers.
bad *adj* **1** defective, faulty, sub-standard, unsatisfactory. **2** dangerous, harmful. **3** corrupt, criminal, evil, vile, wicked. **4** disobedient, mischievous, naughty, unruly. **5** decayed, mouldy, off, rancid, rotten, sour. **6** diseased, ill, sick, unwell. **7** adverse, distressed, gloomy, grim, troubled.
badge *n* brand, device, emblem, identification, insignia, mark, sign, stamp, token.
badger *v* annoy, bother, harangue, pester, torment.
badly *adv* **1** carelessly, poorly, shoddily, wrongly. **2** improperly, wickedly.
baffle *v* **1** amaze, astound, bewilder, confuse, dumbfound, perplex, puzzle, stump, stun. **2** defeat, foil, frustrate, hinder, thwart.
bag *v* capture, catch, get, kill, land, shoot, trap.
baggage *n* bags, belongings, equipment, gear, luggage, suitcases, things.
baggy *adj* billowing, bulging, floppy, ill-fitting, loose, slack.
bail *n* bond, guarantee, security, surety, warranty.
bail *v* dip, drain off, ladle, scoop.
bail out *v* **1** aid, help, relieve, rescue. **2** escape, quit, retreat, withdraw.
bake *v* **1** cook. **2** burn, parch, scorch, sear.
balance *v* **1** level, match, parallel, poise, stabilize, steady. **2** counter-balance, equalize, equate, even up, make up for, steady, support.
balance *n* **1** scales, weighing machine. **2** composure, poise, self-control, stability, steadiness. **3** difference, excess, remainder, residue, rest, surplus. **4** evenness, parity, symmetry.
ball *n* **1** drop, globe, globule, orb, pellet, sphere, spheroid. **2** dance, disco, party.
balloon *n* airship, dirigible, hot air balloon, Zeppelin.
balloon *v* billow, blow up, distend, enlarge, expand, inflate, puff out, swell.
ballot *n* election, poll, polling, referendum, vote.
balm *n* cream, lotion, ointment.
balmy *adj* gentle, mild, peaceful, soothing, summery.
bamboozle *v* cheat, deceive, defraud, fool, swindle, trick.
ban *v* banish, bar, forbid, outlaw, prohibit, restrict.

A hot air balloon filled with helium, can lift people high up into the sky in a basket suspended below.

ban *n* boycott, censorship, embargo, prohibition, restriction, stoppage, suppression.
band *n* **1** belt, binding, cord, line, ribbon, ring, strip, stripe. **2** association, body, clique, club, company, crew, flock, gang, group, herd, party, society, troop. **3** combo, ensemble, group, orchestra.
bandage *n* compress, dressing, gauze, lint, plaster.
bandage *v* bind, cover, dress.
bandit *n* crook, gangster, gunman, highwayman, hijacker, outlaw, pirate, robber, thief.
bang *n* **1** blast, boom, burst, clang, crash, explosion, pop, thud, thump. **2** blow, box, bump, collision, hit, knock, pound, smack, strike.
banish *v* **1** deport, evict, exile, expel, shut out. **2** ban, eliminate, oust, restrict, shake off, stop.
banisters *pl n* **1** balustrade, handrail, railing. **2** balusters.
bank *n* **1** fund, reserve, reservoir, savings, stockpile, store. **2** dike, embankment, mass, mound, pile, rampart, ridge. **3** brink, edge, margin, shore, side. **4** array, collection, display, file, group, line, rank, row, sequence, series, tier.
bank *v* **1** deal with, deposit, keep, save, transact business with. **2** amass, heap, mass, mound, pile, stack. **3** camber, cant, incline, pitch, slant, slope, tilt, tip.
bank on *v* assume, count on, depend on, rely on, trust.
bankrupt *v* broke, cleaned out, destitute, exhausted, failed, insolvent, ruined.
banner *n* colours, flag, pennant, placard, standard, streamer.
banquet *n* dinner, dinner party, feast, meal, repast.
banter *n* gossip, joking, joshing, small talk, teasing.
baptism *n* **1** christening, immersion, purification, sprinkling. **2** beginning, debut, dedication, initiation, introduction, launching, rite of passage.
bar *n* **1** batten, crosspiece, paling, pole, rail, rod, shaft, stake, stick. **2** barricade, barrier, deterrent, obstacle, obstruction, rail, stop. **3** canteen, counter, inn, pub, public house, saloon, tavern. **4** bench, court, courtroom, dock, law court. **5** counsel, court, judgment.
bar *v* **1** barricade, bolt, fasten, latch, lock, secure. **2** ban, exclude, forbid, hinder, keep out, obstruct, prevent, prohibit.
barb *n* point, prong, quill, spike, thorn.
barbarian *n* **1** brute, hooligan, lout, monster, ruffian, savage, vandal. **2** bigot, ignoramus, illiterate, philistine.
barbaric *adj* **1** primitive, rude, uncivilized, wild. **2** brutal, coarse, cruel, savage, vulgar.
barbecue *n* outdoor meal, party, picnic; (*Inf*) barbie.
barbecue *v* broil, charcoal, grill.
bare *adj* **1** exposed, naked, nude, stripped, unclad, unclothed, uncovered, undressed. **2** barren,

Portable gas-fired barbeques and woks are becoming a popular way of cooking food for outdoor eating as they heat up quickly and have a lid to keep food warm.

blank, empty, open, scanty, scarce, unfurnished, vacant.
bargain *n* **1** agreement, arrangement, business, contract, convention, negotiation, pact, promise, transaction, treaty, understanding. **2** discount, giveaway, good buy, good deal, good value, reduction, snip.
bargain *v* **1** agree, contract, negotiate, promise, stipulate, transact. **2** barter, buy, deal, haggle, sell, trade, traffic.
bark *v* **1** bay, growl, howl, snarl, woof, yap, yelp. **2** scream, screech, shout, shriek, yell.
bark *n* casing, coating, cortex, covering, crust, husk, rind, skin.
barn *n* **1** byre, outbuilding, outhouse, shed, shelter. **2** mews, stables.
baron *n* **1** aristocrat, lord, noble, noble-man, peer. **2** captain of industry, executive, financier, industrialist, magnate, tycoon.
barracks *pl n* **1** billet, camp, fort, garrison. **2** quarters.
barrage *n* **1** battery, bombardment, broadside, cannonade, curtain of fire, fusillade, gunfire, salvo, shelling, volley. **2** avalanche, burst, deluge, flood, hail, mass, onslaught, plethora, profusion, storm, torrent.
barrel *n* butt, cask, firkin, hogshead, keg, tank, tub, tun, vat.
barren *adj* **1** childless, infecund, infertile, sterile, unprolific. **2** arid, desert, desolate, dry, empty, uncultivable, unfruitful, unproductive, waste. **3** boring, fruitless, futile, stale, useless.
barricade *n* bar, barrier, blockade, bulwark, fence, obstacle, obstruction, palisade,

The Thames flood barrier was designed to protect London from the effects of high tides in the River Thames.

rampart, roadblock, stockade.
barricade *v* bar, blockade, close up, defend, fence in, fortify, obstruct.
barrier *n* **1** bar, barricade, blockade, boundary, ditch, fence, fortification, obstacle, obstruction, railing, rampart, stop, wall. **2** difficulty, drawback, handicap, hindrance, hurdle, impediment, limitation, obstacle, restriction, stumbling block.
barrister *n* **1** counsel. **2** advocate. **3** attorney.
barter *n* bargain, beatdown, exchange, haggle, sell, swap, trade, trade-off, trafficking.
base *n* **1** bed, bottom, foot, foundation, pedestal, stand, support. **2** basis, core, essential, key, root, source. **3** camp, centre, home, post, settlement, starting point, station.
base *v* build, construct, establish, found, ground, locate, station.
baseless *adj* groundless, unfounded, unjustifiable, unsupported.
basement *n* cellar, crypt, garden flat, vault.
bashful *adj* blushing, coy, easily embarrassed, hesitant, modest, nervous, reserved, reticent, self-conscious, sheepish, shy, timid.
basic *adj* **1** central, crucial, essential, fundamental, key, principle, rudimentary, vital. **2** bottom, ground, lowest-level, starting, without commission. **3** plain, simple, sparse, spartan.
basics *pl n* core, essentials, facts, fundamentals, practicalities, principles, rudiments; (*Inf*) brass tacks, nitty-gritty, nuts and bolts.
basin *n* **1** container, receptacle, vessel. **2** bowl, dish, pan. **3** bed, channel.
basis *n* **1** base, foundation, grounds, reasoning, support. **2** core, essence, fundamental main ingredient, point, premise, starting-point. **3** condition, position, procedure, status.
bask *v* **1** laze, lie, loll, lounge, relax, sunbathe. **2** delight, enjoy, rejoice in, relish, revel, savour, take pleasure.

basket *n* **1** container, receptacle. **2** creel, hamper, pannier, punnet.
batch *n* accumulation, amount, bunch, collection, crowd, group, lot, mass, pack, quantity, set.
bath *n* **1** bath-tub, hip-bath, sauna, sitz-bath, steam bath, tub, whirlpool bath. **2** dip, douche, shower, soak.
bath *v* bathe, clean, douse, scrub down, shower, soak, soap, sponge, wash.
bathe *v* **1** clean, cleanse, cover, dunk, flood, immerse, moisten, rinse, soak, wash, wet. **2** take a dip. **3** envelope, suffuse.
bathe *n* dip, swim, wash.
battalion *n* **1** army, brigade, company, contingent, detachment, division, forces, garrison, legion, platoon, regiment, section, squadron, troops, unit. **2** crowd, herd, horde, host, multitude, protesters, throng.
batten *n* bar, board, bolt, clamp, strip.
batten *v* fasten, fix, secure.
batter *v* **1** assault, bash, beat, hit, pelt, pound, strike, wallop. **2** bruise, crush, demolish, destroy, disfigure, harm, hurt, injure, shatter, smash, wound.
battery *n* **1** assault, attack, beating, grievous bodily harm, mugging, onslaught, physical violence, striking, thrashing, thumping. **2** artillery, cannon, cannonry, gun emplacements.
battle *n* affray, armed conflict, attack, campaign, clash, collision, combat, confrontation, contest, crusade, encounter, engagement, fight, fray, hostilities, meeting, mêlée, skirmish, tussle, warfare.
battle *v* **1** combat, contend, feud, fight, strive, struggle, war. **2** labour, push, struggle. **3** argue, bicker, disagree, feud, quarrel, wrangle.
battlefield *n* battlefront, battleground, battle stations, combat zone, field of operations, front, theatre of war.
battlement *n* **1** balustrade, barbican, batizan, bulwark, fortification, parapet, rampart. **2** breastwork, circumvallation, crenellation, outwork.
battleship *n* capital ship, cruiser, gunboat, man-of-war, warship.
bay *n* **1** arm, basin, bight, cove, firth, gulf, harbour, indentation, inlet, natural harbour, sound. **2** alcove, both, niche, nook, opening, recess. **3** bark, baying, cry, howl.

Lighthouses emit a beam of light to warn shipping of dangerous rocks.

bay *v* bark, bellow, clamour, cry, growl, howl, roar, yelp.
bazaar *n* **1** exchange, market, market place, mart, souk. **2** bring-and-buy, fair, fête, sale of work.
beach *n* coast, coastline, lido, margin, plage, sands, seaboard, seashore, seaside, shingle, shore, water's edge.
beacon *n* beam, bonfire, flare, lighthouse, rocket, sign, signal, signal fire, smoke signal, warning light, watchtower.
beak *n* **1** bill, mandible, nib. nose, proboscis, snout. **2** bow, prow, ram, rostrum, stem.
beam *n* **1** boom, girder, joist, plank, post, rafter, spar, stanchion, support, timber. **2** gleam, ray, shaft, streak.
beam *v* **1** broadcast, emit, glare, gleam, glitter, glow, radiate, shine, transmit. **2** grin, laugh, smile.
bear *v* **1** carry, hold, prop up, shoulder, support. **2** carry, convey, deliver, fetch, move, spread, take, transport. **3** display, exhibit, show. **4** accept, admit, allow, endure, grin and bear, permit, persevere, put up with, stomach, suffer, tolerate, withstand. **5** breed, develop, give birth to, produce, provide, yield. **6** bend, curve, deviate, diverge, fork, go, move, turn.
bear *n* American black, Asiatic black, brown, cinnamon, giant panda, grizzly, Himalayan black, honey, Kodiak, musquaw, polar, sloth, red panda, spectacled, sun.
bearable *adj* admissible, endurable, manageable, passable, supportable, sustainable, tolerable.
bearing *n* **1** attitude, behaviour, carriage, demeanour, manner, posture. **2** course, direction. **3** connection, relation, relevance, significance. **4** location, orientation, position, situation, track, way.

In parts of Canada, polar bears are becoming a nuisance as they scavenge for food when the sea freezes and they can reach populated areas.

bear out *v* confirm, corroborate, endorse, justify, prove, substantiate, support, uphold, vindicate.
bear with *v* be patient, forbear, make allowances, put up with, suffer, tolerate, wait.
beast *n* animal, brute, creature; barbarian, fiend, monster, ogre, sadist, savage, swine.
beastly *adj* **1** barbarous, bestial, brutal, brutish, coarse, cruel, depraved, inhuman, monstrous, repulsive, sadistic, savage. **2** awful, disagreeable, foul, horrible, mean, nasty, rotten, terrible, unpleasant, vile.
beat *v* **1** bang, batter, bruise, flog, hit, knock, lash, punch, smack, slap, strike, thrash, whip. **2** conquer, defeat, excel, outdo, overcome, overwhelm, surpass. **3** quiver, tremble, vibrate. **4** blend, mix, stir, whip, whisk. break against, dash, lap, strike, wash. **5** conquer, defeat, overpower, quash, rout.
beat *n* **1** blow, lit, lash, punch, shake, slap, strike, swing, thump. **2** flutter, palpitation, pulsation, pulse, throb. **3** accent, measure, rhythm, stress, time. **4** circuit, course, itinerary, path, rounds, route, way.
beat *adj* exhausted, fatigued, spent, tired, wearied, worn out.
beaten *adj* **1** defeated, disheartened, frustrated, overwhelmed, quashed, thwarted, trounced. **2** blended, foamy, frothy, mixed, stirred, whipped, whisked.
beautiful *adj* brilliant, elegant, good looking, gorgeous, lovely, magnificent, pretty, stunning.
beckon *v* **1** bid, call, gesticulate, gesture, motion, nod, signal, summon, wave at. **2** attract, call, coax, draw, entice, lure, tempt.
bed *n* **1** bedstead, berth, bunk, cot, couch, divan. **2** area, border, garden, patch, plot, row, strip. **3** base, basis, foundation, substructure, substratum, support.
bed *v* **1** bury, embed, establish, fix into, found, implant, inlay, insert, set. **2** seduce, spend the night with. **3** plant out, set in beds. **4** go to. **5** put to bed, settle down, tuck in.
bedlam *n* chaos, commotion, disarray, disorder, furore, hubbub, hullabaloo, noise, pandemonum, tumult, turmoil, uproar.
bedraggled *adj* dishevelled, messy, scruffy, soaking, soggy, soiled, stained, unkempt, untidy, wet.
bedridden *adj* confined, confined to bed, flat on one's back, housebound, incapacitated.
bedrock *n* **1** bed, bottom, rock bed, solid foundation, substratum, substructure. **2** lowest point, rock bottom.
bee *n* bumble-bee, drone, honey-bee, queen, worker.
beer *n* ale, bitter, bottled, brown ale, canned, draught, keg, lager, lite, mild, pale ale, porter, real ale, shandy, stout, strong ale.
before *adv* **1** earlier, formerly, in the past, previously, sooner. **2** ahead, in advance, in front, in the lead.
before *prep* earlier than, in advance of, in front of, in the presence of, in the sight of, previous to, prior to, under the nose of.
befriend *v* assist, help, look after, stand by, support.
begin *v* **1** commence, set in motion, set on foot, start. **2** get going, go ahead. **3** appear, arise, emerge, happen, occur.

The Taj Mahal in India is undoubtedly one of the most spectacular buildings in the world. Built as a tomb for the Mughal empress Mumtaz Mahal, it is a symbol of India. Reigning in India from 1526 to 1858, the Mughals were a dynasty of emperors who were muslim believers.

beginner *n* amateur, apprentice, cub, fledgling, fresher, freshman, learner, novice, pupil, recruit, student, trainee.

beginning *n* birth, conception, dawn, emergence, inception, initiation, origin, prelude, rise, source, start, starting point.

begrudge *v* be jealous, be reluctant, be stingy, envy, grudge, resent.

behave *v* **1** act, function, operate, perform, run, work. **2** act correctly, conduct oneself properly, mind one's manners.

behaviour *n* **1** actions, conduct, manner, ways. **2** action, functioning, operation, performance.

behead *v* decapitate, guillotine.

behind *prep* **1** after, at the back of, at the rear of, following, later than. **2** at the bottom of, causing, initiating, instigating, responsible for. **3** backing, for, in agreement, in the side of, supporting.

behind *adv* **1** after, afterwards, following, next, subsequently. **2** in arrears, in debt, overdue.

beige *adj* biscuit, buff, coffee, neutral, oatmeal, sand.

belated *adj* behind time, delayed, late, overdue, tardy.

belch *v* **1** break wind, burp, hiccough. **2** discharge, emit, give off, give out, issue, spew out, vent.

beleaguered *adj* beseiged, blockaded, encircled, hemmed in, surrounded, under attack, under seige.

belief *n* **1** admission, assent, assurance, confidence, conviction, credit, feeling, impression, judgment, notion, opinion, persuasion, presumption, reliance, theory, trust, view. **2** credence, doctrine, dogma, faith, ideology, principles.

believe *v* **1** accept, be certain of, count on, credit, depend on, have faith in, place confidence in, presume true, swear by, trust. **2** assume, consider, guess, imagine, judge, maintain, presume, reckon, speculate, suppose, think.

believer *n* adherent, convert, devotee, disciple, follower, proselyte, supporter, upholder, zealot.

belittle *v* decry, deprecate, detract from, minimize, play down, scoff at, sneer at.

belligerent *adj* aggressive, argumentative, militant, quarrelsome, quick-tempered.

bellow *v* call out, howl, scream, screech, shout, shriek, yell.

below *adv* beneath, down, lower, under, underneath.

below *prep* inferior, lesser than, subject, subordinate, unworthy.

belt *n* **1** band, cummerband, girdle, girth, sash, waistband. **2** conveyor, fan. **3** area, district, extent, region, stretch, tract. **4** band, line, stria, stripe. **5** bang, blow, punch, smack, thump.

belt *v* **1** bind, encircle, encompass, fasten, gird, tie. **2** birch, cane, flagelate, flail, flog, lash, scourge, strap, thrash, thump, whip. **3** bang, batter, beat, pound, pummel, punch, smack.

bemused *adj* absent-minded, astonished, bewildered, confused, dazed, engrossed, muddled, perplexed, preoccupied, puzzled, stunned.
bench *n* **1** form, long seat, pew, seat, settle, stall. **2** board, counter, table, trestle table, workbench. **3** bar, court, courtroom, judge, judiciary, magistrate, tribunal.
benchmark *n* criterion, gauge, model, norm, pattern, yardstick.
bend *v* bow, buckle, contort, curve, diverge, flex, incline, lean, swerve, turn, twist, veer, warp.
bend *n* angle, arc, bow, corner, crook, curve, hook, loop, turn, twist, zigzag.
beneath *adv* below, in a lower place, underneath.
beneath *prep* below, inferior to, less than, lower than, underneath, unworthy of.
benefactor *n* backer, donor, patron, philanthropist, promoter, sympathizer, well-wisher.
beneficial *adj* advantageous, favourable, gainful, healthy, helpful, promising, rewarding, salubrious, useful, valuable.
beneficiary *n* heir, inheritor, payee, receiver, recipient.
benefit *n* **1** advantage, aid, asset, assistance, avail, betterment, blessing, boon, favour, gain, good, help, interest, profit. **2** allowance, insurance money, sick pay, social security payment, unemployment benefit.
benefit *v* advance, advantage, aid, ameliorate, assist, better, enhance, further, good to, help, improve, profit, promote, serve.
benevolence *n* charity, generosity, goodness, humanity, humanitarianism, kindness, philanthropism.
bent *adj* **1** angled, arched, bowed, crooked, curved, hunched, stooped, twisted. **2** corrupt, crooked, dishonest, fraudulent.
bent on *adj* determined, disposed, fixed, inclined, insistent, predisposed, resolved, set.
bequest *n* bequeathal, bestowal, dower, endowment, estate, gift, heritage, inheritance, legacy, settlement, trust.
berate *v* castigate, censure, criticize, chide, harangue, lambaste, rebuke, reprimand, reprove, scold.
bereavement *n* **1** deprivation, loss. **2** decease, demise, passing.
berserk *adj* amok, crazed, enraged, frenzied, hysterical, insane, mad, raging, raving, unrestrainable, violent, wild.
berth *n* **1** bed, billet, bunk, cot, hammock. **2** anchorage, dock, harbour, haven, mooring, pier, port, tie up, quay, wharf.
berth *v* **1** anchor, dock, land. **2** accommodate, house, lodge, put up, shelter, sleep.
beside *prep* adjacent to, alongside, close to, near, nearby, neighbouring, next door to, next to, overlooking.
besiege *v* blockade, confine, encircle, encompass, hedge in, hem in, invest, lay siege to, shut in, surround.
best *adj* **1** chief, excellent, finest, first-class, first-rate, leading, outstanding, perfect, principal, superlative, supreme, top, worthiest, unsurpassed; (*Inf*) ace, crack. **2** advantageous, apt, correct, golden, most fitting, right. **3** greatest, largest, most.
best *n* choice, cream, elite, finest, first, pick, prime, top.
bestow *v* allot, apportion, award, commit, confer, donate, entrust, give, grant, honour with, lavish, present, render.

How river bends create lakes

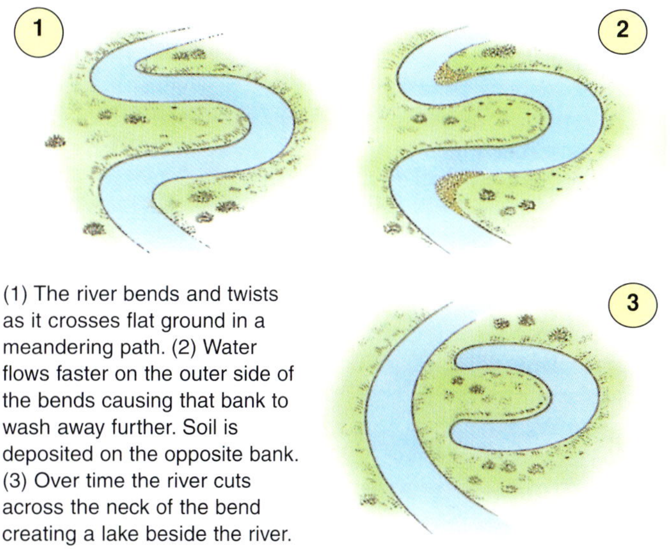

(1) The river bends and twists as it crosses flat ground in a meandering path. (2) Water flows faster on the outer side of the bends causing that bank to wash away further. Soil is deposited on the opposite bank. (3) Over time the river cuts across the neck of the bend creating a lake beside the river.

bet *n* flutter, gamble, hazard, long shot, risk, speculation.
bet *v* chance, gamble, hazard, lay bets, pledge, put money on, risk, speculate, stake, venture, wager.
betray *v* **1** be disloyal, break one's promise, inform on. **2** blurt out, disclose, divulge, expose, lay bare, let slip, manifest, reveal, show, tell, tell on, uncover, unmask. **3** abandon, desert, forsake, jilt, walk out on.
betrayal *n* **1** deception, disloyalty, double-cross, duplicity, falseness, treachery, treason, trickery, unfaithfulness. **2** blurting out, disclosure, divulgence, giving away, revelation, telling.
better *adj* **1** bigger, excelling, finer, fitter, greater, higher-quality, larger, more appropriate, preferable, superior, surpassing, worthier. **2** cured, fitter, fully recovered, healthier, improving, mending, more healthy, on the mend, progressing, recovering, stronger, well. **3** bigger, greater.
beware *v* avoid, be careful, guard against, heed, look out, mind, refrain from, shun, steer clear of, take heed, watch out.
bewilder *v* baffle, befuddle, bemuse, confound, confuse, mystify, perplex, puzzle, stupefy.
bewitch *v* allure, attract, beguile, captivate, charm, enchant, enrapture, entrance, fascinate, hypnotize, spellbind.
beyond *prep* above, apart from, at a distance, away from, before, farther, out of range, out of reach, over, past, remote.
bias *n* **1** aptitude, inclination, intolerance, leaning, liking, partiality, penchant, predilection, preference, prejudice, tendency. **2** bigotry, favouritism, imbalance, injustice, nepotism, one-sidedness, prejudice, racism.
biased *adj* blinkered, distorted, influenced, one-sided, partial, prejudiced, racist, sexist, unfair.
bicycle *n* bike, cycle, penny-farthing, racer, tandem.
bid *v* **1** offer, proffer, propose, submit, tender. **2** call, greet, say, tell, wish. **3** ask, charge, command, desire, direct, instruct, require, solicit, summon, tell.
bid *n* **1** advance, offer, price, proposal, submission, sum, tender. **2** attempt, effort, try.
bidding *n* command, demand, direction, instruction, invitation, order, request, summons.
big *adj* **1** colossal, enormous, gigantic, great, huge, immense, large, massive, sizable, spacious, substantial, vast. **2** important, influential, leading, main, momentous, paramount, powerful, prime, principal, prominent, serious, significant. **3** generous, gracious, unselfish. **4** arrogant, boastful, conceited, proud.
bill *n* **1** account, charges, invoice, note of charge, reckoning, score, statement, tally. **2** advertisement, broadsheet, bulletin, circular, hand-out, leaflet, notice, poster. **3** measure, piece of legislation, projected law, proposal. **4** beak, mandible, neb, nib.
bill *v* charge, debit, figure, invoice, reckon, record.
billow *n* **1** breaker, crest, roller, surge, swell, tide, wave. **2** cloud, deluge, flood, outpouring, rush.
bind *v* **1** attach, fasten, glue, hitch, lash, paste, rope, secure, stick, strap, tie, truss, wrap. **2** compel, constrain, engage, force, necessitate, obligate, oblige, prescribe, require. **3** confine, detain, hamper, hinder, restrain, restrict. **4** bandage, cover, dress, encase, swathe, wrap. **5** border, edge, finish, hem, trim.
binding *adj* compulsory,

By crouching low over their bicycles, riders can increase their speed by reducing air resistance that would normally slow them down.

The development to birth of a baby

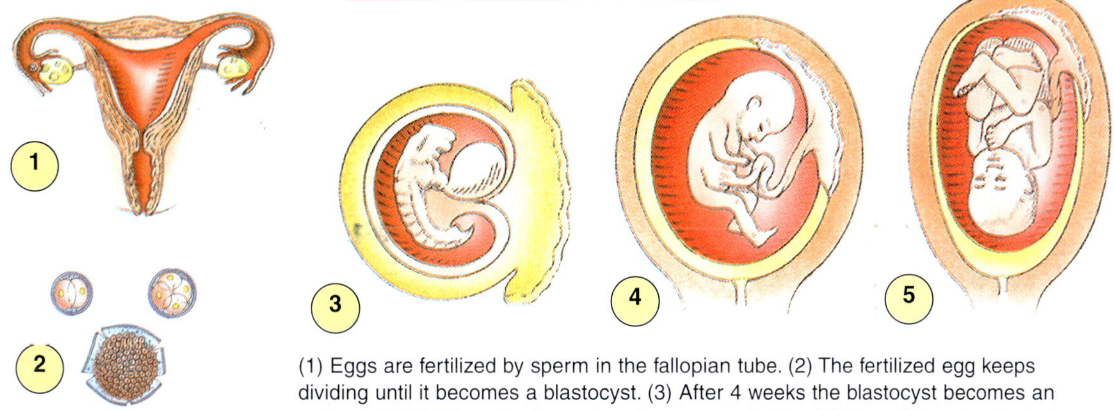

(1) Eggs are fertilized by sperm in the fallopian tube. (2) The fertilized egg keeps dividing until it becomes a blastocyst. (3) After 4 weeks the blastocyst becomes an embryo. (4) At 12 weeks the embryo becomes a foetus. (5) From 38 weeks the baby is ready to be born. The baby is born through the vagina.

conclusive, mandatory, necessary, obligatory.

biography *n* account, life, life story, memoir, memoirs, profile.

birth *n* **1** childbirth, confinement, delivery, nativity. **2** beginning, emergence, fountainhead, genesis, origin, rise, source, start. **3** ancestry, background, blood, breeding, descent, family, genealogy, heritage, origin, lineage, parentage, pedigree, race, stock, strain.

bisect *v* bifurcate, cross, cut across, cut in half, cut in two, divide in two, halve, intersect, separate, split, split down the middle.

bit *n* atom, chip, chunk, crumb, flake, fragment, grain, hunk, iota, jot, lump, mite, morsel, mouthful, part, piece, portion, scrap, segment, shred, slice, sliver, small piece, speck, trace.

bite *v* champ, chew, clamp, crunch, crush, cut, gnaw, hold, masticate, munch, nibble, nip, pierce, pinch, seize, snap, tear, wound.

bite *n* **1** nip, pinch, prick, smarting, sting, tooth marks, wound. **2** food, light meal, morsel, mouthful, piece, snack. **3** edge, kick, piquancy, punch, pungency, spice, spiciness.

biting *adj* **1** bitter, cold, cutting, freezing, harsh, nipping, penetrating, piercing, stinging. **2** acid, bitter, caustic, cutting, mordant, sarcastic, scathing, sharp, stinging, withering.

bitter *adj* **1** acid, acrid, astringent, sharp, sour, tart, unsweetened, vinegary. **2** embittered, hostile, morose, resentful, sore, sour, sullen.

bitterness *n* **1** acerbity, acidity, sharpness, sourness, tartness, vinegariness. **2** animosity, grudge, hostility, pique, rancour, resentment.

bizarre *adj* abnormal, curious, eccentric, extraordinary, odd, peculiar, strange, unusual, weird; (*Inf*) oddball, off-the-wall, wacky, way-out.

black *adj* **1** coal-black, dark, dusky, ebony, inky, jet, murky, pitchy, raven, sable, starless, stygian, swarthy. **2** dark, depressing, dismal, distressing, funereal, gloomy, horrible, pessimistic, sombre. **3** bad, evil, foul, villainous, wicked.

black *v* ban, bar, blacklist, boycott, put an embargo on.

blacklist *v* ban, bar, boycott, debar, exclude, expel, ostracize, preclude, proscribe, reject, repudiate, snub, vote against.

blackmail *n* bribe, exaction, extortion, intimidation, ransom.

blackout *n* **1** coma, faint, loss of consciousness, oblivion, passing out, swoon, unconsciousness. **2** power cut, power failure. 3 censorship.

black sheep *n* disgrace, dropout, outcast, reprobate.

blame *n* **1** accountability, culpability, fault, guilt, liability, onus, responsibility. **2** accusation, censure, charge, complaint, criticism, recrimination, reproach.

blame *v* accuse, charge, find fault with, hold responsible, indict, reprehend, reprove, take to task, upbraid.

blameless *adj* above suspicion, clean, faultless, guiltless, innocent, in the clear, not to blame, perfect, stainless, virtuous.
bland *adj* **1** boring, dull, humdrum, insipid, monotonous, neutral, nondescript, safe, tasteless, tedious, uninspiring, uninteresting. **2** courteous, friendly, gentle, gracious, smooth, suave, unemotional.
blank *adj* **1** bare, clean, clear, empty, plain, spotless, uncompleted, unfilled, unmarked, vacant, void, white. **2** at a loss, bewildered, confused, disconcerted, dumbfounded, empty, expressionless, impassive, muddled, perplexed, puzzled, vacant
blank *n* emptiness, gap, space, vacancy, vacuum, void.
blanket *n* **1** afghan, bedcover, cover, coverlet, rug, spread, throw. **2** carpet, cloak, coat, coating, covering, envelope, film, layer, mantle, sheet, wrapper, wrapping.
blanket *v* cloak, cloud, coat, conceal, cover, eclipse, hide, mask, obscure, suppress, surround.
blare *v* blast, boom, clamour, clang, honk, hoot, roar, scream, sound out, toot, trumpet.
blasé *adj* apathetic, indifferent, lukewarm, offhand, unenthusiastic, uninterested.
blast *n* **1** blow, draught, gale, rush, storm. **2** bellow, blare, boom, clang, honk, peal, screech, toot, wail. **3** blowing up, detonation, discharge, eruption, explosion. **4** attack, castigation, criticism, outburst, rebuke, reprimand, reproof.
blast *v* **1** blare out, boom, roar. **2** blow, demolish, explode, raze to the ground, ruin, shatter. **3** crush, dash, destroy, kill, mar, ruin, shrivel, spoil, wreck, wither. **4** attack, berate, castigate, criticize, rebuke, reprimand. **5** discharge, fire, let fly, shoot.
blatant *adj* barefaced, flagrant, flaunting, glaring, naked, obvious, ostentatious, outright, prominent, pronounced, shameless, sheer, unmitigated.
blaze *n* **1** bonfire, conflagration, fire, flame, flames, holocaust. **2** beam, brilliance, flare, flash, glare, gleam, glitter, glow, light, radiance. **3** burst, eruption, flare-up, outbreak, rush, storm, torrent.
blaze *v* **1** burn, burst into flames, catch fire. **2** beam, flare, glitter. **3** blow up, explode, smoulder. **4** blast, discharge, fire.
bleak *adj* **1** arid, bare, barren, desolate, exposed, open, raw, unsheltered, wind-swept. **2** cheerless, comfortless, depressing, discouraging, disheartening, dismal, dreary, gloomy, grim, hopeless, joyless, miserable, sombre, unpromising, wretched.
blemish *n* birthmark, bruise, fault, flaw, imperfection, mark, naevus, smudge, speck, spot, stain, taint.
blend *v* **1** combine, compound, fuse, merge, mix, unite. **2** complement, fit, go well, suit.
blend *n* alloy, amalgamation, combination, compound, concoction, fusion, mingling, mixture, synthesis, union.
blight *n* canker, decay, disease, fungus, infestation, mildew, pest, pestilence, rot.
blight *v* **1** destroy, ruin, wither. **2** annihilate, crush, destroy, kill, ruin, spoil, wreck.
blind *adj* **1** eyeless, sightless, unsighted, visionless. **2** careless, neglectful, oblivious, unaware of. **3** hasty, rash, reckless, wild.
blind *n* cover, mask, screen.
bliss *n* delight, ecstasy, elation, happiness, heaven, joy, pleasure.
blitz *n* **1** assault, attack, blitzkrieg, bombardment, bombing, offensive, onslaught, raid, strike. **2** set to.

Fireproof clothing often has a shiny surface, because this helps to reflect the radiated heat caused by the blaze away from the body.

blizzard *n* blast, gale, snowstorm, squall, storm, tempest.
bloated *adv* enlarged, full, inflated, puffed up, swollen.
block *n* **1** chunk, cube, ingot, lump, mass, piece, rectangle, square, wedge. **2** bar, barrier, blockage, obstacle, prevent.
block *v* **1** clog, obstruct, plug, stop up. **2** arrest, deter, halt, hinder, impede, prevent, obstruct, stop, thwart.
blockade *n* barricade, barrier, obstacle, restriction.
blockage *n* barrier, clog, jam, obstacle, obstruction, plug.
blond *adj* fair, fair-haired, flaxen, golden, golden-haired.
blood *n* **1** lifeblood, vital fluids. **2** ancestry, birth, descent, family, genealogy, relations.
bloodshed *n* carnage, massacre, murder, violence, war.

Types of blood cells in the body

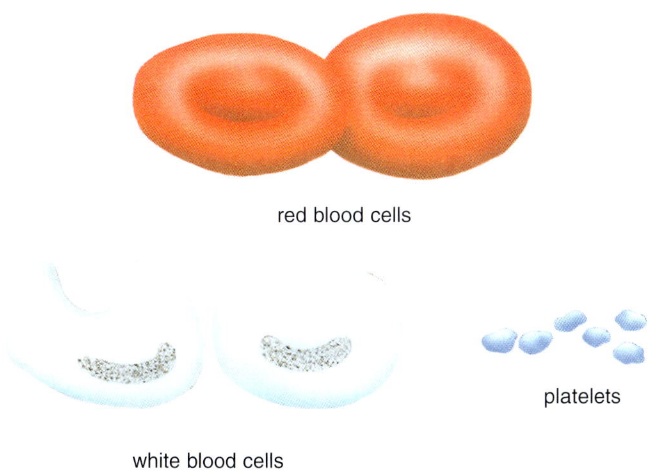

The three kinds of blood cell are carried in a yellowish liquid called plasma. Plasma is 90% water.

blossom *n* bloom, bud, floret, flower, flowers.
blossom *v* bloom, flower. bloom, develop, flourish, get on well, grow, mature, progress, prosper, succeed, thrive.
blot *n* **1** blotch, mark, patch, smear, smudge, speckle, splodge, spot, stain. **2** blemish, blur, defect, disgrace, fault, flaw, spot, stain, taint.
blow *v* **1** blast, breathe, exhale, fan, huff, pant, puff, waft. **2** flow, rush, stream, whirl, whisk. **3** bear, buffet, drive, fling, flutter, sweep, waft, whirl, whisk. **4** blare, mouth, pipe, play, sound, toot, trumpet, vibrate.
blow *n* **1** blast, gale, gust, puff, strong breeze, tempest, wind. **2** bang, bash, belt, knock, punch, smack, thump, whack. **3** bombshell, catastrophe, disaster, misfortune, setback, shock, upset.
blow up *v* **1** bloat, distend, enlarge, expand, fill, inflate, puff up, pump up, swell. **2** blast, bomb, burst, detonate, dynamite, explode, go off, rupture, shatter. **3** enlarge, exaggerate, heighten, magnify.
blue *adj* **1** azure, cobalt, cyan, indigo, navy, sapphire, sky blue, turquoise, ultramarine. **2** dejected, depressed,down hearted, fed up, low, miserable, sad, unhappy; (*Inf*) down in the dumps.
blueprint *n* design, draft, layout, outline, pattern, pilot scheme, plan, project, prototype, scheme, sketch.
bluff *v* con, deceive, defraud, hoax, lie, mislead, pretend, take in, trick.
bluff *n* boast, bragging, bravado, deceit, deception, fake, fraud, humbug, lie, pretence, sham.
bluff *adj* **1** blunt, candid, direct, frank, open, outspoken, plain-spoken. **2** abrupt, acclivitous, perpendicular, sheer, steep.
blunder *n* error, *faux pas*, gaffe, inaccuracy, mistake, oversight, slip; (*Inf*) boo-boo, bloomer, clanger, cock-up, slip-up.
blunder *v* **1** err, make a mistake; (*Inf*) blow it, slip up, screw up. **2** falter, flounder, lurch, stumble. **3** botch, bungle, make a mess of, mismanage.
blunt *adj* **1** dull, pointless, rounded. **2** impolite, out-spoken, plain spoken, rude, straight-forward, tactless, trenchant, uncivil, unpolished.
blur *v* **1** cloud, darken, dim, fog, make hazy, mist-up, obscure, soften, steam up, veil. **2** blot, smear, smudge, spot, stain.
blur *n* blear, blurredness,

cloudiness, confusion, dimness, fog, haze, indistinctness, obscurity.
blush *v* colour, crimson, flush, go pink, redden, turn red, turn scarlet.
board *n* **1** beam, panel, piece of timber, plank, slat, timber. **2** daily meals, food, meals, provisions, victuals. **3** advisers, committee, council, directors, panel, trustees.
board *v* **1** embark, enter, go aboard. **2** accommodate, feed, house, lodge, put up, take in.
boast *v* **1** blow one's own trumpet, brag, exaggerate, show off, strut, swagger. **2** be proud of, congratulate oneself on, exhibit, flatter oneself, possess, pride oneself on, show off; (*Inf*) talk big.
body *n* **1** build, figure, form, frame, physique, shape, torso, trunk. **2** cadaver, carcass, corpse, dead body, remains. **3** bulk, main part, mass. **4** association, authority, committee, company, group, organization, society. **5** crowd, horde, majority, mass, mob, multitude, throng.
bog *n* fen, marsh, marshland, mire, peat bog, quagmire, slough, swamp, wetland.
boil *v* **1** bubble, cook, heat, simmer, stew. **2** fizz, foam, froth. **3** angry, explode, fume, furious, indignant, rage, rant, rave, seethe; (*Inf*) blow a fuse, blow one's top, fly off the handle, go off at the deep end, go up the wall, hit the roof.
boiling *adj* **1** baking, blistering, roasting, scorching, searing, sweltering, very hot. **2** angry, enraged, fuming, furious, incensed, indignant, infuriated, irate, seething; (*Inf*) mad.
boisterous *adj* **1** active, bouncy, exuberant, frisky, lively, noisy, rowdy, unruly, wild. **2** breezy, gusting, raging, rough, stormy.
bold *adj* **1** adventurous, brave, courageous, daring, heroic. **2** bright, colourful, eye-catching, flashy, striking, strong, vivid. **3** barefaced, brash, cheeky, impudent.
bolt *n* **1** bar, catch, fastener, latch, lock, sliding bar. **2** peg, pin, rivet, rod. **3** bound, dart, dash, escape, flight, rush, spring, sprint. **4** arrow, dart, missile, projectile, shaft, thunderbolt.
bolt *v* **1** bar, fasten, latch, lock, secure. **2** gobble, gorge, gulp, guzzle, stuff, swallow whole, wolf down. **3** abscond, escape, flee, jump, make a break, run, run for it, spring.
bomb *n* charge, explosive, grenade, mine, missile, rocket, shell, torpedo.
bomb *v* attack, blitz, blow up, bombard, destroy, shell, strafe, torpedo.
bombard *v* assault, attack, blitz, bomb, cannonade, pepper, fire at, fusillade, pound, shell, strafe.
bond *n* **1** band, binding, chain, cord, fastening, link, manacle, shackle, tie. **2** affiliation, affinity, attachment, connection, ligature, link, nexus, relation, tie, union. **3** agreement, compact, concordat, contract, covenant, guarantee, obligation, pledge, promise, treaty, word.
bond *v* bind, connect, fasten, fix together, fuse, glue, gum, paste.
bonus *n* benefit, commission, extra, gain, perk, premium, prize, reward, tip.
book *v* arrange for, line up, organize, reserve, schedule.

Nuclear bombs were first used in the Second World War. Two bombs were dropped on the Japanese cities of Nagasaki and Hiroshima, killing hundreds of thousands of people.

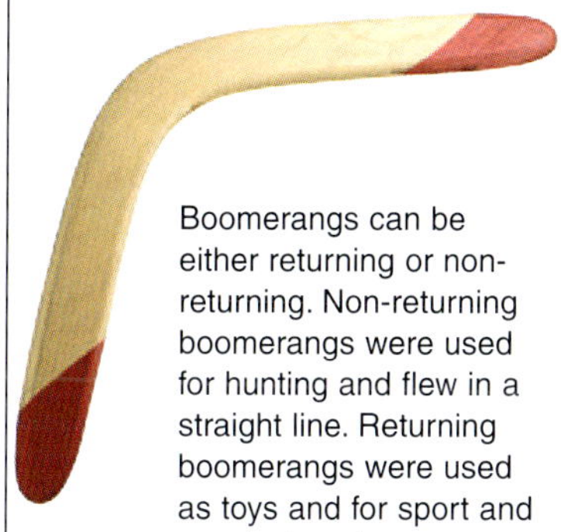

Boomerangs can be either returning or non-returning. Non-returning boomerangs were used for hunting and flew in a straight line. Returning boomerangs were used as toys and for sport and are designed to return to the thrower.

boomerang *v* backfire, come back, rebound, return, reverse, ricochet.
boot *v* **1** kick, knock. **2** dismiss, eject, expel, kick out, oust, sack, throw out. **3** load, make ready, prepare.
booth *n* **1** counter, stall, stand. **2** cubicle, compartment, enclosure.
booty *n* **1** haul, loot, pillage, plunder, spoil. **2** pickings, profits, spoils, takings, winnings; (*Inf*) swag.
border *n* **1** boundary, bounds, edge, limits, lip, margin, rim. **2** boundary, frontier, perimeter.
borderline *adj* doubtful, indefinite, marginal.
bore *v* **1** burrow, drill, mine, penetrate, sink, tunnel. **2** annoy, bother, fatigue, pester, send to sleep, wear out.
bore *n* **1** borehole, calibre, diameter, drill hole, hole, shaft, tunnel. **2** dull person, nuisance, pest; (*Inf*) pain in the neck.
boredom *n* apathy, doldrums, dullness, tedium, weariness.
boring *adj* dull, monotonous, routine, tedious, uninteresting.
borrow *v* **1** scrounge, take on loan, use temporarily. **2** acquire, obtain, steal, take.
boss *n* chief, director, employer, executive, foreman, head, leader, manager, master, owner, superintendent, supervisor.
bottle *n* **1** carafe, decanter, demijohn, flagon, flask, pitcher. **2** bravery, courage, daring, nerve.
bottleneck *n* blockage, congestion, hold up, jam, narrowing, obstruction.
bough *n* branch, limb, twig.
boulder *n* rock, stone.
boulevard *n* avenue, broad road, drive, promenade, roadway, thoroughfare.
bound *adj* **1** cased, fastened, fixed, tied. **2** certain, destined, sure. **3** forced, obliged, required.
bound *v* bob, bounce, caper, frisk, gambol, hurdle, jump, leap, pounce, prance, skip, spring, vault.
bound *n* **1** bounce, jump, hop, hurdle, leap, spring, vault. **2** dance, frolic, prance, skip.
boundary *n* barrier, border, borderline, bounds, brink, confines, edges.
bout *n* **1** battle, boxing match, competition, contest, encounter, engagement, fight, match, set-to, struggle. **2** attack, fit, spell, paroxysm.
bow *v* **1** bend, bob, droop, genuflect, incline, nod, stoop. **2** accept, acquiesce, nod, stoop. **3** concede, give in, submit, surrender, yield.
bowel *n* colon, intestine, large intestine, small intestine.
bowels *pl n* **1** entrails, guts, intestines, viscera. **2** belly, core, depths, inside, interior; (*Inf*) innards, insides.
box *n* **1** bin, carton, case, casket, chest, coffer, container, crate, pack, package, portmanteau, receptacle, trunk. **2** cabin, compartment, cubicle, enclosure, kiosk, hut. **3** cuff, slap, punch, thump.
box *v* **1** bundle up, package, wrap. **2** fight, grapple, spar.

A hurdle is a special kind of fence which runners must clear as they compete around a race track.

Boxers spar and fight against their opponents using special gloves to protect their hands from the impact of punches.

3 batter, buffet, knock, hit, pummel, slap, strike, thump; (*Inf*) belt, clout, slug, whack.
boxer *n* fighter, prizefighter, sparing partner.
boy *n* **1** fellow, junior, kid, lad, schoolboy, stripling, whippersnapper, youngster, youth. **2** garçon, page, servant, waiter.
boycott *v* avoid, ban, bar, black, blacklist, debar, embargo, exclude, ostracize, outlaw, prohibit, proscribe, refrain from, refuse, reject, spurn.
boyfriend *n* admirer, beau, date, follower, lover, man, steady, suitor, swain, sweetheart, toy boy, young man.
bracing *adj* brisk, crisp, energizing, exhilarating, fresh, invigorating, stimulating, strengthening, vitalizing.
bracket *n* **1** buttress, prop, support. **2** angle bracket, brace, parenthesis, round bracket, square bracket. **3** category, class, classification, division, grade, group, order, section, set.
brag *v* boast, show off.
braid *v* entwine, intertwine, inter-weave, plait, twist, wind.
braid *n* **1** tape, thread, twine, yarn. **2** pigtail, plait.
brake *n* constraint, control, curb, rein, restraint.
brake *v* decelerate, halt, reduce speed, slow, stop.
branch *n* **1** arm, bough, limb, off-shoot, prong, shoot, spray, sprig. **2** department, division, office, section, wing. **3** feeder, subsiduary, tributary.
branch *v* **1** divide, fork. **2** diverge, separate. **3** depart from, go off at a tangent to. **4** broaden, diversify, spread out, widen.
brand *n* **1** kind, line, label, registered trade mark, trade mark, name, trade name. **2** kind, sort, style, type, variety. **3** earmark, identification, marker. **4** slur, stigma, taint.
brand *v* **1** burn in, mark, scorch, stamp. **2** engrave, fix, impress, imprint, print. **3** discredit, disgrace, mark, stigmatize, taint.
brave *adj* **1** bold, courageous, daring, fearless, gallant, heroic, intrepid, resolute. **2** showy, spectacular.
brave *n* fighter, soldier, warrior.
bravery *n* courage, daring, gallantry, heroism, spirit, valour.
brawl *n* argument, battle, clash, commotion, fight, row, scuffle.
bray *v* hee-haw, neigh, whinny.
breach *n* **1** aperture, chasm, fissure, gap, opening, split. **2** contravention, infringement, trespass, violation.
break *v* **1** crack, disintegrate, divide, fracture, separate, sever, split, tear. **2** disobey, violate. **3** cripple, incapacitate, tame, weaken. **4** escape, flee, run away. **5** give up, stop, take a break. **6** cushion, lessen.
break *n* **1** rack, gap, gash, hole, opening, split, tear. **2** halt, interval, pause, rest, stop. **3** coffee break, tea break, supper break. **4** holiday, time off, vacation. **5** chance, opportunity, stroke of luck. **6** alteration, change, variation.
breakdown *n* **1** collapse, crackup, disruption, failure, stoppage. **2** analysis, detailed list, diagnosis. **3** going to pieces, loss of control, nervous breakdown.
breaker *n* **1** billow, roller, surf, wave. **2** white horses.
breakneck *adj* dangerous, fast, reckless, speedy.
breakthrough *n* advance, development, discovery, invention, progress, quantum leap, step forward.
breakwater *n* barrier, embankment, groyne, jetty,

mole, sea wall.
breathe *v* inhale and exhale, pant, puff, respire.
breathtaking *adj* amazing, astonishing, impressive, spectacular, stunning, thrilling.
breed *v* **1** give birth, hatch, multiply, procreate, produce young, reproduce. **2**cause, create, generate, give rise to.
breed *n* **1** family, kind, lineage, pedigree, race, sort, species, type, variety. **2** brand, class, kind, strain, type, variety.
breeze *n* **1** air, breath of wind, current of air, draught, gust, light wind, puff of air, waft. **2** land breeze, onshore breeze, sea breeze.
breeze *v* drift, glide, flit, sail, sally, stroll, sweep.
brevity *n* **1** conciseness, curtness. **2** briefness, shortness.
brew *v* **1** boil, ferment, infuse. **2** devise, hatch, plan, plot.
brew *n* **1** ale, beer, liquor, tea. **2** infusion, preparation.
bribe *n* carrot, enticement, inducement; (*Inf*) backhander, boodle, bung, graft, hush money, kickback, protection, sweetner.
bribe *v* buy off, corrupt, get at, influence by gifts, reward, square, suborn; (*Inf*) bung, fix, give a backhander, grease the palm of, sweetener.
bridge *n* **1** arch, flyover, overpass, span, viaduct. **2** band, bonding, bond, connection, cord, link, tie.
bridge *v* arch over, connect, cross over, extend across, go over, join, link, span, unite.
bridle *n* **1** halter. **2** check, control, restraint.
bridle *v* **1** constrain, control, curb, govern, keep control of,

Different kinds of bridges

The earliest bridges were probably tree trunks across streams. Gradually people learned to span wider rivers and ravines by supporting the bridge in the middle. Since then engineers have devised many ways of spanning very wide distances.

Medieval arched bridges had shops built along them.

A bascule bridge can be opened to allow shipping through.

Suspension bridges have towers and cables to support the bridge.

keep in check, hold back, master, moderate, repress, restrain, subdue. **2** bristle, draw oneself up, feel one's hackles rise, get angry.
brief *adj* **1** compressed, concise, condensed, curt, short, succinct, terse, to the point. **2** fading, fast, fleeting, hasty, momentary, quick, short-lived, temporary. **3** abrupt, blunt, brusque, curt, sharp, short, surly.
brief *n* **1** abstract, out-line, precis, summary, synopsis. **2** argument, case, defence, demonstration, evidence, proof. **3** briefing, data, directions, guidance, intelligence, instructions, preparation, priming.
brief *v* advise, explain, fill in, give a rundown, guide, inform, instruct, prepare, prime.
briefing *n* conference, guidance, information, meeting, preparation, priming, rundown.
brigade *n* association, band, body, contingent, crew, force, group, organization, outfit, party, section, squad, team.
brigand *n* bandit, criminal, desperado, gangster, highwayman, marauder, outlaw, pirate, robber.
bright *adj* **1** blazing, brilliant, dazzling, gleaming, glistening, glittering, glowing, intense, luminous, lustrous, phosphorescent, radiant, scintillating, shimmering, shining, sparkling, twinkling, vivid. **2** astute, brilliant, clever, ingenious, intelligent, inventive, sharp, smart. **3** encouraging, excellent, golden, good, optimistic, promising. **4** cheerful, genial, glad, happy, jolly, lively, merry, vivacious.
brighten *v* **1** enliven, gleam, glow, illuminate, make brighter, shine. **2** cheer up, enliven, encourage, gladden, hearten, make happy, perk up.

Television pictures are broadcast from stations after being processed through picture studios where the images are edited together with sound.

bring *v* **1** accompany, bear, carry, convey, deliver, escort, fetch, gather, guide, import, transfer, transport. **2** cause, create, effect, inflict, produce, result in, wreak.
brisk *adj* **1** active, alert, animated, busy, energetic, hectic, lively, quick, rapid, swift. **2** biting, bracing, crisp, exhilarating, fresh, invigorating, refreshing; (*Inf*) nippy.
brittle *adj* breakable, crumbling, delicate, fragile, frail.
broach *v* **1** bring up, mention, propose, propound, put forward, suggest, submit. **2** open, start, uncork. **3** draw off, pierce, puncture, tap.
broad *adj* **1** ample, extensive, large, roomy, spacious, vast, wide-spread. **2** comprehensive, far-reaching, global, nonspecific, sweeping, universal, wide. **3** broad-minded, liberal, progressive, tolerant, unbiased.
broadcast *v* **1** air, beam, cable, radio, relay, show, televise, transmit. **2** advertise, announce, circulate, make public, proclaim, report, spread. **3** disperse, scatter, sow.
broadcast *n* programme, radio show, television show, show, telecast, transmission.
broaden *v* amplify, augment, expand, increase, open up, spread, stretch, supplement, swell, widen.
brochure *n* advertisement, booklet, circular, folder, handbill, hand-out, leaflet, mailshot, pamphlet.
broker *n* agent, broker-dealer, dealer, factor, insurance broker,

intermediary, middleman, negotiator, stockbroker.
brooch *n* breast-pin, clip, pin, tie-clip, tie-pin.
brood *v* **1** dwell upon, fret, mull over, think upon, worry. **2** cover young, hatch eggs, incubate eggs.
brood *n* chicks, children, clutch, family, hatch, infants, issue, litter, nest, offspring, progeny, young.
brook *n* beck, burn, rill, rivulet, stream, streamlet, watercourse.
brother *n* **1** relation, relative, sibling. **2** associate, colleague, companion, compeer, comrade, confrère, fellow member, partner. cleric, friar, monk.
brow *n* **1** forehead, temple. **2** eyebrows. **3** apex, brink, crown, peak, summit, top.
brown *adj* **1** bay, roan, sorrel. **2** brick, bronze, bronzed, browned, brunette, chestnut, chocolate, coffee, cocoa, dark, dun, dusky, ginger, hazel, rust, tawny, umber. **3** browned, sunburnt, tan, tanned, toasted.
brown *v* fry, grill, sauté, seal, sear.
browse *v* **1** dip into, flip through, glance at, leaf through, look through, scan, skim, window shop. **2** crop, eat, feed, graze, nibble, pasture.
bruise *v* blacken, blemish, contuse, damage, injure, mark.
bruise *n* black and blue mark, blemish, contusion, discolouration, injury, mark, swelling.
brutal *adj* barbarous, blood-thirsty, cruel, ferocious, heart-less, merciless, pitiless, ruthless, savage, vicious.
brute *n* **1** animal, beast, creature, wild animal. **2** barbarian, devil, fiend, monster, ogre, sadist, savage, swine.
bubble *n* **1** air cavity, bead, blister, blob, drop, droplet, globule, vesicle. **2** delusion, dream, chimera, fantasy, illusion.
bubble *v* **1** effervesce, fizz, foam, froth, percolate, seethe, sparkle, spume. **2** boil, percolate, seethe, simmer; brim over, be filled.
buccaneer *n* corsair, free-booter, pirate, sea rover, Viking.
bucket *n* can, pail, pitcher, scuttle.
buckle *n* **1** catch, clasp, clip, fastener, fastener, fastening, hasp. **2** bulging, contorted, curved, distorted, kinked, warped.
buckle *v* **1** catch, clasp, clip, fasten, hook, secure, strap, tie. **2** bend, bulge, cave in, collapse, contorted, crumpled, curved, distorted, fold, twisted, warped.
buff *adj* beige, sandy, straw-coloured, yellowish, yellowish-brown.

Bugs have developed different methods of protecting themselves against predators. Some use bright warning colours to deter enemies while others use camouflage to blend into their environment.

buff *v* burnish, polish, rub, rub up, shine, smooth.
buff *n* addict, admirer, enthusiast, expert, fan.
buffer *n* bulwark, bumper, cushion, fender, guard, intermediary, safeguard, screen, shield, shock absorber.
buffet *v* bang, batter, beat, box, bump, clobber, cuff, flail, hit, knock, pound, pummel, push, rap, shove, slap, strike, thump, wallop, whack.
buffet *n* **1** café, caféteria, salad bar, snack bar. **2** cold meal, cold table, self-service, smorgasbord. **3** blow, bump, jolt, knock, push, shove, thump, wallop, whack.
bug *n* **1** flea, insect, mite. **2** disease, germ, infection, micro-organism, virus. **3** craze, fad, mania, obsession, passion. **4** defect, flaw, gremlin, imperfection, obstruction. **5** listening device, phone-tap, tap, wire-tap.
bug *v* **1** phone-tap, wire-tap. **2** eavesdrop on, listen in, spy, tap. **3** anger.
build *v* **1** assemble, construct, erect, fabricate, form, make, manufacture, put up, raise. **2** base, begin, develop, establish, inaugurate, initiate, institute, set up, start.
build *n* body, figure, form, frame, physique, structure.
building *v* **1** domicile, dwelling, edifice, fabric, house, structure. **2** architecture, construction, erection, fabricating, railing.
bullet *n* ball, dumdum bullet, missile, pellet, plastic bullet, projectile, rubber bullet, shot.
bulletin *n* **1** announcement, communication, dispatch, flash, message, newsflash, news report, statement. **2** broadsheet, leaflet, listings, newsletter, newspaper, pamphlet.
bulwark *n* **1** bastion, buttress, defence, fortification, mole, outwork, partition, rampart, redoubt. **2** defence, guard, mainstay, safeguard, support. **3** defendant, protector.
buoy *n* beacon, float, guide, marker, signal.
bureau *n* **1** desk, writing desk. **2** agency, branch, department, division, office, service.
burly *adj* beefy, big, brawny, bulky, hefty, hulking, muscular, powerful, stocky, stout, strapping, strong, sturdy, thickset, well-built.
burrow *n* den, hole, lair, retreat, shelter, tunnel.
burrow *v* delve, dig, excavate, hollow out, scoop out, tunnel.

In hot climates, some animals live underground in burrows, where the temperature is cooler.

bustle *n* activity, commotion, excitement, flurry, fuss, haste, hurry, pother, stir, tumult.
buttress *n* **1** reinforcement, pier, prop, stanchion, support. **2** cornerstone, mainstay, pillar, sustainer, upholder.
buttress *v* back up, brace, defend, prop up, shore up, strengthen, support, uphold, underpin.
buy *v* acquire, invest in, obtain, pay for, procure, purchase.
buy *n* acquisition, bargain, deal, purchase.
by *prep* **1** along, alongside, beside, by way of, close to, in front of, near, next to, over, past, via. **2** through, through the agency of, under the aegis of. **3** at, before, no later than. **4** as a result, because of, through.
by *adv* aside, at hand, away, beyond, close, handy, in reach, near, past, to one side.
bygone *adj* ancient, antiquated, dead, extinct, former, obsolete, outmoded, passé, past, previous.
by-law, bye-law *n* local regulation, regulation, rule, statute.
bypass *n* alternative route, circuitous route, detour, ring road, roundabout way.
bypass *v* **1** go round, make a detour round, pass round. **2** avoid, evade, circumvent, find a way round, get round. **3** avoid, circumvent, go over the head of, ignore, miss out, pass over.
bystander *n* eyewitness, gaper, looker-on, observer, onlooker, passer-by, spectator, viewer, watcher, witness.
byword *n* **1** catchword, example of, motto, slogan. **2** cliché, proverb, saying.

Cc

cake *v* **1** bun, pastry. **2** bar, block, cube, chunk, loaf, lump, mass, slab.
cake *v* **1** bake, coagulate, dry, harden, ossify, solidify, thicken. **2** coat, cover, encrust, plaster.
cab *n* **1** hackney, hackney carriage, minicab, taxi, taxicab. **2** cabin, compartment, cubicle, cubbyhole, quarters.
cabin *n* **1** berth, chalet, cot, cottage, crib, hovel, hut, lodge, shack, shanty, shed, **2** both. **3** berth, compartment, deckhouse, quarters, room.
cabinet *n* **1** case, cupboard, dresser, locker. **2** administration, assembly, council, counsellors, ministers, ministry, senate.
cable *n* **1** cord, cordage, line, rope, wire. **2** cablegram, telegram, telegraph, wire.
cable *v* radio, telegraph, wire
café *n* bistro, cafeteria, coffee bar, coffee shop, lunchroom, restaurant, snack bar, tearoom, teashop, wine bar.
cage *n* **1** coop, enclosure, lock-up, pen, pound. **2** corral. **3** aviary, birdcage, hen coop, sheep pen.
cage *v* confine, coop, coop up, corral, fence in, hem in, immure, impound, imprison, incarcerate, lock up, mew, pen, restrain, restrict, shut in.
calculate *v* adjust, compute, count, estimate, figure, judge, reckon, value, weigh, work out.
calculation *n* answer, computation, estimate, estimation, figuring, forecast, judgment, reckoning, result.
calibre *n* **1** bore, diameter, gauge, measure. **2** ability, capacity, capability, competence, distinction, endowment, excellence, faculty, force, gifts, merit, parts, quality, scope, stature, strengths, talent, worth.
call *v* **1** announce, awaken, cry, hail, proclaim, roar, shout, shriek, waken, yell. **2** assemble, collect, gather, invite, muster, phone, rally, ring up, summon, telephone. **3** christen, denominate, describe as, label, name, term.
call *n* **1** cry, hail, scream, shout, signal, whoop, yell. **2** appeal, command, demand, invitation, notice, order, plea, request, summons, supplication, visit.
callous *adj* **1** apathetic, cold, hard-hearted, heartless, indifferent, insensitive, thick-skinned, unsympathetic. **2** hard, hardened, leathery, thickened.
calm *adj* **1** balmy, mild, pacific, peaceful, placid, quiet, restful, serene, smooth, still, tranquil, windless. **2** composed, cool, relaxed, unemotional, unexcited, unmoved, unruffled.
calm *n* **1** harmony, peace, restfullness, serenity, stillness, tranquillity. **2** composure, coolness, poise, self-control; (*Inf*) cool.
calm *v* **1** allay, alleviate, appease, assuage, hush, lull, mollify, pacify, placate, quieten, relax, soothe, tranquillize. **2** die down, quieten, settle down, still.
camouflage *n* cover, disguise, front, guise, mask, masquerade, mimicry, protective colouring.
camouflage *v* cloak, conceal, cover up, disguise, hide, mask, obscure, screen, veil.
camp *n* **1** bivouac, camping ground, camp site, cantonment, encampment, tents. **2** faction,

Native American lived in camps with tents made from skins and sticks called tepees. A hole in the top let out the smoke from their fires.

group, party, sect, set.
camp *v* **1** encamp, pitch camp, pitch tents, set up camp. **2** behave affectedly, ham it, lay it on, overact, over do it, spread it on thick.
campaign *n* **1** attack, battle, crusade, drive, expedition, movement, offensive, operation, push, war. **2** action, battle plan, course of action, manoeuvre, promotion, strategy.
campaign *v* agitate, battle, crusade, fight, strive, struggle, work.
can *n* container, receptacle, tin.
can *v* bottle, preserve, tin.
canal *n* **1** channel, race, watercourse, waterway. **2** conduit, duct, pipe, tube.
cancel *v* abolish, abort, call off, delete, do away with, eliminate, erase, obliterate, quash, repeal.
cancer *n* **1** growth, malignancy. **2** carcinoma, melanoma, metastasis, sarcoma. **3** blight, canker, corruption, disease, pestilence, plague, scourge, sickness.
candid *adj* blunt, fair, frank, outspoken, straightforward, truthful, unbiased.
candidate *n* applicant, contender, contestant, nominee.
cane *n* alpenstock, reed, rod, shepherd's crook, staff, stave, stick, walking stick.
cane *v* **1** beat, flog, hit, scourge, strap, strike, thrash; (*Inf*) tan one's backside. **2** defeat, rout, thrash, trounce.
canker *n* abcess, blister, lesion, running sore, ulcer, ulceration.
cannibal *n* **1** man-eater, people eater. **2** barbican, savage.
cannon *n* field gun, gun, mounted gun; (*Inf*) big gun.
canopy *n* awning, cover, sunshade, tarpaulin, tester.
canter *n* amble, easy, gallop, jog, lope, saunter, trot.
canvass *v* **1** campaign, drum up support. **2** electioneer, enquire into, examine, explore, find out, inspect, investigate, look into, persuade, poll, scan, scrutinize, sift, solicit, solicit votes, study air, argue, debate, dispute, ventilate.
canvass *n* examination, investigation, poll, scrutiny, survey, tally.
canyon *n* abyss, chasm, gorge, gulf, gully, ravine, valley
cap *n* **1** bonnet, hat, headgear; (*Inf*) lid. **2** bung, cork, lid, plug, stopper, top. **3** apex, crest, peak, pinnacle, summit.
cap *v* **1** beat, better, exceed, excel, outdo, outstrip, top. **2** include, pick, select.
capable *adj* able, clever, efficient, intelligent, qualified, skilful, smart, suited, talented.
capacity *n* **1** dimensions, extent, magnitude, proportions, range, room, scope, size, space, volume. **2** ability, aptitude, capability, competence, gift, intelligence, power, proficiency, readiness, strength. **3** appointment, function, job, office, position, post, province, role, service, sphere.
cape *n* cloak.
cape *n* head, headland, jess, peninsula, point, promontory, tongue.
capital *adj* **1** chief, controlling, essential, foremost, important, leading, main, major, primary, prime, principal, vital. **2** excellent, fine, first, prime, splendid, superb.
capital *n* **1** centre of administration, first city, seat of government. **2** capital letter. **3** cash, financing, funds, hard cash, investment, means, money, principal, property, wealth.
capsize *v* invert, keel over, over turn, tip over, turn over, upset.

In England, barges and narrow boats were often brightly painted with patterns and scenes from life on the canals.

During the 20th century the car evolved enormously. From cars in the early years with top speeds barely over walking pace, to the 230mph Maclaren F1 at the end of the century.

captain *n* boss, chief, chieftain, commander, head, leader, master, officer, pilot, skipper.
captive *n* bondservant, convict, detainee, hostage, internee, prisoner of war, slave.
captive *adj* caged, confined, enslaved, ensnared, imprisoned, incarcerated, locked up, penned, restricted, subjugated.
captivity *v* bondage, confinement, custody, detention, duress, imprisonment, restraint, slavery, thraldom.
capture *v* apprehend, arrest, bag, catch, secure, seize, take, take into custody, take prisoner; (*Inf*) collar.
car *n* auto, automobile, machine, motor, motorcar, vehicle.
carcass *n* body, cadaver, corpse, dead body, framework, remains, shell, skeleton.
care *n* **1** concern, interest, responsibility, trouble, worry. **2** attention, carefulness, consideration, regard, vigilance. **3** charge, control, custody, protection, supervision, ward.
career *n* calling, employment, livelihood, occupation, vocation.
careful *adj* **1** attentive, cautious, conscientious, discreet, precise, thoughtful. **2** thrifty. **3** alert, concerned, mindful, protective, vigilant, wary, watchful.
caretaker *n* concierge, curator, janitor, keeper, porter, superintendent, warden, watchman.
cargo *n* baggage, consignment, freight, goods, load, merchandise, shipment, tonnage.
carnival *n* celebration, fair, festival, fiesta, gala, holiday, jamboree, jubilee, Mardi Gras.
carriage *n* **1** carrying, conveyance, delivery, freight, transport, transportation. **2** cab, coach, vehicle. **3** air, bearing, behaviour, conduct, manner, posture, presence.
carry *v* **1** bear, bring, convey, fetch, haul, lift, lug, move, relay, take, transfer, transport. **2** bear, hold up, shoulder, stand, support, sustain, underpin, uphold.

carton *n* box, case, container, pack, package, packet.
cartoon *n* animated film, animation, caricature, comic strip, lampoon, parody, satire, sketch; (*Inf*) takeoff.
cartridge *n* charge, round, shell.
carve *v* chip, chisel, cut, divide, engrave, etch, fashion, form, indent, mould, sculpt, sculpture, slash, slice, whittle.
cascade *n* avalanche, cataract, deluge, falls, flood, fountain, out-pouring, shower, torrent, waterfall.
case *n* **1** baggage, box, briefcase, bureau, cabinet, carton, casket, chest, container, crate, cupboard, envelope, folder, holder, housing, jacket, luggage, receptacle, sheath, shell, suitcase, tray, trunk, wrapping.
2 condition, context, event, predicament, situation, state.
3 example, instance, occasion, occurrence, specimen. **4** action, dispute, lawsuit, legal cause, legal dispute, legal proceedings, proceedings, process, suit, trial.
5 invalid, patient, sick person.
cash *n* banknotes, bullion, capital, change, currency, finance, funds, money, notes, payment, resources, wherewithal.
cashier *n* accountant, bank clerk, banker, bursar, clerk, purser, teller, treasurer.
casino *n* gambling club, gambling den, gambling house.
cask *n* barrel, firkin, hogshead, keg, pipe, tun, vat, vessel.
casket *n* **1** box, case, chest, coffer, container, receptacle.
2 coffin, pall, sarcophagus; (*Inf*) wooden overcoat.
cast *v* **1** chuck, drop, fling, hurl, launch, let fly, lob, sling, throw, thrust, toss. **2** discard, get rid of, peel off, throw off. **3** direct, send out, shoot, turn. **4** diffuse, emit, give off, radiate. **5** create, form. **6** give, grant. **7** enter, record, register, vote. **8** fashion, form, model, mould, sculpt. **9** allot, appoint, assign, choose, name, pick, select. **10** actors, characters, company, players, troupe.
cast *n* **1** fling, hurl, lob, pitch, shy, throw, toss. **2** sort, stamp, type. **3** figure, form, mould, shape. **4** defect, squint, twist.
castle *n* chateau, citadel, fortress, keep, mansion, palace, stronghold, tower.
casual *adj* **1** accidental, chance, spontaneous, unexpected.
2 apathetic, blasé, indifferent, informal, offhand, relaxed, unconcerned. **3** irregular, part-time, temporary.

This castle has very small windows so that there are few entrances for enemy arrows and bullets. A narrow slit was all that was necessary for the castle's inhabitants to fire on attackers outside.

casualty *n* loss, sufferer, victim.
catalogue *n* directory, gazetteer, index, inventory, list, record, register, roll, roster, schedule.
catastrophe *n* blow, calamity, disaster, fiasco, misfortune, tragedy; (*Inf*) meltdown.
catch *v* **1** apprehend, arrest, capture, entrap, seize, snatch, take. **2** detect, discover, expose, find out, surprise.
catch *n* **1** bolt, clasp, clip, fastener, hasp, hook, hook and eye, latch, lock, sneck, snib.
2 disadvantage, drawback, hitch, snag, stumbling block, trap.
category *n* class, classification, department, division, grade, grouping, head, heading, list, order, rank, section, sort, type
cater *v* provide, provision, supply, victual.
cattle *n* beasts, cows, kine,

livestock, stock.
cause *v* bring about, create, generate, incite, produce, provoke, result in.
caustic *adj* acrid, astringent, biting, burning, corroding, corrosive.
cautious *adj* careful, guarded, heedful, judicious, prudent, tentative, vigilant, wary,
cave *n* cavern, cavity, den, grotto, hollow.
cavern *n* cave, hollow, pothole.
cavity *n* crater, dent, gap, hole, hollow, pit.
cease *v* break off, conclude, culminate, discontinue, end, fail, finish, halt, stay, stop, terminate.
celebration *n* carousal, festival, festivity, gala, jollification, jubilee, junketing, merrymaking, party.
celebrity *n* big name, dignitary, lion, luminary, name, personality, star, superstar, VIP; (*Inf*) celeb.
cell *n* **1** cavity, chamber, compartment, cubicle, dungeon, stall. **2** living matter, organism.
cement *v* attach, bind, bond, glue, join, plaster, seal, solder, stick together, unite, weld.
central *adj* chief, essential, focal, fundamental, mean, median, mid, middle, primary, principal.
centre *n* bull's-eye, core, crux, focus, heart, hub, mid, middle, midpoint, nucleus, pivot.
ceremonial *n* ceremony, rite, ritual.
certain *adj* **1** confident, positive, sure. **2** true, unmistakable, valid. **3** decided, definite, established, fixed, settled.
certainty *n* confidence, conviction, faith, inevitability, sureness, trust, validity.
certificate *n* diploma, document, licence.
certify *v* authenticate, confirm, guarantee, verify.
chain *v* bind, handcuff, manacle, restrain, shackle, tether.
chain *n* **1** bond, coupling, fetter, link, manacle, shackle, union. **2** progression, sequence, series, set, string, succession, train.
challenge *v* dare, demand, provoke, question, require, throw down the gauntlet.
chamber *n* apartment, bedroom, cavity, compartment, cubicle, hollow, room.
champion *n* challenger, conqueror, defender, hero, protector, title holder, upholder, victor, vindicator, warrior, winner
chance *n* **1** likelihood, odds, possibility, probability. **2** coincidence, fate, luck, peril. providence. **3** risk, speculation, uncertainty.
chance *v* **1** happen, occur. **2** endanger, jeopardize, risk, try.
change *v* **1** alter, modify, shift, transform. **2** alternate, exchange, replace, substitute, swap.
change *n* **1** alteration, innovation, metamorphosis, transformation. **2** conversion, exchange, substitution, trade.
channel *n* canal, conduit, groove, gutter, passage, strait.
channel *v* conduct, convey, direct, guide, transmit.
chaos *n* anarchy, bedlam, disorder, pandemonium.
chapter *n* episode, part, period, phase, section, stage, topic.
character *n* **1** attributes, nature, personality, reputation, type. **2** honour, integrity. **3** eccentric. **4** persona,
characteristic *adj* distinctive, peculiar, specific, typical.
characteristic *n* attribute, feature, mark, peculiarity, quality, quirk,trait.
charge *v* **1** accuse, blame. **2** bid, command, instruct, order.
charge *n* **1** accusation, allegation, attack. **2** duty, office, trust. **3** amount, cost, expense, price.
charity *n* assistance, donations, fund, gift, hand-out.

The main parts of a living cell

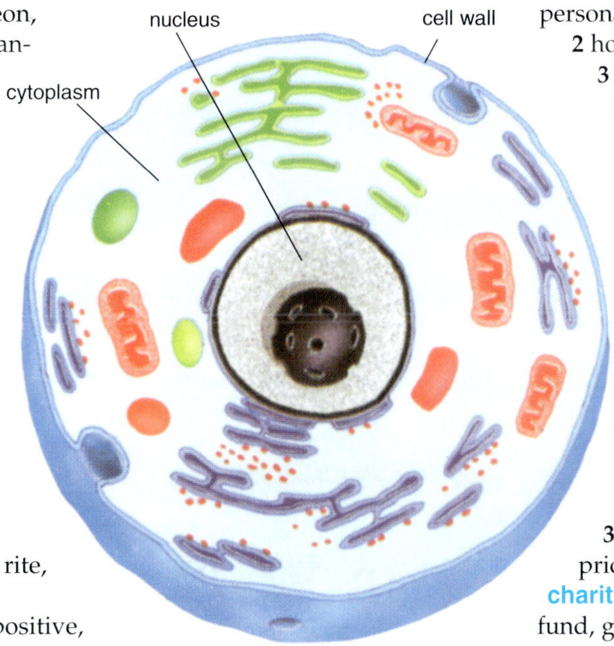

charm *v* attract, captivate, delight, enchant, fascinate, mesmerize, win over.
charm *n* appeal, attraction, fascination, magic.
chart *n* blueprint, diagram, graph, map, plan, table.
chart *v* draft, graph, outline, plot, sketch.
charter *n* contract, document, licence, permit, privilege, right.
chase *v* course, drive, follow, hunt, pursue, run after, track.
chat *n* chatter, gossip, heart-to-heart, natter, talk.
chat *v* chatter, gossip, talk
chatter *n/v* chat, gossip, natter, prattle; (*Inf*) chin wag, natter.
cheap *adj* **1** bargain, cut-price, inexpensive, low-priced, sale. **2** common, inferior, second-rate, shoddy, tatty. **3** base, despicable, low, mean.
cheat *v* **1** con, deceive, double-cross, hoodwink, swindle, trick. **2** baffle, check, defeat, deprive, foil, frustrate, prevent, thwart.
cheat *n* **1** inspection, research, scrutiny, test. **2** control, curb, limitation, restraint, stoppage.
chest *n* box, case, casket, crate, strongbox, trunk.
chew *v* bite, champ, crunch, gnaw, grind, masticate, munch.
chief *adj* central, essential, foremost, main, principal.
chief *n* boss, captain, chieftain, commander, director, governor, head, leader, lord, manager, master, principal, ruler.
child *n* baby, infant, juvenile, minor, toddler, tot, youngster.

By nine months, the human child is on the move, crawling or sliding along. Within a year, they will be able to walk and understand language.

chilly *adj* **1** cool, crisp, draughty, fresh, nippy. **2** frigid, hostile, unfriendly, unwelcoming.
chip *n* dent, flaw, nick, scratch.
choke *v* asphyxiate, block, clog, constrict, dam, obstruct, stifle.
choose *v* adopt, elect, opt for, pick, prefer, select, wish.
chore *n* burden, duty, errand, job, task.
cinema *n* films, motion pictures, movies, pictures; (*Inf*) big screen, flicks.
circle *n* **1** band, circumference, globe, orb, perimeter, ring, sphere, turn. **2** area, enclosure, field, orbit, range, realm, sphere. **3** assembly, class, club, company, fellowship, group, society.
circle *v* belt, curve, encircle, enclose, encompass, envelop, hem in, pivot, revolve, rotate, surround, tour, whirl.
circuit *n* area, compass, course, journey, orbit, perambulation, revolution, round, route, tour.
circumference *n* boundary, edge, fringe, limits, outline, perimeter, periphery, rim, verge.
circumstances *pl n* life style, means, resources, situation, state, state of affairs, status.
city *n* conurbation, megalopolis, metropolis, municipality.
civil *adj* civic, domestic, home, interior, municipal, political.
claim *v* allege, ask, assert, call for, challenge, collect, demand, exact, hold, insist, maintain, need, require, take, uphold.
claim *n* allegation, call, demand, request, requirement, right, title.
clan *n* band, brotherhood, faction, family, fraternity, group, house, race, sect, set, society, tribe.
clap *v* acclaim, applaud, cheer.
clarify *v* clear up, elucidate, explain, illuminate, make plain, resolve, simplify, throw light on.
clarity *n* clearness, definition, precision, simplicity.
clash *v* conflict, cross swords, feud, quarrel, war, wrangle.
clash *n* brush, collision, conflict, confrontation, fight; (*Inf*) showdown.
clasp *v* attack, clutch, embrace, fasten, grasp, grip, hold, hug, seize, squeeze.
clasp *n* brooch, buckle, catch,

clip, fastener, fastening, grip, hook, pin, press stud, snap.
class *n* caste, category, division, grade, group, kind, league, order, rank, set, sort, species, sphere, status, type, value.
classic *adj* best, finest, first-rate.
classify *v* arrange, catalogue, categorize, file, rank, sort.
clause *n* **1** article, chapter, condition, paragraph, passage, section. **2** heading, item, point, provision, proviso, stipulation.
claw *n* nail, talon, tentacle.
clean *adj* **1** fresh, hygienic, pure, spotless, unstained, washed. **2** good, innocent, moral, pure, respectable, upright.
clean *v* bath, cleanse, deodorize, disinfect, launder, vacuum, wash, wipe.
clear *adj* **1** bright, fine, halcyon, light, luminous, shining, sunny. **2** apparent, comprehensible, distinct, evident, obvious, plain. **3** empty, free, open, unimpeded, unobstructed. **4** certain, definite, positive, sure.
clear *v* **1** clean, sweep away, tidy. **2** brighten, clarify, lighten. **3** acquit, excuse, jump, leap, miss, pass over, vault.
clever *adj* able, bright, expert, gifted, intelligent, shrewd, skilful, smart, talented.
cliff *n* bluff, crag, escarpment, face, overhang, precipice, rock face, scar, scarp.
climate *n* **1** country, region, temperature, weather, zone. **2** ambience, disposition, feeling, mood, temper, tendency, trend.
climax *n* acme, apogee, culmination, head, height, highlight, highspot, peak, summit, top, zenith.
climb *v* ascend, clamber, mount, rise, scale, shin up, soar, top.
cling *v* adhere, attach to, embrace, fasten, grasp, grip, hug, twine round.
clip *v* **1** crop, curtail, cut, cut short, pare, prune, shear, shorten, snip, trim. **2** attach, fasten, fix, hold, pin, staple. **3** box, cuff, hit, punch, smack, wallop; (*Inf*) clout. **4** dash, gallop, go like lightning, race, rush, whip along, zoom.
cloak *v* camouflage, conceal, cover, disguise, hide, mask, obscure, screen, veil.
cloak *n* blind, cape, coat, cover, mask, shield, wrap.
close *v* **1** bar, bolt, fasten, latch, padlock, secure, slam, shut. **2** block, obstruct, plug, seal, secure, shut, stop up. **3** cease, conclude, finish, mothball, seal, settle, terminate. **4** connect, couple, join, unite.
close *adj* **1** adjacent, approaching, imminent, near, neighbouring. **2** compact, dense, jam-packed, thick, tight. **3** attached, devoted, intimate, loving. **4** airless, heavy, humid, muggy, oppressive, stifling, suffocating, sweltering, unventilated. **5** mean, miserly, stingy, tight-fisted. **6** alert, attentive, intense, keen, painstaking, vigilant.
close *n* **1** cessation, completion, conclusion, end, finale, finish, termination, wind-up. **2** courtyard, cul-de-sac, enclosure, piazza, quadrangle.
closet *n* cabinet, cupboard, locker, storage room, wardrobe.
closet *adj* concealed, furtive, secret, undisclosed, unrevealed.
closet *v* confine, isolate, seclude, shut away.

Climatic conditions

The climate in different parts of the world varies enormously. The position of each region and its proximity to the sea and mountains, determines what type of conditions will be found in that particular ecosystem.

Tropical rainforest
warm moist climate

Deciduous woodland
part mild, part wet climate

Ice and tundra
freezing cold climate

clothing *n* apparel, attire, costume, dress, garments, habits, outfit, wardrobe, wear.
cloud *n* billow, darkness, fog, haze, mist, nebula, vapour.
cloud *v* darken, eclipse, obscure, overcast, overshadow, shadow.
cloudy *adj* blurred, confused, dim, dull, hazy, murky, overcast.
clown *n* **1** buffoon, comedian, comic, fool, harlequin, jester, joker, pierrot, prankster. **2** fool, half-wit, idiot, nitwit; (*Inf*) clot.
clown *v* fool, joke, mess about; (*Inf*) mess, muck about.
club *n* **1** bat, bludgeon, cosh, stick, truncheon. **2** association, circle, company, fraternity, group, guild, lodge, order, set, society, union.
clue *n* evidence, hint, indication, lead, pointer, sign, suggestion, suspicion, tip, trace.
clumsy *adj* awkward, bungling, heavy, inept, inexpert, ponderous, uncouth, unskilful, unwieldy; (*Inf*) butter-fingered.
cluster *n* batch, bunch, collection, gathering, group, knot.
cluster *v* assemble, collect, flock, gather, group.
coach *n* **1** bus, car, carriage, charabanc, vehicle. **2** instructor, teacher, trainer, tutor.
coach *v* cram, drill, instruct, prepare, train, tutor.
coast *n* beach, coastline, littoral, seaboard, seaside, shore, strand.
coast *v* cruise, drift, freewheel, get by, glide, sail, taxi.
coat *n* **1** fleece, fur, hair, hide, pelt, skin, wool. **2** coating, covering, layer, overlay.
coat *v* apply, cover, plaster, smear, spread.
coax *v* cajole, decoy, entice, flatter, persuade, talk into.

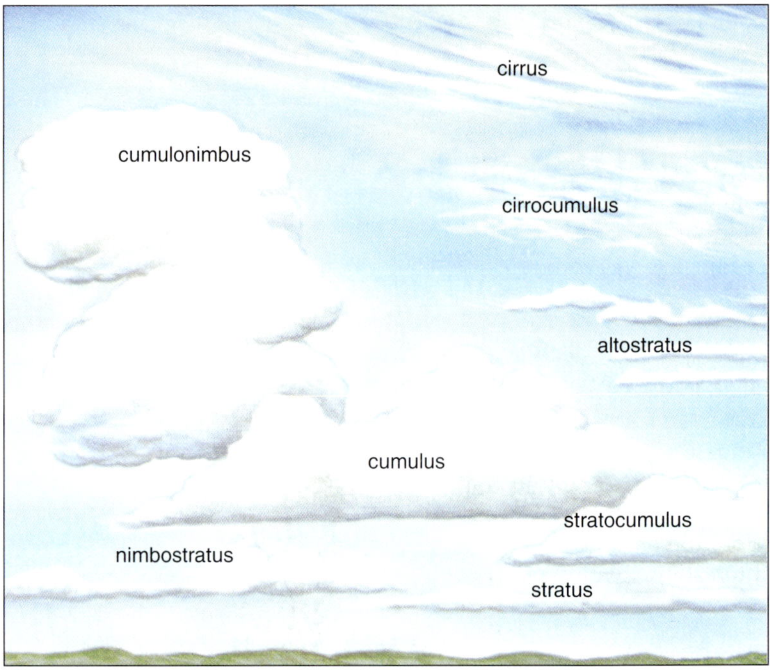

Clouds are formed from water evaporating into the air from rivers, lakes and oceans. As it rises into the air, the vapour is cooled and condenses into clouds. The names given to clouds simply describe their shapes and positions in the sky. Higher levels of cloud are made of ice crystals.

code *n* **1** cipher, cryptograph. **2** convention, custom, ethics, etiquette, manners, regulations, rules, system.
coil *v* convolute, curl, entwine, loop, snake, spiral, twine, twist, wind, wreathe, writhe.
coincidence *n* accident, chance, eventuality, fluke, fortuity, happy accident, luck, stroke of luck.
cold *adj* **1** arctic, biting, bitter, chilly, cool, freezing, frosty, frozen, icy, raw, wintry. **2** chilled, freezing, numbed, shivery. **3** apathetic, dead, distant, frigid, indifferent, lukewarm, passionless, reserved, stony, unfeeling, unsympathetic.
cold *n* chill, chilliness, coldness, frigidity, frostiness, iciness, inclemency.
collapse *v* break down, cave in, crack up, crumple, fail, fall, fold, founder, give way, subsided.
collapse *n* breakdown, cave-in, disintegration, downfall, exhaustion, failure, faint, prostration, subsidence
collect *v* **1** accumulate, aggregate, amass, assemble, gather, heap, hoard, save, stockpile. **2** assemble, cluster, ongregate, convene, converge, rally.
collection *n* **1** anthology, compilation, pile, store. **2** assembly, assortment, cluster, company, congregation, crowd, gathering, group. **3** alms, contribution, offering.

collision *n* accident, bump, crash, impact, pile-up, smash; (*Inf*) prang.
colour *n* **1** colourant, dye, paint, pigment, shade, tincture, tint. **2** animation, bloom, blush, brilliance, glow, rosiness, ruddiness.
colour *v* **1** colourwash, dye, paint, stain, tinge, tint. **2** distort, embroider, exaggerate, misrepresent, pervert, prejudice, slant, taint. **3** blush, burn, crimson, flush, go crimson, redden.
colourful *adj* **1** bright, brilliant, intense, kaleidoscopic, rich, vibrant, vivid. **2** distinctive, interesting, lively, picturesque, rich, stimulating, unusual, vivid.
column *n* **1** file, line, list, procession, queue, rank, row, string, train. **2** pillar, post, shaft, support, upright.
coma *n* black-out, drowsiness, insensibility, lethargy, oblivion, stupor, trance, unconsciousness.
combat *n* action, battle, conflict, contest, encounter, engagement, fight, skirmish, struggle, war.
combine *v* amalgamate, blend, connect, fuse, integrate, join, link, merge, mix, pool, put together, synthesize, unify, unite.
come *v* **1** advance, appear, approach, enter, happen, materialize, move, near, occur, originate, reach, show up, turn out. **2** appear, arrive, attain, enter, materialize, reach. **3** fall, happen, occur, take place. **4** arise, emerge, end up, flow, issue, originate, result, turn out. **5** extend, reach; (*Inf*) show up.
comfortable *adj* **1** ample, cosy, enjoyable, homely, pleasant, relaxing, restful, roomy, snug. **2** affluent, prosperous, well-off, well-to-do. **3** comic, amusing, comical, droll, facetious, farcical, funny, humorous, jocular, joking, light, rich, waggish, witty.
command *v* **1** bid, compel, demand, direct, order, require. **2** control, dominate, govern, head, lead, manage, reign over, rule, supervise.

The colours of the spectrum

Although light appears to be colourless, in fact it is made up of all the colours of the spectrum. Each colour has a different wavelength. The spectrum of colours can be seen if a beam of light is split by a prism. In nature the colours of the spectrum can sometimes be seen as a rainbow.

command *n* bidding, direction, directive, edict, mandate, order, requirement, ultimatum.
commander *n* boss, captain, chief, C in C, CO, commander-in-chief, commanding officer, director, head, leader, officer, ruler.
commence *v* begin, embark on, enter upon, initiate, open, start.
commentary *n* analysis, description, explanation, notes, review, voice-over.
commentator *n* commenter, reporter, special, correspondent, sportscaster.
commit *v* carry out, do, enact, execute, perform, perpetrate
common *adj* **1** average, daily, everyday, familiar, frequent, ordinary, plain, regular, routine, run-of-the-mill, simple, standard, stock, usual. **2** accepted, general, popular, prevailing, prevalent, universal, widespread. **3** coarse, inferior, low, stale, vulgar.
commotion *n* disorder, disturbance, excitement, fuss, riot, rumpus, to-do, turmoil, uproar.
communication *n* **1** connection, contact, conversation, correspondence, link, transmission. **2** announcement, information, intelligence, message, news, report, statement.
communism *n* Bolshevism, collectivism, Marxism, socialism, state socialism.
compact *adj* **1** close, condensed, dense, firm, impenetrable, pressed together, solid, thick. **2** brief, concise, succinct, terse, to the point.
company *n* **1** assembly, band, body, circle, collection, crew, crowd, ensemble, gathering, group, league, party, set, troop, troupe. **2** association, business, concern, corporation, establishment, firm, house, partnership, syndicate.

The world-wide competition for disabled athletes is known as the Paralympics. It was first held in 1960 in Rome.

compartment *n* alcove, bay, berth, booth, cell, chamber, cubicle, locker, pigeonhole.
compel *v* drive, enforce, make, necessitate, oblige, restrain, squeeze, urge; (*Inf*) bulldoze.
compensation *n* damages, payment, recompense, reward, satisfaction.
compete *v* challenge, contest, fight, rival, strive, struggle, vie.
competition *n* **1** contest, opposition, rivalry, struggle. **2** championship, event, puzzle, quiz, tournament.
compile *v* accumulate, amass, collect, gather, organize, put together.
complain *v* find fault, fuss, grieve, groan, grumble, moan, whine; (*Inf*) bellyache.
complaint *n* **1** accusation, charge, criticism, moan, trouble, wail. **2** affliction, ailment, disease, disorder, illness, indisposition, malady, sickness, upset.
complete *adj* **1** all, entire, full, integral, whole. **2** accomplished, concluded, ended, finished. **3** absolute, perfect, thorough, total, utter.
complete *v* accomplish, achieve, cap, close, conclude, discharge, do, execute, finalize, fulfil, perfect, perform, settle, terminate.
complex *adj* complicated, intricate, mingled, mixed, tangled.
complicated *adj* **1** complex, convoluted, elaborate, interlaced, intricate, involved, labyrinthine. **2** difficult, perplexing, problematic,

The chameleon and the Arctic hare can both conceal themselves by changing colour to match their surroundings. The hare is white in winter and changes to brown in summer. The chameleon can tighten or release special skin cells which alter colour during this process.

puzzling, troublesome.
component *n* constituent, element, ingredient, piece, unit.
compose *v* build, compound, comprise, constitute, construct, fashion, form, make, make up, put together.
composition *n* **1** arrangement, design, formation, layout, make up, organization, structure. **2** creation, essay, exercise, literary work, piece, study, work, writing.
compress *v* abbreviate, compact, condense, cram, crowd, crush, shorten, squash, squeeze.
comprise *v* consist of, contain, include, take in.
compulsory *adj* binding, forced, mandatory, obligatory, required.
comrade *n* ally, buddy, colleague, companion, friend, partner; (*Inf*) mate, pal.
conceal *v* bury, camouflage, cover, disguise, dissemble, hide, keep, dark, keep secret, mask, obscure, screen, secrete, shelter
concentrated *adj* **1** deep, hard, intense. **2** boiled down, condensed, reduced, rich, hickened, undiluted.
concept *n* idea, image, theory.
concern *v* **1** affect, apply to, involve, touch. **2** bother, disturb, trouble, worry.
concern *n* **1** affair, business, field, interest, job, occupation, responsibility, task, transaction. **2** anxiety, apprehension, care, consideration, distress, heed, solicitude, worry. **3** company, corporation, firm, house, organization.
concise *adj* brief, compact, condensed, short, summary.
conclusion *n* **1** close, end, finale, finish, result. **2** outcome, result. **3** agreement, decision, judgment, opinion, verdict.
concrete *adj* actual, definite, material, real, sensible, specific, substantial.
condemn *v* **1** blame, censure, disapprove. **2** convict, doom, pass sentence on, sentence.
condense *v* abbreviate, abridge, compact, compress, concentrate, curtail, shorten, summarize.
condensed *adv* compressed, concentrated, curtailed, shortened, shrunken, slimmed down, summarized.
condition *n* **1** plight, position, predicament, state. **2** arrangement, demand, restriction, rule, terms. **3** fitness, health, order, shape.
condition *v* accustom, educate, prepare, train.
conditional *n* provisional, subject to.
conduct *n* control, direction, guidance, leadership, organization, running, supervision.
conduct *v* control, direct, govern, handle, manage, organize, regulate, supervise.
conduct *n* attitude, bearing, behaviour, manners, way.
confess *v* **1** admit, blurt out, confide, divulge, own up. **2** confirm, declare, prove, reveal.
confession *n* admission, disclosure, exposure, revelation.
confIde *v* admit, confess, disclose, divulge, reveal.
confidence *n* **1** belief, faith, trust. **2** assurance, courage, nerve. confidentially, in secrecy, privately.
confidential *adj* off the record, private, secret.
confine *v* bind, bound, cage, enclose, hem in, hold back, imprison, incarcerate, intern, keep, shut-up.
confirm *v* **1** assure, establish, fix, fortify, reinforce, strengthen. **2** approve, corroborate, endorse, ratify, sanction, substantiate, validate, verify.
conflict *n* **1** battle, clash, collision, combat, contest, fight, fracas, strife, war, warfare. **2** antagonism, difference, disagreement, discord,

Global conflict broke out twice during the 20th century. World War I (1914–18) and World War II (1939–45) together were responsible for 50 million deaths worldwide.

dissension, divided loyalties, friction, hostility, interference, opposition, strife, variance.
conflict *v* clash, collide, combat, contest, fight, interfere, struggle.
confuse *v* **1** baffle, bemuse, bewilder, darken, mystify, obscure, perplex, puzzle. **2** embarrass, shame, upset.
confusion *n* **1** mystification, perplexity, puzzlement. **2** chaos, commotion, disorder, jumble, muddle, shambles, turmoil, untidiness, upheaval.
congested *adj* crowded, jammed, overflowing, packed, stuffed, teeming.
connect *v* associate, combine, couple, join, link, relate, unite.
connected *adv* affiliated, allied, associated, combined, coupled, joined, linked, related, united.
connection *n* **1** fastening, link, tie, union. **2** bond, marriage, relationship, relevance, tie-in. **3** acquaintance, ally, associate, contact, friend, sponsor.
conquer *v* beat, crush, defeat, overpower, overthrow, quell, rout, triumph, vanquish.
conqueror *n* champion, conquistador, hero, lord, master, victor, winner.
conscience *n* principles, scruples.
conscientious *adj* careful, diligent, exact, faithful, meticulous, painstaking, particular, thorough.
conscious *adj* **1** alert, aware, sensible. **2** deliberate, premeditated, responsible, wilful.
consent *v* agree, allow, approve, assent, comply, concede, concur, permit, yield.
consent *n* agreement, approval, permission, sanction.
consequence *n* effect, end, event, issue, outcome, result.
conservation *n* custody, maintenance, preservation, protection, safekeeping, saving.
conservative *adj* cautious, guarded, moderate, quiet, right-wing, tory, traditional.
conserve *v* keep, preserve, protect, save, store up, take care of; (*Inf*) go easy on.
consider *v* **1** cogitate, consult, contemplate, ponder, reflect, ruminate, think about. **2** bear in mind, make allowance for, remember, take into account.
considerable *adj* **1** abundant, ample, great, large, lavish, plentiful, sizable, substantial,

tidy. **2** distinguished, important, influential, renowned.
considerate *adj* attentive, charitable, circumspect, concerned, discreet, forbearing, kind, kindly, mindful, obliging, patient, tactful, thoughtful, unselfish
consideration *n* **1** analysis, contemplation, discussion, examination, reflection, review, scrutiny, study. **2** concern, friendliness, kindness, respect, tact, thoughtfulness.
consignment *n* batch, delivery, goods, shipment.
consistent *adj* constant, dependable, persistent, regular, steady, true to type, unchanging.
console *v* calm, cheer, comfort, encourage, express sympathy for, relieve, soothe.
conspiracy *n* collusion, intrigue, league, plot, scheme, treason.
constant *adj* **1** continual, fixed, permanent, regular, stable, steady, unbroken, uniform. **2** continual, endless, eternal, everlasting, never-ending, non-stop, perpetual, persistent, relentless, sustained, unrelenting, unremitting.
constantly *adv* continually, endlessly, incessantly, night and day, nonstop, relentlessly.
constitute *v* comprise, create, establish, form, make up, set up.
constitution *n* composition, establishment, formation, organization.
construct *v* assemble, build, compose, create, design, elevate, engineer, erect, establish, fabricate, fashion, form, formulate, found, frame, make, manufacture, organize, put up, raise, set up, shape.
construction *n* assembly, building, composition, creation, erection, fabrication, form, shape, structure.
constructive *adj* helpful, positive, practical, productive, useful, valuable.
consult *v* ask, confer, consider, debate, deliberate, question, refer to.
consultant *n* adviser, authority, specialist.
consultation *n* appointment, discussion, examination, hearing, interview, meeting.
container *n* holder, receptacle, repository, vessel.
contemplate *v* **1** consider, deliberate, meditate, mull over, ponder, reflect upon, study, turn over in one's mind. **2** aspire to, consider, envisage, expect, foresee, intend, plan, propose.
contempt *n* disrespect, mockery, neglect, scorn.
contend *v* **1** compete, contest, jostle, strive, struggle, vie. **2** allege, argue, debate, dispute, hold, maintain.
content *n* **1** subject matter, text, theme. **2** amount, proportion, quantity. **3** capacity, size, volume. **4** happiness, pleasure, satisfaction.

Conservation is vital in managing the resources of the Earth. By studying the way in which earth's natural systems renew themselves, scientists hope that our planet will provide a home for all living things throughout this century and beyond.

consume *v* absorb, drain, eat up, expend, spend, squander, use up, utilize, vanish, waste, wear out.
consumer *n* buyer, customer, purchaser, shopper, user.
contact *n* **1** junction, union. **2** acquaintance, connection.
contact *v* approach, call, get in touch with, get hold of, phone, ring, speak to, write to.
contain *v* accommodate, enclose, have capacity for, hold, incorporate, seat.
content *adj* at peace, cheerful, comfortable, fulfiled, glad, pleased, satisfied, tranquil.
content *v* delight, gladden, humour, pacify, please, satisfy.
contented *adj* at ease, at peace, comfortable, content, glad, happy, pleased, satisfied, serene.
contents *pl n* **1** elements, ingredients, load. **2** chapters,

divisions, subject matter, themes, topics.
contest *n* competition, game, match, tournament, trial.
contest *v* **1** compete, contend, fight over, vie. **2** argue, call into question, challenge, debate, dispute, doubt, object to, oppose, question.
contestant *n* candidate, competitor, contender, entrant, participant, player, rival.
context *n* background, connection, framework, relation.
continual *adj* constant, endless, everlasting, frequent, perpetual, recurrent, regular, repeated, uninterrupted, unremitting.
continually *adv* all the time, always, constantly, endlessly, forever, incessantly, nonstop, persistently, repeatedly.
continuation *n* addition, extension, furtherance, postscript, sequel, supplement.
continue *v* abide, carry on, endure, last, live on, persist, remain, rest, stay, stay on, survive.
continuity *n* flow, progression, sequence, succession, whole.
continuous *adj* connected, constant, continued, prolonged, unbroken, uninterrupted.
contract *v* **1** abbreviate, abridge, compress, condense, confine, reduce, shrivel, wither. **2** agree, arrange, commission, covenant, engagement, pact, settlement, stipulation, treaty.
contradict *v* challenge, counter, deny, dispute, oppose.
contradictory *adj* antagonistic, conflicting, contrary, inconsistent, irreconcilable, opposite.
contrast *n* comparison, difference, distinction, divergence.
contrast *v* compare, differ, distinguish, oppose, set off.
contribute *v* add, donate, furnish, give, provide, subscribe, supply.
contribution *n* donation, gift, grant, offering, subscription.
contrive *v* concoct, construct, create, design, devise, engineer, fabricate, invent.
contrived *adj* artificial, forced, laboured, overdone, planned, unnatural.
controversy *n* argument, contention, debate, dispute, quarrel, squabble, wrangle.
convenient *adj* **1** appropriate, beneficial, handy, helpful, labour-saving, reasonable, useful, well-timed. **2** accessible, at hand, handy, nearby, within reach.
converge *v* coincide, combine, come together, concentrate, gather, join, meet, merge.
conversion *n* **1** change, metamorphosis, transformation. **2** adaptation, alteration, modification, reconstruction, reorganization. **3** change of heart, rebirth, regeneration.
convert *v* **1** alter, change, interchange, transform, transpose, turn. **2** adapt, apply, appropriate, modify, remodel, reorganize, restyle, revise.
convict *v* condemn, find guilty, imprison, sentence.
convict *n* con, criminal, culprit, felon, jailbird, malefactor, prisoner.
convince *v* assure, bring round, gain the confidence of, persuade, prevail upon, prove to, satisfy, sway, win over.
cool *adj* **1** chilled, chilly, cold-nippy. **2** calm, composed, level-headed, placid, quiet, relaxed, self-controlled, serene; (*Inf*) laid-back. **3** aloof, distant, frigid, indifferent, lukewarm, offhand, reserved, unfriendly,

The metamorphosis of an insect

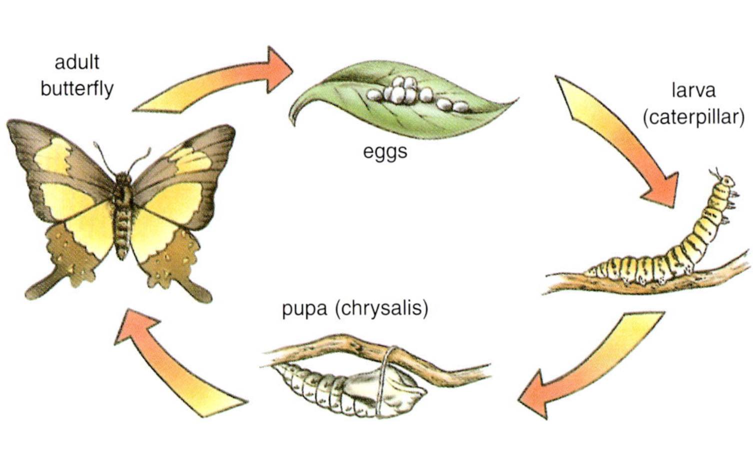

Insects, like butterflies and bees, go through a process called metamorphosis. Their eggs hatch into larvae or caterpillars. These become a pupa or chrysalis, within which an adult insect develops.

uninterested, unresponsive.
cool *v* **1** chill, cool off, freeze, refrigerate. **2** calm, moderate, quiet, temper.
cooperate *v* assist, collaborate, coordinate, help, join forces, pull together, work together.
coordinate *v* correlate, match, organize, relate, synchronize.
cope *v* carry on, get by, manage, survive.
copy *n* archetype, carbon copy, counterfeit, duplicate, facsimile, fake, fax, forgery, image, imitation, likeness, model, pattern, photocopy, print, replica, replication, representation, reproduction, transcription.
copy *v* **1** counterfeit, duplicate, photocopy, reproduce. **2** ape, echo, emulate, follow suit, follow the example of, imitate, mimic, mirror, parrot, repeat, simulate.
cord *n* line rope, string, twine.
core *n* centre, essence, gist, heart, kernel, nub, nucleus, substance.
corner *n* **1** angle, bend, joint. **2** cavity, hide-out, hole, niche, nook, recess, retreat.
corner *v* bring to bay, run to earth, trap.
corpse *n* body, cadaver, carcass, remains.
correct *v* **1** adjust, amend, improve, redress, remedy, right. **2** discipline, punish, reprimand.
correct *adj* accurate, exact, faultless, precise, right, true.
correctly *adv* accurately, precisely, properly, right.
correspond *v* **1** agree, coincide, conform, fit, match, square, tally. **2** communicate, exchange letters, keep in touch, write.

An abacus is a frame of beads and wires or bamboo rods, with five beads at the bottom and two beads at the top.

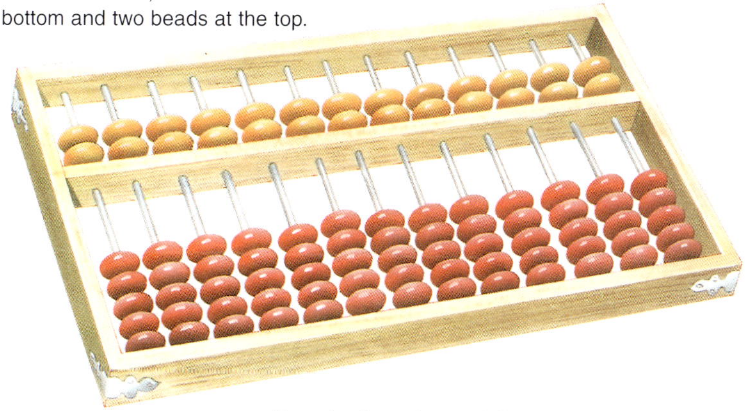

Counting in and around China is still sometimes carried out on an abacus. A skilled abacus user can produce answers to some calculations almost as quickly as someone using an electronic calculator.

corresponding *adj* identical, matching, similar.
corridor *n* aisle, hallway, passage, passageway.
corrosive *adj* biting, caustic, consuming, corroding, erosive, wasting, wearing.
corrupt *adj* dishonest, shady, unethical, unscrupulous.
corrupt *v* bribe, entice, fix, lure, pervert, subvert.
cost *n* **1** charge, damage, expense, outlay, price, rate, worth. **2** damage, expense, injury, loss, penalty, suffering.
cost *v* come to, command a price of, sell at, set back.
costume *n* attire, clothing, dress, fashion, national dress, outfit, uniform.
council *n* assembly, board, cabinet, chamber, committee, congress, convention, governing body, ministry, panel, parliament, synod.
counsel *n* **1** advice, consultation, guidance, information, recommendation, suggestion. **2** advocate, attorney, barrister, lawyer, legal adviser, solicitor.
counsel *v* advise, advocate, caution, instruct, recommend, urge, warn.
count *v* **1** add up, calculate, compute, estimate, reckon, score, tally, tot up. **2** matter, signify, tell, weigh.
counter *adv* against, at variance with, contrarily, contrariwise, conversely, in defiance of, versus.
counter *adj* adverse, against, conflicting, contradictory, contrary, contrasting, obverse, opposed, opposing, opposite.
counter *v* answer, hit back, meet, offset, resist, respond, retaliate, ward off.
counterfeit *v* copy, fabricate, fake, forge, imitate, pretend, simulate.
counterfeit *adj* bogus, faked, false, forged, imitation, sham, simulated.

counterfeit *n* copy, fake, forgery, imitation, reproduction.
countless *adj* endless, limitless, measureless, myriad.
couple *n* brace, duo, item, pair, twain, twosome.
couple *v* buckle, clasp, conjoin, connect, hitch, join, link, marry, pair, unite, wed, yoke.
courageous *adj* brave, daring, fearless, gallant, heroic, valiant.
course *n* **1** advance, flow, march, movement, order, progress, sequence. **2** channel, direction, line, path, route, way. **3** duration, term, time. **4** behaviour, conduct, plan, policy. **5** cinder track, circuit, lap, race, racecourse. **6** classes, curriculum, lectures, studies.
court *n* **1** cloister, courtyard, piazza, plaza, quad, quadrangle, square, yard. **2** hall, manor, palace. **3** attendants, cortege, entourage, retinue, royal household, suite, train. **4** bar, bench, court of justice, lawcourt, tribunal.
court *v* **1** chase, date, go out with, pursue, run after, serenade, take out. **2** cultivate, flatter, seek, solicit.
courtesy *n* civility, elegance, gallantry, good manners, polish, politeness.
courtyard *n* area, enclosure, playground, quadrangle, yard.
cover *v* **1** camouflage, conceal, disguise, eclipse, hide, obscure, screen, shade, shroud, veil. **2** defend, guard, protect, shelter, shield, watch over.
cover *n* **1** disguise, façade, front, mask, obscure, screen, smoke screen. **2** camouflage, defence, guard, hiding place, protection, refuge, sanctuary, shelter, undergrowth, woods. **3** double for, fill in for, relieve, stand in for, substitute, take over. **4** describe, detail, investigate, narrate, report, tell of, write up.
cover *n* compensation, insurance, payment, protection, reimbursement.
covering *n* blanket, casing, clothing, coating, cover, housing, layer, overlay, protection, shelter, top, wrapper, wrapping.

Some amphibians have skins which are coloured and speckled to blend perfectly into their habitation.

covering *adj* accompanying, descriptive, explanatory, introductory.
cover up *v* conceal, cover one's tracks, feign ignorance, hide, hush up, keep dark, keep secret, keep silent about, repress, suppress.
cowardly *adj* chicken, faint-hearted, fearful, gutless, scared, spineless, timorous, weak.
crack *v* break, burst, chip, chop, fracture, snap, splinter, split.
crack *n* **1** breach, break, chink, chip, crevice, fissure, fracture, gap. **2** clap, crash, explosion, pop, report, snap.
crack *v* break down, collapse, give way, go to pieces, lose control, succumb, yield.
crack *n* attempt, opportunity, stab, try.
crack *adj* choice, elite, excellent, first-class, first-rate, hand-picked, superior; (*Inf*) ace.
crafty *adj* artful, calculating, cunning, devious, scheming, shrewd, sly, wily.
cram *v* compact, compress, crowd, crush, force, jam, overcrowd, overfill, pack in, press, ram, shove, squeeze, stuff.
cramp *v* check, clog, confine, constrain, encumber, hamper, hamstring, handicap, hinder, impede, inhibit, obstruct, restrict, shackle, thwart.
cramp *n* ache, contraction, convulsion, pang, shooting pain, spasm, stitch, twinge.
crash *n* bang, boom, clang, clash, clatter, din, racket, smash, thunder.
crash *v* **1** fall headlong, give way, hurtle, lurch, plunge, sprawl, topple. **2** bang, bump, collide, drive into, hit, hurtle into, plough into, wreck.
crash *n* bankruptcy, collapse, downfall, failure, ruin, smash.
crate *n* box, case, container, packing case, tea chest.
crate *v* box, case, enclose, pack, pack up.
crave *v* **1** desire, long for, need, pine for, require, sigh for, thirst for, want, yearn for. **2** ask, beg, plead for, pray for, seek.
craze *n* enthusiasm, fad,

fashion, infatuation, mania, mode, novelty, passion, preoccupation, rage, the latest thing, trend, vogue.
crazy *adj* **1** berserk, crazed, delirious, demented, deranged, idiotic, insane, lunatic, mad, maniacal, mental, of unsound mind, touched, unbalanced, unhinged. **2** bizarre, eccentric, fantastic, odd, outrageous, peculiar, ridiculous, silly, strange, weird.
creak *v* grate, grind, groan, rasp, scrape, scratch, screech, squeak, squeal.
cream *n* **1** cosmetic, emulsion, essence, liniment, lotion, oil, ointment, paste, salve, unguent. **2** best, elite, flower, pick, prime.
crease *v* crinkle, crumple, fold, pucker, ridge, screw up, wrinkle.
crease *n* bulge, corrugation, fold, groove, line, overlap, pucker, ridge, ruck, tuck, wrinkle.
create *v* compose, design, develop, devise, formulate, give birth to, hatch, make, originate, produce, spawn.
creation *n* **1** conception, procreation, siring. **2** development, production, setting up. **3** achievement, concept, invention, production.
creative *adj* artistic, clever, gifted, imaginative, inventive, original, productive, visionary.
creator *n* architect, author, designer, father, God, initiator, inventor, maker, originator.
creature *n* animal, beast, being, living thing, lower animal, quadruped.
credit *n* acclaim, acknowledgement, approval, glory, honour, praise, recognition, thanks.
creek *n* bay, bight, cove, firth, inlet.
creep *v* **1** crawl, crawl on all fours, glide, slither, squirm, worm, wriggle, writhe. **2** approach, unnoticed, skulk, slink, sneak, steal, tiptoe. **3** crawl, dawdle, drag, edge, inch, proceed at a snail's pace.
crest *n* apex, crown, head, height, highest point, peak, pinnacle, ridge, summit, top.
crevice *n* chink, cleft, crack, cranny, fissure, fracture, gap, hole, interstice, opening, rent, rift, slit, split.
crew *n* hands, company, complement, company, corps, gang, party, posse, squad, team, working party.
crime *n* atrocity, offence, outrage, transgression, trespass, unlawful act, violation, wrong.
criminal *n* con man, convict, crook, delinquent, felon, jailbird, lawbreaker, offender, sinner.
criminal *adj* corrupt, crooked,

The crew of sailing ships used to suffer from scurvy due to a lack of vitamin C. This condition caused bleeding gums, weakness and dizziness. In the eighteenth century it was discovered that limes could cure these symptoms.

unlawful, villainous, wrong.
cripple *v* debilitate, disable, incapacitate, lame, mutilate, paralyse, weaken.
crisis *n* **1** critical point, crux, moment of truth, turning point. **2** catastrophe, critical situation, disaster, emergency, mess, plight, predicament, trouble.
crisp *adj* **1** bracing, brisk, fresh, invigorating, refreshing. **2** brief, clear, incisive, short, succinct.
critic *n* **1** analyst, authority, commentator, connoisseur, expert, judge. **2** attacker, censor, censurer, detractor, fault-finder, knocker, reviler, vilifier.
crook *n* criminal, racketeer, rogue, shark, swindler, thief, villain; (*Inf*) cheat.
crop *n* fruits, gathering, harvest, produce, vintage, yield.
crop *v* clip, curtail, cut, lop, mow, pare, prune, reduce, shear, shorten, snip, top, trim.
crop up *v* appear, arise, emerge, happen, occur, spring up.
cross *adj* angry, annoyed, grouchy, grumpy, impatient, irritable, put out, short, snappy.
cross *v* **1** bridge, ford, meet, pass over, span, traverse, zigzag. **2** crisscross, intersect, intertwine. **3** blend, cross-breed, cross-fertilize, cross-pollinate, hybridize.
cross *n* **1** crucifix, rood. **2** crossing, crossroads, intersection, junction. **3** blend, combination, mixture.
cross *adj* crosswise, intersecting, oblique, transverse.
cross-examine *v* interrogate, pump, question, quiz; (*Inf*) grill.
cross out *v* cancel, delete, eliminate, strike out.
crouch *v* bend down, duck, hunch, kneel, squat, stoop.
crowd *n* **1** army, company, flock, herd, horde, mass, mob, pack, rabble, swarm, throng. **2** attendance, audience, gate, house, spectators.
crowd *v* cluster, congregate, cram, flock, gather, huddle, mass, surge, swarm, throng.
crowded *adj* busy, congested, cramped, crushed, full, huddled, jam-packed, mobbed, overflowing, packed, swarming, teeming, thronged.
crude *adj* **1** coarse, dirty, gross, indecent, obscene, smutty, tasteless. **2** makeshift, primitive, rough, sketchy, undeveloped, unfinished, unformed.
cruel *n* **1** brutal, callous, fierce, harsh, heartless, hellish, inhuman, painful, sadistic, savage, unkind. **2** merciless, ruthless, unrelenting.
crumb *n* atom, bit, grain, mite, morsel, particle, scrap, shred, sliver, snippet, soupçon, speck.
crumple *v* **1** crease, crush, rumple, screw up, wrinkle. **2** break down, cave in, collapse, fall, give way, go to pieces.

Which are the world's most widely grown crops?

Wheat is the most widely grown crop as it can be grown in a variety of soils and climates. Harvested wheat is ground into flour tom make bread, pasta and baked goods.

Rice is the main food for over half the world's population. Up to three crops of rice per year can be harvested from the same land. Rice needs a growing-season temperature of over 21°C (70°F).

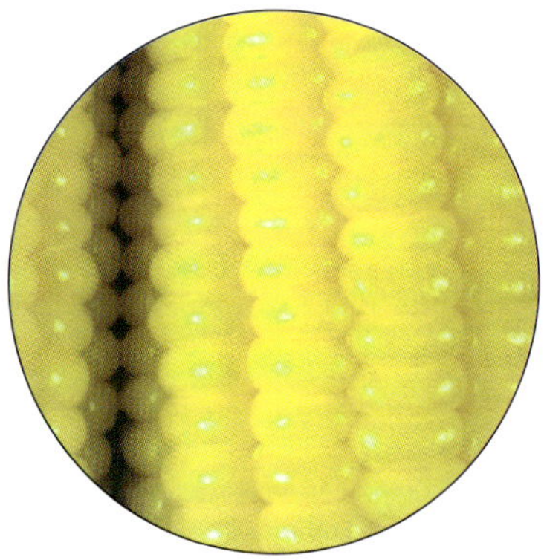

Maize originated from the Americas but is now grown in all warm parts of the world. It is used for human food, as a vegetable and as maize flour and breakfast cereals. It is also milled and fed to animals.

crush *v* **1** bruise, compress, contuse, pulverize, rumple, smash, squeeze, wrinkle. **2** conquer, extinguish, overcome, overwhelm, put down, quell, stamp out, subdue, vanquish.
crush *n* **1** congestion, crowd, huddle, jam. **2** fancy, infatuation, liking, love, passion.
crust *n* caking, coat, coating, covering, film, layer, shell, skin, surface.
cry *v* bawl, greet, shed tears, snivel, sob, wail, weep, whine.
cry *n* **1** bawling, crying, howl, sobbing, wailing, weep. **2** bawl, call out, howl, scream, screech, shriek, yell.
cub *n* **1** offspring, whelp, young. **2** beginner, lad, learner, puppy, recruit, trainee, whipper-snapper, youngster; (*Inf*) babe.
cue *n* catchword, hint, nod, prompt, reminder, sign, signal.
cult *n* **1** body, church, clique, denomination, faction, faith, following, party, religion, school, sect. **2** admiration, craze, devotion, idolization, worship.
cultural *adj* artistic, educational, enlightening, enriching, humane, liberal.
cunning *adj* astute, crafty, devious, foxy, guileful, sharp, shrewd, wily.
cunning *n* artfulness, astuteness, craftiness, deceitfulness, deviousness, guile, shrewdness, slyness, trickery, wiliness.
cure *v* alleviate, ease, heal, help, make better, mend, relieve, remedy, restore to health.
cure *n* antidote, medicine, panacea, remedy, specific treatment.
cure *v* dry, kipper, pickle, preserve, salt, smoke.
curious *adj* **1** inquiring, inquisitive, interested, puzzled, questioning. **2** inquisitive, meddling, nosy, peering, prying. **3** bizarre, exotic, extraordinary, mysterious, novel, odd, peculiar, puzzling, rare, strange, unique, unusual.
curl *v* bend, coil, corkscrew, crimp, crinkle, curve, entwine, meander, spiral, turn, twist.
current *adj* **1** accepted, circulating, going around, in progress, in the news, ongoing, popular, widespread. **2** contemporary, fashionable, in fashion, in vogue, now, present-day, up-to-date, up-to-the-minute; (*Inf*) trendy.

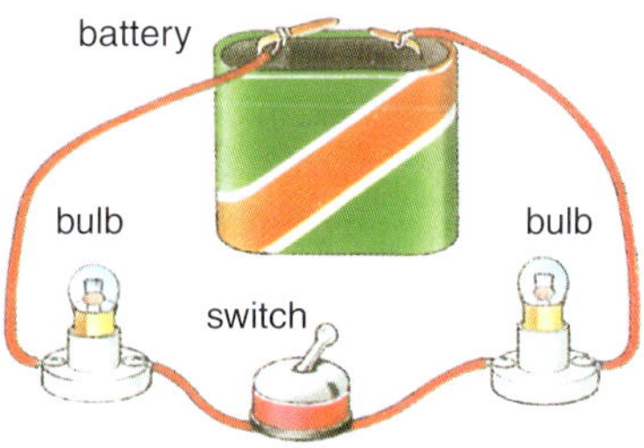

Electric current flows along a circuit each part connected to the next.

current *n* **1** course, flow, jet, progression, river, stream, tide. **2** electrical activity, electrical charge, electricity flow.
curve *v* arc, arch, bend, bow, coil, hook, spiral, twist, wind.
curve *n* arc, bend, half-moon, loop, turn.
custody *n* arrest, confinement, detention, durance, duress, imprisonment, incarceration.
customary *adj* accepted, common, conventional, established, everyday, familiar, fashionable, normal, popular, regular, traditional, usual.
customer *n* buyer, client, consumer, patron, prospect, purchaser, regular, shopper.
cut *v* **1** divide, gash, incise, lacerate, nick, notch, penetrate, pierce, score, sever, slash, slice, slit, wound. **2** carve, chip, chisel, chop, engrave, fashion, form, saw, sculpt, sculpture, shape, whittle. **3** contract, cut back, decrease, ease up on, lower, rationalize, reduce, slash, slim. **4** abbreviate, abridge, condense, delete, edit out, precis, shorten. **5** gash, graze, groove, incision, laceration, nick, rip, slash, slit, stroke, wound. **6** cutback, decrease, fall, lowering, reduction, saving.
cut down *v* fell, hew, level, lop.
cut in *v* break in, butt in, interpose, interrupt, intervene, intrude; (*Inf*) move in.
cut off *v* **1** disconnect, intercept, interrupt. **2** isolate, separate, sever.
cut out *v* delete, extract, give up, remove, sever, stop.
cut-price *adj* bargain, cheap, reduced, sale.
cut short *v* abort, break off, check, halt, interrupt, leave unfinished, postpone, terminate.
cutting *adj* biting, bitter, chill, keen, numbing, penetrating, piercing, raw, sharp, stinging
cycle *n* aeon, age, circle, era, period, phase, revolution, rotation, round (of years).
cynic *n* doubter, pessimist, sceptic.
cynical *adj* distrustful, ironic, mocking, pessimistic, sarcastic, sceptical, scoffing, scornful, sneering, unbelieving.

Dd

dab *n* blot, pat, press, smudge, touch.
daily *adj* diurnal, everyday, day-to-day, everyday, regular, routine.
daily *adv* constantly, every day, often, once a day, regularly.
dale *n* coomb, dell, glen, vale, valley.
dam *n* barrage, barrier, embankment, obstruction, wall.
dam *v* barricade, block, choke, confine, hold back, obstruct.
damage *n* destruction, harm, hurt, injury, loss, mutilation, suffering.
damage *v* abuse, hurt, impair, injure, mutilate, ruin, spoil, tamper with, wreck.
damp *n* darkness, dew, drizzle, fog, mist, moisture, vapour.
damp *adj* **1** clammy, dripping, drizzly, humid, misty, moist, muggy, soggy, wet. **2** dampen, moisten.
dance *v* bob up and down, frolic, hop, jig, pirouette, prance, rock, romp, skip, spin, sway, swing, twirl.
dance *n* ball, disco, discotheque, social.
danger *n* hazard, jeopardy, menace, peril, precariousness, risk, threat, venture.
dangerous *adj* alarming, exposed, hazardous, insecure, menacing, nasty, precarious, risky, threatening, treacherous, unsafe, vulnerable.
dangle *v* **1** droop, hang down, sway, swing, trail. **2** brandish, entice, flaunt, flourish, lure, swing, tantalize, tempt, wave.
dappled *adj* blotched, flecked, marked, mottled, pied, piebald, pinto, spotted.
dare *v* **1** confront, defy, provoke, taunt, throw down the gauntlet. **2** adventure, brave, endanger, risk, stake, venture.
dare *n* challenge, provocation, taunt, ultimatum.
daring *adj* adventurous, bold, brave, daredevil, fearless, impulsive, intrepid, plucky, rash, reckless, valiant, venturesome; (*Inf*) game.

Hydroelectric power station

Hydroelectric power is created by the force of water from the dam surging down to turbines, which in turn spin generators to produce electricity. This electrical power is then carried through cables to wherever it is needed.

daring *n* bottle, bravery, courage, fearlessness, grit, guts, nerve, rashness, spirit; (*Inf*) guts.
dark *adj* **1** black, brunette, dark-haired, dark-skinned, dusky, ebony, jet-black, sable, swarthy. **2** cloudy, dim, dingy, foggy, overcast, pitch-black, shadowy, shady, unlit. **3** concealed, cryptic, deep, enigmatic, hidden, mysterious, obscure, occult, puzzling, secret. **4** bleak, cheerless, dismal, drab, gloomy, grim, joyless, sombre. **5** angry, scowling, sulky, threatening.
dark *n* **1** dusk, gloom, semi-darkness. **2** evening, night, night-fall, night-time, twilight.
darkness *n* blackness, dusk, gloom, nightfall, shadows.
darn *v* mend, patch, repair, sew up, stitch.
darn *n* mend, patch, reinforcement, repair.
dart *n* bolt, bound, dash, flash, fly, race, run, rush, scoot, spring, sprint, start, tear, whistle, whiz.
dash *v* **1** break, crash, shatter, smash. **2** fling, hurl, slam, sling, throw. **3** bolt, bound, dart, hurry, race, run, rush, speed, spring, sprint. **4** confound, disappoint, discourage.
dash *n* brio, flair, flourish, panache, spirit, style, verve, vivacity.
data *pl n* details, documents, facts, figures, information,

input, materials, statistics; (*Inf*) info.
date *n* **1** age, epoch, era, period, stage, time. **2** appointment, engagement, meeting, rendezvous, tryst.
date *v* belong to, come from, originate in.
dated *adj* antiquated, obsolete, old-fashioned, old hat, outdated, out of date, passé, unfashionable, untrendy.
dawdle *v* delay, dilly-dally, hang about, idle, lag, loaf, loiter, potter, trail, waste time.
dawn *n* **1** daybreak, daylight, morning, sunrise, sunup. **2** advent, beginning, birth, rise.
dawn *v* **1** break, brighten, gleam, grow, light, lighten. **2** develop, emerge, rise, start, unfold. **3** come to mind, cross one's mind, hit, register, strike.
day *n* **1** broad daylight, daylight, daylight hours, daytime, twenty-four hours, working day. **2** date, point in time, set time, time.
daybreak *n* break of day, dawn, first light, sunrise.
daydream *n* **1** dream, imagining, musing, stargazing, vision. **2** dream, fancy, fantasy, figment of the imagination, fond hope, pipe-dream, wishful thinking.
daydream *v* dream, envision, fancy, fantasise, hallucinate, imagine, muse, stargaze.
daze *v* **1** bewilder, muddle, numb, paralyse, shock, stun. **2** amaze, astonish, astound, blind, confuse, dazzle, dumbfound, flabbergast, perplex, stagger, startle, surprise.
daze *n* bewilderment, confusion, distraction, shock, stupor, trance, trance-like state.
dazzle *v* **1** blind, blur, confuse, daze, overpower. **2** amaze, astonish, bowl over, fascinate, impress, overwhelm, stupefy; (*Inf*) bowl over, take one's breath away.
dazzle *n* brilliance, flash, gleam, glitter, magnificence, splendour, sparkle; (*Inf*) pizzazz, razzle-dazzle, razzmatazz.
dead *adj* **1** deceased, extinct,

lifeless, perished. **2** cold, indifferent, inert, unresponsive, wooden. **3** boring, dull, flat, insipid, stale.

deadly *adj* **1** dangerous, fatal, lethal, malignant, poisonous. **2** cruel, grim, ruthless, savage, unrelenting. **3** accurate, exact, on target, precise, true.

deaf *adj* **1** hard of hearing, stone deaf. **2** indifferent, oblivious, unconcerned, unhearing, unmoved.

deafening *adj* ear-piercing, ear-splitting, piercing, ringing.

deal *adj* bargain, buy and sell, do business, negotiate, sell, stock, trade, traffic, treat.

deal *n* agreement, arrangement, bargain, buy, contract, pact, transaction, understanding.

deal *v* allot, divide, give, share.

dealer *n* chandler, marketer, merchant, trader, wholesaler.

dear *adj* **1** beloved, favourite, prized, treasured. **2** costly, expensive, overpriced, pricey.

dear *n* beloved, darling, loved one, precious.

death *n* **1** bereavement, decease, departure, dying, loss, passing. **2** destruction, extermination, extinction, grave, ruin.

deathly *adj* **1** gaunt, grim, haggard, pale. **2** deadly, extreme, fatal, intense, mortal, terrible.

debate *v* argue, contest, discuss, dispute, question.

debate *n* **1** argument, contention, controversy, discussion, dispute. **2** deliberation, meditation, reflection.

debris *n* bits, fragments, pieces, remains, ruins, waste.

debt *n* arrears, duty, liability, obligation, score.

debut *n* beginning, entrance, first appearance, launching.

decay *v* **1** deteriorate, shrivel, waste away, wither. **2** corrode, decompose, mortify, perish, rot.

deceased *adj* dead, departed, expired, former, lifeless, lost.

deceit *n* cheating, deception, double-dealing, fraud, pretence, slyness, trickery.

deceitful *adj* crafty, deceiving, dishonest, double-dealing, sneaky, tricky, two-faced, underhand.

deceive *v* betray, cheat, con, double-cross, dupe, entrap, fool, hoodwink, mislead, swindle, trick.

decent *adj* fit, fitting, modest, nice, polite, presentable, proper, respectable, suitable.

deception *n* cunning, deceit, fraud, treachery, trickery.

decide *v* choose, conclude, determine, resolve, settle.

decipher *v* construe, crack, decode, deduce, explain, figure out, interpret, make out, read, reveal, solve, understand, unfold, unravel.

decision *n* conclusion, finding, judgment, outcome, resolution, result, ruling, sentence, verdict.

deck *v* clothe, decorate, dress, embellish, festoon, garland, trim.

decorate *v* **1** deck, trim. **2** colour, paint, paper, renovate, wallpaper. **3** cite, honour, pin a medal on.

decoration *n* **1** garnishing, trimming. **2** flourish, frill, spangle, trimmings. **3** award, badge, colours, emblem, garter, medal, order, ribbon, star.

decoy *n* bait, inducement, lure,

A	• – –
B	– • • •
C	– • – •
D	– • •
E	•
F	• • – •
G	– – •
H	• • • •
I	• •
J	• – – –
K	– • –
L	• – • •
M	– –
N	– •
O	– – –
P	• – – •
Q	– – • –
R	• – •

S	• • •
T	–
U	• • –
V	• • • –
W	• – –
X	– • • –
Y	– • – –
Z	– – • •
1	• – – –
–	
2	• • – –
–	
3	• • • –
–	
4	• • • •
–	
5	• • • •
•	
6	– • • •
•	
7	– – • •
•	
8	– – – •
•	
9	– – – –
•	

Morse code was invented by American engineer Samuel Morse, to send messages via short and long bursts of radio waves along a wire.

pretence, trap.
decoy *v* deceive, ensnare, entice, entrap, lure, tempt.
decrease *v* decline, diminish, drop, dwindle, ease, fall off, lessen, lower, peter out, reduce, shrink, slacken, subside.
decrease *n* contraction, cutback, downturn, ebb, loss, reduction, shrinkage, subsidence.
decree *v* **1** command, decide, dictate, direct, mandate, order, prescribe, proclaim, pronounce, rule. **2** judgement, ruling, verdict. **3** findings.
dedicate *v* commit, devote, pledge, surrender.
deduce *v* conclude, gather, infer, reason, understand.
deduct *v* knock off, reduce by, subtract, take away, take from, take off, take out, withdraw.
deed *n* act, action, exploit, feat, performance, reality, truth.
deep *adj* **1** bottomless, broad, far, profound. **2** extreme, grave, great, intense. **3** bass, full-toned, low-pitched, resonant.
deep *adv* deeply, far down, far into, late.
defeat *v* beat, conquer, overpower, overthrow, quell, repulse, vanquish.
defeat *n* beating, conquest, debacle, overthrow, repulse, rout, trouncing, vanquishment.
defect *n* blemish, blotch, error, failing, fault, flaw, imperfection, mistake, spot, taint, want.
defect *v* abandon, break faith, change sides, desert, go over, rebel, revolt, tergiversate; (*Inf*) walk out on.
defence *n* **1** armament, cover, deterrence, guard, immunity, protection, resistance, safeguard, security, shelter. **2** apology, argument, excuse, exoneration, explanation, extenuation, justification, plea, vindication. **3** alibi, case, declaration, denial, plea, pleading, rebuttal, testimony.
defender *n* **1** bodyguard, escort, guard, protector. **2** advocate, champion, patron, sponsor, supporter, vindicator.
defer *v* adjourn, delay, postpone, put on ice, suspend, table.
deficiency *n* defect, fault, flaw, frailty, weakness.
deficit *n* arrears, deficiency, loss, shortage, shortfall.
define *v* describe, designate, detail, explain, interpret, specify, spell out.
definite *adj* clear, clear-cut, exact, fixed, obvious, particular, precise, specific.
definition *n* clarification, description, explanation.
deflate *n* **1** collapse, contract, empty, flatten, shrink. **2** humble, humiliate, squash, take the wind out of someone's sails; (*Inf*) put down.
deflect *v* bend, deviate, diverge, ricochet, swerve, turn aside, twist, veer.
defy *v* challenge, dare, disregard, provoke, scorn, spurn.
degree *n* **1** class, grade, level, order, position, rank, standing, station, status. **2** calibre, level, measure, quantity, range, rate, scale, standard.
delay *v* defer, postpone, prolong, protract, put off, shelve, stall, suspend, temporize.
delay *n* **1** postponement, stay, suspension. **2** check, detention, hold-up, interruption, setback.
delete *v* blot out, cancel, cross out, cut out, dele, edit out, erase, obliterate, remove, rub out, strike out.
deliberate *v* consult, debate, discuss, meditate, mull over, ponder, reflect, think, weigh.
deliberate *adj* calculated, considered, intentional, planned, prearranged, studied, thoughtful, wilful.
delicate *adj* **1** fragile, frail, sickly, slender, tender, weak. **2** detailed, minute, precise. **3** considerate, discreet, sensitive, tactful. **4** critical, difficult, sensitive.
delicious *adj* appetising, delectable, luscious, mouth-watering, palatable, savoury, tasty; (*Inf*) scrumptious.
delight *n* ecstasy, enjoyment, happiness, joy, pleasure.
delight *v* amuse, charm, cheer,

What makes food taste delicious?

Flavour receptors on different parts of the tongue are best at sensing the basic flavours: sweetness, sourness, bitterness and saltiness. You can test this for yourself with a little sugar for sweetness, salt for saltiness, vinegar for sourness and squeezed lemon for bitterness.

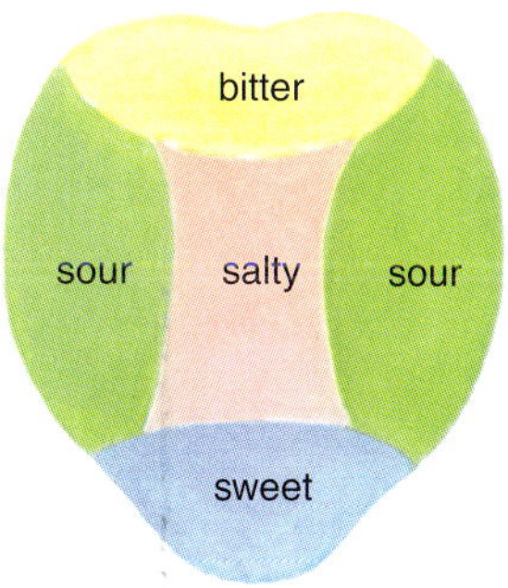

Although our tongues take in information from the food we eat, it is our brains that process it.

enchant, please, satisfy, thrill.
deliver *v* **1** bear, bring, carry, cart, convey, distribute, transport. **2** hand over, relinquish, surrender, transfer, yield. **3** free, liberate, release, save.
de luxe *adj* choice, exclusive, expensive, grand, luxurious, opulent, palatial, plush, rich, sumptuous, superior.
demand *v* **1** ask, challenge, interrogate, question. **2** call for, involve, need, require, want.
democracy *n* commonwealth, government by the people, representative government, republic.
democratic *adj* popular, populist, representative, republican, self-governing.
demonstrate *v* **1** display, exhibit, indicate, prove, show, testify to. **2** describe, explain, illustrate, make clear, show how, teach. **3** march, parade, picket, protest, rally.
den *n* **1** cave, haunt, hideout, lair, shelter. **2** cloister, cubbyhole, hideaway, retreat, sanctuary, sanctum, study.
denial *n* contradiction, disclaimer, dismissal, dissent, negation, prohibition, rebuff, refusal, rejection, renunciation, repudiation, repulse, retraction, veto.
denomination *n* **1** belief, creed, religious group, school, sect. **2** grade, size, unit, value.
denote *v* designate, express, imply, indicate, mean, show.
dense *adj* close, compact, compressed, condensed, heavy, solid, substantial, thick, thickset.
dent *n* chip, crater, depression, dimple, dip, hollow, impression, indentation, pit.
dent *v* depress, hollow, imprint, make a dent in, make concave, press in, push in.
deny *v* **1** contradict, disagree with, oppose, refute. **2** disclaim, disown, repudiate, revoke.
department *n* **1** district, division, province, region, sector. **2** branch, bureau, office, section, station, subdivision, unit. **3** area, domain, function, line, province, realm, responsibility, speciality, sphere.
departure *n* **1** exit, going away, leaving, retirement, withdrawal. **2** branching out, change, difference, innovation, novelty, shift.
depend *v* **1** bank on, count on, lean on, rely upon, trust in. **2** be based on, be subject to, hang on, hinge on, rest on, revolve around.
dependent *adj* **1** defenceless, reliant, vulnerable, weak. **2** conditional, determined by, liable to, relative, subject to.
deplete *v* bankrupt, drain, exhaust, expend, lessen, milk, reduce, use up.
depose *v* **1** dismiss, displace, oust, remove from office. **2** demote, dethrone.
deposit *v* drop, lay, locate, place, precipitate, put, settle, sit down.
deposit *n* down payment, install ment, part payment, pledge, retainer, security, stake.
depress *v* dishearten, dispirit, oppress, sadden, weigh down.
deprived *adj* destitute, in need, lacking, needy, poor.
depth *n* **1** abyss, deepness, drop, extent. **2** bowels of the earth, deepest, inner-most, remotest part, middle, midst.
deputy *n* agent, ambassador, commissioner, delegate, representative, second-in-command, substitute.
derelict *adj* deserted, neglected, ruined.
derive *v* draw, extract, gather, infer, obtain.
descend *v* **1** alight, dismount, fall. **2** ancestry, family tree, genealogy, heredity, origin, parentage.
describe *v* depict, explain, illustrate, portray, relate, report.
description *n* account, explanation, portrayal, report.
desert *n* solitude, waste, wasteland, wilderness, wilds.
desert *adj* arid, barren, desolate, infertile, uncultivated, waste.
desert *v* abandon, abscond,

More than a third of the world's surface is covered by desert. This desert in Utah has a surface of weathered rocks rather than sand.

defect, leave, maroon, quit, resign, run out on, vacate; (*Inf*) walk out on.
design *v* **1** describe, draft, draw, outline, plan, sketch, trace. **2** create, fabricate, invent, originate, think up. **3** aim, contrive, devise, intend, plan, project, propose, scheme, tailor.
design *n* **1** blueprint, draft, drawing, model, outline, plan, scheme, sketch. **2** aim, end, goal, intent, intention, object, point, purpose, target, view.
designer *n* architect, couturier, creator, inventor, stylist.
desire *v* **1** aspire to, fancy, long for, set one's heart on, want, wish for. **2** ask, petition, request.
desire *n* **1** appetite, aspiration, craving, hankering, longing, need, want, wish, yearning. **2** appetite, passion.
desolate *adj* **1** barren, bleak, desert, waste. **2** abandoned, depressing, dismal, gloomy, miserable, wretched.
despair *v* give up, lose heart, lose hope.
despair *n* anguish, dejection, despondency, gloom, hopelessness, misery, wretchedness.
despise *v* detest, loathe, look down on, scorn, slight, spurn.
destination *n* harbour, haven, journey's end, landing-place, resting-place, station, stop, terminus.
destiny *n* cup, divine decree, doom, fate, fortune, karma, kismet, lot.
detach *v* cut off, disconnect, disengage, divide, free, separate, sever, tear off, uncouple, unhitch.
detail *n* aspect, component, count, element, fact, factor, feature, item, particular, point, respect, specific, technicality.
detail *v* allocate, appoint, assign, charge, commission, delegate, detach, send.
detain *v* **1** check, delay, hinder, hold up, impede, keep back, slow up, stay, stop. **2** arrest, confine, hold, intern, restrain.
detect *v* **1** catch, identify, notice, observe, recognize, scent, spot. **2** discover, expose, find, reveal, track down, uncover.
detective *n* CID, constable, copper, investigator, private eye, private investigator; (*Inf*) sleuth.
deter *v* discourage, intimidate, prevent, put off, talk out of.
deteriorate *v* **1** decline, degenerate, depreciate, slump, spoil, worsen. **2** be the worse for wear, crumble, decline, decompose, disintegrate, ebb, fail, fall apart, wear away.
determined *adj* bent on, intent, persistent, resolute, set on, single-minded, tenacious, unflinching, unwavering.
deterrent *n* curb, defensive measures, discouragement, hindrance, impediment, obstacle, restraint.
detest *v* despise, feel disgust, hate, loathe, recoil from.
detour *n* bypass, byway, deviation, diversion, indirect course, roundabout way.
detract *v* diminish, lessen, lower, reduce, take away from.
detrimental *adj* adverse, destructive, harmful, mischievous, unfavourable.
devastating *adj* deadly, destructive, effective, keen, overpowering, overwhelming, savage, stunning, withering.
develop *v* **1** advance, cultivate, evolve, flourish, grow, mature, progress, prosper. **2** amplify, broaden, elaborate, enlarge, expand, unfold. **3** come about, ensue, follow, happen, result.

British policemen wear a distinctive helmet and uniform.

development *n* **1** advance, evolution, expansion, progression, spread. **2** change, outcome, result, turn of events, upshot.
deviate *v* bend, deflect, diverge, drift, stray, swerve, turn aside, vary, veer, wander.
device *n* **1** apparatus, appliance, gadget, implement, instrument, invention, tool, utensil. **2** design, plan, project, purpose, scheme, strategy, stunt.
devious *adj* calculating,

dishonest, double-dealing, insincere, scheming, sly, underhand, wily.
devise *v* conceive, construct, design, dream up, formulate, invent, plan, project, scheme, think up, work out.
devoid *adj* destitute, empty, free from, lacking, vacant, void, wanting, without.
devour *v* bolt, consume, cram, dispatch, eat, gobble, gorge, gulp, guzzle, polish off, stuff, swallow, wolf.
dexterity *n* expertise, finesse, knack, mastery, neatness, nimbleness, proficiency, skill, smoothness, touch.
diagram *n* **1** chart, drawing, layout, outline, plan, sketch.
differ *v* contrast, depart form, diverge, run counter to, stand apart, vary.
different *adj* **1** altered, changed, clashing, contrasting, deviation disparate, dissimilar, divergent, diverse, inconsistent, opposed, unlike. **2** assorted, divers, diverse, manifold, many, miscellaneous, numerous, several, some, sundry, varied, various.
differentiate *v* **1** contrast, distinguish, separate, set off, tell apart.
dig *v* **1** break up, burrow, delve, excavate, gouge, hollow out, mine, quarry, tunnel. **2** delve, dig down, go into, investigate, probe, research, search.
dig *n* **1** jab, poke, prod, punch, thrust. **2** crack, cutting remark, sneer, taunt, wisecrack.
dilapidated *adj* crumbling, decayed, falling apart, in ruins, neglected, ramshackle, rickety, rundown, shabby, tumble down.
dilemma *n* difficulty, fix, jam, mess, plight, predicament, quandary, strait, tight corner.
dilute *v* cut, thin, water down, weaken.
dim *adj* **1** cloudy, dark, dusky, grey, overcast, poorly lit, shadowy. **2** blurred, fuzzy, ill-defined, indistinct, shadowy, unclear. **3** dense, dull, obscure.
diminish *v* contract, cut, decrease, lessen, lower, reduce, shrink, weaken.
dingy *adj* dark, drab, dreary, dull, faded, gloomy, murky, seedy, shabby, soiled, tacky.
dip *v* **1** bathe, douse, duck, dunk, immerse, plunge, rinse, souse. **2** ladle, scoop, spoon.
dip *n* **1** drenching, ducking, immersion, plunge, soaking. **2** bathe, dive, plunge, swim. **3** infusion, mixture, preparation, solution, suspension. **4** basin, concavity, depression, hole, hollow, incline, slope. **5** decline, fall, lowering, sag, slip, slump.
diplomat *n* go-between, mediator, negotiator, politician.
diplomatic *adj* discreet, polite, sensitive, subtle, tactful.
direct *v* **1** advise, engineer, govern, lead, manage, oversee, preside over, regulate, run, supervise; (*Inf*) be the boss. **2** bid, charge, command, dictate, instruct, order. **3** guide, lead, point the way, show.
direct *adj* **1** blunt, frank, honest, matter-of-fact, outspoken, plain-spoken, sincere, straight to the point. **2** blunt, explicit, plain, point-blank. **3** non-stop, shortest, straight through, unbroken, uninterrupted.
direction *n* **1** command, control, government, guidance, leadership, management, order, oversight, supervision. **2** aim, bearing, course, line, path, road, route, track, way.
dirt *n* **1** dust, filth, grime, muck, mud, slime, stain, tarnish. **2** clay, earth, loam, soil.
disability *n* affliction, ailment, complaint, defect, disorder, handicap, impairment.

Disabled atheletes from all over the world have been taking part in the Paralympics, the Olympic Games for athletes with disabilities, since 1960.

disable *v* cripple, damage, debilitate, handicap, immobilize, incapacitate, paralyse, put out of action, unfit, weaken.
disabled *adj* crippled, handicapped, infirm, paralysed, weak.
disagree *v* **1** contradict, counter, differ, diverge, vary. **2** argue, bicker, contest, debate, differ, dispute, dissent, fall out, have words, object, oppose, quarrel, take issue with.
disappear *v* **1** drop out of sight, fade away, retire, vanish from sight, withdraw. **2** cease, die out, end, evaporate, expire, fade, melt away, pass away, perish, vanish.
disappoint *v* deceive, delude, disenchant, dishearten, dismay, fail, let down, sadden, vex.
disapprove *v* **1** blame, condemn, dislike, find unacceptable, frown on, object to, take exception to. **2** disallow, set aside, turn down, veto.
disarray *n* **1** confusion, disharmony, disorder, disorganization, indiscipline, unruliness, upset. **2** chaos, clutter, jumble, mess, mix-up, muddle, shambles, tangle, untidiness.
disastrous *adj* adverse, catastrophic, detrimental, dire, dreadful, fatal, harmful, ill-fated, ill-starred, terrible, tragic, unfortunate, unlucky, untoward.
discharge *n* **1** acquittal, exoneration, pardon, release. **2** blast, detonation, explosion, firing, salvo, shot, volley. **3** emmision, exuding, oozing, release.
discharge *v* **1** discard, dismiss, eject, expel, fire, give, the sack, oust, remove, sack. **2** detonate, explode, fire, let off, set off, shoot. **3** accomplish, carry out, do, execute, fulfil, observe, perform. **4** clear, honour, meet, pay, relieve, satisfy, settle, square up. **5** absolve, acquit, clear, exonerate, free, pardon, release, set free. **6** emmision, exuding oozing, release. 7 emit, excrete. give out, leak.
disclose *v* broadcast, communicate, confess, divulge, make public, publish, reveal, spill the beans about, tell, utter.
discolour *v* fade, mark, rust, soil, stain, streak, tarnish, tinge.
disconnect *v* cut off, detach, disengage, divide, part, separate, sever, take apart, uncouple.
discontinue *v* abandon, break off, cease, end, finish, give up, halt, interrupt, leave off, pause, put an end to, quit, refrain from, stop, suspend, terminate.
discount *v* **1** brush off, disregard, ignore, overlook, pass over. **2** deduct, lower, mark down, rebate, reduce, take off.
discount *n* allowance, concession, cut price, deduction, rebate, reduction.
discourage *v* dash, demoralize, depress, dishearten, dismay, dispirit, frighten, intimidate, put a damper on, scare, unnerve.
discouragement *n* dejection, despair, despondency, dismay, hopelessness, loss of confidence, low spirits, pessimism.
discover *v* **1** bring to light, come upon, locate, turn up, unearth. **2** disclose, find out, learn, notice, perceive, realize, recognize, reveal, spot, turn up, uncover.
discrepancy *n* difference, disparity, variation.
discretion *n* care, caution, judgement, maturity, tact.
discriminate *v* **1** favour, show prejudice, single out, treat differently. **2** distinguish, evaluate, separate, sift, tell the difference.

The pollutants discharged by factories and power stations into the atmosphere leads to pollution over a wide area, as nitrogen oxide and sulphur dioxide fall as 'acid rain' on vegetation.

discrimination *n* bias, bigotry, favouritism, intolerance, prejudice, unfairness.
discuss *v* confer, consider, consult with, debate, talk about, thrash out, weigh up the pros and cons.
discussion *n* consultation, debate, dialogue, examination, review, scrutiny, symposium.
disease *n* affliction, ailment, complaint, condition, disorder, ill health, illness, indisposition, infection, infirmity, malady, sickness, upset.
diseased *adj* ailing, infected, rotten, sick, sickly, tainted, unhealthy, unsound, unwell.
disembark *v* arrive, get off, go ashore, land, step out of.
disfigure *v* damage, deface, deform, distort, injure, maim, make ugly, mar, mutilate, scar.
disgraceful *adj* disreputable, infamous, low, mean, scandalous, shameful, shocking.
disguise *v* **1** camouflage, conceal, cover, hide, mask, screen, secrete, shroud, veil. **2** deceive, falsify, gloss over, misrepresent.
disgusting *adj* abominable, distasteful, foul, grotty, nasty, nauseous, obnoxious, offensive, repellent, revolting, sickening, stinking, vile, vulgar.
dish *n* **1** bowl, plate, platter, salver. **2** fare, food, recipe.
dishonest *adj* corrupt, crooked, deceitful, disreputable, double-dealing, false, fraudulent, lying, swindling, unfair, unscrupulous, untrustworthy, untruthful.
dishonourable *adj* despicable, disgraceful, shameful.
disinfect *v* cleanse, deodorize, fumigate, sanitize, sterilize.
disintegrate *v* break apart, break up, crumble, disunite, fall apart, fall to pieces, reduce to fragments, separate, shatter.
dislike *n* animosity, disgust, hatred, hostility, loathing.

Some fish are able to disguise themselves just as land animals do. When they are still, it is very difficult to see them.

dislike *v* despise, detest, hate, loathe, object to, shun.
disloyal *adj* false, treacherous, unfaithful, unpatriotic.
dismal *adj* bleak, cheerless, dark, depressing, dreary, gloomy, sad.
dismay *v* alarm, appal, distress, frighten, horrify, paralyse, scare, terrify, unnerve.
dismissal *n* **1** adjournment, end, permission to go, release. **2** discharge, expulsion, notice, removal, the sack.
disobedient *adj* defiant, naughty, undisciplined, unruly, wayward, wilful.
dispatch *v* discharge, dispose of, finish, perform, settle.
dispatch *n* account, bulletin, document, instruction, letter, message, news, report, story.
dispense *v* **1** allocate, distribute, dole out, share. **2** administer, carry out, enforce, execute, operate, undertake.
disperse *v* **1** diffuse, scatter, spread. **2** break up, disband, dismiss, dissolve, scatter, send off, separate, vanish.
display *v* **1** demonstrate, exhibit, present, reveal, show, unveil. **2** model, open out, spread out, unfold, unfurl.
disposal *n* **1** clearance, ejection, removal, scrapping, throwing away. **2** arrangement, grouping, placing, position.
dispose of *v* **1** deal with, decide, determine, end, finish, settle. **2** give, make over, part with, sell, transfer. **3** discard, dump, get rid of, jettison, scrap, throw out, unload.
dispute *v* **1** argue, debate, discuss, quarrel, squabble. **2** challenge, question.
disqualify *v* **1** invalidate, unfit. **2** debar, ineligible, prohibit, rule out.
dissent *v* differ, disagree, object, protest, refuse.
dissertation *n* essay, thesis.
dissolution *n* breaking, up, disintegration, divorce, parting, separation.
dissolve *v* **1** melt, soften, thaw. **2** decompose, disintegrate, disperse, evaporate, fade, melt away, perish, vanish.
distance *n* extent, gap, interval, length, range, span, width.
distance *v* dissociate oneself, separate oneself.

distant *adj* **1** far, far-flung, far-off, remote. **2** aloof, cold, cool, formal, reserved, standoffish, stiff, unfriendly.
distil *v* condense, evaporate, extract, press out, purify, rectify, refine, vaporize.
distinct *adj* **1** apparent, clear, clearcut, evident, lucid, obvious, recognizable, sharp. **2** detached, different, individual, separate, unconnected.
distort *v* **1** bend, buckle, contort, deform, twist. **2** bias, falsify, misrepresent, slant.
distress *n* agony, anguish, grief, heartache, misery, pain, sadness, suffering, torment.
distribute *v* allocate, allot, deal, dispense, divide, dole out, give, measure out, share.
district *n* area, community, locality, neighbourhood, parish, quarter, region, sector, ward.
ditch *n* channel, drain, dyke, furrow, gully, moat, trench, watercourse.
ditch *v* **1** dig, drain, excavate, gouge, trench. **2** abandon, discard, dispose of, drop, get rid of, jettison, scrap, throw out.
diversion *n* **1** deviation, redirection. **2** alternative route, detour.
divide *v* **1** bisect, cut, disconnect, partition, separate, split, sub-divide. **2** allocate, deal out, distribute, measure out, share.
dividend *n* bonus, cut, extra, gain, portion, share, surplus.
division *n* **1** bisection, dividing, separation, splitting up. **2** distribution, sharing, border, boundary, dividing line, partition. **3** branch, class, compartment, department, group, head, part, section, sector, segment.
divorce *n* annulment, breach, break, decree, dissolution, rupture, separation.
divorce *v* annul, disconnect, dissolve, divide, part, separate, sever, split up.
divulge *v* betray, disclose, leak, let slip, reveal, tell, uncover.
dizzy *adj* faint, giddy, light-headed, off balance, reeling, shaky, wobbly; (*Inf*) woozy.

In the colder areas of the Earth, tortoises are dormant during winter. They spend the cold months hibernating until the temperature rises once again.

do *v* **1** accomplish, carry out, execute, perform, work. **2** be of use, satisfy, suffice. **3** adapt, render, transpose. **4** behave, carry oneself. **5** fare, get along, get on, make out, manage, proceed. **6** bring about, cause, create, effect, produce. **7** cheat, deceive, dupe, swindle, trick.
do *n* affair, event, function, gathering, occasion, party.
dock *n* harbour, pier, quay, waterfront, wharf.
dock *v* anchor, berth, drop anchor, land, moor, tie up.
doctor *n* general practitioner, GP, medic, physician.
doctor *v* **1** apply medication to, treat. **2** fix, mend, patch up, repair. **3** alter, change, falsify, tamper with.
document *n* certificate, legal form, paper, record, report.
document *v* back up, certify, detail, instance, validate, verify.
dominant *adj* assertive, authoritative, commanding, controlling, governing, leading, presiding, ruling, superior, supreme
dominate *v* control, direct, govern, lead, master, monopolize, overbear, rule, tyrannize. **2** stand over, tower above.
donation *n* contribution, gift, grant, gratuity, offering, present.
donor *n* benefactor, contributor, donator, philanthropist.
dormant *adj* asleep, comatose, hibernating, inactive, sleeping.
double-cross *v* betray, cheat, defraud, mislead, swindle, trick; (*Inf*) two-time.
doubt *v* **1** distrust, fear, mistrust, query, question, suspect. **2** be uncertain, hesitate, waver.
doubt *n* **1** apprehension, distrust, fear, mistrust, suspicion. **2** confusion, difficulty, dilemma, problem, quandary.
doubtful *adj* **1** dubious, unclear, vague. **2** distrustful, hesitating, in two minds, sceptical, unsure.
down *adj* blue, depressed, low, miserable, sad, unhappy.
downfall *n* collapse, descent, fall, overthrow.
downpour *n* cloudburst, deluge, flood, rainstorm, torrential rain.
drain *v* **1** bleed, draw off, dry, empty, evacuate, milk, pump off, remove, tap, withdraw. **2** consume, empty, exhaust, sap,

strain, use up.
drain *n* **1** channel, culvert, ditch, pipe, sewer, sink, trench, water-course. **2** depletion, exhaustion, sap, strain, withdrawal.
drama *n* **1** play, stage play, stage show, theatrical piece. **2** acting, dramatic art, stagecraft, theatre. **3** crisis, scene, spectacle, turmoil.
drastic *adj* extreme, forceful, harsh, radical, severe, strong.
draw *v* **1** drag, haul, pull, tow, tug. **2** depict, design, paint, portray, sketch, trace. **3** attract, entice, persuade. **4** extend, lengthen, stretch. **5** compose, draft, frame, prepare, write.
draw *n* **1** attraction, lure, pull. **2** deadlock, impasse, stalemate, tie. **3** lottery, raffle, sweepstake.
drawing *n* cartoon, illustration, outline, picture, portrayal, representation, sketch, study.
dream *n* **1** daydream, fantasy, hallucination, illusion, imagination, pipe dream, speculation, trance, vision. **2** ambition, aspiration, desire, goal, hope, wish.

Bonsai derives from the Chinese words *pun-sai*, meaning tree in a pot. Bonsai are artistic replicas of natural trees in miniature form.

dream *v* build castle in the air, conjure up, daydream, fancy, fantasize, imagine, visualize.
dress *n* **1** costume, ensemble, garment, outfit, robe, suit. **2** attire, clothing, costume, garb, garments, guise, togs.
dress *v* **1** change, clothe, don, garb, put on, slip on. **2** bandage, bind up, plaster, treat.
drill *v* **1** coach, instruct, practise, rehearse, teach, train. **2** bore, penetrate, perforate, pierce, puncture, sink in.
drill *n* **1** discipline, exercise, instruction, practice, repetition, training. **2** bit, borer, boring-tool, rotary tool.
drink *v* **1** absorb, drain, gulp, guzzle, sip, suck, sup, swallow, swig, swill, wash down. **2** pub-crawl, revel, tipple; (*Inf*) booze.
drink *n* **1** beverage, liquid, potion, refreshment. **2** alcohol, liquor, spirits; (*Inf*) the bottle.
driving *v* compelling, sweeping, vigorous, violent.
drop *n* **1** bead, droplet, globule, pearl, tear. **2** mouthful, pinch, taste, tot, trickle. **3** decline, fall-off, reduction, slump.
drop *v* **1** decline, diminish, fall, lower, plummet, plunge, sink. **2** cease, discontinue, give up, quit, terminate.
drought *n* dehydration, dryness, dry spell, dry weather.
drug *n* **1** medication, medicine, poison, remedy. **2** dope, narcotic, opiate, stimulant.
drug *v* administer a drug, treat.
dry *adj* **1** arid, dehydrated, desiccated, parched, thirsty. **2** boring, dull, monotonous, plain, tedious, uninteresting.
dry *v* dehumidify, dehydrate, desiccate, drain, make dry, parch, sear.
due *adj* **1** outstanding, unpaid. **2** deserved, fitting, just, justified, proper, rightful, well-earned. **3** expected to arrive, scheduled.
due *adv* dead, direct, directly, exactly, straight.
duel *n* **1** affair of honour, single combat. **2** clash, competition, contest, encounter, fight.
dull *adj* **1** dense, dim-witted, slow, stupid, thick, unintelligent. **2** apathetic, dead, lifeless, slow, sluggish. **3** boring, dreary, dry, flat, humdrum, monotonous, plain, run-of-the-mill, tedious, tiresome, uninteresting. **4** cloudy, dim, dismal, gloomy, leaden, opaque, overcast, turbid.
duly *adv* **1** accordingly, correctly, deservedly, fittingly, properly, rightfully, suitably. **2** at the proper time, on time, punctually.
durable *adj* constant, dependable, firm, hard-wearing, long-lasting, permanent, reliable, stable, strong, sturdy, tough.
dwarf *n* bantam, Lilliputian, midget, pygmy, Tom Thumb.
dwarf *adj* baby, bonsai, dwarfed, miniature, petite, pocket, small, tiny, undersized.
dwarf *v* dominate, overshadow, tower above.
dwell *v* inhabit, lodge, reside, rest, settle, stay, stop.
dynamic *adj* active, energetic, forceful, go-ahead, lively, magnetic, powerful, vital, zippy.
dynasty *n* empire, government, house, regime, rule, sovereignty.

Ee

each *pron* each and every one, each one, every one, one and all.
each *adv* apiece, for each, from each, individually, per person.
eager *adj* anxious, avid, earnest, enthusiastic, fervent, greedy, hot, hungry, impatient, keen, longing, raring, yearning.
carly *adj* advanced, forward, premature, untimely.
early *adv* ahead of time, beforehand, in advance, in good time, prematurely, too soon.
earn *v* **1** bring in, collect, draw, get, gross, net, procure, receive. **2** acquire, attain, be entitled to, deserve, merit, warrant, win.
earnest *adj* determined, firm, intent, resolute, sincere, solemn, stable, steady, thoughtful.
earnings *pl n* income, pay, proceeds, profits, remuneration, reward, salary, takings, wages.
earth *n* **1** globe, orb, planet, sphere, terrestrial, sphere, world. **2** clay, clod, dirt, ground, land, loam, sod, soil, topsoil, turf.
earthenware *n* ceramics, crockery, crocks, pots, pottery, terracotta.
earthly *adj* **1** mundane, worldly. **2** human, mortal, non-spiritual.
ease *n* calmness, comfort, enjoyment, happiness, peace, quiet, rest, restfulness, tranquillity.
ease *v* alleviate, lighten, pacify, quiet, relieve, soothe, still.
easily *adv* comfortably, effortlessly, readily, smoothly, with ease, without difficulty.
easy *adj* clear, effortless, no trouble, painless, simple, smooth, straightforward, uncomplicated, undemanding; (*Inf*) a piece of cake.
easygoing *adj* carefree, casual, easy, flexible, happy-go-lucky, laid-back, placid, relaxed, tolerant.
eat *v* **1** chew, consume, devour, gobble, ingest, munch, swallow. **2** dine, feed, have a meal.
eavesdrop *v* listen in, monitor, overhear, tap; (*Inf*) bug, snoop, spy.
cbb *v* **1** fall away, fall back, recede, retire, retreat, sink, subside, withdraw. **2** decrease, diminish, drop, fade away, fall away, shrink, slacken, weaken.
eccentric *adj* bizarre, odd, peculiar, quirky, strange, weird.
echo *v* repeat.
echo *n* **1** answer, repetition. **2** copy, imitation, mirror image, reflection.
eclipse *v* blot out, cloud, darken, dim, extinguish, obscure, overshadow, shroud, veil.
eclipse *n* **1** darkening, dimming, extinction, shading. **2** decline, failure, fall, loss.
economical *adj* **1** cost-effective, efficient, money-saving. **2** frugal, saving, sparing, thrifty.
ecstasy *n* bliss, delight, elation, enthusiasm, euphoria, joy.
ecstatic *adj* blissful, delirious, elated, entranced, euphoric, joyful, on cloud nine, over-joyed.
eddy *n* counter-current, counter-flow, swirl, vortex, whirlpool.
eddy *v* swirl, whirl.
edge *n* **1** border, boundary, brink, fringe, limit, margin, perimeter, periphery, rim, side, verge. **2** bite, sting. **3** advantage, head start, lead, upper hand. **on edge** edgy, nervous, tense, uneasy.
edible *adj* digestible, good, wholesome.
edit *v* adapt, check, correct, rephrase, revise, rewrite.
edition *n* copy, issue, number, version.
education *n* coaching, development,

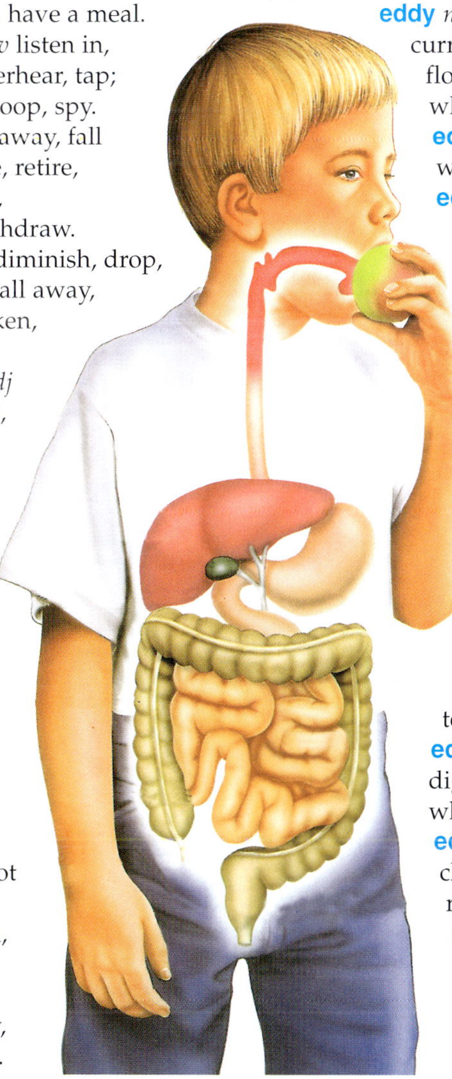

The food that we eat travels slowly through our bodies, a journey of up to ten metres.

The cheetah has an effortless running style and can reach top speeds of 105km/h (65mph) when sprinting over short distances.

drilling, instruction, schooling, teaching, training, tuition.
eerie *adj* awesome, creepy, frightening, mysterious, scary, strange, unearthly, weird.
effect *n* **1** aftermath, conclusion, consequence, outcome, result, upshot. **2 in effect** actually, effectively, essentially, in reality, in truth, really. **3 take effect** become law, begin, come into force, produce results, work.
effect *v* accomplish, achieve, bring about, carry out, complete, create, execute, fulfil, initiate, make, perform, produce.
effective *adj* **1** adequate, capable, efficient, real. **2** active, actual, current, in effect, in force, in operation, operative.
effervesce *v* bubble, ferment, fizz, foam, froth, sparkle.
efficient *adj* adept, business-like, capable, competent, organized, proficient, skilfull, well-organized, workmanlike.
effort *n* application, endeavour, energy, exertion, force, labour, pains, power, strain, stress, stretch, striving, struggle, toil, trouble, work.
effortless *adj* easy, painless, simple, smooth, uncomplicated, undemanding, untroublesome.
eject *v* **1** cast out, discharge, expel, throw out. **2** discharge, dislodge, dismiss, get rid of, oust, throw out.
elaborate *adj* **1** careful, detailed, exact, intricate, painstaking, skilful. **2** complex, complicated, detailed, extravagant, fussy, involved, ornate, ostentatious, showy.
elaborate *v* add detail, develop, embellish, enhance, enlarge, expand, improve, ornament, produce, refine, work out.
electrify *v* amaze, astonish, astound, excite, fire, invigorate, rouse, startle, take one's breath away, thrill.
elegant *adj* beautiful, chic, exquisite, fine, luxurious, refined, stylish, tasteful.
element *n* basis, component, constituent, factor, feature, hint, ingredient, part, section, subdivision, unit.
elevate *v* **1** heighten, hoist, lift, lift up, raise, uplift. **2** advance, prefer, promote, upgrade.
elicit *v* bring to light, cause, derive, evolve, exact, extort, give rise to, obtain.
eliminate *v* cut out, dispose of, eradicate, expel, exterminate, get rid of, remove, stamp out.
elite *n* aristocracy, cream, high society, nobility, upper class.
elope *v* abscond, bolt, escape, leave, run away, run off.
embargo *n* ban, bar, barrier, blockage, check, hindrance, impediment, interdict, prohibition, proscription, restraint, restriction, stoppage.
embark *v* **1** board ship, go aboard, take on board, take ship. **2** begin, commence, engage, initiate, launch, set out, start, take up, undertake.
embarrass *v* confuse, distress, mortify, shame, show up.
embarrassing *adj* awkward, humiliating, shameful, touchy, tricky, uncomfortable.
embarrassment *n* **1** awkwardness, distress, humiliation, mortification, shame. **2** difficulty, dilemma, mess, predicament; *(Inf)* bind, fix, pickle, quandary, scrape.
embellish *v* adorn, deck, decorate, dress up, embroider, enrich, garnish, gild, varnish.
embezzle *v* filch, have one's hand in the till, misappropriate, pilfer, purloin, steal.
emblem *n* badge, crest, device, figure, image, insignia, mark, representation, sign, symbol.

The ancient emblem of the salmander in flames is a reminder of the belief that salamanders could live in the middle of fires as the cold of their bodies extinguished the surrounding flames.

embrace *v* **1** canoodle, cuddle, grasp, hold, hug, seize, squeeze. **2** accept, adopt, grab, make use of, seize, take up.
embrace *n* clasp, clinch, cuddle, hug, squeeze.
emerge *v* **1** appear, become visible, come into view, rise, spring up, surface. **2** become known, come to light, crop up, develop, get around, materialize, transpire, turn up.
emergency *n* crisis, danger, difficulty, extremity, necessity, pass, plight, predicament, quandary, scrape.
emigrate *v* migrate, move, move abroad, remove.
eminent *adj* celebrated, distinguished, famous, great, outstanding, prominent, renowned, well-known.
emit *v* breathe forth, discharge, exhale, give off, give out, issue, radiate, send out, transmit, vent.
emotion *n* ardour, excitement, feeling, passion, sentiment.
emphasis *n* accent, attention, importance, intensity, power, significance, strength, stress, underscoring, weight.
empire *n* commonwealth, domain, imperium, kingdom, realm.
employ *v* **1** commission, engage, hire, retain, take on. **2** engage, fill, keep busy, make use of, occupy, spend, take up, use up.
employee *n* hand, job-holder, staff member, wage-earner, worker, workman.
employer *n* boss, business, company, establishment, firm, gaffer, organization, outfit, owner, patron, proprietor.
empty *adj* **1** bare, blank, clear, deserted, desolate, vacant. **2** futile, senseless, worthless. **3** absent, blank, expressionless.

Some birds migrate many hundreds of miles to breed each year. The longest migration is that of the Arctic tern, which flies at least 15,000km (9,000 miles).

empty *v* clear, consume, deplete, discharge, drain, dump, evacuate, exhaust, gut, pour out, unburden, unload, use up, vacate, void.
enable *v* allow, authorize, license, permit, qualify, sanction, warrant.
enchanting *adj* appealing, attractive, captivating, charming, delightful, endearing, lovely, pleasant.
enclose *v* **1** bound, cover, encase, encircle, fence, hedge, hem in, pen, shut in, wall in, wrap. **2** include, insert, put in, send with.
encounter *v* **1** bump into, come upon, confront, face, meet, run, run into. **2** attack, combat, come into conflict with, cross swords with, do battle with, engage, fight, grapple with, struggle.
encounter *n* **1** chance meeting, rendezvous. **2** battle, brawl, brush, clash, combat, conflict, confrontation, contest, dispute, engagement, scuffle, skirmish.
encourage *v* cheer, comfort, console, inspire, rally, reassure, rouse, stimulate.
end *n* **1** boundary, edge, extent, limit, point, tip. **2** close, culmination, finish, outcome, result, stop, termination, upshot. **3** aim, aspiration, goal, objective, point, purpose, reason. **4** death, demise, destruction, extinction.
end *v* **1** cease, close, conclude, culminate, discontinue, dissolve, expire, fade away, finish, peter out, resolve, stop, terminate; (*Inf*) wind up. **2** annihilate, destroy, put an end to.
endless *adj* **1** continual, eternal, ever-lasting, infinite, limitless, perpetual, unbroken, unlimited. **2** monotonous. **3** continuous, unbroken, undivided, whole.
endorse *v* advocate, authorize, back, confirm, ratify, sanction, support, sustain, vouch for.
endow *v* award, bequeath, bestow, confer, donate, furnish, give, grant, invest, leave, provide, settle on, supply, will.
endure *v* **1** bear, brave, cope

with, experience, go through, stand, suffer, sustain, weather, withstand. **2** abide, permit, put up with, stand, stick, stomach, submit to, suffer, swallow, take, patiently, tolerate.

enemy *n* **1** competitor, foe, opponent, rival, the opposition, **2** competition, opposition.

energy *n* drive, fire, go, liveliness, power, stamina, strength, vigour, vitality, zest.

enforce *v* administer, carry out, execute, implement, impose, put into effect, reinforce, require.

engage *v* **1** appoint, employ, hire, take on. **2** book, charter, hire, lease, rent. **3** attack, combat, fight with, take on. **4** activate, apply, set going, switch on.

engagement *n* **1** appointment, job, post, situation. **2** booking, charter, lease, rent, reservation. **3** betrothal, marriage pledge. **4** agreement, bond, contract, obligation, pledge, promise, undertaking, vow, word. **5** arrangement, commitment, date, interview, meeting. **6** action, battle, combat, conflict, confrontation, encounter, fight, hostilities, struggle, warfare.

engineer *n* architect, designer, inventor, manager, planner.

engineer *v* bring about, cause, contrive, create, devise, mastermind, originate, plan, plot, scheme; (*Inf*) wangle.

engrave *v* carve, chase, chisel, cut, etch, grave, inscribe.

enjoy *v* **1** appreciate, delight in, like, revel in, take joy in, take pleasure in. **2** be blessed with, experience, own, possess, use.

enlarge *v* add to, expand, extend, increase, inflate, make larger, multiply, stretch, widen.

What are the different kinds of energy

enlist *v* engage, enroll, join up, muster, obtain, recruit, register, secure, sign up, volunteer.
enormous *adj* colossal, gigantic, gross, huge, immense, jumbo, mammoth, massive, titanic, tremendous, vast.
enough *adj* abundant, adequate, ample, plenty, sufficient.
enough *adv* adequately, amply, moderately, reasonably, sufficiently, tolerably.
enrage *n* anger, annoy, incense, infuriate, irritate, make one's blood boil, make one see red, provoke.
en route *adv* in transit, on the way, on the road.
enter *v* **1** arrive, come into, introduce, pass into, penetrate, pierce. **2** begin, commence, enlist, enroll, join, sign up, start, take part in. **3** inscribe, list, log, note, record, register. **4** offer, present, put forward, submit, tender.
entertain *v* **1** amuse, charm, delight, occupy. **2** accommodate, be host to, have guests, lodge, put up, treat.
entice *v* attract, lure, persuade, seduce, tempt.
entire *adj* **1** complete, full, gross, total, whole. **2** absolute, outright, thorough, unreserved. **3** intact, undamaged, unimpaired.
entrance *n* **1** access, avenue, door, doorway, entry, gate, inlet, opening, passage, portal, way in. **2** appearance, arrival, coming in, introduction. **3** admission, admittance, entrée, permission to enter.
entrance *v* bewitch, captivate, charm, delight, enchant, enthral, fascinate, spellbind.
entry *n* **1** appearance, coming in, entering, entrance, initiation, introduction. **2** access, avenue, door, doorway, entrance, gate, ingress, inlet, opening, passage, passageway, portal, way in. **3** access, admission, entrance, entree, free passage, permission, to enter. **4** attempt, candidate, competitor, contestant, effort, entrant, participant, player, submission.
envelop *v* blanket, conceal, cover, embrace, encase, encircle, enclose, encompass, engulf, shroud, surround, swathe, veil, wrap.
envelope *n* case, casing, coating, cover, covering, jacket, sheath, shell, skin, wrapper, wrapping.
envious *adj* begrudging, green with envy, grudging, jealous, resentful, spiteful.
envy *n* grudge, hatred, jealousy, malice, resentment, spite, the green-eyed monster.
envy *v* be envious, begrudge, be jealous, covet, grudge, resent.
epidemic *adj* prevalent, rampant, rife, sweeping, wide-ranging, widespread.
epidemic *n* growth, outbreak, plague, rash, spread, upsurge, wave.
epilogue *n* concluding speech, conclusion, postscript.
episode *n* **1** adventure, affair, business, circumstance, event, experience, incident, occurrence. **2** chapter, installment, part, passage, scene, section.
equal *adj* **1** alike, identical, like, proportionate, the same, uniform. **2** balanced, even, evenly matched, level pegging, matched, regular, symmetrical, uniform. **3** able, capable, competent, fit, ready, strong enough, suitable, up to.

Entry into the City of London is guarded by Tower Bridge. The lower bascule sections of the bridge must be raised before shipping can proceed up the river Thames to the Houses of Parliament and beyond.

equal *n* brother, counterpart, equivalent, fellow, match, mate, parallel, peer, rival, twin.
equal *v* **1** amount to, come to, correspond to, make, total. **2** match, measure up to, parallel, rival. **3** achieve, come up to, measure up to, reach.
equip *v* arm, attire, dress, fit out, kit out, outfit, prepare, provide, rig, stock, supply.
equipment *n* apparatus, furniture, material, outfit, rig, supplies, tackle, tools.
equivalent *adj* alike, corresponding, equal, even, same, similar.
era *n* age, cycle, date, day, days, epoch, period, stage, time.
erect *adj* elevated, perpendicular, raised, standing, stiff, straight, upright, vertical.
erect *v* build, construct, elevate, lift, put up, set up, stand up.
erode *v* corrode, destroy, deteriorate, disintegrate, eat away, grind down, wear down.
errand *n* job, message, task.
erratic *adj* changeable, fitful, inconsistent, unpredictable, unreliable, variable.
error *n* bloomer, blunder, fault, flaw, miscalculation, mistake, oversight, slip.
erupt *v* blow up, burst out, discharge, explode, flare up, gush, spout, throw off, vent.
eruption *n* discharge, ejection, explosion, flare up, outbreak, outburst.
escalate *v* amplify, enlarge, expand, extend, grow, increase, intensify, magnify, mount, rise.
escape *v* **1** abscond, bolt, break free, get away, run away, skip, slip away. **2** avoid, circumvent, dodge, duck, elude, evade, pass, shun, slip. **3** discharge, drain, flow, gush, leak, seep, spurt.
escape *n* **1** bolt, break, break-out, flight, getaway. **2** avoidance, circumvention, elusion, evasion. **3** discharge, drain, gush, leak, outpour, spurt.
escort *n* bodyguard, company, convoy, entourage, guard, protection, retinue, train.
escort *v* accompany, chaperon, conduct, defend, guide, lead, partner, protect, shepherd, usher.
essay *n* article, composition, dissertation, paper, piece.
essence *n* **1** core, heart, soul, spirit. **2** concentrate, extract, spirits, tincture.
essential *adj* **1** crucial, necessary, vital. **2** basic, fundamental, key, main.
essential *n* basic, fundamental, must, necessity, principle.
establish *v* base, create, fix, form, implant, install, institute, organize, plant, root, secure, settle, set up, start.
estate *n* **1** area, holdings, lands, manor, piece of land, property. **2** land, region. **3** development. **4** assets, belongings, effects, fortune, possessions, resources, wealth. **5** caste, class, rank, status. **6** condition, position, situation, state.
estimate *v* **1** assess, calculate, evaluate, gauge, guess, judge, number, reckon, value. **2** assess, believe, conjecture, consider, form an opinion, guess, judge, rank, rate, reckon, surmise.
estimate *n* appraisal, approximate calculation, assessment, evaluation, guess, judgment, reckoning, valuation.
estuary *n* bay, cove, creek, firth, fjord, inlet, river mouth.

Eruption of volcanoes occur mainly along fault lines. Molten rock and gases are forced out through a gap in the Earth's crust to release pressure. Over thousands of years, cooled rocks sometimes build up around the fissure in the ground to form the familiar conical shape of a volcano.

Water is constantly evaporating from the Earth, forming clouds and falling back to Earth as rain or snow. Ponds and rivers are part of the evaporation process know as the water cycle.

evaporate *v* **1** dehydrate, dry up. **2** disappear, disperse, dissolve, fade, melt, vanish.
evasion *n* avoidance, dodge, escape, shirking (*Inf*) waffle.
even *adj* **1** flat, level, parallel, smooth, straight, true, uniform. **2** calm, peaceful, placid, stable. **3** balanced, equitable, fair, just, unbiased, unprejudiced.
even *adv* much, still, yet.
event *n* adventure, business, episode, happening, incident, matter, milestone, occurrence.
eventful *adj* active, busy, full, important, momentous, notable, significant.
eventually *adv* finally, in the long run, one day, sooner or later, ultimately.
ever *adv* always, constantly, continually, relentlessly.
evict *v* chuck out, dislodge, dispossess, eject, expel, oust, put out, throw on to the streets, throw out, turn out.
evidence *n* data, grounds, indication, proof, testimony, token, witness.
evil *adj* bad, corrupt, malicious, vicious, vile, wicked, wrong.
evil *n* sin, wickedness, wrong.
evil *adj* catastrophic, disastrous, harmful, painful.
evolution *n* development, evolvement, growth, progress, progression.
evolve *v* develop, expand, grow, increase, mature.
exact *adj* **1** accurate, definite, precise. **2** careful, meticulous, painstaking, scrupulous, strict.
exact *v* claim, demand, insist upon, require.
exactly *adv* **1** accurately, precisely, strictly. **2** absolutely, indeed, precisely, quite.
exaggerate *v* embellish, embroider, inflate, magnify, overdo, overstate.
examination *n* analysis, inquiry, inspection, investigation, probe, quiz, review, search, study, test.
examine *v* analyse, check out, consider, investigate, look over, pore over, scan, scrutinize, study, survey, test, vet, weigh.
example *n* **1** case, illustration, specimen. **2 for example** as an illustration, by way of illustration, e.g., for instance, to cite an instance, to illustrate.
exasperate *v* anger, annoy, enrage, excite, incense, infuriate, irritate, provoke, try the patience of, vex; (*Inf*) aggravate, bug, rile.
excavate *v* burrow, dig out, dig up, gouge, hollow, mine, quarry, scoop, tunnel, uncover, unearth.

Archaeologists and historians excavate ancient historical sites to help build a picture of the past. They can tell how old ancient substances are, fairly accurately, by a process known as carbon dating.

excel *v* beat, be superior, better, exceed, outdo, outshine, pass, surpass, top.
excellent *adj* brilliant, capital, champion, first-class, first-rate, great, outstanding, superb, superior, tiptop, worthy.
except *prep* apart from, besides, but, excluding, leaving out, omitting, other than, with the exception of.
except *v* bar, exclude, leave out, pass over, omit, rule out.
exception *n* anomaly, departure, deviation, freak, inconsistency, irregularity, oddity, quirk, special case.
exceptional *adj* excellent, extraordinary, marvellous, outstanding, phenomenal, remarkable, special, superior.
excitement *n* activity, adventure, agitation, elation, enthusiasm, furore, heat, passion, warmth.
exciting *adj* exhilarating, moving, rousing, sensational, stimulating, stirring, thrilling.
exclude *v* **1** ban, bar, embargo, forbid, prohibit, refuse, shut out, veto. **2** eliminate, ignore, leave out, omit, pass over, reject, rule out, set aside.
exclusive *adj* **1** clannish, closed, limited, private, restricted, select. **2** confined, peculiar, unique.
excursion *n* day trip, jaunt, journey, outing, pleasure trip, ramble, tour, trip.
excuse *v* **1** acquit, forgive, make allowances for, overlook, pardon, tolerate. **2** exempt, free, let off, liberate, release, spare.
excuse *n* apology, explanation, grounds, justification, mitigating circumstances, poor substitute, pretence, pretext, reason, subterfuge, travesty, vindication; (*Inf*) cop out.
execute *v* **1** behead, decapitate, electrocute, guillotine, kill, put to death, send to the electric chair, send to the gas chamber, shoot, stone to death. **2** achieve, carry out, engineer, implement, perform, put into effect.
exercise *v* **1** apply, practise, use, utilize, wield. **2** discipline, drill, practise, train, work out.

Exercise and training improves fitness by building up stamina, flexibility and strength.

exercise *n* **1** action, activity, discipline, drill, drilling, effort, labour, toil, training, work, work-out. **2** drill, practice, schoolwork, task, work.
exert *v* employ, exercise, make use of, use, utilize, wield.
exhaust *v* **1** bankrupt, cripple, drain, sap, tire out, wear out. **2** consume, deplete, finish, run out of, use up, waste. **3** drain, dry, empty.
exhibit *v* demonstrate, display, present, put on view, show.
exhibit *n* demonstration, display, exhibition, model, presentation, show, viewing
exile *n* **1** banishment, deportation, expulsion. **2** deportee, outcast, refugee.
exile *v* banish, deport, eject, expel, oust.
exist *v* abide, be, be extant, be living, be present, breathe, continue, endure, happen, last, live, obtain, occur, prevail, remain, stand, survive.
existence *n* being, continuation, life, survival.
exit *n* door, gate, outlet, passage out, way out.
expand *v* amplify, blow up, develop, distend, enlarge, extend, fatten, fill out, grow, heighten, increase, inflate, lengthen, magnify, multiply, swell, thicken, widen.
expect *v* **1** assume, believe, foresee, imagine, presume, reckon, suppose. **2** anticipate, await, envisage, look ahead to, look for, predict, watch for.
expectation *n* assumption, assurance, belief, likelihood, presumption, probability.
expedition *n* excursion, exploration, journey, mission, quest, safari, tour, trek, trip, undertaking, voyage.
expel *v* **1** belch, discharge, drive out, eject, throw out. **2** banish, bar, blackball, dismiss, drum out, evict, exclude, exile, oust, send packing, turf out.
expenditure *n* charge, cost, expense, outgoings, outlay, spending, use.

expense *n* charge, cost, expenditure, outlay, payment, spending, toll, use.
expensive *adj* costly, dear, exorbitant, extravagant, high-priced, lavish, over-priced, rich, steep.
experience *n* **1** involvement, participation, practice, proof, training, trial, understanding. **2** adventure, affair, encounter, episode, event, happening, incident, occurrence, ordeal, test, trial.
experience *v* feel, go through, live through, participate in, sense, taste, try, undergo.
experienced *adj* accomplished, adept, capable, competent, expert, master, professional, qualified, seasoned, skilful, trained, tried, well-versed.
expert *n* ace, adept, authority, connoisseur, dab hand, master, past master, pro, professional, specialist, virtuoso, wizard.
expert *adj* clever, experienced, handy, knowledgeable, masterly, practised, professional, skilful, trained, virtuoso.

In recent years, explosions in minefields have caused dreadful injuries to civilians long after war has ended. Clearing them is extremely dangerous and is sometimes carried out by robots.

expertise *n* cleverness, command, deftness, dexterity, expertness, facility, judgment, knack, knowledge, masterliness, mastery, proficiency, skill.
expire *v* **1** cease, conclude, end, finish, run out, stop, terminate. **2** decease, depart, die, kick the bucket, pass away, perish.
explain *v* clarify, define, describe, disclose, illustrate, interpret, make clear, resolve, solve, teach, unfold.
explanation *n* **1** clarification, definition, description, illustration, interpretation. **2** answer, cause, excuse, meaning, motive, reason, sense, significance.
explode *v* **1** blow up, detonate, discharge, erupt, go off, set off. **2** discredit, disprove, refute.
exploit *n* achievement, deed, feat, stunt.
exploit *v* abuse, manipulate, misuse, take advantage of.
exploration *n* analysis, examination, inquiry, research, scrutiny, search, study.
explore *v* analyse, examine, inquire into, inspect, investigate, look into, probe, prospect, research, scrutinize, search.
explosion *n* bang, blast, burst, clap, crack, detonation, discharge, outburst, report.
explosive *adj* **1** unstable, volatile. **2** stormy, violent.
expose *v* **1** display, exhibit, manifest, present, put on view, reveal, show, uncover, unveil. **2** betray, bring to light.

The Bullet Train of Japan is one of the fastest express trains in the world.

exposure *n* display, exhibition, presentation, publicity, revelation, showing, uncovering, unveiling.
express *v* articulate, communicate, declare, phrase, pronounce, put across, speak, state, tell, utter, voice.
express *adj* **1** learcut, especial, particular, singular, special. **2** direct, fast, high-speed, non-stop, quick, rapid, speedy, swift.
expression *n* **1** communication, declaration, mention, statement, utterance. **2** demonstration, exhibition, indication, representation, show, sign, symbol, token, choice of words, delivery, diction, emphasis, execution, intonation, language, phraseology, phrasing, speech, style, wording. **3** phrase, term, turn of phrase, word.
exquisite *adj* **1**beautiful, dainty, delicate, elegant, fine, lovely.
extension *n* addendum, addition, annexe, appendix, branch, supplement, wing.
extensive *adj* all-inclusive, broad, comprehensive, far-flung,

far-reaching, huge, lengthy, long, protracted, spacious, sweeping, thorough, vast, widespread.
extent *n* **1** bounds, range, reach, scope. **2** amount, area, breadth, duration, expansion, length, measure, quantity, size, time, volume, width.
exterior *n* appearance, aspect, coating, covering, façade, finish, outside, shell, skin, surface.
exterior *adj* external, outer, outward, superficial, surface.
exterminate *v* annihilate, destroy, eliminate, eradicate.
external *adj* exterior, outer, outward, surface.
extinct *adj* dead, defunct, gone, lost, vanished.
extinction *n* annihilation, death, destruction, dying out, extermination, obliteration.
extra *adj* accessory, additional, auxiliary, supplemental, supplementary.
extra *n* addition, attachment, bonus, extension, supplement.
extra *adv* extraordinarily, extremely, remarkably, uncommonly, unusually.
extract *v* **1** draw, pull out, take out, uproot, withdraw. **2** elicit, evoke, gather, get, glean, obtain.
extract *n* **1** concentrate, distillate, essence, juice. **2** abstract, clipping, cutting, excerpt, passage, quotation, selection.
extraction *n* **1** drawing out, pulling out, removal, uprooting. **2** extortion. **3** distillation.
extraordinary *adj* amazing, bizarre, exceptional, fantastic, marvellous, outstanding, phenomenal, remarkable, special, unique, unusual, wonderful.

How the human eye works

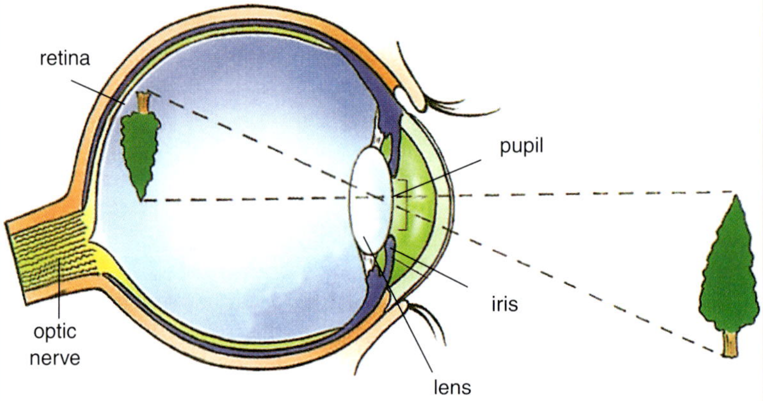

The lens throws an upside down image onto the retina at the back of the eye. The brain sorts out the image so you can see it the right way up.

extravagant *adj* **1** excessive, imprudent, lavish, wasteful. **2** costly, excessive, expensive, extortionate, overpriced, steep; (*Inf*) unreasonable.
extreme *adj* **1** acute, greatest, highest, maximum, supreme, ultimate, worst. **2** faraway, far-off, farthest, final, remotest, terminal, ultimate, utmost.
extreme *n* boundary, depth, edge, excess, height, limit, maximum, minimum, pinnacle, top, ultimate.
extremely *adv* acutely, awfully, excessively, extraordinarily, highly, intensely, severely, utterly, very.
extremity *n* **1** boundary, brink, edge, frontier, limit, margin, maximum, minimum, pinnacle, pole, rim, terminal, terminus, tip, top, ultimate, verge, zenith. **2** extremities fingers and toes, hands and feet, limbs.
eye *n* **1** eyeball, optic, orb. **2** appreciation, discrimination, judgment, perception, recognition, taste; (*Inf*) peeper. **3 keep an eye on** guard, keep in view, keep under surveillance, monitor, observe, watch over. **4 see eye to eye** accord, agree, back, be in unison, coincide, concur, fall in, get on, go along, harmonize, jibe, subscribe to. **5 up to one's eyes** busy, fully occupied, inundated, overwhelmed, wrapped up in.
eye *v* contemplate, glance at, have a look at, inspect, look at, scan, scrutinize, stare at, study, survey, view, watch.
eyesight *n* observation, perception, sight, vision.
eyesore *n* blemish, blight, blot, disfigurement, disgrace, horror, mess, monstrosity, sight.
eyewitness *n* bystander, looker-on, observer, onlooker, passer-by, spectator, viewer, watcher, witness.

Ff

fabric *n* **1** cloth, material, textile, web. **2** constitution, construction, foundations, framework, infrastructure, organization, structure.
fabulous *adj* **1** amazing, astounding, breathtaking, incredible, legendary, unbelievable. **2** fantastic, imaginary, invented, made-up, mythical, unreal.
façade *n* appearance, exterior, face, front, frontage, guise, mask, pretence, semblance, show, veneer.
face *n* **1** clock, features, visage; (*Inf*) dial, mug. **2** appearance, aspect, expression, frown, look, scowl, smirk. **3 face to face** confronting, eyeball. **4 on the face of it** apparently, to the eye.
face *v* **1** be confronted by, brave, come up against, confront, encounter, experience, meet, oppose. **2** be opposite, front onto, give towards, look onto, overlook.
facet *n* angle, aspect, face, part, phase, plane, side, slant, surface.
facetious *adj* amusing, comical, funny, humorous, jesting, merry, tongue in cheek, witty.
face up to *v* accept, acknowledge, come to terms with, confront, cope with, deal with, meet head on.
facilitate *v* ease, forward, help, promote, smooth the path of, speed up.
facility *n* ability, ease, efficiency, gift, knack, proficiency, quickness, readiness, skilfulness, skill, smoothness, talent
facing *adj* fronting, opposite, partnering.
facsimile *n* carbon copy, copy, duplicate, fax, photocopy, print, replica, reproduction.
fact *n* **1** event, happening, incident, occurrence, performance. **2** certainty, gospel, naked-truth, reality, truth. **3 in fact** actually, indeed, in point of fact, in reality, in truth, really, truly.
faction *n* bloc, cabal, caucus, clique, coalition, combination, confederacy, contingent, coterie, division, gang, ginger group, group, junta, lobby, minority, party, pressure group, section, sector, set, splinter group.
factor *n* aspect, cause, circumstance, component, consideration, determinant, element, influence, item, part, point, thing.
factory *n* **1** manufacturing building, mill, plant, works. **2** foundry, mill, workshop.
facts *pl n* data, details, information, the whole story.
factual *adj* accurate, authentic, correct, credible, exact, faithful, genuine, literal, matter-of-fact, objective, precise, real, sure, true, true-to-life, unadorned, unbiased, veritable.
fad *n* craze, fancy, fashion, mania, rage, trend, vogue.
fade *v* **1** bleach, discolour, dull, lose colour, pale, wash out. **2** decline, die away, diminish, disappear, disperse, dissolve, dwindle, fail, perish, shrivel, vanish, waste away, wilt, wither.
fail *v* **1** be defeated, be in vain, be unsuccessful, break down, come to grief, come to nothing, fall, fall short, fall through, founder, go astray, go down, miscarry, misfire, miss, not make the grade, turn out badly. **2** abandon, break one's word, disappoint, forget, let down, neglect, omit.

The arrival of the Industrial Revolution brought enormous changes to methods of production in factories. In textile production, machines were invented which could be operated by one person but spin several threads at the same time.

Family photographs can provide clues when tracing your ancestors. Names and addresses of photographers can pinpoint the location of the family, and the style of dress can help provide an approximate date.

failure *n* **1** breakdown, collapse, defeat, downfall, frustration, miscarriage, overthrow, wreck. **2** black sheep, disappointment, loser, no-good. **3** neglect, shortcoming, stoppage. **4** decay, decline, deterioration, failing, loss. **5** bankruptcy, crash, downfall, insolvency, ruin.
faint *adj* **1** bleached, faded, hazy, ill-defined, indistinct, light, low, muted, soft, vague. **2** frail, remote, slight, unenthusiastic, weak. **3** dizzy, exhausted, faltering, giddy, lightheaded, muzzy; (*Inf*) woozy.
faint *v* black out, collapse, fade, fail, flake out, languish, lose consciousness, pass out, weaken.
fair *adj* **1** equal, even-handed, honest, just, lawful, proper, trustworthy, unbiased, upright. **2** blond, blonde, fair-haired, light. **3** average, moderate, OK, passable, reasonable, satisfactory. **4** beautiful, handsome, lovely, pretty.
fair *n* bazaar, carnival, expo, exposition, festival, gala, market, show.
fairy *n* brownie, elf, hob, leprechaun, pixie, Robin Goodfellow, sprite.
fake *v* assume, copy, counterfeit, forge, pretend, sham, simulate.
fake *n* copy, forgery, hoax, imitation, impostor.
fall *v* **1** cascade, collapse, crash, descend, dive, nose-dive, pitch, plummet, plunge, sink, subside, topple, trip, tumble. **2** decline, decrease, depreciate, diminish, dwindle, flag, slump, subside. **3** be overthrown, capitulate, give in, give way, go out of office, pass into enemy hands, resign, succumb, surrender, yield.
fall *n* **1** descent, dive, droop, nose dive, plummet, plunge, slip, spill, tumble. **2** cut, decline, decrease, dip, drop, dwindling, falling off, lowering, reduction, slump. **3** collapse, defeat, destruction, downfall, overthrow, resignation, surrender. **4** descent, incline, slant, slope.
fall apart *v* break up, crumble, disband, disintegrate, disperse, dissolve, fall to bits, go to pieces, lose, cohesion, shatter.
fall back on *v* call upon, employ, make use, of, press into service, resort to.
fall behind *v* be in arrears, drop back, get left behind, lose one's place, trail.
fall out *v* altercate, argue, clash, differ, disagree, fight, quarrel, squabble.
false *adj* **1** inaccurate, incorrect, mistaken, unreal, wrong. **2** lying, unreliable, untrue. **3** artificial, counterfeit, forged, imitation, mock, sham, synthetic.
falsify *v* alter, distort, doctor, forge, tamper with.
falter *v* break, hesitate, shake, stammer, stutter, tremble, waver.
fame *n* celebrity, credit, eminence, glory, honour, name, prominence, public esteem, renown, reputation, repute, stardom.
familiar *adj* **1** accustomed, common, everyday, routine. **2 familiar with** at home with, aware of, conscious of, knowledgeable, well up in. **3** amicable, close, confidential, easy, free-and-easy, friendly, informal, near, open, relaxed.
family *n* brood, children, descendants, household, kin, offspring, relations, relatives.
famine *n* death, destitution, hunger, scarcity, starvation.
famous *adj* celebrated, distinguished, eminent, excellent, far-famed, glorious, honoured, illustrious, legendary, much-publicized, notable, noted,

prominent, remarkable, renowned, signal, well-known.
fanatic *n* activist, addict, bigot, enthusiast, extremist, militant.
fancy *v* **1** believe, conceive, guess, imagine, reckon, suppose, think, think likely. **2** be attracted to, crave, desire, dream of, hanker after, long for, wish for, would like, yearn for.
fancy *adj* baroque, decorated, decorative, elaborate, elegant, embellished, extravagant, intricate, ornamental, ornate.
far *adv* **1** a great distance, a long way, deep, miles. **2** considerably, decidedly, extreme. **3 so far** thus far, to date, until now, up to now, up to the present.
far *adj* distant, faraway, far-flung, far-off, far removed, long, outlying, out-of-the-way, remote, removed.
fare *n* **1** charge, price, ticket money, transport cost. **2** diet, food, meals, menu, provisions, rations, victuals.
fare *v* do, get along, get on, make out, manage, prosper.
far-fetched *adj* doubtful, dubious, fantastic, incredible, unbelievable, unlikely, unrealistic.
farm *n* acreage, acres, croft, farmstead, holding, homestead, land, plantation, ranch.
farm *v* bring under cultivation, cultivate, plant, till the soil.
fascinate *v* captivate, charm, delight, enchant, enthral, intrigue, spellbind, transfix.
fascination *n* attraction, charm, lure, magnetism, pull, spell.
fashion *n* **1** convention, craze, custom, fad, latest style, look, mode, rage, style, trend, usage, vogue. **2** attitude, demeanour, manner, method, mode, style, way.
fashion *v* create, design, forge, make, manufacture, mould, shape, work.
fashionable *adj* all the rage, chic, current, customary, hip, in vogue, latest, modern, popular, prevailing, stylish, trend-setting, up-to-the-minute, usual.
fast *adj* **1** brisk, flying, hasty, hurried, nippy, quick, rapid, speedy, swift. **2** immoral, loose, promiscuous, wild.

Downhill skiing is one of the fastest unassisted sports, with participants reaching incredibly frightening speeds.

fast *adv* **1** hastily, hurriedly, presto, quickly, rapidly, speedily, swiftly. **2** extravagantly, loosely, recklessly, wildly.
fast *v* abstain, go hungry, go without food, practise abstention, refrain from food.
fast *n* abstinence, fasting.
fasten *v* affix, anchor, attach, bind, bolt, chain, connect, fix, grip, join, link, lock, make firm, seal, secure, tie, unite.
fat *adj* **1** beefy, elephantine, gross, heavy, obese, over-weight, plump, podgy, portly, rotund, solid, stout. **2** fatty, greasy, oily, suety.
fat *n* blubber, cellulite, fatness, flab, flesh, obesity, overweight, paunch, weight problem.
fatal *adj* **1** deadly, destructive, final, incurable, killing, lethal, malignant, mortal, terminal. **2** catastrophic, disastrous, lethal.
fate *n* chance, destiny, divine, will, fortune, kismet, nemesis. **3** end, future,outcome, upshot.
father *n* **1** dad, pater, patriarch, sire. **2** ancestor, forefather, predecessor, Progenitor. **3** abbé, padre, pastor, priest.
father *v* beget, procreate, sire.
fatherly *adj* affectionate, benevolent, kind, kindly, paternal, protective, supportive, tender.
fault *n* **1** blemish, defect, drawback, failing, flaw, imperfection, infirmity, shortcoming, snag,

weakness, weak point. **2** frailty, misconduct, misdeed, misdemeanour, offence, peccadillo, sin, wrong.
favour *n* **1** approval, backing, bias, esteem, favouritism, friendliness, goodwill, kindness, kind regard, patronage, support. **2** benefit, courtesy, good turn, indulgence, kindness, service.
favour *v* esteem, indulge, pamper, reward, spoil, value.
favourable *adj* advantageous, auspicious, encouraging, fair, fit, good, helpful, opportune, promising, suitable, timely.
favourite *adj* best-loved, choice, dearest, esteemed, favoured, preferred.
favourite *n* beloved, darling, idol, pet, preference, teacher's pet, the apple of one's eye.
fear *n* **1** alarm, apprehensiveness, awe, consternation, dread, fright, horror, panic, terror, trepidation. **2** horror, nightmare, phobia, spectre.
fear *v* apprehend, be afraid, dread, have a horror of, have a phobia about, have qualms, live in dread of, shake in one's shoes, shudder at, take fright.
feasible *adj* achievable, attainable, likely, possible, reasonable, viable, workable.
feast *n* banquet, barbecue, carousal, carouse, dinner, entertainment, festive board, jollification, junket, repast, revels, treat; (*Inf*) spread.
feat *n* accomplishment, achievement, act, exploit, performance.
feather *n* down, pinion, plumage, quill.
faulty *adj* broken, damaged, defective, flawed, impaired, imperfect, not working, out of order, unsound, weak, wrong.
feature *n* **1** aspect, characteristic, factor, hallmark, peculiarity, point, quality, trait. **2** article, column, comment, item, piece, report, story.
feature *v* accentuate, emphasize, give prominence to, headline, present, promote, spotlight, star.
federation *n* alliance, association, coalition, combination, confederacy, entente, federacy, league, syndicate, union.
fee *n* account, bill, charge, compensation, hire, pay, payment, recompense, remuneration, reward, toll.
feeble *adj* debilitated, delicate, doddering, failing, frail, infirm, sickly, weak, weakened.
feed *v* **1** cater for, nourish, provide for, supply, wine and dine. **2 feed on** devour, eat, exist on, graze, live on, nurture, pasture.
feel *v* **1** caress, fondle, handle, paw, run one's hands over, stroke, touch. **2** endure, enjoy, experience, go through, notice, perceive, suffer, take to heart, undergo. **3** explore, fumble, grope, sound, test, try. **4** be convinced, have a hunch, have the impression, sense. **5** believe, consider, deem, hold, judge, think. **6** appear, resemble, seem, strike one as. **7** desire, fancy, feel inclined, feel the need for, feel up to, want.
feeling *adj* **1** feel, perception, sensation, sense, sense of touch, touch. **2** hunch, idea, impression, inkling, notion, sense, suspicion. **3** inclination, instinct, opinion, point of view, view.
fell *v* cut down, demolish, flatten, floor, knock down, level, raze, strike down.

The feathers of the peacock are used to attract the female. Despite the weight of the tail feathers, a peacock can still fly.

fen *n* bog, holm, marsh, morass, quagmire, slough, swamp
fence *n* **1** barbed wire, barricade, barrier, defence, guard, hedge, paling, palisade, railings, rampart, shield, stockade, wall. **2 fence in** bound, confine, coop, defend, enclose, fortify, hedge, pen, protect, restrict, secure, surround.
ferocious *adj* fierce, predatory, savage, violent, wild.
ferry *n* ferryboat, packet boat.
ferry *v* carry, chauffeur, convey, run, ship, shuttle, transport.
fertile *adj* abundant, flowering, plentiful, prolific, rich, teeming.

festival *n* **1** anniversary, commemoration, fiesta, holiday, holy day, saint's day. **2** carnival, celebration, entertainment, festivities, field day, gala, jubilee.
festive *adj* carnival, celebratory, cheery, happy, hearty, holiday, jolly, jovial, joyful, jubilant, light-hearted, merry.
festoon *v* array, bedeck, deck, decorate, drape, garland, hang, swathe, wreathe.
fetch *v* **1** bring, carry, conduct, convey, deliver, escort, get, obtain, retrieve, transport. **2** bring in, earn, go for, make, realize, sell for, yield.
feud *n* argument, bad blood, bickering, conflict, disagreement, discord, dissension, falling out, grudge, quarrel, vendetta.
feud *v* be at odds, bicker, brawl, clash, contend, dispute, duel, fall out, quarrel, row, squabble, war.
fever *n* agitation, excitement, fervour, frenzy, heat, intensity, passion, turmoil, unrest.
few *adj* hardly any, insufficient, meagre, negligible, not many, rare, scanty, scarcely any, sparse, sporadic, thin.
few *pron* handful, scarcely any, scattering, small number, some.
fiasco *n* catastrophe, disaster, failure, flap, mess, rout, ruin.
fib *n* fiction, lie, story, untruth, white lie; (*Inf*) whopper.
fibre *n* fibril, filament, pile, staple, strand, texture, thread.
fibre *n* essence, nature, quality, spirit, substance.
fiction *n* **1** fable, fantasy, legend, myth, novel, romance, story, tale; (*Inf*) yarn. **2** fantasy, figment of the imagination, imagination, invention, lie, tall story, untruth; (*Inf*) cock and bull story.

The prairie grasslands of North America once supported huge roaming herds of bison. Early white settlers killed enormous numbers of them, depriving the Native Americans of one of their vital sources of food and clothing.

field *n* **1** grassland, green, meadow, pasture. **2** area of activity.
field *v* catch, pick up, retrieve, return, stop.
fierce *adj* brutal, cruel, ferocious, menacing, murderous, savage, threatening, vicious, wild.
fight *v* **1** assault, battle, box, brawl, come to blows, conflict, do battle, feud, grapple, spar, struggle, wrestle. **2** contest, defy, dispute, oppose, resist, stand up to, strive, struggle, withstand. **3** argue, bicker, dispute, fall out, squabble, wrangle. **4** carry on, conduct, engage in, prosecute, wage.
fight *n* action, affray, battle, brawl, clash, conflict, dispute, dogfight, duel, encounter, engagement, exchange of blows, fracas, hostilities, riot, scuffle, skirmish, sparring match, tussle, war.
fighter *n* **1** fighting man, man-at-arms, soldier, warrior. **2** boxer, prize fighter.
figure *n* **1** character, cipher, digit, number, numeral, symbol. **2** amount, cost, price, sum, total, value. **3** form, outline, shadow, shape, silhouette. **4** body, build, frame, physique, proportions, shape, torso. **5** celebrity, character, dignitary, force, leader, notability, personality, presence, somebody, worthy.
figurehead *n* front man, mouthpiece, name, puppet, token.
file *v* polish, refine, rub down, scrape, shape, smooth.
file *n* case, data, documents, dossier, folder, portfolio.
file *v* document, enter, pigeonhole, put in place, register.
fill *v* cram, crowd, furnish, glut, gorge, inflate, pack, replenish, satisfy, store, supply.
fill in *v* **1** answer, complete, fill out, fill up. **2** deputize, replace, represent, stand in, substitute, take the place of.
filling *n* contents, filler, innards, insides, padding, stuffing, wadding.
filling *adj* ample, heavy, satisfying, square, substantial.
film *n* **1** coat, coating, covering, dusting, layer, membrane, scum, skin, tissue. **2** flick, motion picture, movie.
film *v* photograph, shoot, take, video, videotape.
filter *v* clarify, filtrate, purify,

refine, screen, sieve, sift, strain, winnow.
filter *n* gauze, membrane, mesh, riddle, sieve, strainer.
final *adj* **1** closing, concluding, end, eventual, last, last-minute, latest, terminal, terminating, ultimate. **2** absolute, conclusive, decided, decisive, definite, finished, settled.
finale *n* climax, close, conclusion, final curtain, final scene, finish, last act; (*Inf*) wind up.
finance *n* accounts, banking, business, commerce, economics, financial affairs, investment, money management.
finance *v* back, bankroll, float, fund, pay for, provide, security, for, set up in business, subsidize, support, underwrite.
find *v* **1** catch sight of, come across, discover, encounter, meet, recognize, spot, stumble upon, track down, turn up, uncover, unearth. **2** get back, recover, regain, retrieve.
find *n* acquisition, asset, bargain, catch, discovery, good buy.

fine *adj* **1** beautiful, excellent, first-class, great, magnificent, outstanding, splendid, supreme. **2** bright, clear, cloudless, fair, pleasant, sunny. **3** delicate, exquisite, fragile. **4** pure, refined, solid, sterling. **5** acceptable, all right, good, OK, suitable.

How the film in a camera works

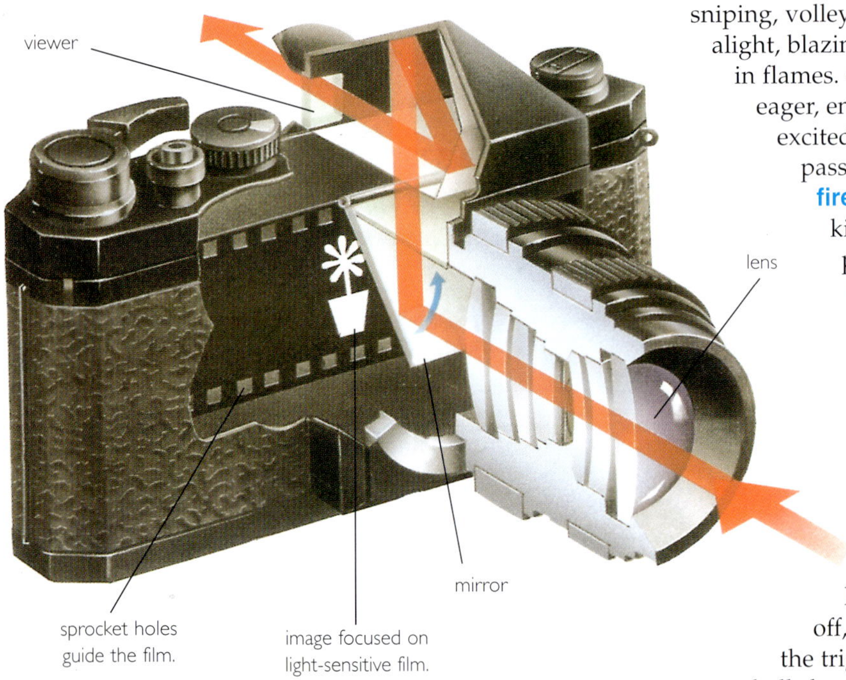

finish *v* **1** accomplish, achieve, cease, close, complete, conclude, culminate, end, finalize, stop, terminate, wrap up. **2** elaborate, perfect, polish, refine. **3** coat, face, gild, lacquer, polish, stain, texture, veneer, wax. **4 finish off** bring down, defeat, destroy, kill, overcome, overpower, ruin.
finish *n* **1** completion, conclusion, culmination, finale, last stage, termination. **2** annihilation, bankruptcy, death, defeat, end, end of the road, liquidation, ruin. **3** cultivation, culture, elaboration, perfection, polish, refinement. **4** appearance, grain, lustre, patina, polish, shine, smoothness, surface, texture.
fire *n* **1** blaze, flames, inferno. **2** barrage, flak, salvo, shelling, sniping, volley. **3 on fire** alight, blazing, burning, in flames. **4** ardent, eager, enthusiastic, excited, inspired, passionate.
fire *v* **1** ignite, kindle, light, put a match to, set ablaze, set aflame, set alight, set fire to, set on fire. **2** detonate, discharge, eject, explode, hurl, launch, let off, loose, pull the trigger, set off, shell shoot, touch off.
firm *adj* **1** compact, compressed, dense, inflexible, rigid, set, solid, stiff. **2** anchored, cemented, embedded, fastened, fixed, immovable, rivetted, secured, stable, sturdy. **3** constant, definite, fixed, set on, settled, staunch, steadfast, strict, true.
firm *n* business, company, corporation, enterprise, organization, partnership.
first *adj* **1** chief, head, leading, principal. **2** earliest, initial,

The flag of the United States of America – the number of stars represents the number of states – 50.

introductory, maiden, opening. **3** basic, elementary, key, primary.
first *adv* at the beginning, at the out-set, before all else, before-hand, firstly, initially, in the first place, to begin with, to start with
first-rate *adj* admirable, elite, excellent, exceptional, exclusive, first class, outstanding, prime, second to none, superb, tiptop. (*Inf*) topnotch, tops.
fissure *n* breach, crack, crevice, fault, fracture, gap, hole, opening, rift, rupture, split.
fit *adj* **1** able, competent, correct, prepared, qualified, ready, suitable, trained. **2** able bodied, hale, healthy, in good condition, robust, toned up, trim.
fit *v* **1** agree, belong, join, match, meet, suit. **2** adapt, adjust, alter, arrange, place, position, shape.
fitting *adj* appropriate, becoming, correct, decent, desirable, proper, right, suitable.
fitting *n* accessory, attachment, component, connection, part, piece, unit.
fix *v* **1** anchor, embed, establish, implant, install, locate, place, plant, position, root, set, settle. **2** attach, cement, connect, fasten, glue, pin, secure, stick, tie. **3** agree on, arrange, conclude, decide, establish, limit, name, resolve, set, settle, specify.
fix *n* difficult situation, dilemma, mess, predicament, quandary, tricky situation; (*Inf*) bind, hole, jam, pickle, scrape, spot.
flag *v* decline, droop, fade, fail, fall off, sag, sink, slump, taper off, weaken, wilt.
flag *n* banner, colours, ensign, jack, pennant, pennon, standard, streamer.
flair *n* **1** ability, aptitude, gift, knack, talent. **2** chic, elegance, panache, style, taste.
flamboyant *adj* **1** elaborate, extravagant, ornate, ostentatious, over the top, rich, showy, theatrical. **2** brilliant, colourful, dashing, dazzling, exciting, glamorous, swashbuckling.
flame *v* blaze, burn, flare, flash, glare, glow, shine.
flame *n* **1** blaze. **2** brightness, glow. **3** fire, light. **4** affection, passion, warmth. **5** boyfriend, girlfriend, lover, partner.
flap *v* agitate, beat, thrash, vibrate, wave.
flap *n* apron, cover, fly, fold, lapel, overlap, skirt, tab, tail.
flare *v* blaze, burn up, dazzle, flicker, flutter, glare, waver.
flash *v* **1** blaze, flare, flicker, gleam, glint, glisten, light, shimmer, sparkle, twinkle. **2** bolt, dash, fly, race, shoot, speed, sprint, streak.
flash *n* **1** blaze, dazzle, flare, flicker, gleam, ray, spark, sparkle, streak, twinkle. **2** instant, jiffy, moment, second, shake, split second, trice, twinkling, twinkling of an eye. **3** instant, jiffy, moment, second, split second, trice, twinkling, twinkling of an eye.
flashy *adj* cheap, garish, gaudy, in poor taste, loud, ostentatious, showy, tasteless.
flatten *v* compress, even out, iron out, level, raze, smooth off, squash, trample.
flatter *v* butter up, compliment,

The Olympic flame is carried by runners from Greece and is used to light the main flame at the opening ceremony of each Olympic Games.

humour, praise, softsoap, sweet-talk, wheedle.
flavour *n* aroma, essence, extract, flavouring, odour, seasoning, tang, taste, zest, zing.
flavour *v* ginger up, infuse, lace, leaven, season, spice.
flaw *n* **1** blemish, defect, fault, imperfection, spot, weakness. **2** breach, break, crack, crevice, fissure, fracture, split, tear.
flawed *adj* blemished, broken, chipped, cracked, damaged, defective, faulty, unsound.
fleck *n* mark, speckle, spot
fleck *v* dot, freckle, mark, mottle, speckle, sprinkle, streak.
flee *v* abscond, bolt, escape, make a quick exit, run away, scarper, take flight, vanish.
fleet *n* armada, flotilla, naval force, sea power, squadron, task force, vessels, warships.
fleet *adj* fast, like the wind, nimble, quick, speedy, swift-footed.
fleeting *adj* brief, flying, fugitive, momentary, passing, short-lived, temporary.
flexible *adj* **1** bendable, elastic, mouldable, pliable, supple. **2** adjustable, variable. **3** docile, gentle, manageable, responsive.
flicker *v* blink, flare, flash, glimmer, glint, glitter, quiver, sparkle, twinkle, vibrate, waver.
flight *n* **1** flying, soaring, winging. **2** journey, trip, voyage. **3** bevy, cloud, covey, flock, formation, squadron, swarm, unit, wing migration. **4** absconding, departure, escape, exit, exodus, fleeing, departure, getaway, retreat, running away. **5** aviation, aerial navigation. **6** aeronautics. **7** journey, shuttle; (*Inf*) plane trip. **8** flight of stairs.
flimsy *adj* **1** delicate, fragile, frail, make-shift, rickety, shaky, shallow, slight, superficial. **2** feeble, poor, thin, trivial,weak.
flinch *v* cower, cringe, duck, flee, recoil, retreat, shrink, shy away, swerve, wince.
fling *v* cast, catapult, heave, hurl, jerk, let fly, pitch, precipitate, propel, send, shy, sling, throw, toss.
float *v* **1** lie on the surface, displace water, hang, hover, poise, rest on water, stay afloat. **2** bob, drift, glide, sail, slide, slip along. **3** get going, launch, promote, push off, set up.
flock *v* collect, congregate, converge, crowd, gather, group, herd, huddle, mass, throng, troop.
flock *n* **1** colony, drone, flight, gaggle, herd, skein. **2** assembly, collection, congregation, convoy, crowd, group, herd, host, mass, multitude, throng.
flood *v* **1** deluge, overflow, pour over, submerge. **2** engulf, flow, gush, overwhelm, surge, swarm. **3** choke, fill, glut, saturate.
flood *n* **1** deluge, downpour,

The Italian fleet are pictured setting sail in the Mediterranean during World War II prior to the Battle of Matapan, where most of the Italian ships were sunk by the British Navy.

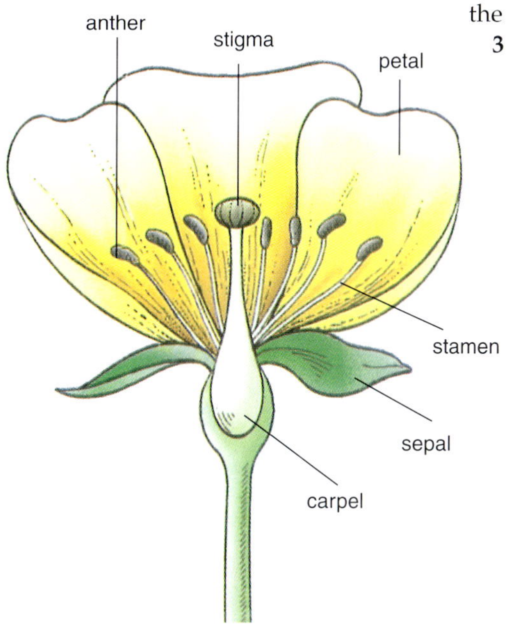

Flowers are the reproductive part of a plant. The male parts are the stamens which produce pollen. The female part of the flower is called the carpel and contains a stigma. Not all flowers have male and female parts and to reproduce, they must be fertilized by another plant.

flash flood, overflow, tide, torrent. **2** abundance, flow, glut, multitude, outpouring, profusion, rush, stream.
floor *n* deck, level, storey, tier.
floor *v* **1** fell, ground, knock down, prostrate. **2** baffle, beat, bewilder, defeat, dumbfound, overthrow, perplex, puzzle, stump; (*Inf*) throw.
flop *v* **1** dangle, droop, sag. **2** fail, fall flat, go down like a lead balloon, miss the mark.
flop *n* debacle, disaster, failure, fiasco, loser; (*Inf*) dud, lemon, no-hoper, washout.
flourish *v* bear fruit, be successful, bloom, blossom, develop, do well, flower, get on, go up in the world, grow, increase, prosper, succeed, thrive.
flourish *n* brandishing, dash, display, fanfare, parade, shaking, show, showy, gesture, twirling, wave.
flow *v* circulate, course, glide, gush, move, pour, purl, ripple, roll, run, rush, slide, surge, sweep, swirl, whirl.
flower *n* bloom, blossom, efflorescence.
flower *v* bloom, blossom, blow, flourish, mature, open, unfold.
flowing *adj* continuous, easy, fluent, smooth, unbroken.
fluctuate *v* alternate, change, go up and down, oscillate, rise and fall, seesaw, swing, undulate, vary, waver.
fluid *adj* **1** liquid, molten, runny, watery. **2** adaptable, changeable, flexible.
fluid *n* liquid, liquor, solution.
flush *v* blush, burn, colour, colour up, crimson, flame, glow, go red, redden, suffuse.
flush *n* bloom, blush, colour, glow, redness, rosiness.
flush *adj* **1** even, flat, level, plane, square, true. **2** abundant, full, generous, overflowing.
flush *adv* even with, hard against, in contact with, level with, squarely, touching.
flutter *v* agitate, bat, beat, flap, flicker, flit, flitter, fluctuate, hover, palpitate, quiver, ripple, ruffle, shiver, tremble, vibrate.
flutter *n* palpitation, quiver, quivering, shiver, shudder, tremble, tremor, twitching, vibration.
fly *v* **1** flutter, hover, soar, take to the air, take wing. **2** aviate, be at the controls, manoeuvre, pilot. **3** display, flap, show, wave. **4** elapse, glide, pass swiftly, roll on, run its course, slip away. **5** bolt, career, dart, dash, hasten, hurry, race, rush, scamper, scoot, shoot, speed, sprint, tear, whiz; (*Inf*) be off like a shot, zoom.
foam *n* bubbles, froth, head, lather, spray, spume, suds.
foam *v* boil, bubble, effervesce, fizz, froth, lather.
focus *n* bull's eye, centre, centre of activity, centre of attraction, core, focal point, heart, hub, target.
fog *n* gloom, mist, murkiness, smog.
fold *v* **1** bend, crease, crumple, dog-ear, pleat, tuck, turn under. **2** do up, enclose, enfold, envelop, wrap up.
fold *n* bend, crease, double thickness, folded, portion, furrow, knife-edge, layer, overlap, pleat, turn, wrinkle.
folder *n* binder, envelope, file, portfolio.
follow *v* **1** come after, come next, step into the shoes of, succeed, take the place of. **2** chase, dog, pursue, run after, shadow, stalk, tail, track. **3** act in accordance with, be guided by, conform, heed, note, obey, observe, regard, watch.
food *n* bread, chow, cooking, cuisine, diet, edibles, foodstuffs, larder, meat, menu,

nourishment, nutriment, nutrition, provender, provisions, rations, refreshment, stores, sustenance.
fool *n* **1** ass, blockhead, dunce, halfwit, idiot, ignoramus, nitwit, numskull, silly. **2** buffoon, clown, comic, jester, pierrot, punchinello; (*Inf*) dimwit, twit.
fool *v* **1** bamboozle, bluff, cheat, deceive, dupe, hoax, hoodwink, make a fool of, mislead, play a trick on, trick. **2** act the fool, cut capers, feign, jest, joke, make believe, pretend, tease.
foolish *adj* **1** absurd, ill-advised, senseless, silly, unwise. **2** brainless, crazy, idiotic, mad, ridiculous, senseless, stupid.
foolproof *adj* certain, guaranteed, safe; (*Inf*) sure-fire.
forbid *v* ban, disallow, exclude, hinder, inhibit, outlaw, preclude, prohibit, rule out, veto.
force *n* **1** impact, might, muscle, power, pressure, strength. **2** effectiveness, influence, weight; (*Inf*) bite, drive, emphasis, intensity, persistence.
force *v* **1** bring pressure to bear upon, compel, drive, impose, make, necessitate, oblige, overcome, press-gang, pressure, urge; (*Inf*) strong-arm. **2** blast, break, open, prise, propel, push, thrust, use violence on, wrench, wrest. **3** drag, extort, wring.
forecast *v* anticipate, calculate, estimate, plan, predict, prophesy.
forecast *n* anticipation, guess, outlook, planning, prediction, prognosis, projection, prophecy.
foreign *adj* alien, distant, exotic, external, imported, overseas, remote, strange, unfamiliar,
forfeit *n* **1** damages. **2** fine, loss, penalty **3** confiscation, loss.
forfeit *v* be deprived of, be stripped of, give up, lose, relinquish, renounce, surrender.
forge *v* coin, copy, counterfeit, fake, falsify, feign, imitate.
forget *v* leave behind, lose sight of, omit, overlook.
forgive *v* absolve, acquit, excuse, exonerate, pardon.
form *v* **1** assemble, build, concoct, construct, create, devise, fabricate, fashion, forge, found, make, manufacture, model, mould, produce, put together, set up, shape. **2** arrange, combine, design, dispose, draw up, frame, organize, plan, think up.
form *n* **1** appearance, cast, construction, cut, fashion, formation, model, mould, pattern, shape, structure. **2** format, frame-work, order, plan, proportion, structure, symmetry. **3** application, document, paper, sheet.
formal *adj* ceremonial, fixed, lawful, legal, official, prescribed, regular, rigid, ritualistic, set.
formation *n* **1** accumulation, compilation, development, establishment, evolution, generation, manufacture, production. **2** arrangement, configuration, design, disposition, figure, grouping, patter, rank, structure.
formidable *adj* **1** daunting, dreadful, horrible, intimidating, menacing, shocking, terrifying,

The foods required for a balanced diet

The framework and systems of the human body

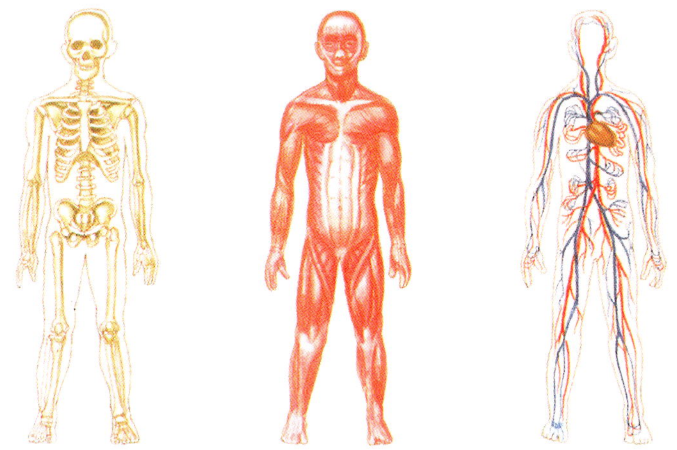

The skeleton supports and protects the soft parts of the body.

The muscular system enables the body to move.

The circulatory system allows blood to flow around the body.

threatening. **2** challenging, difficult, mammoth, overwhelming, staggering.

formula *n* **1** form of words, ritual, **2** blueprint, method, recipe, rule, way.

fortress *n* castle, citadel, fastness, fort, redoubt, stronghold.

fortune *n* **1** affluence, gold mine, property, prosperity, riches, treasure, wealth. **2** accident, chance, contingency, destiny, fate, luck, providence.

forward *adj* advanced, early, onward, premature, progressive, well-developed.

forward *v* advance, aid, assist, back, encourage, favour, foster, further, help, hurry, promote, speed, support.

foster *v* **1** cultivate, encourage, feed, nurture, promote, stimulate, support, uphold. **2** bring up, mother, nurse, raise, rear, take care of. **3** accommodate, entertain, harbour, sustain.

foul *adj* **1** contaminated, dirty, filthy, offensive, polluted, putrid, rank, repulsive, revolting, rotten, stinking. **2** bad, disagreeable, foggy, murky, rainy, rough, stormy, wet, wild.

foul *v* contaminate, pollute, smear, soil, stain, sully, taint.

foundation *n* **1** base, basis, bottom, footing, groundwork, substructure. **2** establishment, inauguration, institution.

fountain *n* font, fount, jet, reservoir, spout, spray, spring, well.

fracture *n* breach, break, cleft, crack, fissure, gap, opening, rent, rift, rupture, split.

fracture *v* break, crack, rupture, splinter, split.

fragile *adj* breakable, brittle, dainty, delicate, feeble, fine, flimsy, frail, infirm, slight, weak.

fragrance *n* aroma, bouquet, perfume, scent, smell.

fragrant *n* aromatic, balmy, perfumed, sweet-smelling.

frail *adj* breakable, brittle, delicate, flimsy, fragile, infirm, slight, tender, vulnerable, weak.

frame *v* **1** assemble, build, constitute, construct, fabricate, invent, make, manufacture, model, mould, put together.
2 block out, compose, conceive, concoct, contrive, cook up, devise, draft, draw up, form, formulate, hatch, map out, plan, shape, sketch. **3** case, enclose, mount, surround.

frame *n* **1** casing, construction, fabric, framework, scheme, shell, structure, system. **2** anatomy, body, build, carcass, physique, skeleton. **3** mounting, setting.

framework *n* core, fabric, foundation, frame, groundwork, plan, shell, skeleton, structure, the bare bones.

frantic *adj* berserk, beside oneself, distraught, fraught, frenzied, furious, hectic, mad, overwrought, raging, raving, wild.

fraud *n* **1** cheat, deceit, deception, hoax, sharp practice, swindling, treachery. **2** bluffer, cheat, counterfeit, double-dealer, fake, forgery, hoaxer, impostor.

free *adj* **1** complimentary, free of charge, gratis, on the house, unpaid, without charge. **2** at large, footloose, independent, loose, off the hook, on the loose, unrestrained. **3** able, allowed, permitted, unrestricted.
4 free of exempt from, immune to, safe from, unaffected by.
5 independent, self-governing, self-ruling, sovereign.
6 available, empty, extra, idle, not tied down, spare, unused. **7** generous, hospitable, lavish, open-handed, unsparing, willing.

8 free and easy casual, easy-going, informal, laid-back, relaxed, tolerant.
free *adv* **1** for love, without charge. **2** freely, idly, loosely.
free *v* **1** deliver, discharge, let go, loose, release, set at liberty, set free, uncage, unfetter, unleash, untie. **2** clear, cut loose, deliver, disengage, disentangle, exempt, extricate, ransom, redeem, relieve, rescue, rid, unburden, undo, unshackle.
freedom *n* **1** home rule, independence, liberty, release, self-government. **2** exemption, immunity. **3** discretion, free rein, licence, opportunity, play, power, range, scope.
freeze *v* **1** chill, harden, ice over, stiffen. **2** fix, hold up, inhibit, stop, suspend.
freezing *adj* arctic, biting, bitter, chilled, cutting, frosty, glacial, icy, numbing, penetrating, polar, raw, Siberian, wintry.
freight *n* cargo, consignment, goods, load, merchandise, payload, tonnage.
frequent *adj* common, constant, everyday, numerous, persistent, recurring, usual.
frequent *v* attend, be a regular customer of, patronize, visit.
fresh *adj* **1** different, modern, new, novel, original, recent, up-to-date. **2** added, additional, auxiliary, extra, supplementary. **3** bracing, brisk, clean, clear, cool, crisp, invigorating, pure, refreshing, sparkling. **4** blooming, fair, glowing, good, hardy, healthy, rosy, ruddy, wholesome. **5** green, inexperienced, natural, new, raw, uncultivated, untrained, untried, youthful.
fright *n* alarm, dismay, dread, fear, horror, panic, scare, shock, terror, trepidation.
frighten *v* alarm, daunt, dismay, intimidate, petrify, scare, scare stiff, scare the living daylights out of someone, shock, startle, terrify, terrorise, throw into a fright, throw into a panic, unnerve.
front *n* **1** façade, facing, foreground. **2** beginning, frontline, head, lead, top, vanguard. **3** blind, cover, disguise, mask, pretext, show. **4 in front** ahead, before, first, in advance, in the lead, leading, preceding.
front *adj* first, foremost, head, lead, leading, topmost.
frown *v* **1** glare, scowl. **2 frown upon** disapprove of, dislike, show disapproval.
frozen *adj* **1** arctic, chilled, frosted, ice-bound, ice-covered, icy, numb. **2** fixed, petrified, turned to stone.
full *adj* **1** brimming, complete, entire, gorged, intact, stocked, sufficient. **2** ample, copious, extensive, maximum, plentiful. **3** chock-a-block, chock-full, crammed, crowded, jammed, packed.
fully *adv* **1** absolutely, entirely, thoroughly, totally. **2** abundantly, adequately, sufficiently.
fumes *pl n* exhaust, gas, haze, pollution, smog, smoke, vapour.
funny *adj* **1** amusing, comical, entertaining, hilarious, humorous, laughable, side-splitting, witty; (*Inf*) killing. **2** curious, mysterious, odd, peculiar, puzzling, remarkable, strange, suspicious, unusual, weird.
future *n* expectation, outlook, prospect, time to come.
future *adj* coming, expected, forthcoming, impending, later, to come.
fuzzy *adj* **1** blurred, indistinct, misty, out of focus, unclear, unfocused. **2** confused, muddled, foggy, shadowy.

The freezing regions known as the North and South Poles are covered by thick layers of snow and ice. But the two areas are very different. South Pole Antarctica has land far under the ice while the Arctic North Pole is actually frozen sea.

The Arctic

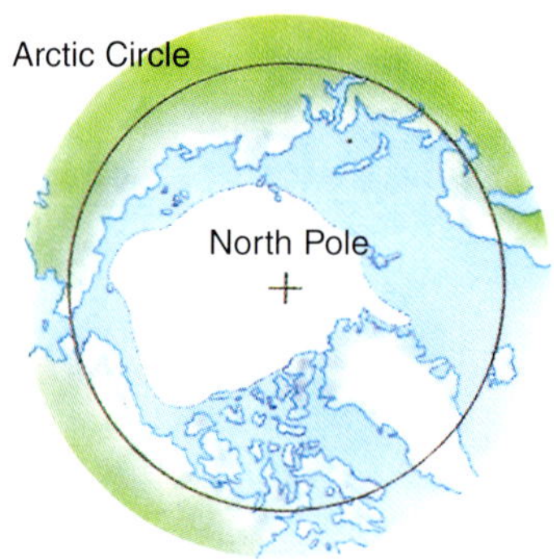

Antarctica

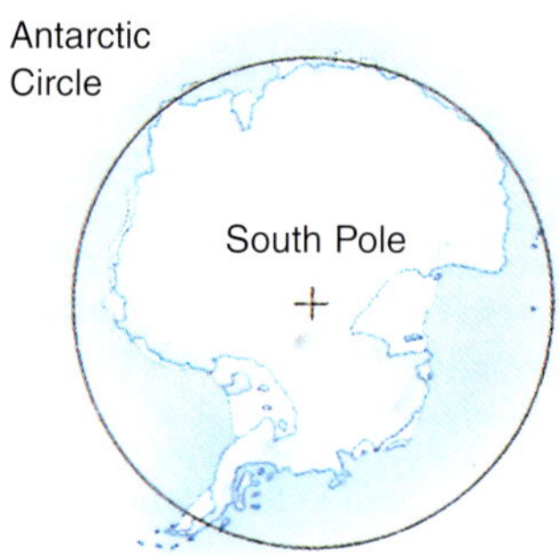

Gg

gadget *n* contraption, device, invention, tool.
gag *v* curb, silence, stifle, still, suppress, throttle.
gain *v* **1** acquire, attain, build up, collect, gather, harvest, obtain, pick up, reap, secure, win. **2** bring in, clear, earn, get, make, net, produce, realize, yield.
gain *n* achievement, acquisition, advance, advantage, benefit, dividend, earnings, growth, headway, improvement, income, produce, profit, return, rise.
gala *n* carnival, celebration, festival, fete, jamboree, pageant.
galaxy *n* **1** constellation, stars, the heavens. **2** brilliant gathering, host, illustrious group.
gale *n* blast, cyclone, hurricane, squall, storm, tempest, tornado, typhoon.
gallantry *n* bravery, courage, daring, heroism, nerve, valour.
gallop *v* bolt, career, dart, dash, fly, hasten, hurry, race, run, rush, sprint, tear along, zoom.
gamble *v* **1** back, bet, game, make a bet, play, punt, stake, try one's. **2** chance, hazard, risk, speculate, take a chance, venture.
gamble *n* **1** chance, leap in the dark, lottery, risk, speculation, venture. **2** bet, flutter, wager.
gambol *v* caper, cavort, frisk, frolic, hop, jump, prance, skip.
game *n* **1** amusement, entertainment, fun, joke, lark, play, recreation, sport. **2** competition, contest, event, match, meeting, round, tournament. **3** chase, prey, quarry, wild animals.
game *adj* brave, courageous, fearless, heroic, intrepid, plucky.
gang *n* band, circle, clique, club, company, crew, crowd, group, herd, horde, lot, mob, pack, party, ring, set, shift, squad, team, troupe.
gangster *n* bandit, brigand, crook, desperado, gang member, racketeer, robber, ruffian, thug.
garbage *n* bits and pieces, debris, junk, litter, odds and ends, rubbish, scraps.
garland *n* coronet, crown, deck, festoon, headband, honours, laurels, wreath.
garments *pl n* apparel, articles of clothing, clothes, clothing, costume, dress, garb, gear, habit, outfit, robes, togs, unform.
garnish *v* adorn, beautify, bedeck, deck, decorate, embellish, enhance, grace, ornament, set off, trim.
garrison *n* **1** armed force, command, detachment, militia, troops, unit. **2** base, camp, encampment, fort, fortification, fortress, post, station, stronghold. **3** barracks.
gash *v* cut, gouge, lacerate, slash, slit, split, tear, wound.
gasp *v* catch one's breath, choke, fight for breath, gulp, pant, puff.
gasp *n* gulp, pant, puff.
gate *n* access, barrier, door, door way, entrance, exit, gateway, opening, passage, portal.
gather *v* **1** accumulate, amass, collect, convene, group, hoard, marshal, mass, muster, pile up, round up, stack up, stockpile. **2** assume, be led to believe, conclude, deduce, draw, hear, infer, learn, make, surmise, understand. **3** crop, cull, garner, harvest, pick, pluck, reap, select.
gaze *v* look, stare, view, watch.

The garbage discarded in enormous amounts by human beings can provide nourishment for insects, birds and animals.

To germinate successfully, some trees rely on animals or birds eating their seeds, carrying them in their digestive systems and then depositing them far away in their droppings.

gaze *n* fixed look, look, stare.
gear *n* **1** cogwheel, gearwheel, toothed wheel. **2** equipment, instruments, outfit, rigging, supplies, tackle, tools, trappings. **3** baggage, belongings, effects, kit, luggage, stuff, things.
gem *n* **1** jewel, precious stone, semiprecious stone, solitaire, stone. **2** flower, jewel, masterpiece, pearl, pick, prize, treasure.
generate *v* bring about, cause, create, engender, form, give rise to, initiate, make, originate, procreate, propagate, spawn.
generation *n* **1** breeding, creation, formation, origination, procreation, reproduction. **2** age, epoch, era, period, time, times.
generosity *n* bountiful, charitable, free, hospitable, kind, lavish, liberal, open-handed, princely, ungrudging,unstinting. **2** big-hearted, disinterested, good, high-minded, lofty, noble, unselfish.
genius *n* **1** expert, maestro, master-mind, virtuoso. **2** ability, aptitude, brilliance, flair, gift, knack, talent.
gentle *adj* **1** compassionate, kind, mild, peaceful, placid, quiet, soft, sweet-tempered, tender. **2** calm, moderate, muted, serene, smooth, tranquil.
genuine *adj* authentic, bona fide, honest, legitimate, natural, original, real, true.
germ *n* **1** bacterium, bug, microbe, micro-organism, virus. **2** beginning, embryo, origin, root, seed, source, spark.
germinate *v* bud, develop, grow, sprout, swell.
get *v* **1** achieve, acquire, bring, earn, gain, inherit, make, net, obtain, receive, secure, win. **2** arrest, capture, collar, grab, lay hold of, seize, take, trap. **3** become, grow, turn. **4** arrive, come, make it, reach. **5** arrange, contrive, fix, manage, succeed, wangle. **6** convince, influence, persuade, talk into.
get across *v* communicate, convey, get over, make clear, put over, transmit.
get along *v* **1** agree, get on, hit it off. **2** cope, develop, make out, manage, shift.
get around *v* **1** bypass, outwit; (*Inf*) out-smart. **2** coax, persuade, sway, talk round, win over; (*Inf*) cajole. **3** circulate, socialize, visit.
get at *v* **1** gain access to, get, get hold of, reach. **2** hint, imply. **3** annoy, blame, find fault with, irritate, nag, pick on, taunt.
get down *v* alight, bring down, climb down, descend, disembark, dismount, get off, lower, step down.
get off *v* descend, disembark, dismount, escape, exit, leave.
get on *v* **1** board, climb, embark, mount. **2** advance, get along, progress, prosper, succeed. **3** agree, get along, hit it off.
ghost *n* apparition, phantom, spirit, spook.
giant *adj* colossal, elephantine, enormous, extraordinary, gargantuan, gigantic, huge, immense, jumbo, large, mammoth, titanic, vast. (*Inf*) mega.
gift *n* **1** bequest, donation, grant, legacy, present. **2** aptitude, capability, capacity, flair, genius, knack, power, talent.
gifted *adj* able, accomplished, brilliant, clever, intelligent, skilled, talented.
gigantic *adj* colossal, elephantine, enormous, extraordinary, gargantuan, giant, herculean,

The gigantic cranes that make modern construction possible are made of steel and are capable of carrying enormous weights.

huge, immense, mammoth, massive, monstrous, titanic, tremendous, vast. (*Inf*) mega.
give *v* **1** allow, award, confer, donate, grant, present, provide, suppl. **2** display, indicate, manifest, offer, provide, show. **3** allow, grant, lend, surrender.
give away *v* **1** betray, disclose, divulge, leak, let slip, reveal; (*Inf*) blow the whistle on, grass on, rat on. **2** bestow, donate, gift.
give in *v* admit defeat, capitulate, collapse, comply, concede, quit, submit, surrender.
give off *v* discharge, emit, produce, release, send out.
give up *v* abandon, hand over, quit, resign, stop, surrender, throw in the towel.
glad *adj* cheerful, contented, delighted, happy, joyful, overjoyed, pleased, willing.
glamorous *adj* alluring, attractive, beautiful, bewitching, captivating, charming, dazzling, elegant, enchanting, entrancing, exciting, fascinating, glittering, glossy, lovely, prestigious, smart.
glance *v* gaze, glimpse, look, peek, peep, scan, view.
glance *n* **1** brief look, gander, glimpse, look, peek, peep, quick look, squint, view. **2** flash, gleam, glimmer, glint, reflection, sparkle, twinkle. **3** allusion, passing mention, reference.
glare *v* frown, give a dirty look, glower, look daggers, lower, scowl, stare angrily.
glare *n* **1** angry stare, black look, dirty look, frown, glower, lower, scowl. **2** blaze, brilliance, dazzle, flame, flare, glow.
glasses *pl n* bifocals, binoculars, eyeglasses, field-glasses, lorgnette, monocle, opera-glasses,

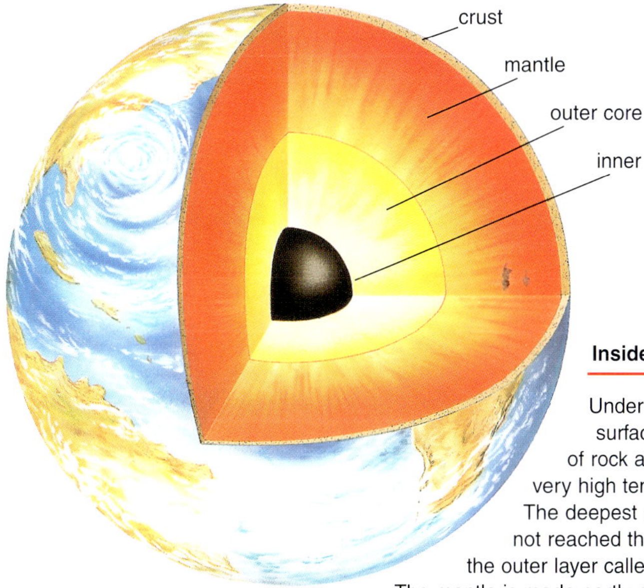

Inside the globe

Under the Earth's surface lie layers of rock and metal at very high temperatures. The deepest mines have not reached the bottom of the outer layer called the crust. The mantle is made partly of solid rock and partly molten rock. At the centre is an outer core of molten metal and an inner core of solid metal, probably iron.

pince-nez, spectacles, sun-glasses.
glaze *v* burnish, coat, enamel, furbish, gloss, lacquer, polish, varnish.
glaze *n* coat, enamel, finish, gloss, lacquer, lustre, patina, polish, shine, varnish.
glide *v* coast, drift, float, flow, fly, roll, run, sail, skate, skim, slide, slip, soar.
glimmer *v* blink, flicker, gleam, glisten, glitter, glow, shimmer, shine, sparkle, twinkle.
glimmer *n* blink, flicker, gleam, glow, ray, shimmer, sparkle, twinkle.
glimpse *n* brief view, glance, look, peek, peep, quick look, sight, sighting, squint.
glimpse *v* catch sight of, descry, espy, sight, spot, spy, view.
glitter *v* flash, glimmer, glint, glisten, shimmer, shine, sparkle, twinkle.
global *adj* **1** international, planetary, universal, worldwide. **2** all-inclusive, comprehensive, exhaustive, thorough, unlimited.
globe *n* ball, earth, orb, planet, round, sphere, world.
globule *n* bead, bubble, drop, droplet, particle, pearl, pellet.
gloomy *adj* **1** dark, dim, dismal, dull, murky, obscure, overcast. **2** black, depressing, sombre. **3** blue, crest-fallen, dejected, despondent, down in the mouth, glum, miserable, moody, sad.
glorious *adj* **1** distinguished, excellent, famous, grand, magnificent, majestic, renowned. **2** enjoyable, fine, great, splendid, wonderful; (*Inf*) delightful, marvellous.
glory *n* **1** distinction, fame, honour, prestige. **2** adoration, gratitude, praise, worship. **3** grandeur, magnificence, pageantry, pomp, splendour.

The yellow-orange glow given off by streetlights is caused by the sodium vapour inside the lights.

glow *n* **1** burning, gleam, glimmer, light. **2** brilliance, **3** excitement, intensity, passion, warmth.
glow *v* **1** burn, gleam, smoulder. **2** blush, colour, flush, radiate, thrill, tingle.
glue *n* adhesive, cement, gum, mucilage, paste.
glue *v* affix, cement, fix, gum, paste, seal, stick.
glut *n* excess, overabundance, saturation, surplus.
gnaw *v* **1** bite, chew, munch, nibble. **2** consume, devour, eat away, erode, fret, wear away.
go *v* **1** depart, journey, leave, move out, proceed, set off, travel. **2** move, operate, perform, run. **3** develop, happen, proceed, result, turn out, work out. **4** die, expire, pass away, perish. **5** elapse, flow, lapse, slip away.
go *n* attempt, effort, essay, shot.
goal *n* aim, ambition, design, destination, end, intention, limit, mark, object, objective, purpose, target.
go along *v* agree, cooperate, follow.
go away *v* depart, exit, leave, move out, withdraw.
go back *v* return, revert.
gobble *v* bolt, cram, gorge, gulp, guzzle, stuff, swallow, wolf.
go-between *n* agent, broker, dealer, intermediary, mediator, middleman.
go by *v* **1** elapse, exceed, flow on, move onward, pass, proceed. **2** adopt, be guided by, follow, heed, judge from, observe.
gone *v* **1** ended, finished, over, past. **2** absent, astray, away, lost, missing, vanished. **3** dead, deceased, extinct. **4** consumed, done, finished, used up.
good *adj* **1** acceptable, capital, excellent, fine, first-rate, great, pleasant, pleasing, positive, splendid, worthy. **2** admirable, honourable, praise-worthy, right, trustworthy. **3** able, capable, competent, proficient, reliable, satisfactory, serviceable, skilled, sound, suitable, talented, thorough, useful. **4** authentic, genuine, honest, legitimate, real, reliable, sound, true, valid. **5** decorous, dutiful, obedient, polite, proper, well-behaved. **6** ample, extensive, full, large.
good *n* **1** behalf, benefit, profit, use, worth. **2** excellence, merit, morality, right, uprightness, virtue, worth.
goodbye *interject* adieu, farewell, parting.
good-for-nothing *n* black sheep, layabout, waster.
good-humoured *adj* cheerful, congenial, good-tempered, happy, pleasant.
good-looking *adj* attractive, fair, handsome, pretty.
good-natured *adj* friendly, good-hearted, helpful, kind, tolerant, willing to please.
goods *pl n* **1** belongings, effects, furnishings, furniture, gear, possessions, property, things, trappings. **2** commodities, stock, stuff, wares.
goodwill *n* favour, friendliness, friendship, kindliness.
go off *v* blow up, detonate, explode, fire; (*Inf*) go bad, go stale, rot.
go on *v* continue, endure, happen, occur, persist, stay.
go out *v* **1** depart, exit, leave. **2** die out, expire, fade out.
go over *v* **1** examine, inspect, rehearse, reiterate, review, revise, study. **2** peruse, read, scan, skim.
gorge *n* canyon, chasm, clough, crevice, fissure, pass, ravine.
gorge *v* bolt, cram, devour, feed, gobble, gulp, guzzle, overeat, stuff, swallow, wolf.
gorgeous *adj* beautiful, brilliant, dazzling, elegant, glittering, grand, magnificent, splendid, stunning, superb.
gossip *n* **1** blether, chat, hearsay, idle talk, prattle, scandal, small talk, tittle-tattle. **2** busybody, gossipmonger, telltale.
gossip *v* blather, blether, chat, gabble, jaw, prattle, tattle.
go through *v* **1** bear, brave, endure, experience, undergo, withstand. **2** consume, exhaust, squander, use. **3** check, examine, explore, hunt, look, search.
govern *v* **1** administer,

command, control, direct, guide, lead, manage, order, pilot, reign, rule, steer, supervise. **2** decide, determine, guide, influence, rule, sway.
government *n* **1** administration, authority, law, rule, sovereignty, state. **2** executive, regime. **3** command, control, direction, management, regulation, restraint, supervision.
governor *n* administrator, boss, chief, commander, director, executive, leader, manager, ruler, superintendent, supervisor.
go with *v* **1** accompany, blend, complement, correspond, fit, harmonize, match, suit. **2** agree, concur.
go without *v* abstain, be deprived of, deny oneself, do without, go short, lack.
gown *n* costume, dress, frock, garment, habit, robe.
grab *v* bag, capture, catch, grasp, grip, latch on to, nab, pluck, seize, snap up, snatch, take hold of.
graceful *adj* beautiful, charming, elegant, fine, flowing, pleasing, smooth, tasteful.
grade *n* brand, category, class, condition, degree, group, level, mark, position, quality, rank, station, step.
grade *v* arrange, brand, classify, evaluate, group, order, rank, rate, sort, value.
gradient *n* bank, grade, hill, incline, rise, slope.
gradually *adv* bit by bit, evenly, gently, piece by piece, piecemeal, slowly, steadily, step by step.
graduate *v* calibrate, grade, mark off, measure out, proportion, regulate.
grain *n* **1** cereals, corn. **2** grist, kernel, seed.
grant *v* admit, agree to, allocate, allow, assign, bestow, concede, consent to, donate, give, permit.
grant *n* allocation, allotment, allowance, award, bequest, donation, gift, subsidy.
grasp *v* **1** catch, clasp, clinch, clutch, grab, hold, seize, snatch. **2** catch the drift of, catch on, comprehend, follow, realize, see, take in, understand.
grasp *n* **1** clasp, clutches, grip, hold, possession. **2** awareness, comprehension, knowledge, perception, understanding.
grate *v* **1** creak, grind, rub, scrape. **2** annoy, exasperate, get one down, irritate, jar, nettle, peeve, rankle, rub one up the wrong way. **3** set one's teeth on edge, vex; (*Inf*) get on one's nerves.
grateful *adj* appreciative, beholden, indebted, obliged, thankful.
gratitude *n* appreciation, gratefulness, indebtedness, obligation, recognition, sense of obligation, thankfulness, thanks.
gratuitous *adj* complimentary, free, unpaid, unrewarded, voluntary.
gravity *n* **1** importance, severity, significance, urgency. **2** the force of gravity, the magnetic force of the Earth, the pull of the Earth's gravity.
greasy *adj* **1** fatty, oily, slick, slimy, slippery. **2** glib, grovelling, smooth.
great *adj* **1** big, bulky, colossal, enormous, gigantic, huge, immense, large, mammoth, stupendous, tremendous, vast. **2** extended, lengthy, prolonged, protracted. **3** chief, grand, main, major, principal. **4** excessive, extreme, high, strong. **5** critical, crucial, grave, important. **6** celebrated, distinguished, eminent, famous, illustrious, outstanding, prominent, talented. **7** chivalrous, dignified, grand, impressive. **8** devoted, keen. **9** able, expert, skilful; (*Inf*) fantastic, first-rate, good, marvellous, terrific, wonderful.

There is no gravity in space so astronauts float, even wearing suits and equipment which on Earth would be as difficult to walk in as a suit of armour.

greedy *adj* **1** hungry, insatiable, ravenous. **2** craving, grasping, hungry, impatient, selfish.
green *adj* **1** blooming, grassy, leafy, new. **2** fresh, immature, raw, unripe.
green *n* common, grass, lawn, turf, village green.
greenhouse *n* conservatory, glass-house, hothouse.
grey *adj* **1** ashen, colourless, pale, pallid. **2** cloudy, dark, depressing, dismal, drab, dreary, dull, foggy, gloomy, misty, murky, overcast, sunless. **3** aged, ancient, elderly, experienced, hoary, mature, old.
ground *n* clod, dirt, dry, land, dust, earth, field, land, loam mould, sod, soil, terra firma, terrain, turf.
group *n* band, batch, bunch, category, circle, class, cluster, collection, crowd, gang, pack, party, set, troop.
group *v* arrange, assemble, class, classify, gather, marshal, order, organize, put together, sort.
grow *v* **1** develop, increase, spread, stretch, swell, thicken, widen. **2** develop, flourish, germinate, shoot, spring up, sprout. **3** advance, expand, improve, progress, prosper, succeed, thrive. **4** breed, cultivate, farm, produce, propagate.
growl *v* bark, howl, snarl, yelp.
grown-up *adj* adult, fully-grown, mature, of age.
gruesome *adj* ghastly, grim, hideous, horrendous, horrible, horrid, horrific, horrifying, repulsive, shocking, terrible.

By studying, in a greenhouse environment, the way Earth's systems work, scientists hope to be able to create successful ecosystems on other planets.

guarantee *n* assurance, bond, certainty, collateral, covenant, earnest, guaranty, pledge, promise, security, undertaking, warranty, word of honour.
guarantee *v* answer for, assure, certify, ensure, insure, maintain, make certain, pledge, promise, protect, secure, stand behind, swear, vouch for, warrant.
guard *v* cover, defend, escort, keep, mind, oversee, patrol, police, preserve, protect, safeguard, save, screen, secure, shelter, shield, supervise, tend, watch, watch over.
guard *n* **1** defender, lookout, sentry, warder, watchman. **2** defence, protection, rampart, safeguard, screen, security shield. **3** attention, care, caution, vigilance, wariness.
guess *v* estimate, predict, solve, speculate, work out.
guess *n* feeling, notion, prediction, suspicion, theory.
guide *v* **1** direct, escort, lead, pilot, shepherd, show the way, steer, usher. **2** command, control, direct, handle, manage. **3** advise, counsel, educate, instruct, rule, supervise, teach, train.
guide *n* **1** adviser, conductor, controller, counsellor, escort, leader, mentor, pilot, teacher, usher. **2** catalogue, directory, guidebook, handbook, instructions, key, manual.
guild *n* association, club, order, society, union.
guile *n* art, craft, deceit, deception, slyness, treachery, trickery.
guilt *n* **1** blame, responsibility, wrong. **2** bad conscience, guilty conscience, remorse, shame.
guilty *adj* at fault, convicted criminal, responsible, to blame.
gulf *n* **1** bay, blight, sea inlet. **2** abyss, breach, chasm, cleft, gap, opening, split, void.
gullible *adj* easily taken in, foolish, green, innocent, naive, trusting, unsuspecting.
gulp *v* bolt, devour, gobble, guzzle, knock back, wolf.
gulp *n* draught, mouthful, swallow; (*Inf*) swig.
gum *n* adhesive, cement, glue, paste, resin.
gush *v* burst, cascade, flood, flow, jet, pour, run, rush, spout, spurt, stream.
gush *n* burst, cascade, flood, flow, jet, outburst, outflow, rush, spout, spurt, stream, torrent.
gust *n* blast, blow, breeze, flurry, gale, puff, rush, squall.
guts *pl n* audacity, backbone, courage, daring, nerve, spirit, willpower.
gutter *n* channel, conduit, ditch, drain, duct, pipe, sluice, trench, trough, tube.

Hh

Modern intensive farming methods have led to the destruction of the hedgerows and natural habitats of birds and animals to accommodate large fields.

habit *n* **1** custom, practice, way. **2** convention, custom, mode, routine, rule, second nature. **3** dress, garment, riding dress.

habitat *n* abode, environment, locality, natural setting.

habitation *n* dwelling, home, house, living quarters, lodging, quarters, residence.

haggle *v* **1** bargain, barter, beat down. **2** bicker, dispute, quarrel, squabble, wrangle.

hail *n* **1** barrage, bombard, pelt, rain, rain down on, shower, storm, volley. **2** frozen rain, hailstones, sleet.

hail *v* **1** acknowledge, applaud, cheer, greet, salute, welcome. **2** call, flag down, make a sign to, wave down. **3** be a native of, come from, originate in. **4** batter, bombard, pelt, pepper, rain down, shower, volley.

hair *n* head of hair, locks, mane, mop, shock, tresses.

half *n* bisection, division, equal part, fifty per cent, fraction, hemisphere, portion, section.

half *adj* divided, fractional, halved, incomplete, partial.

half *adv* barely, incompletely, in part, partially, partly, slightly.

halfway *adv* **1** midway, in the middle. **2** almost, just about, nearly, incompletely, moderately, nearly, partially. **3** establish a middle ground with, meet halfway, reach a compromise with; (*Inf*) go fifty-fifty with, go halvers with.

halfway *adj* central, equidistant, intermediate, mean, medial, median, mid, middle, midway.

hall *n* **1** corridor, entrance hall, entry, foyer, hallway, lobby, passage, passageway, vestibule. **2** assembly room, auditorium, chamber, church hall, concert hall, conference hall, meeting place.

halt *v* **1** break off, call it a day, cease, close down, come to an end, desist, draw up, pull up, rest, standstill, stop, wait. **2** arrest, block, check, curb, cut short, end, hold back, obstruct, terminate. **3** falter, hobble, limp, stumble. **4** be unsure, hesitate, pause, think twice.

halt *n* break, breathing space, discontinue, interruption, pause, rest, stop, stoppage, termination, time out.

halve *v* bisect, cut in half, divide equally, reduce by fifty per cent, share equally, split in two.

hammer *v* **1** bang, beat, club, hit, knock, strike, tap. **2** bear out, fabricate, fashion, forge from, make, mould, shape. **3** batter, beat, bludgeon, club, hit, pound, slap, strike, thrash; (*Inf*) beat, clobber. **4** grind away, keep on, labour, plod away, slog away; (*Inf*) beaver away, plug away, stick at. **5** accomplish, complete, negotiate, resolve, settle, sort out, work out.

hammer *n* beetle, claw-hammer, gavel, mallet, sledgehammer.

hamper *v* curb, embarrass, handicap, hinder, hold up, impede, interfere with, obstruct, prevent, restrict, thwart.

hand *n* **1** fist, palm, paw. **2** direction, influence, share. **3** aid, assistance, help, support. **4** craftsman, employee, hired man, labourer, workman. **5 in hand** receiving attention, under control. **6** available for use, in reserve, put by, ready.

hand *v* **1** deliver, hand over, pass. **2** aid, assist, conduct, convey, guide, help, lead, present, transmit.

handbook *n* guide, guidebook, instruction book, manual.

handcuff *v* manacle, shackle.

handicap *n* **1** barrier, drawback, obstacle, restriction, stumbling block. **2** defect, disability, impairment.
handicap *v* block, curb, hold back, limit, restrict.
handle *n* grip, handgrip, helve, hilt, knob, shaft, stock.
handle *v* **1** feel, grasp, hold, maul, pick up, poke, touch. **2** control, direct, guide, manage, manipulate, manoeuvre, operate, steer, use, wield. **3** administer, conduct, cope with, deal with, supervise, take care of, treat.
hand-outs *pl n* **1** charity, dole, gifts. **2** bulletin, circular, free sample, leaflet, literature, mailshot, pamphlet, press release.

In harbour at night, ships show a green light on their starboard (right) side and a red light on their port (left) side.

hand out *v* deal out, disburse, dish-out, dispense, disseminate, distribute, give out.
hand over *v* deliver, donate, present, release, surrender, transfer, turn over, yield.
hand-picked *adj* choice, elect, élite, select, specially chosen.
handwriting *adj* calligraphy, chirography, longhand, scrawl, script.
handy *adj* **1** accessible, at hand, convenient, nearby, within reach. **2** easy to use, helpful, manage-able, neat, practical, serviceable, useful, user-friendly. **3** adept, clever, expert, nimble, proficient, ready, skilful, skilled.
hang *v* **1** dangle, depend, droop, suspend. **2** execute, sent to the gallows, string up. **3** adhere, cling, hold, rest, stick. **4** attach, cover, deck, decorate, drape, fasten, furnish.
hang about *adj* dally, linger, loiter, roam, tarry, waste time.
hang back *adj* be backward, be reluctant, demur, hesitate, hold back, recoil.
hanging *adj* dangling, drooping, floppy, pendent, suspended, swinging, unsupported.
happen *v* **1** appear, arise, come about, crop up, develop, follow, occur, result, take place. **2** become of, befall, betide. **3** chance, fall out, have the fortune to be, turn out.
happy *adj* blissful, cheerful, contented, delighted, ecstatic, elated, glad, jolly, joyful, merry, over the moon, pleased, thrilled.
happy-go-lucky *adj* carefree, casual, easy-going, heedless, irresponsible, light-hearted, unconcerned, untroubled.
harass *v* annoy, badger, bait, bother, disturb, exasperate, exhaust, fatigue, hound, persecute, pester, plague, tease, torment, trouble, vex, weary, worry.
harbour *n* **1** haven, port. **2** asylum, covert, refuge, retreat, sanctuary, shelter.
harbour *v* conceal, hide, lodge, protect, provide, refuge, relieve, secrete, shelter, shield.
hard *adj* **1** compact, dense, firm, rigid, solid, stiff, strong, tough. **2** arduous, back-breaking, exhausting, tough. **3** complex, difficult. **4** callous, cold, cruel, harsh, severe, unkind.
hard *adv* **1** intensely, powerfully, severely. **2** intently, persistently, steadily. **3** badly, painfully, severely, with difficulty. **4** bitterly, reluctantly, resentfully.
harden *v* **1** bake, cake, freeze, set, solidify. **2** brace, buttress, fortify, reinforce, strengthen, toughen.
hardened *adj* **1** chronic, fixed, habitual, set. **2** accustomed, seasoned, toughened.
hardly *adv* barely, by no means, not at all, not quite, no way, only just, scarcely.
hard-working *adj* conscientious, diligent, energetic, zealous.

hardy *adj* fit, healthy, hearty, robust, rugged, sound, strong, sturdy, tough, vigorous.
harm *n* abuse, damage, hurt, ill, injury, loss, misfortune.
harm *v* abuse, damage, hurt, ill-treat, injure, wound.
harmful *adj* damaging, detrimental, hurtful.
harmless *adj* gentle, innocent, not dangerous, safe.
harness *n* equipment, gear, tack, tackle, trappings.
harness *v* **1** couple, hitch up, put in harness, saddle, yoke. **2** apply, channel, control, employ, exploit, utilize.
harsh *adj* **1** coarse, croaking, grating, rasping, rough. **2** abusive, austere, bleak, grim, hard, ruthless, sever, stern, unkind, unpleasant.
harvest *n* **1** harvesting, harvest-time, reaping. **2** crop, produce, yield.
hastily *adv* **1** fast, hurried, rapid, speedy, swift, urgent. **2** heedless, impulsive, reckless.
hatch *v* breed, bring forth, incubate, conceive, contrive, cook up, design, devise, dream up, plan, plot, scheme, think up.
hate *v* be repelled by, be sick of, despise, detest, dislike, to loathe.
hatred *n* animosity, antagonism, aversion, dislike, hate, ill will, repugnance, revulsion.
haul *v* drag, draw, hale, heave, lug, pull, tow, trail, tug.
haul *n* booty, catch, find, gain, harvest, loot, spoils, takings, yield.
haunt *v* **1** visit, walk. **2** come back, plague, prey on, stay with, torment. **3** frequent, hang around, visit.
haunt *n* den, gathering place, hangout, meeting place, resort, stamping ground.
haven *n* **1** anchorage, harbour, port, roads. **2** asylum, refuge, retreat, sanctum, shelter.
haversack *n* backpack, kitbag, knapsack, rucksack, satchel.

Harvest of crops is not always for human food. Cotton, flax and jute are grown to made into fabric. Esparto grass may be cultivated for the manufacture of rope or paper, while tobacco is grown for smoking. Other non-food crops, such as the lavender in the picture is grown for the perfume and cosmetics industries.

havoc *n* **1** damage, destruction, devastation, ruin, wreck. **2** chaos, confusion, disruption, mayhem; (*Inf*) shambles.
hazardous *adj* dangerous, difficult, precarious, risky, unsafe.
haze *n* cloud, dimness, film, fog, mist, smog, smokiness, vapour.
hazy *adj* **1** blurry, cloudy, dim, faint, misty, obscure, overcast. **2** fuzzy, indistinct, unclear, vague.
head *n* **1** cranium, crown, skull. **2** boss, captain, chief, chieftain, commander, director, head-master, headmistress, head teacher, leader, manager, master, principal, supervisor. **3** apex, crest, crown, height, peak, pitch, summit, tip, top, vertex. **4** ability, aptitude, brains, intellect, mind, talent, thought, understanding. **5** branch, department, division, heading, section, subject, topic.
head *adj* chief, first, highest, leading, main, pre-eminent, premier, prime, principal.
head *v* **1** be first, cap, crown, lead, lead the way, precede, top. **2** be in charge of, command, control, direct, govern, guide, lead, manage, rule, supervise.
headache *n* **1** migraine. **2** bane, bother, bugbear, inconvienience, pest, trouble, vexation.
heal *v* **1** lure, make well, mend, regenerate, remedy, restore, treat. **2** patch up, reconcile, settle, soothe.
health *n* fitness, good condition, soundness, strength, wellbeing.
healthy *adj* active, blooming, fit, flourishing, hale and hearty, hardy, in good condition, physically fit, robust, sound, strong, well.

During a storm, electrical energy is released in a flash of light. There is usually thunder at the same time. As light travels faster than sound, we see the lightning flash before we hear the thunder.

hear *v* **1** catch, eavesdrop, give attention, heed, listen in, listen to, overhear. **2** ascertain, be informed, be told of, discover, find out, gather, learn, pick up, understand; (*Inf*) get wind of. **3** consider, examine, inquire into, investigate, judge, try.

hearing *n* **1** audition, ear, perception. **2** chance to speak, interview. **3** auditory range, earshot, hearing distance, range, sound. **4** inquiry, investigation, trial.

heartbreaking *adj* agonizing, bitter, desolating, disappointing, distressing, grievous, heart-rending, pitiful, poignant, sad, tragic.

heartbroken *adj* brokenhearted, dejected, disappointed, miserable.

heat *n* **1** fever, high temperature, hot spell, warmth. **2** excitement, fever, passion.

heat *v* **1** become warm, cook, grow hot, reheat, warm up. **2** arouse, enrage, excite, inflame, stimulate, stir.

heated *adj* angry, bitter, excited, fierce, furious, intense, raging, stormy, violent.

heave *v* **1** drag up, elevate, haul, heft, hoist, lever, lift, pull, raise, tug. **2** cast, fling, hurl, pitch, send, sling, throw, toss.

heaven *n* ecstasy, Eden, happiness, happy hunting-ground, paradise, seventh heaven, sheer bliss, utopia.

heavy *adj* **1** bulky, massive, weighty. **2** awkward, difficult, harsh, severe. **3** laden, loaded. **4** fat, overweight, obese, stout, tubby. **5** dense, solid, thick. **6** boggy, difficult, muddy. **7** intense, serious, severe. **8** rough, tempestuous, squally, turbulent, wild. **9** cloudy, dark, dreary, gloomy, grey, overcast.

hedge *n* **1** hedgerow. **2** barrier, boundary, protection, screen, windbreak. **3** cover, guard, insurance cover, safeguard.

hedge *v* **1** border, edge, enclose, fence, surround. **2** block, confine, hem in, hinder, obstruct, restrict. **3** dodge, duck, evade, sidestep.

heel *n* **1** crust, end, remainder, rump, stub, stump. **2** platform heel, stiletto, wedge heel. **3 Achilles' heel** weak spot. **4 down at heel** run-down, seedy, shabby, worn.

height *n* **1** altitude, elevation, highness, loftiness, stature, tallness. **2** apex, crest, crown, hill, mountain, peak, summit, top, vertex.

help *v* **1** aid, assist, lend a hand, promote, support. **2** cure, heal, improve, relieve, restore.

help *n* advice, aid, assistance, guidance, support.

helper *n* aide, assistant, deputy, mate, partner, right-hand man, second, subsidiary, supporter.

helpful *adj* **1** beneficial, constructive, fortunate, practical, useful. **2** accommodating, caring, considerate, cooperative, friendly, kind, neighbourly, supportive, sympathetic.

helping *n* piece, plateful, portion, ration, serving.

hem *n* border, edge, fringe, margin, trimming.

herd *n* collection, crowd, crush, flock, horde, mass, mob, multitude, pack, swarm, throng.

herd *v* assemble, associate, collect, congregate, flock, gather, huddle, rally, round up.

heritage *n* **1** background, history, tradition. **2** bequest, birthright, endowment, estate, inheritance, tradition. **3** ancestry,

The Statue of Liberty is a symbol of America's heritage. Standing on Liberty Island in Manhattan Bay, New York 'the green lady' is a monument to freedom unveiled in 1886 by President Grover Cleveland.

birth, descent, dynasty, lineage.
hermit *n* monk, recluse.
hero *n* **1** cavalier, champion, great man, idol, knight, shining example, star, superstar. **2** lead actor, leading man, male lead, principal male character. **3** ideal man, idol; (*Inf*) heart-throb.
heroic *adj* bold, brave, daring, gallant, intrepid, valiant.
heroine *n* **1** celebrity, goddess, ideal, woman of the hour. **2** diva, female lead, lead actress, leading lady, paragon, prima donna, principal female character.
heroism *n* boldness, bravery, courage, daring, fearlessness, gallantry, manliness, prowess, spirit, valour, virililty.
hesitate *v* be uncertain, dither, doubt, hang back, pause, stall, swither, wait; (*Inf*) dillydally.
hesitation *v* **1** delay, doubt, hesitancy, indecision, stalling, uncertainty. **2** misgivings, reluctance, unwillingness.
hidden *adj* clandestine, concealed, covered, covert, cryptic, obscure, secret.
hide *v* **1** conceal, go into hiding, go to ground, go underground, take cover. **2** camouflage, cloak, cloud, conceal, cover, darken, disguise, mask, obscure, obstruct, shelter, shroud, veil.
hide *n* coat, fleece, fur, pelt, skin.
hideaway *n* den, hermitage, hiding-place, lair, refuge, retreat, shelter.
hideous *adj* **1** disgusting, ghastly, grim, grisly, grotesque, gruesome, macabre, monstrous, repellant, repulsive, revolting, ugly, unsightly. **2** abominable, appalling, contemptible, foul, frightening, heinous, horrific, horrifying, monstrous, odius, outrageous, terrifying.

We are still unsure how the Egyptians were able to build the pyramids so high without machines. But the answer must be that they used huge numbers of slaves to shape and haul the enormous stones with which they are built.

high *adj* **1** elevated, steep, tall, towering. **2** extreme, great, strong. **3** chief, eminent, high-ranking, important, influential, leading, main, powerful, principal, ruling. **4** costly, dear, exorbitant, expensive, high-priced; (*Inf*) steep. **5** forceful, potent, sharp, vigorous. **6** acute, high-pitched, penetrating, piercing, piping, soprano, treble. **7** extravagant, grand, high-living, lavish, luxurious, rich. **8** boisterous, elated, happy, jolly, overexcited. **9** delirious, drugged, hallucinating, intoxicated; (*Inf*) freaked out, on a trip, spaced out, stoned, tripping, turned on. **10** going bad, going off, rotting, smelling, tainted; (*Inf*) ponging, niffy, whiffy.
high *adv* aloft, altitude, at great height, far up, high up, way up.
high *n* apex, height, peak, ummit, top, zenith.
high-class *adj* choice, elegant, élite, first-rate, posh, superior, up market, upper class. (*Inf*) classy, super, super duper.
high-handed *adj* arbitrary, arrogant, autocratic, dictatorial, domineering, haughty, inconsiderate, lordly, oppressive, overbearing, peremptory, selfwilled, tyrannical, wilful; (*Inf*) bossy.
highland *n* mountainous region, hilly country, plateau, ridge, tableland, uplands.
highlight *n* best part, high point, main feature, peak, outstanding feature.
highlight *v* accentuate, bring home, emphasize, feature, focus attention on, give prominence to, place emphasis on, spotlight, stress, underline.
highly-strung *adv* edgy, excitable, irritable, neurotic,

nervous, over-wrought, stressed, temperamental, wound up.

high-powered *adj* dynamic, energetic, fast-track, forceful, go-getting, highly capable, vigorous.

high-spirited *adj* boisterous, bold, daring, dashing, energetic, full of life, fun-loving, lively, spirited, vibrant.

high spirits *pl n* animation, boisterousness, bounciness, dynamism, exhilaration, exuberance, liveliness, vitality.

hijack *v* car-jack, commandeer, expropriate, seize, skyjack, steal, take over.

hike *v* back-pack, ramble, tramp, trek, walk, wander.

hike *n* march, ramble, tramp, trek, trudge, walk.

hilarious *adj* a great laugh, amusing, comical, entertaining, funny, humorous, jolly, merry, mirthful, noisy, rollicking, side-witty, zany.

hill *n* **1** brae, elevation, eminence, fell, heights, high land, hillock, hilltop, hummock, knoll, mound, mount, prominence, ridge, tor. **2** acclivity, gradient, incline, rise, slope. **3** drift, heap, mound, mountain, pile.

hire *v* **1** appoint, commission, employ, engage, enlist, sign up, take on. **2** charter, engage, lease, let, rent.

hire *n* **1** charge, cost, earnings, fee, pay, price, renumeration, salary, stipend, wage. **2** lease, rent, rental.

hiss *n* **1** buzz, wheeze, whistle. **2** boo, catcall, hoot, jeer; (*Inf*) raspberry.

hiss *v* **1** rasp, shrill, wheeze, whirr, whistle, whiz. **2** boo, catcall, condemn, hoot, jeer, mock, ridicule, taunt; (*Inf*) blow raspberries.

Easter Island is famous for its historic gigantic stone statues of which there are more than 600. The island is approx. 2,200 miles west of Chile in the Pacific and the statues, known as moais, were carved between 1000 and 1689 AD.

historic *adj* celebrated, famous, important, memorable, momentous, notable, outstanding, remarkable, significant.

history *v* **1** account, autobiography, biography, chronicle, memoirs, records, story. **2** background, experiences, fortunes. **3** antiquity, bygones, former times, yesterday.

hit *v* **1** bang, beat, box, hammer, knock, pound, punch, slap, smack, strike, swat, thrash, thump; (*Inf*) biff, clobber, clout, sock, wallop, whack. **2** bang into, bump, clash with, collide with, crash against, meet head-on, run into, smash into.

hit *n* **1** beating, blow, box, bump, clash, collision, knock, punch, rap, shot, slap, smack, stroke, thump; (*Inf*) bashing, belting, clout, swipe, wallop. **2** sellout, sensation, smash, success, triumph, winner.

hoarse *adj* croaky, gruff, husky, ough, throaty.

hoax *n* cheat, deception, fraud, practical joke, prank, trick; (*Inf*) con, scam, spoof.

hobble *v* limp, reel, shuffle, stagger, totter.

hobby *n* activity, amusement, diversion, game, leisure pursuit, occupation, pastime, recreation, relaxation, sport.

hold *v* **1** adhere, clasp, cleave, clinch, cling to, clutch, cradle, embrace, enfold, fondle, grasp, grip, hold on to, hug. **2** have, keep, own, possess, retain. **3** arrest, bind, confine, curb, detain, imprison, restrain, stay, stop, suspend. **4** assume, believe, presume, think. **5** continue,

endure, last, persevere, persist, remain, stay. **6** assemble, call, carry on, celebrate. **7** bear, carry, prop, support. **8** contain, take.
hold *n* **1** clasp, clutch, grasp, grip. **2** anchorage, foothold, stay, support. **3** control, grip, power. **4** influence, sway; (*Inf*) clout, pull. **5** delay, pause, postponement.
hold-up *n* **1** bottleneck, hitch, setback, stoppage, traffic jam, wait. **2** mugging, robbery.
hold-up *v* **1** delay, hinder, set back, slow down, stop. **2** brace, jack up, prop, shore up, support. **3** mug, rob, snatch.
hole *n* **1** break, crack, fissure, gap, notch, opening, outlet, perforation, puncture, slit, split, tear. **2** cave, cavern, chamber, crater, depression, dug-out, excavation, hollow, mine, pit, scoop, shaft. **3** defect, error, fault, flaw, inconsistency, loophole. **4** burrow, covert, earth, den, lair, nest, set, shelter. **5** hovel, slum; (*Inf*) dive, dump, joint. **6** cell, dungeon, prison. **7** crack, discrepancy, error, fault, flaw, inconsistency. **8** dilemma, mess, muddle, plight, predicament, tangle, trouble; (*Inf*) fix, jam, hot water, pickle, scrape.
hole *v* gash, lacerate, perforate, pierce, puncture, spike, stab.
holiday *n* **1** break, leave, recess, sabbatical, time off, vacation. **2** anniversary, bank holiday, carnival day, celebration, feast, festival, festivity, gala, public holiday, saint's day.
hollow *adj* **1** empty, not solid, unfilled, vacant. **2** cavernous, concave, deep-set, depressed, indented, sunken. **3** deep, dull, expressionless, low, muted, rumbling, toneless. **4** empty, fruitless, futile, meaningless, pointless, specious, useless, vain, worthless.
hollow *n* **1** basin, bowl, cave, cavern, cavity, concavity, crater, cup, den, dent, depression, dimple, excavation, hole, indentation, pit, trough. **2** bottom, dale, dell, dingle, glen, valley.
holocaust *n* **1** fire, inferno. **2** carnage, ethnic cleansing, extermination, genocide, massacre, slaughter.
home *n* **1** abode, house, residence. **2** birth-place, family, home town, household. **3** habitat, range, stamping ground, territory. **4 at home** available, in, present. **5** at ease, comfortable, familiar, relaxed. **6 at home in**, familiar with, knowledgeable.
honest *adj* **1** honourable, law-abiding, reliable, reputable, trustworthy, truthful, upright. **2** fair, fair and square, just. **3** candid, direct, forthright, frank, open, plain, sincere, straightforward, undisguised.
honour *v* **1** fame, glory, prestige, rank, reputation. **2** acclaim, praise, respect. **3** fairness, goodness, honesty, integrity, morality, principles. **4** compliment, credit, favour, pleasure, privilege. **5** chastity, innocence, modesty, purity, virginity, virtue.
honour *v* admire, glorify, respect,

Rainwater, seeping through holes in the Earth's surface into caves and caverns below, is slightly acidic and reacts with limestone to form the stange rock formations known as stalagmites (rising from the floor) and stalactites (hanging from the ceiling).

value, worship.
honourable *adj* ethical, fair, honest, moral, principled, true, trustworthy, trusty, upstanding, virtuous.
hope *n* ambition, anticipation, assumption, belief, confidence, desire, dream, expectancy, expectation, faith, longing.
hope *v* anticipate, count on, desire, expect, look forward to.

Houses built before the sixteenth century usually have very small windows, in which little panes of glass were fitted. It is only recently that techniques have been devloped for making large sheets of glass for windows.

horrible *adj* **1** appalling, awful, dreadful, ghastly, gruesome, horrid, revolting, shocking, terrible. **2** awful, cruel, mean, nasty, unpleasant.
horrify *v* **1** frighten, scare, terrify, terrorize. **2** appal, disgust, dismay, outrage, shock, sicken.
horror *n* **1** alarm, dread, fear, fright, panic, terror. **2** disgust, hatred, loathing, revulsion.
hospitable *adj* friendly, kind, welcoming.
host *n* **1** hotelier, landlord. **2** party-giver. **3** anchorman, anchorwoman, compère, entertainer, master of ceremonies, MC, presenter. **4** army, horde, legion, multitude, swarm, throng.
hostile *adj* alien, inhospitable, unfriendly, unwelcoming.
hostilities *pl n* conflict, fighting, state of war, war, warfare.
hostility *n* animosity, hatred, ill will, opposition, resentment.
hot *adj* **1** blistering, boiling, burning, fiery, flaming, heated, piping hot, roasting, scalding, scorching, searing, sweltering, warm. **2** acrid, biting, peppery, sharp, spicy.
house *n* **1** dwelling, home, residence. **2** family, household. **3** clan, dynasty, family tree, lineage, race, tribe. **4** business, company, establishment, firm, organization. **5** hotel, inn, public house, tavern.
huge *adj* bulky, colossal, enormous, extensive, giant, gigantic, great, immense, large, massive, mega, monumental, titanic, tremendous, vast.
humour *n* **1** amusement, comedy, fun, funniness, wit. **2** comedy, joking, wittiness. **3** frame of mind, mood, spirits.
hunger *n* **1** appetite, famine, ravenousness, starvation. **2** appetence, appetite, craving, desire, greediness, itch, lust, yearning.
hunger *v* crave, desire, hanker, long for, pine, starve, thirst, want, wish, yearn.
hunt *v* **1** chase, hound, pursue, stalk, track, trail. **2** ferret about, forage, look high and low, rummage through, scour, search, seek, try to find.
hurricane *n* cyclone, gale, storm, tempest, tornado, typhoon, windstorm.
hurry *v* **1** dash, fly, lose no time, rush, scoot. **2** accelerate, push on, speed up, urge; (*Inf*) get a move on.
hurry *n* bustle, commotion, dispatch, flurry, haste, rush, speed, urgency.
hurt *v* **1** bruise, damage, disable, harm, impair, injure, mar, spoil, wound. **2** ache, be sore, burn, pain, smart, sting, throb. **3** annoy, distress, grieve, pain, sadden, sting, upset, wound.
hurt *n* **1** distress, pain, soreness, suffering. **2** bruise, sore, wound.
hustle *v* bustle, crowd, elbow, force, hasten, hurry, impel, jog, jostle, push, rush, shove, thrust.
hygiene *n* cleanliness, hygienics, sanitary measures, sanitation.
hypnotize *v* **1** mesmerize, put in a trance, put to sleep. **2** entrance, fascinate, spellbind.
hypocrite *n* fraud, impostor, pretender.
hysteria *n* agitation, frenzy, hysterics, madness, panic attack.
hysterical *adj* **1** agitated, crazed, distraught, frantic, frenzied, in a panic, out of control, uncontrollable. **2** amusing, hilarious, side-splitting, very funny.

Ii

ice *n* ice age, ice box, ice breaker, ice-cap, ice-cream, ice-cube, ice-hockey, ice-lolly, ice-pick, ice-rink, ice-skater; on ice, on thin ice, break the ice, cut no ice.

icy *adj* **1** chilly, cold, freezing, frosty, glacial, ice-cold, Siberian, slippery. **2** aloof, distant, hostile, indifferent, reserved, unfriendly.

idea *n* **1** concept, impression, judgment, thought. **2** belief, opinion, teaching, view.

ideal *n* example, model, pattern, prototype, standard.

identical *adj* alike, duplicate, equal, equivalent, like, matching, similar, twin.

identify *v* classify, diagnose, distinguish, label, name, pinpoint, place, recognize, single out, tag.

idiot *n* ass, blockhead, cretin, dimwit, fool, imbecile, moron, nin-compoop, nitwit, pillock.

idiotic *adj* absurd, crazy, daft, foolish, insane, lunatic, sense-less, stupid, unintelligent; (*Inf*) daft, dumb.

idle *adj* **1** sluggish. **2** inactive, mothballed, unused. **3** out of work, redundant, unemployed; (*Inf*) on the dole. **4** empty, unoccupied, vacant. **5** baseless, groundless. **6** foolish, insignificant, superficial, trivial. **7** fruitless, futile, pointless. **8** frivolous, worthless.

idle *v* **1** laze, mark time, potter, shirk, sit back and do nothing, shirk, stroll, vegetate, waste. **2** tick over.

Living on the ice

Animals living on and under the ice are specially adapted to live in the coldest parts of the world. In fact, at the North and South Poles almost nothing can survive, but around the edges of the Arctic and Antarctic there are seas rich in plant and animal life. This means that larger animals living on the edge of the ice can find food in the teeming waters.

No one is quite sure why the narwhal has such a long tusk. It is a mammal giving birth to live young underwater.

idol *n* **1** effigy, god, icon, image. **2** darling, favourite, hero, hero-ine, pet, superstar; (*Inf*) pin-up.

idolize *v* admire, adore, look up to, love, revere, worship, worship to excess.

The Sun is our nearest star. It illuminates the Earth and generates heat and light energy which makes life on earth possible.

ignite *v* burn, burst into flames, catch fire, set alight, set fire to.
ignorance *n* **1** blindness, denseness, illiteracy, lack of education, mental darkness, stupidity. **2** greenness, inexperience, innocence, unawareness.
ignorant *adj* **1** innocent, in the dark about, oblivious, unaware, unconscious. **2** green, naive, uneducated, unread, untrained.
ignore *v* disregard, give the cold shoulder to, neglect, overlook, pass over, pay no attention to, turn a blind eye to, turn a deaf ear to, turn one's back on.
ill *adj* **1** diseased, off-colour, sick, under the weather, unwell. **2** bad, damaging, evil, foul, harmful, unlucky, wicked, wrong. **3** disturbing, ominous, sinister, threatening.
ill-defined *adj* blurred, dim, fuzzy, indistinct, vague.
illegal *adj* banned, black-market, criminal, illicit, prohibited, proscribed, unlawful.
illegible *adj* faint, obscure, scrawled, unreadable.
ill-fated *adj* doomed, unlucky.
ill feeling *n* animosity, bad blood, bitterness, hostility, ill will, resentment.
ill-founded *adj* baseless, empty, groundless, unjustified, unproven, unreliable, unsubstantiated, unsupported.
illicit *adj* **1** black-market, bootleg, contraband, criminal, illegal, illegitimate, prohibited, unauthorized, unlawful. **2** clandestine, forbidden, furtive, guilty, improper, wrong.
ill-mannered *adj* badly behaved, ill-behaved, rude.
illness *n* complaint, disability, disease, disorder, ill health, infirmity, poor health, sickness.
illogical *adj* absurd, faulty, invalid, irrational, senseless.
ill-treat *v* abuse, handle roughly, harass, harm, injure, knock about, maltreat, misuse.
illuminate *v* **1** brighten, light, light up. **2** clarify, explain, instruct, shed light on.
illuminating *adj* enlightening, helpful, informative, instructive, revealing.
illumination *n* awareness, insight, inspiration, perception, revelation, understanding.
illusion *n* **1** daydream, figment of the imagination, mirage. **2** deception, delusion, error, false impression, misconception.
illustrate *v* **1** clarify, demonstrate, explain, make clear, show. **2** decorate, depict, draw, picture, sketch.
illustration *n* **1** analogy, example. **2** decoration, picture, sketch.
illustrious *adj* celebrated, eminent, famous, prominent, renowned, splendid.
image *n* **1** effigy, figure, icon, idol, likeness, picture, portrait, reflection, representation, statue. **2** concept, figure, idea, impression, mental picture.
imaginable *adj* believable, likely, possible.
imaginary *adj* assumed, fictional, invented, made-up, unreal.
imagination *n* creativity, insight, inspiration, inventiveness, originality, vision, wit.
imaginative *adj* clever, creative, ingenious, inventive, visionary.
imagine *v* conceive, conjure up, create, devise, invent, picture, think up, visualize.
imitate *v* ape, copy, echo, mimic,

mock, simulate; (*Inf*) spoof.
imitation *n* **1** duplication, likeness, resemblance. **2** forgery, impersonation, impression, replica, reproduction.
imitation *adj* artificial, man-made, reproduction, simulated, synthetic; (*Inf*) phoney.
imitator *n* follower, mimic, parrot, shadow; (*Inf*) copycat.
immaculate *adj* **1** clean, impeccable, spick-and-span, spruce. **2** above reproach, flawless, guiltless, perfect, pure, spotless, stainless, uncontaminated.
immaterial *adj* insignificant, irrelevant, of no consequence, trivial, unimportant.
immature *adj* **1** adolescent, green, imperfect, raw, undeveloped, unripe, young. **2** babyish, childish, inexperienced, juvenile; (*Inf*) wet behind the ears.
immediate *adj* **1** instant, instantaneous. **2** adjacent, close, near, next, primary, recent.
immediately *adv* at once, now, right now, straight away, this instant, this very minute.
immense *adj* colossal, enormous, giant, gigantic, great, huge, large, mammoth, massive, monstrous, monumental, titanic, tremendous, vast.
inconsiderate *adj* insensitive, intolerant, rude, tactless, thoughtless, uncharitable, unkind, unthinking.
inconsistent *adj* **1** at odds, conflicting, contradictory, out of step. **2** changeable, erratic, fickle, irregular, unpredictable, unstable, variable.
inconspicuous *adj* camouflaged, hidden, ordinary, unassuming, unnoticeable, unobtrusive.
inconvenient *adj* awkward, tiresome, troublesome, unsuitable.
incorporate *v* absorb, amalgamate, blend, combine, fuse, integrate, merge, mix, unite.
increase *v* add to, boost, build up, develop, enlarge, expand, extend, grow, inflate, intensify, magnify, mount, multiply, proliferate, prolong, raise, snowball, spread, strengthen, swell.
increase *n* addition, augmentation, boost, expansion, extension, gain, growth, i ntensification, rise, upsurge.
incredible *adj* absurd, beyond belief, far-fetched, implausible, impossible, improbable, preposterous, unbelievable.
incurable *adj* **1** hopeless, incorrigible. **2** fatal, terminal.
indecision *n* doubt, hesitation, indecisiveness, uncertainty.
indecisive *adj* doubtful, hesitating, uncertain, undecided.
indeed *adv* absolutely, actually, certainly, doubtlessly, in fact, in point of fact, in reality, in truth, positively, really, strictly, surely, to be sure, truly, undeniably, undoubtedly.
indefinite *adj* doubtful, general, uncertain, unclear, unlimited, unsettled, vague.
independence *n* **1** freedom, home-rule, liberty, self-rule; (*Inf*) standing on one's own feet. **2** free-thinking, individualistic, liberated, unrestrained.
independent *adj* absolute, free, liberated, separate, unconnected, unconstrained, uncontrolled.
independently *adv* alone, by oneself, individually, on one's own, separately, solo, unaided.

The immense structure known as the Great Wall of China stretches for over 3640km (2150 miles) across China. Originally built to fortify the country's distant borders against rampaging hordes of invading tribesmen, it is the only human structure that can be seen from space.

An indicator to measure acidity or alkalinity

An indicator is a substance that changes colour when it comes into contact with something acid or alkali. Several materials in nature will do this, including litmus which comes from lichen. Using a range of different dyes, a universal indicator can be matched to pH numbers to show how acidic or alkali a substance is. Below 7 indicates acid, above 7 indicates alkali, exactly 7 is neutral.

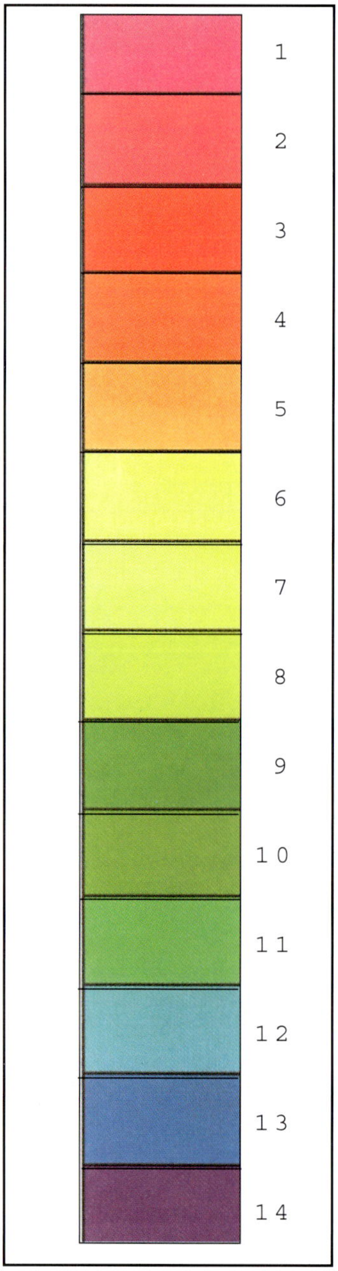

indestructible *adj* durable, enduring, everlasting, immortal, non-perishable, permanent, unbreakable.
index *n* **1** catalogue, directory, guide, key. **2** clue, hint, indication, mark, sign, symptom, token. **3** hand, indicator, needle, pointer.
indicate *v* denote, imply, point to, reveal, show, signify, suggest; (*Inf*) add up to.
indication *n* clue, evidence, explanation, hint, note, omen, sign, signal, warning.
indicator *n* display, gauge, guide, index, mark, pointer, sign, signal, signpost, symbol.
indictment *n* accusation, allegation, charge, impeachment, prosecution, summons.
indifferent *adj* **1** cold, detached, distant, uncaring, unconcerned, unsympathetic. **2** average, fair, ordinary.
indignation *n* anger, fury, rage, resentment, righteous, scorn, umbrage, wrath.
indirect *adj* long-drawn-out, meandering, roundabout, wandering, winding, zigzag.
indiscreet *adj* foolish, hasty, heedless, ill-judged, naive, rash, reckless, tactless, unwise.
indispensable *adj* crucial, essential, key, necessary, vital.
indisposed *adj* ailing, confined to bed, ill, sick, unwell; (*Inf*) laid up, poorly.
indistinct *adj* blurred, dim, faint, hazy, misty, obscure, out of focus, unclear, vague, weak.
indistinguishable *adj* alike, identical, same, twin.
individual *adj* characteristic, exclusive, identical, peculiar, separate, single, specific, unique.
individual *n* being, body, character, creature, person, soul, type.
induce *v* encourage, incite, influence, persuade, talk into.
indulge *v* cater to, give way to, satisfy, treat oneself to, yield to.
indulgence *n* **1** excess, fondness, spoiling. **2** courtesy, good will, patience, understanding.
industrious *adj* active, busy, hard-working, productive.
industry *n* business, enterprise, manufacturing, production, trade.
ineffective *adj* futile, useless, vain, worthless.
inefficient *adj* disorganized, incompetent, wasteful.
ineligible *adj* disqualified, ruled out, unacceptable, unsuitable.
inequality *n* difference, disparity, diversity, lack of balance, unevenness.
inert *adj* dead, dormant, inactive, lifeless, motionless, passive, sluggish, static, still, unmoving, unresponsive.
inevitable *adj* certain, destined, fixed, inescapable, necessary, ordained, settled, sure, unavoidable, unpreventable.
inexcusable *adj* indefensible, outrageous, unforgivable, unjustifiable, unpardonable, unwarrantable.
inexpensive *adj* bargain, budget, cheap, economical, low-cost, low-priced, modest, reasonable
inexperienced *adj* amateur,

fresh, green, immature, raw, unfamiliar, untrained, unused.
infant *n* babe, baby, child, little one, neonate, newborn child, toddler, tot.
infatuated *adj* besotted, captivated, fascinated, head over heels in love with, obsessed, spellbound, swept off one's feet, under the spell of.
infect *v* affect, blight, contaminate, corrupt, defile, poison, pollution, septicity, virus.
infectious *adj* catching, contagious, infective, spreading, transmittable, virulent.
inferior *adj* junior, lesser, lower, minor, secondary, subordinate, subsidiary, underneath.
infertile *adj* barren, sterile, unfruitful, unproductive.
infest *v* flood, invade, overrun, penetrate, swarm, throng.
infiltrate *v* creep in, filter through, penetrate, work one's way into.
infinite *adj* absolute, immense, limitless, never-ending, vast, without end.
infinity *n* boundlessness, endlessness, eternity.
infirm *adj* ailing, debilitated, decrepit, doddery, frail, weak.
inflamed *adj* angry, fevered, heated, hot, infected, red, septic, sore, swollen.
inflammable *adj* combustible, flammable, incendiary.
inflate *v* aerate, blow up, expand, increase, pump, swell.
inflation *n* enlargement, expansion, extension, increase, rise, spread, swelling.
inflexible *adj* firm, fixed, hard and fast, immovable, set.
inflict *v* administer, apply, deliver, exact, impose, levy, visit.
influence *n* **1** control, credit, direction, guidance, power, rule, weight. **2** connections, hold, importance, leverage, power, prestige, weight.
influence *v* act upon, affect, control, direct, guide, induce, lead to believe, persuade, prompt, rouse, sway.
inform *v* advise, instruct, let know, notify, send word to, teach, tell, tip off.
informal *adj* casual, familiar, natural, relaxed, simple.
information *n* advice, blurb, data, facts, instruction, material, message, news, report.
informer *n* accuser, betrayer, grass, sneak, stool pigeon.
infrequent *adj* few and far between, occasional, rare, sporadic, uncommon, unusual.

The highly inflammable fuel mixture of liquid hydrogen and oxygen gives the rocket power to escape Earth's gravity.

infringe *v* break, contravene, disobey, violate.
infuriating *adj* aggravating, annoying, exasperating, irritating, provoking.
ingenious *adj* brilliant, clever, creative, inventive, resourceful, shrewd, skilful.
ingredient *adj* component, constituent, element, part.
inhabit *v* abide, dwell, live, lodge, occupy, reside, take up residence in, tenant.
inhabited *v* colonized, held, occupied, populated, settled, tenanted.
inherit *v* accede to, be left, come into, fall heir to, succeed to.
inhibition *n* bar, check, embargo, obstacle, restriction, self-consciousness, shyness.
inhospitable *adj* **1** cool, unfriendly, unkind, unsociable, unwelcoming. **2** bare, barren, bleak, desolate, empty, forbidding, hostile, lonely, sterile, uninhabitable.
inhuman *adj* barbaric, brutal,

cold-blooded, cruel, heartless, ruthless, savage, vicious.
inhumane *adj* brutal, cruel, heartless, pitiless, uncompassionate, unfeeling, unkind, unsympathetic.
initial *adj* beginning, first, inaugural, introductory, opening, primary.
initiative *n* advantage, beginning, commencement, first move, first step, lead.
inject *v* **1** inoculate, jab, vaccinate. **2** bring in, infuse, insert, instil, interject, introduce.
injunction *n* command, instruction, mandate, order, ruling.
injure *v* abuse, blemish, blight, break, damage, disable, harm, hurt, ruin, spoil, tarnish, undermine, weaken, wound, wrong.
injustice *n* bias, discrimination, favouritism, inequality, one-sidedness, prejudice, unfairness, unjustness, unlawfulness.
inland *adj* domestic, interior, internal, upcountry.
inlet *n* bay, bight, cove, creek, entrance, ingress, loch, passage, sea.
inner *adj* central, essential, inside, interior, internal, inward, middle.
innermost *adj* basic, buried, central, deepest, intimate, personal, private, secret.
innocent *adj* **1** blameless, honest, in the clear, not guilty. **2** immaculate, pristine, pure, spotless, virgin. **3** childlike, naive, simple; (*Inf*) wet behind the ears.
innovation *n* change, departure, introduction, modernization.
inquest *n* inquiry, inquisition, investigation, probe.
inquiry *n* examination, inquest, investigation, probe, research, scrutiny, search, study, survey.
inquisition *n* cross-examination, examination, inquest, inquiry, investigation.
inquisitive *adj* curious, inquiring, intrusive, probing, prying, questioning, scrutinizing; (*Inf*) snooping.
insane *adj* crazy, demented, deranged, mad, mentally ill, out of one's mind, unhinged.
inseparable *adj* **1** conjoined, indivisible, inseverable. **2** close, devoted.
insert *n* embed, implant, place, put, stick in, tuck in, work in.
inside *n* **1** contents, inner part, interior. **2** insides belly, bowels, entrails, guts, innards, internal organs, stomach, vitals.
inside *adv* indoors, into the building, under cover, within.
inside *adj* **1** inner, innermost, interior, internal, inward. **2** classified, confidential, private, privileged, privy, secret.
insight *n* awareness, intuition, judgment, observation, perception, understanding, vision.
insignia *n/pl n* badge, crest, decoration, emblem, ensign, symbol.
insignificant *adj* immaterial, irrelevant, minor, negligible, petty, trivial, unimportant.
insincere *adj* deceitful, devious, dishonest, false, lying, untrue.
insinuation *n* hint, implication, innuendo, slur, suggestion.
insist *v* **1** be firm, demand, lay down the law, persist, stand firm, take a stand, urge. **2** assert, claim, contend, hold, maintain, repeat, swear, urge, vow.
insistent *adj* demanding, emphatic, forceful, persevering, persistent, pressing, unrelenting, urgent.
insolvent *adj* bankrupt, failed, gone bust, in receivership, in the hands of the receivers, on the rocks, ruined.

The innovation of aerial photography has made map making more accurate, but it cannot tell you the name of a street or the height of a hill. This information has still to be added by the map makers themselves, known as cartographers.

The difference between being a winner and being beaten in boxing depends not only on fast hands, but also instant reactions and split-second timing.

insomnia *n* restlessness, sleeplessness, wakefulness.
inspect *v* audit, check, examine, go over, investigate, look over, oversee, scan, scrutinize, search, supervise, survey, vet.
inspection *n* checkup, examination, investigation, scrutiny, search, survey.
inspector *n* censor, checker, critic, examiner, investigator, overseer, scrutineer, scrutinizer, superintendent, supervisor.
inspiration *n* influence, spur, stimulus.
inspire *v* be responsible for, encourage, enliven, galvanize, hearten, imbue, influence, infuse, inspirit, instil, spark off, spur, stimulate.
inspired *adj* brilliant, dazzling, enthralling, exciting, marvellous, memorable, outstanding, supreme, thrilling, wonderful.
instability *n* frailty, imbalance, unpredictability, unsteadiness, volatility, weakness.
install *v* **1** fix, lay, place, put in, set up. **2** establish, institute, introduce, set up.
installation *n* **1** inauguration, induction, investiture, ordination. **2** equipment, machinery, plant, system. **3** camp, post, station.
instalment *n* chapter, division, episode, part, portion, section.
instance *n* case, case in point, example, illustration, occasion, situation, time.
instance *v* mention, name, quote, specify.
instant *n* flash, moment, second, split second; (*Inf*) jiffy, two shakes of a lamb's tail.
instant *adj* direct, immediate, instantaneous, prompt, quick, split-second, urgent.
instantaneous *adj* direct, immediate, instant, on-the-spot.
instantly *adv* at once, directly, immediately, instantaneously, now, right away, right now, straight away, there and then, this minute, without delay.
instead *adv* alternatively, in preference to, on second thoughts, preferably.
instinct *n* aptitude, feeling, gift, intuition, natural, inclination, predisposition, sixth sense, talent, tendency, urge.
instinctive *adj* automatic, inborn, intuitive, mechanical, natural, spontaneous, unlearned, unpremeditated, unthinking.
institute *n* academy, college, conservatory, foundation, guild, institution, school, seat of learning, society.
institution *n* **1** constitution, creation, enactment, establishment, formation, foundation, initiation, introduction, investment, organization. **2** academy, college, hospital, institute, school, seminary, society, university. **3** convention, custom, law, practice, ritual, rule, tradition.
instruct *v* **1** bid, charge, command, direct, order, tell. **2** coach, discipline, drill, educate, enlighten, ground, guide, inform, school, teach.
instruction *n* coaching, education, guidance, information, schooling, teaching, training, tuition.
instructions *pl n* advice, directions, guidance, orders, recommendations, rules.
instructor *n* adviser, coach, guide, master, mentor, mistress, schoolmaster, schoolmistress, teacher, trainer, tutor.
instrument *n* apparatus, appliance, contraption, device, gadget, implement, mechanism, tool, utensil.
instrumental *adj* assisting, helpful, influential, of help.
insufficient *adj* inadequate, incapable, lacking, short, unfitted, unqualified.

A crew of up to eight people has to train for several months to become familiar with the instruments and controls of a spacecraft.

Internal combustion engine - how it works

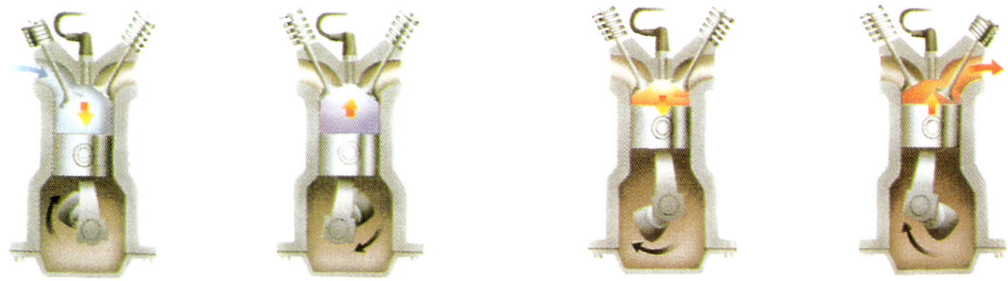

1. As the piston moves down, it sucks air and fuel into the cylinder.
2. As the piston goes up, it compresses the air and fuel mixture, causing it to heat up.
3. A spark ignites the fuel, causing the gases to expand and push the piston down.
4. As the piston rises again, exhaust gases are pushed out of the cylinder.

insulate *v* **1** close off, cocoon, cushion, cut off, isolate, protect, shield. **2** cover, encase, envelop, heatproof, pad, seal, shockproof, soundproof, wrap.
insult *n* abuse, insolence, offence, outrage, rudeness, slap in the face, slight, snub.
insult *v* abuse, call names, offend, outrage, slander, snub.
insurance *n* assurance, cover, guarantee, indemnification, indemnity, protection, provision, safeguard, security, warranty.
insure *v* cover, guarantee, indemnify, underwrite, warrant.
intact *adj* all in one piece, complete, entire, perfect, unbroken, undamaged, whole.
integral *adj* **1** basic, component, constituent, elemental, essential, fundamental, indispensable, intrinsic, necessary, requisite. **2** complete, entire, full, intact, undivided, whole.
integrate *v* accommodate, amalgamate, blend, combine, fuse, incorporate, join, knit, merge, unite.
intellectual *adj* bookish, highbrow, intelligent, studious, thoughtful.
intellectual *n* academic, highbrow, thinker.
intelligent *adj* apt, bright, clever, discerning, knowing, sharp, smart, well-informed.
intelligible *adj* clear, comprehensible, distinct, lucid, open, plain, understandable.
intend *v* aim, contemplate, determine, have in mind, mean, plan, propose, scheme.
intercept *v* arrest, block, catch, cut off, deflect, head off, interrupt, seize, stop, take.
interest *n* **1** affection, attention, attraction, curiosity, suspicion. sympathy. **2** concern, relevance, significance, weight. **3** activity, pastime, pursuit. **4** advantage, benefit, gain, good, profit.
interest *v* **1** amuse, arouse one's curiosity, attract, fascinate, hold the attention of, intrigue, touch. **2** affect, concern, engage, involve.
interesting *adj* absorbing, appealing, compelling, curious, entertaining, gripping, intriguing, stimulating, thought-provoking, unusual.
interfere *v* butt in, get involved, intermeddle, intervene, intrude, meddle, tamper.
interference *n* **1** intervention, intrusion, meddling, prying. **2** collision, conflict, obstruction, opposition.
interior *adj* **1** inner, inside, internal. **2** central, inland, remote, upcountry. **3** hidden, inner, intimate, personal, private, secret, spiritual.
interior *n* centre, heartland, upcountry.
intermediate *adj* halfway, in between, intermediary, interposed, intervening, mean, mid, middle, midway, transitional.
intermittent *adj* broken, fitful, occasional, recurring, sporadic,
internal *adj* inner, inside, interior, intimate, private.
international *adj* cosmopolitan, global, intercontinental, universal, worldwide.
interpret *v* adapt, clarify, decipher, decode, define, explain, explicate, expound, make sense of, paraphrase, read, render, solve, spell out, take, throw light on, translate, understand.
interpretation *n* **1** analysis, diagnosis, explanation, meaning,

understanding. **2** deciphering, decoding. **3** paraphrase, translation. **4** depiction, enactment, execution, presentation.
interpreter *n* annotator, commentator, exponent, performer, portrayer, transcriber, translator.
interrogation *n* cross-examination, cross-questioning, enquiry, examination, grilling, inquiry, inquisition, questioning.
interrupt *v* barge in, break, break in, break off, cut short, delay, discontinue, halt, hold up, interfere, postpone, separate, sever, stay, stop, suspend; (*Inf*) butt in on, chime in on, chip in, muscle in on.
interruption *n* break, cessation, disruption, division, halt, hitch, obstacle, obstruction, pause, severance, stoppage, suspension.
intersection *n* crossing, crossroads, interchange, junction, meeting, road junction, roundabout; (*Inf*) spaghetti junction.
interval *n* break, delay, distance, gap, hiatus, interim, interlude, intermission, interspace, meantime, meanwhile, opening, pause, period, playtime, rest, season, space, spell, term, time, wait.
intervention *n* interference, intrusion, mediation.
interview *n* audience, conference, consultation, dialogue, evaluation, meeting, oral examination, press conference, talk.
intimate *adj* **1** bosom, cherished, close, confidential, dear, friendly, innermost, near, nearest and dearest, warm. **2** confidential, personal, private, privy, secret, thorough; (*Inf*) comfy, cosy, thick. **3** friendly, informal, warm.
intimate *v* announce, declare, drop a hint, imply, indicate, inform, let it be known, make known, remind, signal, warn.
intimidation *n* bullying, fear, menaces, pressure, terror, threats; (*Inf*) arm-twisting
intrepid *adj* audacious, bold, brave, courageous, daring, dauntless, doughty, fearless, gallant, heroic, lion-hearted, nerveless, plucky, resolute, stalwart, stouthearted, unafraid, undaunted, unflinching, valiant, valourous.
intricate *adj* complicated, difficult, elaborate, fancy, involved, tangled.
intrigue *v* **1** arouse the curiosity of, attract, fascinate, interest, tickle one's fancy, titillate. **2** conspire, plot, scheme.
intriguing *adj* absorbing, compelling, exciting, fascinating, interesting, tantalizing.
introduce *v* **1** acquaint, make known, make the introduction, present. **2** begin, commence, establish, initiate, institute, launch, organize, pioneer, set up, start, usher in. **3** announce, lead into, open, preface.
introduction *n* **1** debut, launch, presentation. **2** commencement, lead-in, opening, opening remarks, overture, preface, prelude.
intruder *n* burglar, housebreaker, prowler, raider, thief, trespasser; (*Inf*) gate-crasher.
intrusion *n* infringement, interference, invasion, trespass.
intuition *n* hunch, insight, instinct, perception, sixth sense.
invade *v* assault, attack, burst in, descend upon, occupy, raid.
invader *n* aggressor, alien, attacker, looter, plunderer,

The Roman invaders left many legacies in Britain. One of the most important was the road system. The Roman Empire stretched from North Africa to Scotland and in order to govern successfully, the occupying forces had to be able to reach trouble spots quickly. Roman roads were built so that the armies could march rapidly for hundreds of miles.

raider, trespasser.
invalid *adj* ailing, bedridden, disabled, feeble, frail, ill, infirm, sickly, weak.
invalid *adj* false, ill-founded, irrational, not binding, null and void, unsound, void, worthless.
invasion *n* assault, attack, foray, incursion, offensive, raid.
invent *v* coin, come up with, conceive, contrive, create, design, devise, discover, dream up, imagine, think up; (*Inf*) cook up.
invention *n* **1** contraption, creation, device, discovery, gadget; (*Inf*) brainchild. **2** deceit, fabrication, fake, falsehood, fantasy, fiction, forgery, lie, sham, story, untruth, yarn.
inventive *adj* creative, fertile, gifted, imaginative, ingenious, innovative, inspired, original, resourceful.
inventor *n* architect, author, creator, designer, father, framer, maker, originator.
inventory *n* account, catalogue, checklist, description, file, list, record, register, roll, schedule, statement, stock book, tally.
invert *v* capsize, overturn, reverse, turn inside out, turn upside down, upset, upturn.
investigation *n* analysis, enquiry, examination, fact finding, inquest, inquiry, probe, review, search, study, survey.
investigator *n* examiner, detective, private eye, researcher, reviewer, sleuth.
investment *n* asset, investing, speculation, transaction.
invigorate *v* enliven, fortify, freshen, liven up, nerve, pep up, perk up, refresh, rejuvenate, revitalize, stimulate, strengthen.

The invention of the railway

Since George Stephenson's Rocket in 1829, trains have developed enormously. However, steam trains are still running scheduled services in some parts of the world. The steam engine in the picture above is still working every day in Sumatra.

Maglev trains in Japan run just above, not on, their tracks. Both the bottom of the train and the track itself are magnets. The magnets repel each other, so the trains hover just above the track, enabling them to run with less friction and so reach higher speeds with no sound of rattling wheels on tracks.

invincible *adj* impregnable, indestructible, indomitable, inseparable, insuperable, invulnerable, unassailable, unbeatable, unconquerable, unsurmountable, unyielding
invisible *adj* **1** out of sight, unseen. **2** concealed, disguised, hidden.
invitation *n* **1** asking, begging, call, request, summons. **2** challenge, enticement, incitement, inducement, open door, overture, provocation.
invite *v* **1** ask, beg, bid, call, request the pleasure of someone's company, solicit, summon. **2** ask for, attract, bring on, draw, encourage, entice, lead, leave the door open to, provoke, solicit, tempt, welcome.
involve *v* **1** entail, imply, mean, necessitate, require. **2** affect, associate, concern, connect, draw in, implicate, incriminate, touch. **3** absorb, bind, commit, engage, engross, grip, hold.
inward *adj* **1** entering, incoming, penetrating. **2** confidential, hidden, innermost, internal, personal, private, secret.
iron out *v* clear up, erase, get rid of, put right, resolve, settle, simplify, smooth over, sort out.
irrational *adj* absurd, crazy, foolish, illogical, injudicious, nonsensical, preposterous, silly, unreasonable, unreasoning, unsound, unthinking, unwise.
irregular *adj* **1** erratic, fluctuating, intermittent, out of order, random, variable. **2** asymmetrical, bumpy, craggy, crooked, elliptic, elliptical, jagged, lopsided, lumpy, pitted, ragged, rough, unequal, uneven, unsymmetrical.
irregular *n* guerrilla, mercenary, partisan, resistance fighter, under-ground fighter, volunteer.
irrelevant *adj* beside the point, immaterial, neither here nor there, unconnected, unrelated.
irresistible *adj* **1** compelling, overpowering, overwhelming, potent. **2** enchanting, fascinating, ravishing, tempting.
irresponsible *adj* careless, flighty, hare-brained, ill-considered, immature, reckless, thoughtless, wild.
irreversible *adj* final, incurable, irreparable.
irrigate *v* flood, inundate, moisten, water, wet.
irritable *adj* bad-tempered,

The irresistible force of a nuclear explosion produces a mushroom shaped cloud. With the development of nuclear weapons, human beings, for the first time, possessed the power to destroy the living world within seconds.

cantankerous, crabby, cross, exasperated, fiery, hasty, hot, ill-humoured, oversensitive, prickly, snappish, snappy, snarling, tense, testy, touchy.

irritate *v* **1** aggravate, annoy, bother, drive one up the wall, enrage, inflame, infuriate, offend, provoke, raise one's hackles, ruffle. **2** chafe, fret, intensify, pain, rub.

irritating *adj* annoying, disturbing, infuriating, provoking.

irritation *n* anger, annoyance, displeasure, exasperation, illhumour, ill temper, impatience, indignation, irritability, resentment, shortness, snappiness, testiness, vexation, wrath.

isolate *v* cut off, detach, disconnect, divorce, insulate, quarantine, segregate, separate, sequester, set apart.

issue *n* **1** affair, concern, matter, point, problem, question, subject, topic. **2** copy, edition, impression, installment, number, printing. **3** children, descendants, heirs, offspring, progeny.

issue *v* **1** announce, broadcast, deliver, distribute, give out, publish, put out, release. **2** flow, originate, proceed, rise, spring,.

itch *v* **1** irritate, tickle, tingle. **2** burn, crave, hanker, hunger, long, lust, pant, pine, yearn.

itch *n* **1** irritation, itchiness, prickling, tingling. **2** craving, desire, hunger, longing, lust, passion, restlessness, yearning.

item *n* **1** article, detail, entry, matter, point. **2** account, bulletin, dispatch, feature, notice, paragraph, piece, report.

itemize *v* detail, document, inventory, list, number, record, register, set out, specify, tabulate.

itinerary *n* **1** circuit, course, journey, line, programme, route, schedule, timetable, tour, travel plan. **2** daybook, diary, record.

Most normal ants cause itching and irritation when they come in contact with humans. However, stinging ants of South America produce an acid called methanoic acid (formic acid) which they use to immobilize and kill their prey.

Jj

jab *v* box, dig, elbow, lunge, poke, prod, punch, stab, thrust.
jab *n* dig, nudge, poke, prod, punch, stab.
jacket *n* case, casing, coat, covering, envelope, folder, sheath, skin, wrapper.
jackpot *n* award, bonanza, kitty, pool, prize, reward, winnings.
jaded *adj* **1** exhausted, fatigued, spent, tired-out, weary. **2** bored; (*Inf*) bushed, done in, pooped.
jagged *adj* barbed, broken, ragged, ridged, rough, serrated, snaggy, spiked.
jail, gaol *n* borstal, detention, lock up, penitentiary, prison, reformatory; (*Inf*) inside, nick.
jail, gaol *v* confine, detain, imprison, incarcerate, intern, lock up, put away, send down.
jailer, gaoler *n* captor, guard, keeper, warden, warder.
jam *v* **1** cram, crowd, crush, force, pack, press, ram, squeeze, stuff, throng, wedge. **2** block, cease, clog, congest, halt, obstruct, stall, stick.
jam *n* **1** crowd, horde, mass, mob, pack, swarm, throng. **2** dilemma, plight, predicament, quandary, scrape, trouble.
jamb *n* doorjamb, doorpost, pillar, post, upright.
jangle *v* **1** chime, clank, clash, clatter, jingle, rattle, vibrate. **2** grate on, jar on, irritate.
jangle *n* clink, rattle.
janitor *n* caretaker, concierge, custodian, doorkeeper, porter.
jar *n* carafe, container, flagon, flask, jamjar, jug, pitcher, pot, receptacle, urn, vase, vessel.
jar *v* **1** clash, disagree, interfere, oppose, quarrel. **2** agitate, disturb, grate, irritate, offend, rock, shake, vibrate. **3** annoy, grind, upset, vex. **4** conflict, be at odds, be in opposition.
jargon *n* dialect, idiom, patois, slang, tongue, usage.
jaunt *n* excursion, expedition, outing, tour, trip.
jealous *adj* envious, green, green-eyed, resentful, rival.
jealousy *n* envy, mistrust, possessiveness, resentment, spite.
jeer *v* barrack, boo, heckle, hiss, mock, ridicule, taunt, tease.
jeopardize *v* endanger, expose, hazard, menace, risk, threaten.
jerk *v* **1** bounce, bump, jolt, pull, shake, throw, thrust, tremble, tug, wrench, yank. **2** snap.
jerk *n* **1** bump, jar, start. **2** dim-wit, dope, fool, idiot, scoundrel; (*Inf*) creep, nerd.
jerry-built *adj* cheap, defective, faulty, flimsy, insubstantial, ramshackle, rickety, shoddy.
jersey *n* jumper, pullover, sweater, top; (*Inf*) woolly.
jest *n* hoax, joke, prank, wise-crack, witticism.
jest *v* jeer, joke, kid, mock, scoff, sneer, tease.
jester *n* **1** comedian, comic, humorist, joker. **2** clown, fool.
jet *n* **1** flow, fountain, gush, spout, spray, spring, stream. **2** atomizer, nose, nozzle, rose, spout, sprayer, sprinkler.
jet *v* flow, gush, issue, rush, shoot, spew, spout, squirt, stream, surge.
jettison *v* abandon, discard, dump, eject, expel, heave, scrap, throw overboard, unload.
jetty *n* breakwater, dock, groyne, pier, quay, wharf.
jewel *n* **1** gemstone, ornament, precious stone, trinket; (*Inf*) rock. **2** charm, gem, pearl, prize, rarity, treasure, wonder.
jiffy *n* flash, instant, minute, moment, split second, trice; (*Inf*) two shakes of a lamb's tail.
jingle *v* chime, clink, jangle, rattle, ring, tinkle.
jingle *n* **1** clang, clink, rattle, ringing, tinkle. **2** chorus, ditty, limerick, melody, song, tune.
jinx *n* black magic, curse, evil eye, plague, voodoo.
jinx *v* bewitch, curse.
job *n* **1** assignment, chore, duty, function, responsibility, role, stint, task, undertaking, venture, work. **2** business, calling, career, craft, employment, livelihood, occupation, position, post,

These jet planes are moving in formation, at the same speed and in the same direction, displaying the pillots skills.

profession, trade, vocation.
jog *v* **1** activate, arouse, nudge, prod, prompt, push, remind, shake, stimulate, stir, suggest. **2** canter, dogtrot, lope, run, trot. **3** plod, traipse, tramp, trudge.
join *v* **1** accompany, add, combine, connect, splice, tie, unite. **2** enlist, enroll, sign up.
joint *n* connection, hinge, junction, knot, seam, union.
joint *adj* collective, combined, communal, concerted, consolidated, cooperative, joined, mutual, shared, united.
jointly *adv* as one, collectively, in common, in conjunction, in league, in partnership, mutually, together, unitedly.
joke *n* jest, lark, play, wisecrack, witticism, yarn.
joke *v* banter, frolic, jest, mock, ridicule, taunt, tease.
jolly *adj* cheerful, funny, jovial, joyful, merry, playful.
jolt *v* **1** jar, jerk, jostle, knock, push, shake, shove. **2** astonish, disturb, perturb, startle, stun, surprise, upset.

When a parachutist jumps from a plane, their descent from high altitude, is slowed by friction caused by the enormous surface area of the parachute which allows them to land safely.

jolt *n* **1** bump, jar, jerk, jump, lurch, shake, start. **2** blow, bolt from the blue, bombshell, setback, shock, surprise.
jostle *v* bump, elbow, jog, jolt, push, shove, thrust.
journal *n* **1** chronicle, daily, gazette, magazine, monthly, newspaper, paper, periodical, record, register, review, tabloid, weekly. **2** diary, log, record.
journalist *n* broadcaster, columnist, contributor, correspondent, hack, newsman, newspaperman, pressman, reporter.
journey *n* excursion, expedition, jaunt, outing, pilgrimage, ramble, tour, trek, trip, voyage.
joy *n* delight, elation, gladness, pleasure, rapture, satisfaction.
joyful *adj* delighted, elated, glad, happy, jolly, jovial, jubilant, merry, pleased, satisfied.
judge *n* **1** arbitrator, referee, umpire. **2** assessor, evaluator, expert. **3** justice, magistrate.
judge *v* **1** adjudicate, arbitrate, decide, mediate, referee, umpire. **2** assess, consider, estimate, examine, review, value.
judgment *n* **1** commonsense, intelligence, wisdom. **2** award, conclusion, finding, ruling, sentence, verdict. **3** assessment, diagnosis, finding, opinion, valuation, view.
judicial *adj* legal, official.
jug *n* carafe, container, crock, decanter, ewer, jar, pitcher, receptacle, urn, vessel.
juggle *v* alter, change around, manipulate, rig, tamper with.
juicy *adj* **1** moist, succulent. **2** interesting, sensational, spicy, suggestive, vivid.
jumble *v* confuse, disorder, disorganize, entangle, mix, muddle, shuffle, tangle.
jumble *n* chaos, clutter, disarray, disorder, litter, mess, mishmash, mixture, muddle.
jump *v* **1** bounce, bound, caper, hop, hurdle, leap, skip, spring, vault. **2** avoid, evade, miss, omit, overshoot, skip, switch.
jump *n* **1** bound, hop, leap, skip, spring, vault. **2** advance, boost, increase, increment, rise, upsurge, upturn.
jumper *n* jersey, pullover, sweater, top.
jumpy *adj* agitated, anxious, apprehensive, fidgety, nervous, on edge, restless, shaky, tense.
junction *n* alliance, connection, coupling, joint, seam, union.
junior *adj* inferior, lesser, lower, minor, secondary, younger.
junk *n* debris, garbage, leftovers, litter, rubbish, scrap, trash.
just *adj* **1** honest, honourable, lawful, pure, right. **2** deserved, justified, rightful, well-deserved.
justice *n* **1** fairness, honesty, justness, law, right. **2** amends, compensation, penalty.
justify *v* acquit, confirm, defend, excuse, explain, legitimize, maintain, substantiate, support, sustain, uphold, validate, vindicate, warrant.
juvenile *n* adolescent, boy, child, girl, infant, minor, youth.
just *adv* **1** completely, entirely, exactly, precisely. **2** hardly, lately, only now, recently, scarcely.

Kk

kaleidoscope *adj* **1** psychedelic, variegated. **2** changeable, fluid, mobile, variable, varying.
keel *n* **1** bottom, underside. **2** boat, craft, ship, vessel.
keen *adj* **1** avid, conscientious, eager, enthusiastic, willing. **2** astute, bright, clever, sharp, smart, wise. **3** razor-sharp, sharp-edged, sharp. **4** eager to, impatient to, longing to.
keep *v* **1** hold, possess, retain. **2** accumulate, deposit, heap, pile, stack, stock, store, trade in. **3** care for, defend, guard, look after, maintain, manage, mind, protect, safeguard, watch over. **4** board, feed, nourish, nurture, provide for, support. **5** hold, honour, obey, observe, respect.
keep *n* **1** board, food, means, nourishment, support. **2** castle, citadel, donjon, dungeon, fort, inner sanctum, stronghold, tower.
keeper *n* caretaker, curator, custodian, defender, gaoler, guard, jailer, steward, warden, warder.
keepsake *n* emblem, memento, relic, remembrance, reminder, souvenir, symbol, token.
keg *n* barrel, butt, cask, container, drum, firkin, hogshead, tun, vessel.
kernel *n* **1** germ, grain, seed, stone. **2** centre, core, essence, gist, heart, nucleus.
key *n* **1** latchkey, opener, passkey, skeleton key. **2** answer, clue, explanation, guide, pointer, solution. **3** pitch tone. **4** mood, spirit, style, tone.
key *adj* basic, crucial, decisive, essential, fundamental, major, pivotal, principal.
keynote *n* centre, core, essence, gist, heart, nucleus, theme.
keystone *n* **1** cornerstone. **2** basis, foundation, linchpin, principle.
kibosh *v* bring to an end, check, crack down on, curb, nip in the bud, quash, quell, suppress.
kick *v* **1** boot, punt. **2** recoil, spring back. **3** abandon, give up, quit, stop. **4** object, oppose, rebel, resist; (*Inf*) beef about, gripoe about. **5 kick around** debate, discuss, talk over, thrash out. **6 kick off** begin, commence, get underway, initiate, start, start the ball rolling. **7 kick out** dismiss, eject, evict, expel, force out, throw out; (*Inf*) fire, sack, send packing, throw out on one's ear.
kick *n* **1** boot, punt. **2** force, intensity, power, punch, strength, zest, zip. **3** energy, enthusiasm, force, vigour.
kick-off *n* beginning,

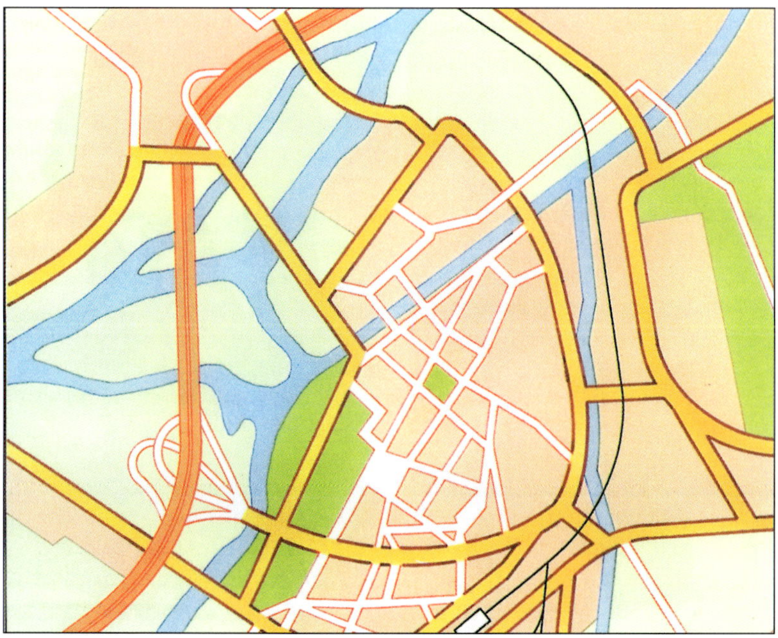

What is a Key?

A map must be as easy to read as possible, which means that symbols and colours can often give more information. A key explains what the symbols and colours mean, as the one below does for the map on the left.

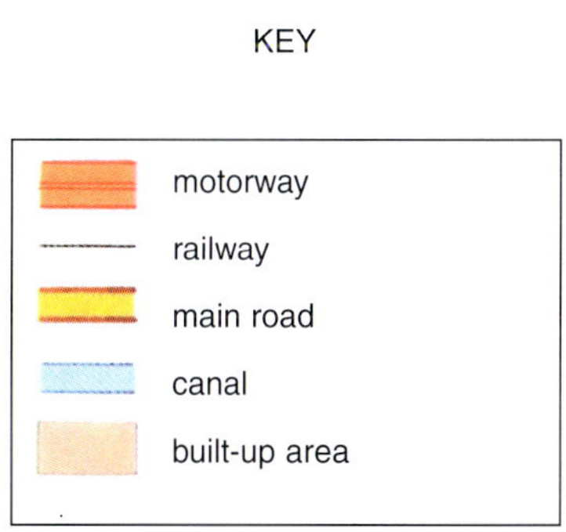

commencement, initiation, opening, start.
kid *n* baby, bairn, boy, child, girl, infant, lad, little one, teenager, tot, young person, youngster, youth.
kid *v* bamboozle, beguile, cozen, delude, fool, hoax, hoodwink, jest, joke, mock, plague, pretend, ridicule, tease, trick.
kidnap *v* abduct, capture, hijack, hold to ransom, seize, steal.
kill *v* **1** annihilate, assassinate, butcher, destroy, execute, exterminate, massacre, murder, slaughter. **2** cancel, deaden, extinguish, quash, quell, scotch, smother, stifle, stop, suppress.
killer *n* assassin, butcher, executioner, gunman, hangman, murderer, poisoner, strangler.
killing *n* bloodshed, execution, homicide, manslaughter, massacre, murder, slaughter.
killjoy *n* spoilsport; (*Inf*) party-pooper, wet blanket.
kilter *n* condition, fitness, order, shapoe, state, working order.
kin *n* blood, connection, lineage, relationship, stock.
kind *n* brand, breed, class, family, race, species, variety.
kind *adj* affectionate, charitable, compassionate, considerate, courteous, friendly, generous, gentle, kind-hearted, loving, neighbourly, obliging, sympathetic, thoughtful, understanding.
kindle *v* **1** fire, ignite, inflame, light, set fire to, torch. **2** arouse, awaken, incite, inspire, provoke, stimulate, stir.
kindly *adj* beneficial, gentle, good-natured, hearty, helpful, kind, mild, pleasant, polite, sympathetic, warm.

In the past, wealthy people could pay for an artist to paint pictures of themselves. Before photography, we could only see a mirror image of ourselves in a mirror. Today, most people have family photographs taken so that we can see ourselves as others see us.

kindly *adv* agreeably, cordially, graciously, politely, tenderly, thoughtfully.
kindred *n* family, kin, people, relations, relatives.
kindred *adj* **1** connected, related. **2** corresponding, matching, resembling, similar.
king *n* crowned head, emperor, majesty, monarch, prince, ruler, sovereign.
kingdom *n* **1** dominion, dynasty, empire, monarchy, realm, reign, sovereignty. **2** commonwealth, county, division, nation, province, state, territory, tract.
kink *n* **1** bend, coil, corkscrew, knot, tangle, twist, wrinkle. **2** eccentricity, quirk, whim.
kiosk *n* bookstall, booth, counter, news-stand, refreshments kiosk, stall, stand, telephone kiosk.
kismet *n* destiny, fate, fortune, God's will, one's lot, the writing on the wall, what is to come.
kiss *n* greetings with the lips, hand kiss; (*Inf*) canoodle, neck, peck, smacker, smooch, snog.
kit *n* apparatus, equipment, gear, instruments, outfit, provisions, rig, supplies, tackle, tools, trappings, utensils.
kit *v* arm, accoutre, deck out, equip, fit out, fix up, furnish, outfit, provide, supply.
kitchen *n* bakehouse, cook-house, galley, scullery.
knack *n* ability, aptitude, expertise, flair, gift, ingenuity, skill, talent.
knead *v* form, manipulate, massage, press, rub, shape, squeeze, work.
kneel *v* bow, curtsy, get down on one's knees, kowtow, stoop.
knell *v* announce, chime, herald, peal, ring, sound, toll.
knickers *pl n* briefs, cami-knickers, Directoire knickers, drawers, lingerie, pants, smalls, underwear.
knick-knack *n* bauble, bric-à-brac, ornament, trinket.
knife *n* blade, carving knife,

chopper, cutter, cutting tool, dagger, flick-knife, penknife, sheath knife, Stanley knife.
knife *v* bayonet, cut, lacerate, pierce, run through, slash, stab.
knit *v* **1** bind, connect, crochet, draw together, fasten, gather in, heal, interlace, intertwine, join, link, loop, mend, secure, tie, unite, weave. **2** make, purl, sew, stitch, weave.
knit *n* cardigan, jersey, pullover, sweater; (*Inf*) cardi, wooly.
knock *v* **1** cuff, hit, punch, rap, slap, smack, strike, tap, thump, thwack; (*Inf*) clip, clout, whack. **2** bang, crash, jolt, smash, thud. **3** censure, condemnation, criticism, fault-finding; (*Inf*) panning, lambasting. **4** failure, rejection, reversal, set-back.
knock *n* **1** blow, box, clip, clout, cuff, hammering, punch, rap, slap, smack, thump. **2** censure, condemnation, criticism. **3** bad luck, defeat, failure, misfortune, rejection, set-back.
knock around *v* abuse, beat up, hit, mistreat, punch.
knock down *v* demolish, level, pull down, raze.
knock into *v* bump into, collide with, crash into, dash against, run into.
knock off *v* **1** clock off, close shop, finish work, shut down. **2** kill, murder; (*Inf*) bump off, do in, top. **3** pilfer, rob, steal, thieve.
knock out *v* **1** floor, render unconscious; (*Inf*) kayo, KO. **2** defeat, eliminate, overthrow.
knock up *v* **1** build rapidly, put together quickly. **2** achieve, attain; (*Inf*) clock up. **3** have a practice game, hit a ball around, warm up.
knoll *n* barrow, hill, hillock, hummock, hump, mound.
knot *v* bind, entangle, knit, lash, loop, secure, tether, tie.
knot *n* **1** bow, braid, connection, joint, ligature, loop, rosette, tie, twist. **2** gnarl, lump, node, nodule, protuberance.
know *v* **1** comprehend, experience, fathom, feel certain, learn, notice, perceive, realize, recognize, see, undergo, understand. **2** associate with, be familiar with, fraternize with, recognize. **3** distinguish, identify, make out, recognize, see, tell.
knowing *adj* astute, clever, competent, discerning, experienced, expert, intelligent, qualified, skilful, well-informed.
know-how *n* aptitude, capability, knack, skill, talent.
knowing *adj* clever, expert, qualified, skilful, well informed.
knowledge *n* **1** education, instruction, intelligence, schooling, wisdom. **2** ability, grasp, judgment, understanding.
knowledgeable *adj* aware, conscious, familiar, understanding, well-informed; (*Inf*) in the know.
known *adj* acknowledged, familiar, famous, noted, popular, recognized, well-known.

What is the difference between knitting and weaving?

Both knitting and weaving are methods of making threads into cloth, but knitting involves looping one long thread together, while weaving usually involves passing threads lying in one direction over and under threads lying at right angles to them.

Threads in woven fabrics can be criss-crossed in hundreds of different ways to add texture to the cloth.

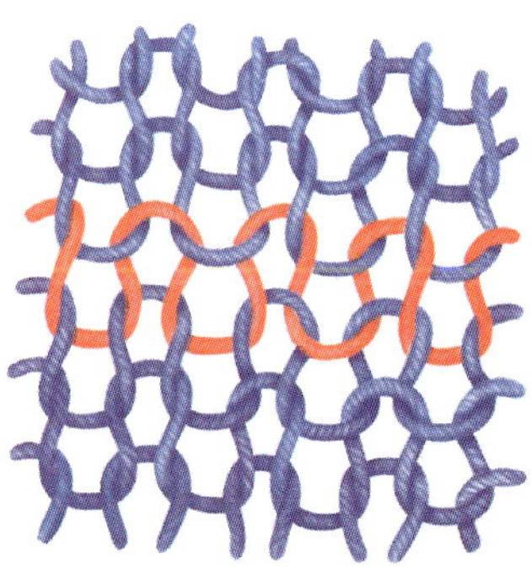

It is not only woollen jumpers that are knitted. The fabric that T-shirts are made from is knitted cotton.

Ll

label *n* **1** docket, sticker, tag, tally, ticket. **2** brand, company, mark, trademark.
label *v* **1** docket, mark, stamp, sticker, tag, tally. **2** brand, call, characterize, classify, define, describe, identify, name.
laborious *adj* **1** difficult, hard, heavy, strenuous, tedious. **2** careful, diligent, meticulous, painstaking, scrupulous.
labour *n* **1** industry, toil, work. **2** employees, hands, labourers, workers, work force, workmen. **3** donkey-work, drudgery, effort, exertion, toil. **4** childbirth, contractions, delivery, labour pains, pains.
labour *v* dwell on, elaborate, overdo, strain.
laboured *adj* difficult, forced, heavy, strained.
labourer *n* blue-collar worker, manual worker, unskilled worker, working man, workman.
labyrinth *n* **1** jungle, maze, network, warren. **2** problem, puzzle, tangle.
lace *n* **1** filigree, meshwork, netting, tatting. **2** bootlace, cord, shoelace, string, thing, tie, twine.
lace *v* **1** close, do up, fasten, secure, thread. **2** compress, confine, constrict, squeeze. **3** band streak, striate, stripe. **4** blend, flavour, fortify, stiffen, strengthen; (*Inf*) spike.

The most widely spoken languauge of all, Mandarin Chinese, does not use an alphabet. Instead, it has over 50,000 characters, each representing a word or part of a word.

lacerate *v* **1** claw, cut, cut open, gash, hurt, maim, mangle, mutilate, rend, rip, slash, tear, wound. **2** afflict, crucify, distress, hurt, torture, wound.
lack *n* absence, deficiency, need, shortage, want.
lack *v* be deficient in, be lacking in, be short of, be without, miss, need, require, want.
lacking *adj* defective, deficient, flawed, impaired, inadequate, missing, needing, without.
lacklustre *adj* boring, drab, dull, lifeless, unimaginative.
laden *adj* burdened, full, heavily-laden, loaded, oppressed, taxed, weighed down.
lag *v* be behind, dawdle, delay, drag one's feet, linger, loiter, saunter, straggle, trail.
laid-back *adj* easy-going, free and easy, relaxed, unhurried.
laid-up *adj* bedridden, disabled, housebound, immobilized, incapacitated, out of action, sick.
lair *n* **1** cave, hollow, tunnel. **2** den, hide-away, refuge, retreat, sanctuary, snug, study.
lame *adj* **1** crippled, disabled, handicapped, hobbling. **2** feeble, flimsy, inadequate, insufficient, poor, thin, unconvincing, weak.
land *n* **1** dry land, earth, ground, terra-firma. **2** dirt, ground, loam, soil. **3** acres, estate, grounds, property. **4** country, district, fatherland, motherland, nation, province, region, territory.
land *v* arrive, berth, disembark, dock, touch down.
landlord *n* host, hotelier, hotel-keeper, innkeeper.
landmark *n* **1** feature, monument. **2** crisis, milestone, turning point, water-shed.
landscape *n* countryside, outlook, panorama, prospect, scene, scenery, view, vista.
language *n* **1** communication, conversation, speech, talk, words. **2** dialect, jargon, native tongue, patter, speech, tongue. **3** diction, expression, phrasing, style, wording. **4** rhetoric, style, terminology, wording.
lap *n* **1** knee, knees. **2** comfort, protection, refuge. **3** circle, circuit, course, distance, loop, orbit, round, tour.
lap *v* **1** cover, envelop, fold, turn, twist, wind, wrap. **2** beat, splash, wash. **3** drink up, sip.

lapse *n* error, fault, mistake, omission, oversight, slip.
lapse *v* **1** decline, degenerate, deteriorate, drop, fail, fall, sink, slide, slip. **2** become obsolete, become void, end, expire, run out, stop, terminate.
larder *n* cooler, pantry, scullery, still-room, store-room.
large *adj* **1** big, bulky, colossal, enormous, giant, gigantic, great, high, huge, immense, massive, monumental, stupendous, vast; (*Inf*) jumbo, whopping. **2** ample, hefty, heavy-set, thick-set. **3** abundant, broad, capacious, comprehensive, copious, corpulent, extensive, full, generous, grand, roomy, spacious, wide. **4** far-reaching, wide-ranging.
lark *n* antic, caper, escapade, game, prank, revel, romp.
lash *n* blow, bullwhip, cat-o'-nine-tails, hit, horsewhip, stripe, stroke, swipe, whip.
lash *v* **1** beat, birch, chastise, flog, hammer, scourge, strike, thrash, whip. **2** buffet, dash, hit, knock, pound, smack. **3** berate, castigate, condemn, criticize, scold; (*Inf*) lambaste, pitch into. **4** bind, fasten, make fast, secure, strap, tether, tie.
last *adj* **1** at the end, hindmost, rearmost. **2** latest, most recent. **3** closing, final, ultimate.
last *adv* after, behind, bringing up the rear, in the end.
last *v* abide, carry on, continue, endure, hold on, hold out, keep, keep on, persist, remain, stand up, survive, wear.
lasting *adj* abiding, continuing, durable, enduring, indelible, life-long, long-standing, long-term, permanent, unending.
latch *n* bar, bolt, catch, clamp, fastening, hasp, hook, lock.
late *adj* **1** behind, belated, delayed, last-minute, overdue, slow. **2** advanced, fresh, modern, new, recent. **3** dead, deceased, departed, ex-, former, old, past, preceding, previous.
later *adv* after, afterwards, in a while, in time, later on, next, subsequently, thereafter.
latest *adj* current, fashionable, in, modern, most recent, newest, now, up-to-date, up-to-the-minute; (*Inf*) with it.
lather *n* bubbles, foam, froth, soap, soapsuds, suds.
latitude *n* **1** breadth, extent, range, space, span, spread, sweep, width. **2** elbow-room, freedom, liberty.
lattice *n* fretwork, grating, grille, latticework, mesh, trellis, web.
laugh *v* **1** be in stitches, chuckle, giggle, snigger, split one's sides. **2 laugh at** belittle, deride, jeer, make fun of, mock, ridicule, taunt; (*Inf*) take the mickey out of.
laugh *n* chortle, chuckle, giggle, roar, snigger, titter; (*Inf*) belly laugh.
launch *v* **1** cast, dispatch, fire, project, propel, send off, throw. **2** begin, commence, initiate, instigate, introduce, open, start.
lavish *adj* **1** abundant, profuse, prolific, sumptuous. **2** generous, liberal.
law *n* **1** charter, code, constitution. **2** act, code, command, decree, edict, order, rule, statute.
law-abiding *adj* dutiful, good, honest, lawful, obedient, orderly, peaceful.
lawsuit *n* action, argument, case, dispute, litigation, proceedings, prosecution, suit, trial.
lawyer *n* advocate, attorney, barrister, counsel, counsellor, legal adviser, solicitor.
lax *adj* careless, casual, easy-going, lenient, negligent, remiss, slack, slipshod.
lay *v* **1** deposit, leave, place, put, set down, spread. **2** arrange,

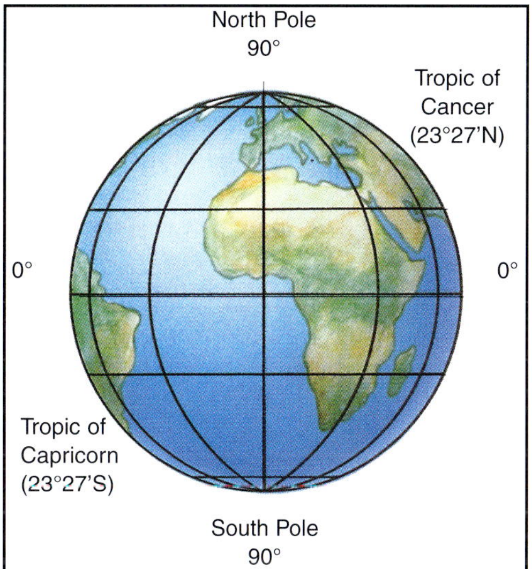

How are latitude and longitude measured?

We cover the Earth with a grid of imaginary lines, measured in degrees. Lines of longitude run North to South, while lines of latitude run East to West. The line of longitude running through Greenwich, England, is taken as 0° and lines on either side of it are so many degrees East or West. The line of latitude that is counted as 0° runs around the equator.

locate, position, set out. **3** bear, deposit, produce. **4** allocate, assign. **5** concoct, contrive, design, devise, hatch, plan, plot, prepare, work out. **6** bet, gamble, hazard, risk, stake, wager.

layer *n* bed, ply, row, seam, stratum, thickness, tier.

lay-off *n* discharge, dismissal, drop, let go, make redundant, pay off, unemployment.

lay on *v* cater, furnish, give, provide, supply.

layout *n* arrangement, design, draft, formation, geography, outline, plan.

lay out *v* arrange, design, display, exhibit, plan, spread out.

lazy *adj* **1** idle, inactive, slack, slow, workshy. **2** drowsy, lethargic, sleepy, sluggish,

lead *v* **1** conduct, escort, guide, pilot, show the way, steer, usher. **2** induce, influence, persuade, prompt. **3** command, direct, govern, head, manage, preside over, supervise. **4** be ahead, come first, excel, outdo, outstrip, surpass. **5** experience, have, live, pass, spend, undergo.

lead *n* **1** advance, cutting edge, first place, margin, priority, start. **2** direction, guidance, leader-ship, model. **3** clue, guide, hint, suggestion, tip. **4** leading role, principal, star part, title role.

leader *n* boss, captain, chief, chieftain, commander, conductor, director, guide, head, principal, ringleader, ruler, superior.

leadership *n* **1** administration, direction, directorship, guidance, management, running. **2** authority, control, influence, sway.

leaf *n* **1** blade, bract, flag, frond, needle, pad. **2** folio, page, sheet.

leaflet *n* booklet, brochure, circular, mailshot, pamphlet.

league *n* alliance, association, coalition, confederation, consortium, federation, fellowship, group, guild, union.

leak *n* **1** aperture, crack, crevice, cut, fissure, gash, hole, opening, puncture, slit. **2** drip, escape, leakage, oozing, seepage. **3** disclosure, divulgence.

leak *v* **1** drip, escape, ooze, seep, spill, trickle. **2** disclose, divulge, give away, let slip, let the cat out of the bag, make known, make public, pass on, reveal, tell; (*Inf*) spill the beans.

lean *v* **1** be supported, prop, recline, repose, rest. **2** bend, incline, slant, slope, tilt, tip.

lean *adj* **1** angular, bony, lank, scrawny, skinny, thin, wiry. **2** bare, meagre, pitiful, poor, scanty, sparse.

leap *v* **1** bound, frisk, hop, jump, skip, spring, vault. **2** hasten, hurry, hurtle. **3** escalate, mount, rise up, rocket, soar.

learn *v* **1** acquire, attain, grasp, master, pick up. **2** commit to memory, get off pat, learn by heart, memorize, word-perfect. **3** determine, find out, gain, gather, hear, understand.

learner *n* **1** apprentice, beginner, novice. **2** disciple, pupil, student.

leave *v* **1** abandon, desert, go away, move, pull out, quit, retire, withdraw. **2** abandon, desert, evacuate, surrender. **3** commit, consign, entrust, give over. **4** bequeath, hand down, transmit, will.

leave *n* **1** allowance, consent, permission, sanction. **2** holiday, leave of absence, sabbatical, time off, vacation.

lecture *v* **1** address, speak, talk, teach. **2** censure, reprimand, scold; (*Inf*) tell off.

lecture *n* censure, dressing-down, reprimand, scolding.

leech *n* barnacle, bloodsucker, parasite, sponger.

Leeches attach themselves to animals and suck their blood. Scientists are looking at the leech's ability to produce a chemical which stops blood from clotting, to see how this could help human beings.

How do levers work?

There are three different kinds of lever, depending on where the force applied and the load are in relation to each other. A lever is a rod that can turn on a pivot, or fulcrum.

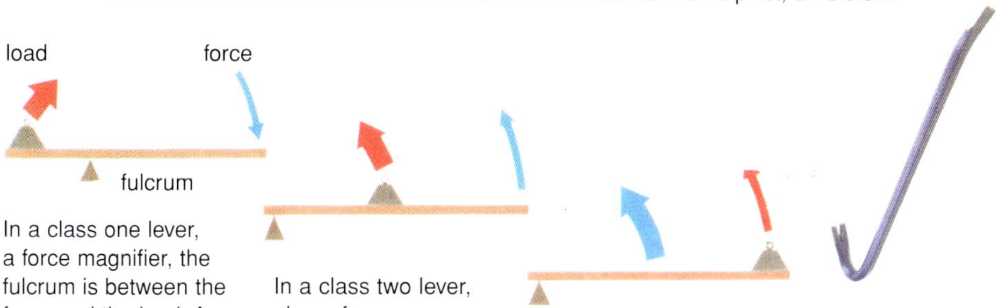

In a class one lever, a force magnifier, the fulcrum is between the force and the load. A crowbar is an example of such a lever.

In a class two lever, also a force magnifier, the load is between the effort and the fulcrum. Nutcrackers are class two levers.

A class three lever is a distance magnifier. It has the force between the fulcrum and the load. Tweezers are class three levers.

The further from the fulcrum the force is applied, the larger the load that can be moved, which is why a crowbar has a long handle.

legacy *n* **1** bequest, estate, gift, inheritance. **2** birthright, endowment, heritage, throwback.
legalize *v* allow, approve, authorize, license, permit.
legend *n* **1** fable, fiction, myth, narrative, saga, story. **2** caption, device, inscription, motto.
legendary *adj* fabled, famous, mythical, romantic, traditional.
legible *adj* clear, decipherable, distinct, easily read, easy to read, neat, plain, readable.
legion *n* army, brigade, company, division, force, troop.
legislate *v* constitute, establish, make laws, ordain, pass laws, prescribe, put in force.
legislation *n* **1** lawmaking, regulation. **2** act, bill, charter, law, regulation, ruling, statute.
legitimate *adj* authentic, genuine, legal, proper, rightful, statutory, true.
lend *v* **1** advance, loan. **2** afford, give, grant, present, provide, supply.
length *n* **1** distance, extent, longitude, measure, reach, span. **2** duration, period, space, stretch, term.
lengthen *v* continue, draw out, extend, increase, make longer, prolong, spin out, stretch.
lenient *adj* compassionate, forgiving, kind, merciful, tolerant.
less *adj* **1** shorter, smaller. **2** inferior, minor, secondary.
less *adv* barely, little.
lessen *v* decrease, diminish, dwindle, ease, grow less, lower, reduce, shrink.
lesson *n* **1** class, coaching, instruction, period, schooling, teaching, tutoring. **2** deterrent, example, message, moral.
let *v* **1** allow, authorize, give permission, permit, sanction. **2** hire, lease, rent.
let-down *n* disappoint, fail, fall short, leave stranded.
lethal *adj* dangerous, deadly, fatal, poisonous.
lethargic *adj* apathetic, drowsy, , indifferent, lazy, slow.
let in *v* admit, allow to enter, greet, receive, take in, welcome.
let off *v* **1** detonate, discharge, emit, explode, exude, fire, give off, leak, release. **2** absolve, discharge, excuse, exempt, forgive, pardon, release, spare.
let out *v* **1** emit, produce. **2** free, let go, liberate, release. **3** disclose, leak, let slip, make known, reveal.
level *adj* **1** even, flat, horizontal, plain, plane, regular, smooth, uniform. **2** aligned, balanced, even, flush, in line, neck and neck, on a par. **3** constant, even, stable, steady.
level *v* **1** even off, flatten, make flat, plane, smooth. **2** demolish, destroy, knock down, pull down, raze, tear down, wreck.
level *n* **1** altitude, height. **2** floor, layer, storey, zone.
level-headed *adj* balanced, calm, composed, cool, reasonable, sane, sensible, steady, together; (*Inf*) unflappable.
lever *n* bar, crowbar, handle, handspike, jemmy.
lever *v* force, jemmy, move,

prise, pry, purchase, raise.
levy *v* charge, collect, demand, gather, impose, tax.
levy *n* collection, gathering.
liable *adj* **1** accountable, answerable, bound, responsible. **2** susceptible, vulnerable. **3** inclined, likely, prone.
liaison *n* **1** contact, go-between, intermediary. **2** affair, love affair, romance.
libel *n* slander, smear.
libel *v* blacken, drag someone's name through the mud, malign, slander, slur, smear.
liberal *adj* **1** advanced, radical, reformist. **2** charitable, free-handed, generous, kind, open-hearted, unstinting. **3** ample, bountiful, handsome, lavish, plentiful, profuse, rich.
liberate *v* deliver, emancipate, free, let loose, release, set free.
liberty *n* **1** freedom, independence, liberation, release, self-determination, sovereignty. **2** carte blanche, freedom, leave, permission, privilege, right.
licence *n* **1** authorization, carte blanche, certificate, entitlement, leave, permission, permit, privilege, right. **2** abandon, anarchy, disorder, excess, indulgence, lawlessness, unruliness. **3** freedom, option.
license *v* allow, authorize, permit, sanction, warrant.
lick *v* brush, lap, taste, tongue, touch, wash.
lie *v* falsify, fib, tell a lie.
lie *n* deceit, fib, invention, untruth, white lie.
lie *v* **1** couch, loll, lounge, recline, rest, sprawl, stretch out. **2** be buried, be found, belong, be placed, exist, remain.
life *n* **1** breath, growth, viability.

Does light always move in a straight line?

Beams of light do travel in straight lines, but lines can be deflected. Light travels at varying speeds in different substances. When the light passes from one substance to another, its beam bends. This is called refraction.

2 course, duration, time. **3** human being, individual, person, soul. **4** autobiography, biography, career, confessions, history, life story, memoirs, story. **5** behaviour, conduct, lifestyle. **6** activity, energy, sparkle, spirit, vitality, zest; (*Inf*) get-up-and-go, go, oomph.
lifeless *adj* cold, dead, dead to the world, out cold, out for six, unconscious.
lifelike *adj* authentic, faithful, realistic, true-to-life, vivid.
lifelong *adj* constant, enduring, for life, lifetime, long-lasting, perennial, permanent, persistent.
lift *v* **1** elevate, hoist, pick up, raise, rear, uplift. **2** climb, disperse, mount, rise, vanish.
lift *n* **1** car ride, drive, ride, run, transport. **2** boost, pick-me-up, reassurance; (*Inf*) shot in the arm.
light *n* **1** brightness, brilliance, flash, glare, glow, illumination, radiance, shine, sparkle. **2** beacon, bulb, candle, flare, lamp, lantern, lighthouse, taper, torch. **3** dawn, daybreak, daylight, daytime, morning, sun, sunrise, sunshine. **4** example, guiding light, model, shining example. **5** flame, lighter, match. **6 bring to light** discover, expose, reveal, show, uncover, unearth, unveil. **7 come to light** appear, be disclosed, be discovered, be revealed, come out, transpire, turn up. **8 in the light of** bearing in mind, because of, considering, in view of, taking into account.
light *adj* **1** bright, brilliant, glowing, luminous, shining, sunny, well-lit. **2** bleached, blond, fair, pale, pastel. **3** delicate, flimsy, lightweight, portable, soft, weak. **4** minute, scanty, small, thin, tiny, trivial, wee. **5** easy, effortless, simple; (*Inf*) cushy. **6** agile, graceful, nimble. **7** amusing, entertaining, funny, witty. **8** carefree, cheery, merry, sunny. **9** digestible, modest, not heavy, restricted, small.
light *v* **1** fire, ignite, kindle, set a match to. **2** brighten, floodlight, flood with light, illuminate, light up, switch on, turn on. **3** brighten, cheer.
lighten *v* **1** brighten, illuminate, light up, shine. **2** reduce in weight, unload. **3** ease, lessen, reduce, relieve.
light-headed *adj* giddy, silly, superficial; (*Inf*) bird-brained.
light-hearted *adj* carefree, cheerful, happy-go-lucky, jolly, joyful, merry; (*Inf*) upbeat.
lightweight *adj* insignificant, petty, slight, trivial, worthless.
like *adj* alike, corresponding, resembling, similar.
like *v* **1** be fond of, be keen on,

be partial to, delight in, enjoy, love, relish, revel in; (*Inf*) adore. **2** admire, appreciate, approve, prize; (*Inf*) take a shine to.
likely *adj* anticipated, expected, on the cards, possible, probable, to be expected.
likely *adv* in all probability, no doubt, probably; (*Inf*) like as not.
liken *n* compare, equate, juxtapose, match, parallel, relate, set beside.
likeness *n* **1** resemblance, similarity. **2** copy, image, model, photograph, picture, portrait, replica, representation, study.
limelight *n* attention, fame, public eye, publicity, recognition, stardom, in the spotlight.
limit *n* **1** bound, cutoff point, deadline, end, furthest point, **2** border, boundary, edge, perimeter, periphery. **3** ceiling, limitation, maximum, restriction.
limit *v* confine, curb, fix, hem in, hinder, restrict.
limitless *adj* countless, endless, infinite, unlimited, vast.
limp *v* hobble, shuffle.
line *n* **1** band, mark, rule, stripe, **2** crease, furrow, mark, wrinkle. **3** border, boundary, edge, limit. **4** contour, figure, outline, profile, silhouette. **5** cable, cord, rope, string, thread, wire. **6** course, direction, path, route, track. **7** approach, course of action, policy, position, procedure, scheme, system. **8** activity, area, business, calling, department, employment, field, job, profession, trade. **9** column, queue, row, series. **10** family, race, stock, strain. **11** card, letter, message, note, postcard, report, word. **12** draw the line, lay down the law, object, prohibit, put one's foot down, restrict.
line *v* **1** crease, draw, inscribe, mark, rule, score, trace. **2** border, edge, fringe, rim, skirt, verge.
line-up *n* arrangement, array, row, selection, team.
line up *v* **1** fall in, form ranks, queue up. **2** assemble, organize, prepare, produce, secure.
linger *v* **1** hang around, loiter, remain, stay, wait. **2** continue, endure, persist.
link *n* **1** division, member, part, piece. **2** association, connection, relationship, tie.
link *v* **1** attach, connect, couple, fasten, join, tie. **2** associate, bracket, connect, identify, relate.
liquid *n* fluid, juice, solution.
liquid *adj* fluid, melted, molten, runny, thawed.
liquidate *v* **1** pay off, settle, square. **2** abolish, annul, cancel, dissolve, terminate. **3** convert to cash, realize, sell off, sell up. **4** destroy, eliminate, exterminate, finish off, get rid of, kill, murder, remove, silence; (*Inf*) blow away, bump off, do in, wipe out.
list *n* **1** catalogue, directory, file, index, inventory, invoice, listing, record, register, roll, schedule, series, syllabus, tabulation, tally. **2** cant, leaning, slant, tilt.
list *v* **1** catalogue, enter, file, index, note, prepare. **2** incline, lean, tilt, tip.
listen *v* **1** be all ears, be attentive, hang on someone's words, hear, lend an ear; (*Inf*) pin back one's ears, prick up one's ears. **2** concentrate, do as one is told, pay attention, take notice.
literate *adj* cultivated, cultured, educated, learned, lettered, scholarly, well-read.

How are races on a circular track made fair?

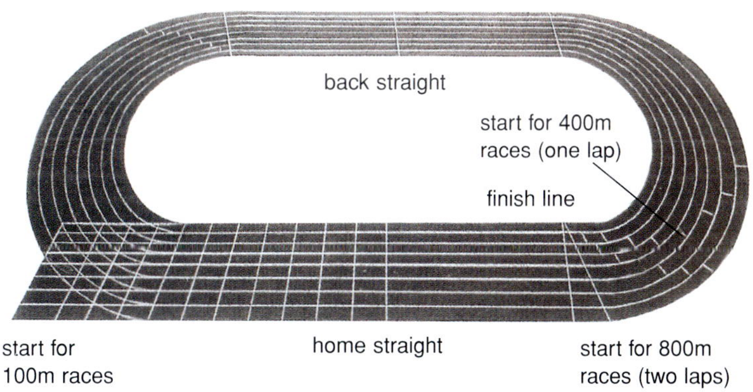

In order to ensure that everyone runs the same distance, the start is staggered, so that those on the inside appear to start much further back than those on the outside. Not until the final straight is it is really possible to see who is winning. Longer races often start from a simple curved line. Atheletes break out of their lanes quickly and each runs to the inside of the track as quickly as possible.

litigation *n* action, case, contending, disputing, lawsuit, process, prosecution.
litter *n* **1** debris, fragments, garbage, muck, refuse, rubbish, shreds. **2** clutter, disarray, mess, untidiness. **3** family, offspring, progeny, young. **4** bedding, couch, floor cover, mulch, straw bed. **5** stretcher.
litter *v* clutter, disorder, mess up, scatter, strew.
little *adj* **1** dwarf, mini, miniature, minute, petite, pygmy, short, small, tiny, wee. **2** babyish, immature, infant, junior, young. **3** hardly any, insufficient, meagre, scant, skimpy, sparse. **4** brief, fleeting, insignificant, negligible.
little *adv* **1** barely, hardly, not much, not quite, only just. **2** hardly ever, not often, rarely, scarcely, seldom.
live *v* **1** breathe, exist, have life. **2** be permanent, be remembered, last, persist, prevail, remain alive. **3** earn a living, endure, make ends meet, pass, remain, subsist, support oneself, survive. **4 live in** dwell, inhabit, lodge, occupy.
live *adj* **1** alive, breathing, living. **2** active, burning, current, hot, topical, vital. **3** brisk, dynamic, energetic, lively, wide-awake.
livelihood *n* employment, income, job, occupation, work.
lively *adj* **1** active, agile, alert, brisk, energetic, keen, nimble, perky, quick; (*Inf*) full of beans, full of pep. **2** cheerful, frisky. **3** busy, buzzing, crowded. **4** colourful, exciting, vivid.
livid *adj* **1** angry, fuming, furious, incensed, infuriated, outraged; (*Inf*) mad. **2** bruised, contused, discoloured, purple. **3** ashen, greyish, pale, pasty.
living *adj* active, alive, animated, breathing, existing, lively, strong, vigorous, vital; (*Inf*) in the land of the living.
living *n* **1** existing, life. **2** job, livelihood, occupation, work.
load *n* **1** bale, cargo, consignment, freight, lading, shipment. **2** burden, millstone, weight.

Ships transport over 90% of the freight that travels around the globe. Air travel is faster but more expensive and weight is always a problem. Although ships may be slower than aircraft, they can carry enormous loads. The loads are carried in steel containers, which can be stacked on the ship and then lifted by crane directly onto the back of a truck in the port.

load *v* **1** cram, fill, heap, pack, stack, stuff. **2** burden, weigh down. **3** make ready, prepare to fire, prime.
loaded *adj* **1** full, laden. **2** at the ready, charged, primed, ready to shoot. **3** rich, wealthy, well-off; (*Inf*) flush, rolling, well-heeled.
loathing *n* disgust, horror, revulsion.
lobby *n* corridor, entrance hall, foyer, hall, hallway, passage, passageway, porch, vestibule; pressure group.
lobby *v* campaign for, exert influence, persuade, press for, pressure, promote, push for; (*Inf*) pull strings.
local *adj* **1** community, district, neighbourhood, parish, regional. **2** confined, limited, narrow, provincial, small-town.
local *n* inhabitant, native, resident; (*Inf*) neighbourhood pub.
locate *v* come across, detect, discover, find, lay one's hands on, pin down, pin point, run to earth, track down, unearth.
lodge *n* **1** cabin, chalet, cottage, gatehouse, house, hunting lodge, hut, shelter. **2** association, branch, chapter, club, group, society.
lodge *v* **1** accommodate, board, put up, shelter, stay, stop. **2** catch, implant, stick.
location *n* bearings, position, site, situation, spot, venue, whereabouts.
lock *n* bolt, clasp, fastening, padlock.
lock *v* bolt, close, fasten, latch, seal, secure, shut.
lodger *n* boarder, guest, paying guest, tenant.
lodging *n* accommodation,

As felled trees are very heavy, the logs are floated down river to the sawmill where possible. There, they are ground up into fibres, and then mixed with water. Special machinery processes this mixture to form smooth paper.

boarding, quarters, residence, rooms, shelter; (*Inf*) digs.
log *n* **1** chunk, piece of timber, stump, trunk. **2** account, chart, daybook, journal, listing, logbook, record, tally.
logic *n* **1** argument, reasoning. **2** comon sense, judgement, relevance, wisdom.
logical *adj* clear, reasonable, sound, valid, well-organized.
logo *n* design, device, emblem, seal, stamp.
loiter *v* dawdle, delay, hang about or around, idle, lag, linger, saunter, stroll; (*Inf*) dilly-dally.
lone *adj* by oneself, deserted, isolated, lonesome, one, only, separate, separated, single, sole, solitary, unaccompanied.
loneliness *n* desolation, isolation, seclusion, solitude.
lonely *adj* **1** abandoned, destitute, outcast. **2** alone, by oneself, lone, single, solitary, withdrawn. **3** deserted, desolate, isolated, out-of-the-way, remote, secluded, solitary, uninhabited; (*Inf*) off the beaten track.
long *adj* elongated, expanded, extended, extensive, far reaching, lengthy, spread out, stretched.
long *v* crave, desire, dream of, hanker, hunger, want, wish.
long-winded *adj* lengthy, long-drawn-out, rambling, tedious.
look *v* **1** consider, examine, eye, glance, inspect, observe, scan, scrutinize, see, study, survey, view, watch; (*Inf*) check out, take a gander at. **2** appear, display, evidence, exhibit, look like, make clear, present, seem to be. **3** forage, hunt, search, seek.
look *n* **1** examination, glimpse, inspection, peek, review, sight, squint, survey, view; (*Inf*) eyeful, once over, squiz. **2** appearance, bearing, effect, expression, face, manner.
look down on *v* despise, scorn, sneer, treat with contempt; (*Inf*) look down one's nose at, turn one's nose up at.
look forward to *v* anticipate, await, count on, expect, hope for, long for, look for, wait for.
look into *v* check out, delve into, examine, explore, inquire about, inspect, investigate, look over, probe, research, study.
lookout *n* **1** readiness, vigil, watch. **2** guard, sentinel, sentry, vedette, watchman. **3** beacon, citadel, observation post, post, tower, watchtower.
look out *v* be alert, be on guard, be vigilant, keep an eye out, pay attention, watch out; (*Inf*) keep one's eyes peeled.
loop *n* bend, circle, coil, curl, curve, eyelet, hoop, kink, loophole, noose, ring, spiral, twirl, twist, wind round.
loophole *n* **1** gap, slot. **2** escape, escape clause, escape route, let-out, means of escape.
loose *adj* **1** free, unattached, unbound, unsecured, untied, wobbly. **2** baggy, loosened, slack.
loose *v* detach, disconnect, free, let go, release, unfasten, untie.
loosen *v* **1** detach, let out, separate, slacken, undo, untie. **2** deliver, free, let go, liberate, release, set free.
lopsided *adj* crooked, off balance, one-sided, out of shape, squint, tilting, uneven, warped.
lord *n* **1** commander, governor, king, leader, master, monarch, prince, ruler, sovereign. **2** earl, noble, nobleman, peer, viscount.
lose *v* **1** drop, forget, mislay, misplace. miss. **2** fail, fall short, forfeit; (*Inf*) lose out on, pass up. **3** be defeated, be the loser, come to grief, suffer defeat; (*Inf*) come a cropper, take a licking.
loser *n* failure, underdog; (*Inf*) flop, lemon, no-hoper, washout.
loss *n* **1** bereavement, disappearance, failure, waste. **2** cost, damage, defeat, harm, hurt, injury, ruin.
lost *adj* **1** misplaced, missing, strayed, vanished. **2** adrift, off-course, off-track. **3** baffled,

confused, helpless, mystified, puzzled; (*Inf*) clueless. **4** absent, dreamy, engrossed, preoccupied, spellbound. **5** dead, extinct, forgotten, gone, obsolete, past.
lot *n* **1** batch, collection, group, quantity; (*Inf*) bunch. **2** chance, destiny, fate. **3** allowance, part, percentage, piece, portion, quota, ration, share; (*Inf*) cut. **4** abundance, large amount, plenty; (*Inf*) heaps, loads, masses, oodles, piles, stacks.
lotion *n* balm, cream, embrocation, liniment.
lottery *n* **1** draw, raffle, sweepstake. **2** chance, gamble, hazard, risk. (*Inf*) toss-up.
loud *adj* **1** booming, deafening, ear-piercing, noisy. **2** garish, gaudy, lurid, tasteless, vulgar. **3** brash, crude, loud, offensive, vulgar; (*Inf*) loud-mouthed.
lounge *v* laze, lie about, recline, relax, sprawl; (*Inf*) take it easy.
lovable *adj* adorable, attractive, cuddly, endearing, likeable, sweet; (*Inf*) fetching.
love *v* **1** adore, cherish, idolize, worship. **2** appreciate, desire, enjoy, fancy, like. **3** caress, embrace, fondle, kiss, pet; (*Inf*) canoodle, neck.
love *n* affection, devotion, fondness, infatuation, passion, tenderness, warmth.
lovely *adj* **1** attractive, beautiful, charming, exquisite, graceful, handsome, pretty, sweet, winning. **2** delightful, nice, pleasant, pleasing.
low *adj* **1** inferior, poor, second-rate, worthless. **2** common, crude, rude, vulgar. **3** blue, dejected, depressed, disheartened, down, miserable; (*Inf*) brassed off, down in the dumps, fed up. **4** gentle, muted, quiet, soft. **5** cheap. **6** mean, nasty, vile, vulgar.
lower *adj* minor, secondary, second-class, subordinate.
lower *v* **1** drop, fall, let down, sink, submerge. **2** disgrace, humiliate, stoop.
loyal *adj* dependable, devoted, dutiful, faithful, trusty.
lubricate *v* grease, make slippery, make smooth, moisturize, oil, oil the wheels, smear, smooth the way.
lucid *adj* clear, crystal-clear, explicit, obvious, plain, transparent.
luck *n* **1** accident, chance, fate, fortune. **2** fluke, good fortune, success, windfall; (*Inf*) break.
lucky *adv* advantageous, blessed, fortunate, prosperous, successful.
luggage *n* baggage, bags, cases, gear, suitcases, trunks.
lukewarm *adj* cold, cool, half-hearted, indifferent.
luminous *adj* bright, lit, luminescent, radiant, shining.
lump *n* **1** ball, chunk, mass, nugget, piece, wedge. **2** bulge, growth, swelling, tumour.
lump *v* batch, bunch, combine, group, mass, pool, unite.
lunge *n* charge, jab, pounce, stab, swing, swipe, thrust.
lunge *v* charge, dash, dive, hit at, jab, pitch into, pounce, set upon, strike at, thrust.
lure *v* attract, draw, ensnare, entice, invite, tempt.
lure *n* attraction, bait, decoy, enticement, temptation; (*Inf*) carrot, come-on.
lurk *v* conceal oneself, crouch, hide, lie in wait, prowl, sneak.
luxury *n* **1** opulence, richness, splendour. **2** bliss, comfort, delight, enjoyment, pleasure, satisfaction. **3** extravagance, frill, indulgence, treat.
lying *n* deceit, dishonesty, double-dealing, fibbing, perjury.
lying *adj* **1** deceitful, dishonest, double-dealing, false, two-faced. **2** fame, glory, honour, prestige.

In an oil refinery, crude oil is separated into usable compounds. By mixing these with other substances and treating them in a variety of ways, literally thousands of useful materials can be made.

Mm

machine *n* **1** appliance, device, engine, instrument, mechanism, tool. **2** agency, machinery, organization, party, structure, system; (*Inf*) setup.
machinery *n* **1** apparatus, equipment, gear, instruments, mechanism, tools. **2** agency, procedure, structure, system.
mad *adj* **1** beserk, deranged, frantic, insane, lunatic, off one's head, psychotic, rabid, raving, unbalanced, unstable. **2** absurd, foolish, ludicrous, senseless, unsafe, wild; (*Inf*) bananas, barmy, batty, bonkers, crackers, crazy, cuckoo, daft, loony, loopy, mental, nuts, nutty, off one's chump, off one's nut, off one's rocker, off one's trolley, round the bend, screwy.
made-up *adj* fabricated, false, fictional, imaginary, invented, make-believe, unreal, untrue.
magazine *n* **1** journal, pamphlet, paper, periodical. **2** ammunition dump, arsenal, depot, store, storehouse, warehouse.
magic *adj* bewitching, charming, enchanting, entrancing, spell-binding.
magistrate *n* bailie, JP, judge, justice, justice of the peace, provost.
magnet *n* **1** bar magnet, electro magnet, field magnet, solenoid. **2** focal point, focus. **3** attraction, charm, fascination, temptation.
magnetic *adj* attractive, captivating, charismatic, charming, entrancing, fascinating, hypnotic, mesmerizing, seductive.
magnificent *adj* brilliant, excellent, gorgeous, grand, imposing, impressive, lavish, luxurious, majestic, outstanding, regal, splendid, stately, superb.
magnify *v* **1** amplify, augment, blow up, boost, enlarge, expand, heighten, increase, intensify. **2** blow up out of all proportion, dramatize, exaggerate, inflate, make a mountain out of a mole-hill, overdo, overestimate.
mail *n* **1** correspondence, letters, packages, parcels, post. **2** postal service, postal system.
mail *v* dispatch, forward, post, send, send by post.
maim *v* cripple, disable, hurt, incapacitate, injure, lame, mar, put out of action, wound.
main *adj* capital, cardinal, central, chief, critical, crucial, essential, foremost, head, leading, necessary, outstanding, paramount, predominant, premier, prime, principle, special, supreme, vital.
main *n* cable, channel, conduit, duct, line, pipe.
maintain *v* **1** care for, carry on, conserve, finance, keep up, look after, nurture, preserve, prolong, retain, supply, support, sustain, take care of, uphold. **2** allege, assert, claim, declare, hold, insist, profess, state. **3** advocate, argue for, back, defend, fight for, justify, plead for, stand by, uphold, vindicate.
maintenance *n* **1** conservation, looking after, preservation, provision, repairs, supply, support, upkeep. **2** food, keep, livelihood, living, sustenance.

What is a magnetic field?

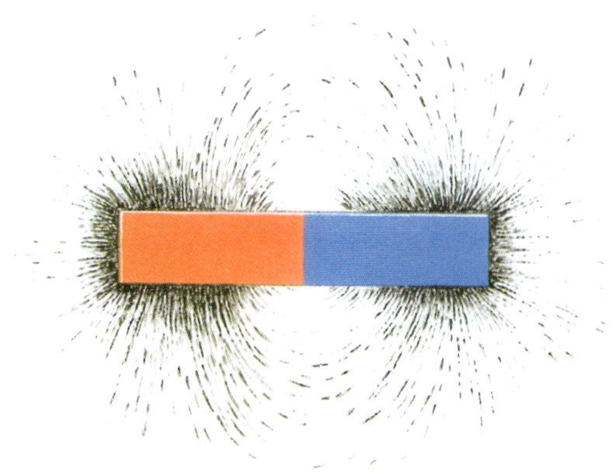

A magnetic field is the area around a magnet in which its magnetic force operates. A magnetic object that is placed within the field will be attracted or repelled by the magnet. When iron filings (tiny slivers of iron) are placed near a magnet, they line up to show its magnetic field. In fact, each tiny piece of iron has become a small magnet. The mini-magnets show how strongly each part of the large magnet attracts them.

majesty *n* **1** dignity, glory, grandeur, impressiveness, kingliness, magnificence, nobility, pomp, queenliness, royalty, splendour, state, stateliness, sublimity. **2** authority, dominion, power, supremacy.
major *adj* better, bigger, chief, elder, greater, higher, larger, leading, main, most, senior, superior, supreme, uppermost.
majority *n* **1** best part, bulk, greater number, mass, more, most. **2** adulthood, manhood, maturity, seniority, womanhood.
make *v* **1** assemble, build, construct, create, fabricate, fashion, forge, manufacture, mould, originate, put together, shape. **2** accomplish, generate, lead to, produce. **3** cause, drive, force, press, require. **4** appoint, assign, designate, elect, install, invest, nominate, ordain. **5** draw up, enact, establish, fix, form, frame, pass. **6** add up to, amount to, constitute, represent. **7** calculate, estimate, judge, reckon, suppose. **8** acquire, clear, earn, gain, get, obtain, realize, secure, win. **9** put together.
make *n* brand, build, character, composition, constitution, construction, cut, designation, form, kind, make-up, mark, model, shape, sort, structure, style, type, variety.
make do *v* cope, get by, improvise, manage, muddle through, scrape by.
make off *v* abscond, beat a hasty retreat, bolt, cut and run, flee, fly, run away, run off, run for it, take to one's heels.
make out *v* **1** detect, discover, distinguish, perceive, recognize, see. **2** comprehend, decipher, fathom, follow, grasp, perceive, realize, see, understand, work out. **3** complete, draw up, fill in, fill out, inscribe, write out.

Cosmetics contain many organic compounds. Solvents dissolve other ingredients to produce a liquid consistence. Pigments give the cosmetics a wide range of colours. Oils give a smooth texture that is resistant to moisture.

makeshift *adj* make-do, provisional, rough and ready, stopgap, substitute, temporary.
makeshift *n* stand-by, stopgap, substitute.
make-up *n* **1** blusher, cosmetics, eyebrow pencil, eye-liner, eye-shadow, foundation, greasepaint, lipstick, lip gloss, powder, rouge; (*Inf*) face paint, war paint. **2** arrangement, assembly, composition, configuration, constitution, construction, form, format, formation, organization, structure. **3** character, disposition, mould, nature, personality, stamp, temper, temperament; (*Inf*) what makes someone tick.
make up *n* **1** compose, comprise, constitute. **2** coin, concoct, construct, create, devise, dream up, fabricate, formulate, frame, hatch, invent, originate, trump up, write; (*Inf*) cook up, complete, fill, meet, supply. **3** forgive and forget, make peace, mend fences, settle differences, shake hands. **4** mix, prepare, put together. **5** decide, resolve.
malfunction *v* breakdown, develop a fault, fail, go wrong.
malfunction *n* breakdown, defect, failure, fault, flaw, glitch.
malice *n* animosity, bad blood, bitterness, evil intent, hate, ill will, spite, vindictiveness.
malicious *adj* bitter, hateful, ill-natured, mischievous, resentful, spiteful; (*Inf*) bitchy, catty.
malign *adj* bad, destructive, evil, harmful, hurtful, injurious, malevolent, malignant, pernicious, vicious, wicked.
maltreat *v* abuse, bully, damage, harm, hurt, ill-treat, injure, man handle roughly, mistreat.

man *n* **1** gentleman, male. **2** adult, human being, person, somebody. **3** Homo sapiens, humanity, human race, mankind. **4** attendant, employee, follower, retainer, servant, soldier, subject, valet, worker, workman; (*Inf*) bloke, chap, guy.

man *v* crew, fill, furnish with staff, garrison, occupy, people.

manage *v* **1** administer, be in charge of, command, direct, govern, guide, manipulate, oversee, preside over, rule, supervise. **2** arrange, bring about, carry on, cope with, deal with, succeed. **3** control, dominate, govern, handle, influence, manipulate, operate, pilot, ply, steer, train, use, wield.

management *n* administration, board, directors, employers, executives; (*Inf*) bosses.

manager *n* administrator, conductor, controller, director, executive, governor, head, organizer, proprietor, superintendent, supervisor; (*Inf*) boss, gaffer.

mandatory *adj* binding, compulsory, essential, obligatory, necessary, required, requisite.

mangle *v* butcher, cripple, crush, cut, deform, destroy, disfigure, distort, hack, lacerate, maim, mar, maul, mutilate, rend, ruin, spoil, tear, wreck; (*Inf*) murder.

manhandle *v* **1** handle roughly, knock about, maul, paw, pull, push, rough up. **2** carry, haul, heave, hump, lift, manoeuvre, pull, push, shove, tug.

mania *n* craziness, dementia, derangement, disorder, frenzy, insanity, lunacy, madness.

maniac *n* lunatic, madman, madwoman, psychopath.

manifestation *n* appearance, demonstration, disclosure, display, exhibition, exposure, expression, indication, instance, mark, materialization, revelation, show, sign, symptom, token.

manipulate *v* **1** employ, handle, operate, ply, use, utilize, wild, work. **2** conduct, control, direct, engineer, guide, influence, manoeuvre, negotiate, steer.

mankind *n* Homo sapiens, humanity, humankind, human race, man, people.

man-made *adj* artificial, imitation, simulated, synthetic, synthesized; (*Inf*) plastic.

manner *n* **1** air, appearance, aspect, bearing, behaviour, conduct, demeanour, look, presence, tone. **2** approach, custom, fashion, form, habit, means, method, mode, practice, procedure, process, routine,

What is a projection?

Globes can represent the Earth in miniature, with features shown in a true relationship to each other. Paper maps, though, are much easier to use, but an adjustment needs to be made in order to show a curved land surface on a flat map. The adjustment chosen is called a projection. Several different projections can be used, depending on the purpose of the map.

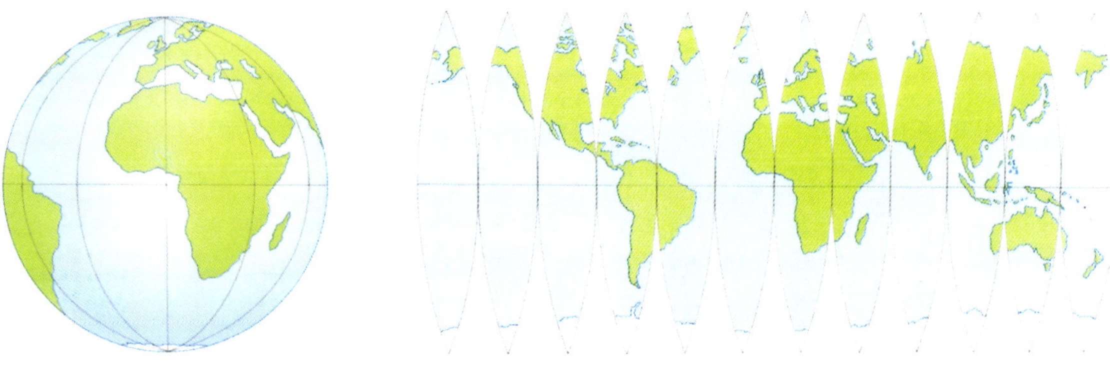

In order to flatten out the earth's surface, it can be thought of as being divided into segments, like peeling an orange. But that leaves gaps at the top and bottom that make the map impossible to use.

style, tack, tenor, usage, way.
mannerism *n* characteristic, habit, idiosyncrasy, peculiarity, quirk, trait, trick.
manners *pl n* **1** bearing, behaviour, breeding, carriage, conduct, demeanour, deportment. **2** ceremony, courtesy, decorum, etiquette, formalities, good form, posh, politeness, proprieties, protocol, refinement, social graces, the done thing.
manoeuvre *n* action, device, dodge, intrigue, move, movement, plan, plot, ploy, ruse, scheme, stratagem, subterfuge, tactic, trick.
manoeuvre *v* **1** contrive, devise, engineer, intrigue, manage, manipulate, plan, plot, pull strings, scheme. **2** direct, guide, navigate, negotiate, pilot, steer. **3** deployment, exercise.
mansion *n* abode, castle, château, dwelling, habitation, hall, manor, manor-house, palace, residence, seat, stately home, villa.
manual *adj* done by hand, hand-operated, human, physical.
manual *n* bible, guide, guidebook, handbook, instructions, workbook.
manufacture *v* assemble, build, compose, construct, create, fabricate, forge, form, make, mass-produce, mould, process, produce, put together, shape, turn out.
manufacture *n* assembly, construction, creating, fabrication, making, mass-production, processing, produce, production.
manure *n* compost, droppings, dung, excrement, fertilizer, guano, muck, ordure.
many *adj* abundant, copius, countless, frequent, innumerable, manifold, multifarious, multifold, multitudinous, myriad, numerous, profuse, sundry, varied, various; (*Inf*) oodles, umpteen.
mar *v* blemish, blight, blot, damage, deface, detract from, disfigure, harm, hurt, impair, injure, maim, mangle, mutilate, ruin, scar, spoil, stain, sully, taint, tarnish, vitiate.
march *v* file, footslog pace, parade, stalk, stride, strut, tramp, tread, walk.
march *n* **1** hike, routemarch, tramp, trek, walk. **2** demonstration, parade, procession.
margin *n* **1** border, bound, boundary, brim, brink, confine, edge, limit, perimeter, periphery, rim, side, verge. **2** allowance, compass, elbow room, extra, latitude, leeway, play, room, scope, space, surplus.
marginal *adj* bordering, borderline, on the edge, peripheral.
marine *adj* **1** maritime, nautical, naval, ocean-going, oceanic, seafaring, seagoing. **2** acquatic, oceanic, pelagic, saltwater, sea, seawater, thalassic.
mariner *n* bluejacket, hand, Jack Tar, navigator, sailor, salt, sea dog, seafarer, seafaring man, seaman; (*Inf*) limey, matelot, tar.
maritime *adj* marine, nautical, naval, oceanic, sea, seafaring.
mark *n* **1** blemish, blot, blotch, bruise, dent, impression, line, nick, pock, scar, spot, stain, streak. **2** badge, brand, characteristic, device, emblem, evidence, feature, hallmark, impression, indication, label, note, print, proof, seal, sign, stamp, symbol, symptom, token. **3** aim, end, goal, objective, purpose, target. **4** footmark, footprint, sign, trace, track, trail.
mark *v* **1** blemish, blot, blotch, brand, bruise, dent, impress, imprint, nick, scar, scratch, smudge, splotch, stain, streak. **2** brand, characterize, identify, label, stamp. **3** attend, mind, note, observe, pay attention, pay heed, regard, remark, watch.
marked *adj* apparent, clear, distinct, evident, notable, noticeable, obvious, prominent, pronounced, striking.
market *n* bazaar, fair, mart.

Why is the sea salty?

The sea is salty because there are many minerals dissolved in it. Some people prefer to use sea salt to flavour their food. This is obtained simply by boiling sea water, so that it evaporates. The water escapes as steam, while the salt is left behind as crystals.

market *v* offer for sale, retail, sell, vend.
maroon *v* **1** abandon, cast ashore, cast away, desert, leave, strand; (*Inf*) high and dry.
marrow *n* core, cream, essence, gist, heart, kernel, pith, quick, soul, spirit, substance.
marry *v* **1** become man and wife, wed; (*Inf*) get hitched, get spliced, take the plunge, tie the knot, walk down the aisle. **2** bond, join, knit, link, match, merge, splice, tie, unify, unite.
marsh *n* bog, fen, morass, moss, quagmire, slough, swamp.
marshal *v* align, arrange, array, assemble, collect, deploy, draw up, gather, group, line up, muster, organize.
marshy *adj* boggy, quaggy, swampy, waterlogged, wet.
marvel *v* be amazed, be awed, be filled with surprise, goggle at, wonder.
marvel *n* amazing, genius, phenomenon, whiz; (*Inf*) wonder.
marvellous *adj* amazing, astonishing, astounding, breathtaking, extraordinary, miraculous, phenomenal, remarkable, stupendous.
masculine *adj* **1** male, manly, mannish, virile. **2** bold, brave, macho, powerful, resolute, strapping, strong, vigorous, well-built; (*Inf*) butch.
mass *n* **1** block, chunk, hunk, lump, piece. **2** aggregate, body, collection, entirety, sum total, totality, whole. **3** accumulation, batch, bunch, collection, heap, load, pile, quantity, stack. **4** band, body, crowd, group, horde, host, lot, mob, number, throng; (*Inf*) bunch. **5** body, bulk, lion's share, majority. **6** dimension, greatness, magnitude, size.
mass *adj* extensive, general, indiscriminate, large-scale, popular, wholesale, widespread.
mass *v* accumulate, amass, assemble, gather, muster, rally, swarm, throng.
massacre *n* annihilation, blood bath, carnage, extermination, holocaust, killing, mass slaughter, murder.
massacre *v* annihilate, blow away, butcher, cut to pieces, exterminate, kill, mow down, slaughter, slay, wipe out.
massage *n* **1** manipulation, pummeling.

The Holocaust
Although six million is the most quoted figure for the massacre of Jews during the Holocaust, it remains impossible to apply an exact figure. There may have been fewer – or far more – killed as Hitler implemented 'the Final Solution'.
These women and children are pictured at the Auschwitz camp just hours after the camp was liberated.

2 acupressure, aromatherapy, reflexology, shiatsu.
massive *adj* big, bulky, colossal, enormous, gigantic, great, heavy, huge, immense, mammoth, substantial, titanic, vast; (*Inf*) ginormous, mega, whopping.
master *n* **1** captain, chief, commander, controller, director, employer, governor, head, lord, manager, over-lord, overseer, owner, principle, ruler, skipper, superintendent; (*Inf*) big cheese, boss, top dog. **2** expert, genius, grandmaster, maestro, virtuoso, wizard; (*Inf*) ace, dab hand, pro.
master *adj* expert, masterly, proficient, skilful, skilled; (*Inf*) crack.
master *v* **1** acquire, grasp, learn. **2** bridle, check, conquer, curb, defeat, overcome, over-power, quash, quell, subdue, suppress, tame, triumph over, vanquish; (*Inf*) get clued up on, get the hang of.
match *n* **1** competition, contest, game, trial. **2** competitor, rival. **3** copy, double, duplicate, looka-like, replica, twin. **4** affiliation, alliance, combination, couple, duet, marriage, pair, partner-ship, union; (*Inf*) dead ringer, item, spitting image.
match *v* **1** combine, couple, join, link, marry, mate, pair, unite. **2** adapt, agree, correspond, fit, go with. **3** compare, compete, equal, measure up to, oppose, pit against, rival, vie.
matching *adj* comparable, coordinating, corresponding, double, duplicate, equal, equivalent, identical, like, paired, parallel, same, toning, twin.

Why are there very few trees on areas of grassland?

Large areas of grassland have soil that is too poor for trees to grow as well as insufficient rainfall. When grazing animals frequently pass over newly growing forest, young trees are soon killed by nibbling and trampling so that the trees never have a chance to become established again.

material *n* **1** body, matter, stuff, substance. **2** data, evidence, facts, information, notes, work. **3** cloth, fabric, stuff.
material *adj* essential, grave, important, serious, significant, vital, weighty.
materialize *v* appear, come about, happen, occur, take place, take shape, turn up.
matter *n* **1** body, material, stuff, substance. **2** affair, business, concern, event, incident, issue, question, situation, subject, topic. **3** consequence, import, importance, moment, note, significance, weight.
matter *v* be important, carry weight, count, have influence, make a difference, signify.
matter-of-fact *v* deadpan, dry, dull, emotionless, flat, lifeless, mundane.
mature *adj* adult, full-grown, fully-fledged, grown-up, of age, ready, ripe, ripened, seasoned.
mature *v* **1** age, become adult. **2** come of age, develop, grow up, mellow, reach adulthood, ripen, season.
maul *v* **1** abuse, ill-treat, manhandle, molest, paw. **2** batter, beat, claw, knock about, lacerate, mangle, pummel, rough up, thrash; (*Inf*) beat up.
maximum *n* ceiling, extremity, height, peak, pinnacle, summit, top, upper limit, utmost, zenith.
maximum *adj* greatest, highest, maximal, most, paramount, supreme, topmost, utmost.
maybe *adv* perhaps, possibly.
mayhem *n* chaos, commotion, confusion, destruction, disorder, fracas, havoc, trouble, violence.
maze *n* **1** labyrinth. network. **2** confusion, mesh, puzzle, snarl, tangle, uncertainty, web.
meadow *n* field, grassland, ley, pasture.
meagre *adj* deficient, exiguous, inadequate, insubstantial, little, paltry, poor, puny, scanty, scrimpy, short, skimpy, slender, slight, small, spare, sparse.
mean *v* **1** convey, drive at, hint at, imply, indicate, represent, say, signify, spell, stand for, suggest, symbolize. **2** aim, contemplate, desire, have in mind, intend,

plan, propose, set out.
mean *adj* **1** miserly, penny-pinching, stingy, tight-fisted. **2** callous, despicable, hard-hearted, narrow-minded, petty, shameful, sordid, vile, wretched. **3** grungy, miserable, poor, run-down, scruffy, seedy, shabby, squalid, wretched; (*Inf*) near.
mean *adj* average, intermediate, medial, median, medium, middle, normal, standard.
meander *v* ramble, snake, stray, stroll, wander, wind, zigzag.
meander *n* bend, coil, curve, loop, turn, twist, zigzag.
meaning *n* **1** explanation, gist, interpretation. **2** aim, design, idea, intention, object, plan, point, purpose, trend. **3** effect, point, thrust, use, usefulness, validity, value, worth.
meaningful *adj* **1** important, relevant, significant, useful, valid, worthwhile. **2** expressive, suggestive.
means *pl n* **1** channel, course, instruction, measure, method, mode, process, way. **2** affluence, capital, estate, funds, income, money, property, resources, riches, wealth.
measure *n* **1** allotment, amount, capacity, degree, extent, portion, quota, range, ration, reach, share, size. **2** gauge, metre, rule, scale, yardstick. **3** method. **4** example, model, norm, standard, test, touchstone, yardstick. **5** action, course, manoeuvre, procedure, proceeding, step. **6** act, bill, law, statute. **7** beat, foot, metre, rhythm, verse.
measure *v* assess, calculate, calibrate, compute, estimate, gauge, judge, quantify, rate, size, sound, survey, value, weigh.

What were the first measurements?

The first measurements were based on human bodies. As everyone had a body, they could use themselves as references! People vary in size, so this was not an accurate system.

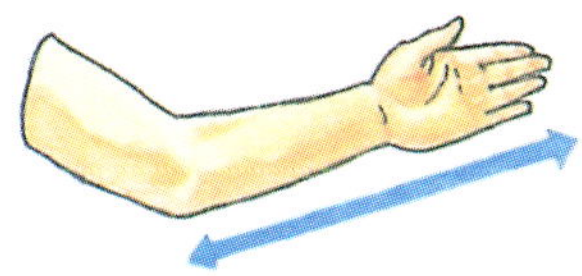

From elbow to fingertips was one cubit.

The width of the hand was four fingers.

measure up to *v* be adequate, be capable, be equal to, be fit, be suitable, come up to standard, equal, fit the bill, match, meet, rival; (*Inf*) come up to scratch, make the grade.
mechanical *adj* **1** automated, automatic, machine-driven. **2** cold, emotionless, impersonal, lifeless, machine-like, matter-of-fact, routine, unconscious, unfeeling, unthinking.
mechanism *n* **1** device, instrument, machine, structure, system, tool. **2** agency, execution, medium, method, operation, procedure, process, system, technique, workings.
meddle *v* butt in, interfere, intervene, intrude, pry, tamper; (*Inf*) stick one's nose in.
medicine *n* cure, drug, medication, remedy.
medieval *adj* antiquated, antique, archaic, old fashioned, unenlightened.
mediocre *adj* average, inferior, insignificant, ordinary, passable, run-of-the-mill, second-rate, tolerable, uninspired; (*Inf*) fair to middling, so-so.
meditate *v* consider, contemplate, deliberate, muse, ponder, reflect, study, think.
medium *adj* average, fair, intermediate, mean, medial, median, mediocre, middle, mid-way.
medium *n* **1** average, centre, compromise, mean, middle, middle course, middle ground, middle path, middle way, mid-point. **2** agency, avenue, channel, instrument, means, mode, organ, vehicle, way.
meet *v* **1** bump into, come across, encounter, find, run into. **2** come together, connect, converge, intersect, join, link, touch, unite. **3** answer, carry out, come up to, comply, equal, fulfil, match, measure up, perform, satisfy. **4** assemble, collect, congregate, gather, rally.
mellow *adj* **1** delicate, full-flavoured, juicy, mature, rich, ripe, soft, sweet. **2** full, rounded, smoothe, sweet, tuneful. **3** cheerful, happy, jolly, jovial, merry, relaxed.
melt *v* **1** diffuse, dissolve, fuse, liquefy, soften, thaw. **2** disarm, relax, soften, touch.

member *n* **1** associate, fellow, representative. **2** arm, component, constituent, element, extremity, leg, limb, organ, part, portion.
memoirs *pl n* autobiography, diary, experiences, journals, life story, memories, recollections, reminiscences.
memorable *adj* celebrated, famous, historic, illustrious, important, notable, remarkable, significant, unforgettable.
memorial *n* cairn, memento, monument, plaque, record, remembrance, souvenir.
mend *v* **1** cure, darn, fix, heal, patch, rectify, refit, reform, remedy, renovate, repair, restore, retouch. **2** ameliorate, amend, better, correct, improve, rectify, reform, revise.
mend *n* darn, repair, stitch.
menial *adj* boring, dull, humdrum, routine, unskilled.
mentality *n* **1** brainpower, brains, intellect, intelligence quotient, IQ, mental age, mind, understanding, wit. **2** attitude, character, psychology; (*Inf*) grey matter.
mention *v* acknowledge, cite, declare, disclose, divulge, hint at, make known, reveal, speak about, state, tell, touch upon.
mention *n* **1** acknowledgment, recognition, tribute. **2** announcement, notification, observation, reference, remark.
merchandise *n* goods, produce, products, stock, wares.
merchant *n* broker, dealer, distributor, retailer, salesman, seller, shop-keeper, trader, tradesman, trafficker, vendor, wholesaler.
merge *v* amalgamate, blend, combine, consolidate, fuse, join, meet, melt into, mingle, mix, tone with, unite.
merger *n* amalgamation, coalition, combination, fusion, incorporation, union.
merit *v* be entitled to, be worthy of, deserve, earn, have a right to, incur, rate, warrant.
merry *adj* **1** care-free, cheerful, festive, fun-loving, happy, jolly. **2** amusing, comic, comical, funny, hilarious, humorous.
mesh *n* **1** net, netting, network, reticulation, web. **2** entanglement, snare, tangle, trap, web.
mesh *v* **1** catch, ensnare, net, snare, tangle, trap. **2** combine, come together, connect, dovetail, engage, fit together, harmonize, interlock, knit.
mess *n* **1** chaos, clutter, jumble, litter, shambles, turmoil, untidiness. **2** difficulty, dilemma, mix-up, muddle. (*Inf*) fix, jam, pickle, stew.
mess *v* botch, bungle, clutter, dirty, disarrange, dishevel, foul, litter, muddle, pollute, scramble; (*Inf*) make a hash of, muck up.
message *n* **1** bulletin, communiqué, letter, memorandum, note, notice, tidings, word. **2** idea, import, meaning, moral, point, theme.
messenger *n* agent, courier, delivery boy, emissary, envoy, errand-boy, go-between, runner.
messy *adj* chaotic, cluttered, confused, dirty, dishevelled,

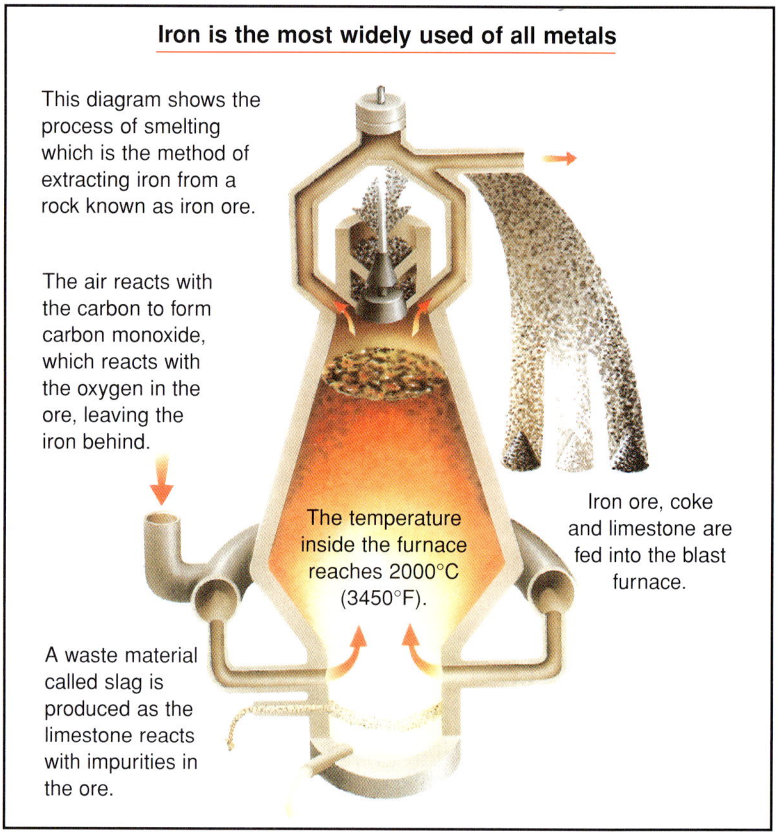

grubby, littered, muddled, shambolic, sloppy, untidy.
metal *n* **common metals and alloys:** aluminium, brass, bronze, copper, gold, iron, lead, magnesium, platinum, potassium, silver, sodium, stainless steel, tin, zinc.
metaphor *n* figure of speech, image, symbol.
method *n* **1** approach, course, manner, mode, plan, routine, scheme, style. **2** design, form, order, pattern, planning, structure, system.
methodical *adj* businesslike, efficient, meticulous, neat, organized, precise, tidy.
meticulous *adj* details, exact, fussy, pain-staking, particular, precise, strict, thorough.
microscopic *adj* infinitesimal, minuscule, minute, tiny.
midday *n* noon, noonday, noontide, noontime, twelve noon, twelve o'clock.
middle *adj* central, halfway, inside, intermediate, mid.
middle *n* centre, focus, halfway point, heart, inside, mean, midpoint, midsection, midst, thick.
midget *n* dwarf, gnome, pygmy, Tom Thumb.
midget *adj* **1** baby, dwarf, miniature. **2** minute, pocket, tiny, toy, very small.
migrant *n* drifter, emigrant, gypsy, immigrant, itinerant, nomad, rover, tinker, transient, traveller, vagrant, wanderer.
migrate *v* drift, journey, move, roam, rove, shift, travel, trek, voyage, wander.
migration *adj* emigration, journey, movement, shift, travel, trek, voyage, wandering.
mild *adj* calm, compassionate, docile, gentle, indulgent, kind, meek, merciful, moderate, pacific, peaceable, placid, pleasant, serene, smooth, soft, temperate, tender, tranquil, warm.
military *adj* armed, martial, soldierlike, soldierly, warlike.
military *n* armed forces, army, forces, services.
mill *n* **1** factory, foundry, plant, shop, works. **2** crusher, grinder.
mimic *v* ape, caricature, imitate, impersonate; (*Inf*) take off.
mimic *n* caricaturist, copycat, impersonator, impressionist, parrot.
mind *n* **1** intelligence, mentality, reason, sense, understanding, wits. **2** memory, recollection; (*Inf*) brains, grey matter. **3** brain, head, imagination, psyche. **4** desire, fancy, inclination, leaning, notion, purpose, tendency, urge, will, wish. **5** attention, concentration, thinking. **6** attention, concentration, thinking, thoughts. **7 make up one's mind.** come to a decision, decide, determine, reach a decision, resolve. **8 bear in mind** remember, take note of.
mind *v* **1** care, disapprove, dislike, object, resent, take offense. **2** adhere to, comply with, follow, heed, listen to, mark, notice, obey, observe, pay attention, respect, watch. **3** attend to, guard, have charge of, keep an eye on, look after, take care of, tend, watch.
mine *n* **1** coalfield, colliery, deposit, excavation, pit, shaft, vein. **2** abundance, fund, hoard, reserve, source, stock, store,

What is opencast mining?

Opencast mines are used when the deposit lies near the surface. Although this method is cheaper than digging deep mines, some people feel that the environmental costs of it are high, as large areas of land are laid bare and wildlife destroyed.

supply, wealth.
mine *v* dig for, dig up, excavate, extract, quarry, unearth.
mingle *v* **1** amalgamate, blend, combine, fuse, join, merge, mix, unite. **2** associate with, circulate, hang around, socialize.
miniature *adj* baby, dwarf, little, midget, mini, minute, pocket, pygmy, reduced, scaled-down, small, tiny, toy, wee.
minimal *adj* least, least possible, littlest, minimum, nominal, slightest, smallest, token.
minimize *v* **1** abbreviate, decrease, diminish, miniaturize, reduce, shrink. **2** belittle, decry, discount, make little of, play down, underestimate, underrate.
minimum *n* bottom, depth, least, lowest, nadir, slightest.
minimum *adj* least possible, littlest, lowest, minimal, slightest, smallest.
minister *n* **1** chaplain, churchman, clergyman, cleric, parson, pastor, preacher, priest, rector, vicar. **2** administrator, ambassador, cabinet member, delegate, diplomat, envoy, executive, office-holder, official.
minister *v* administer, answer, attend, cater to, pander to, serve, take care of, tend.
minor *adj* inferior, insignificant, junior, lesser, light, negligible, petty, slight, smaller, trivial.
mint *adj* brand-new, excellent, first-class, perfect, unblemished, undamaged.
mint *v* cast, coin, make, produce, punch, stamp, strike.
minute *n* flash, instant, moment, second; (*Inf*) jiffy, tick, trice.
minute *adj* little, microscopic, miniature, minuscule, slender, small, tiny.
minutes *pl n* memorandum, notes, proceedings, record, transactions, transcript.
miracle *n* marvel, phenomenon, prodigy, wonder.
miraculous *adj* amazing, astonishing, extraordinary, incredible, marvellous, phenomenal, superhuman, unbelievable, wonderful.
mirage *n* hallucination, illusion, optical illusion.
mirror *n* **1** glass, looking-glass, reflector. **2** clone, copy, double, exact likeness, image, reflection, replica, representation, twin; (*Inf*) dead ringer for, spitting image.
mirror *v* copy, depict, echo, emulate, follow, reflect, show.
misbehaviour *n* bad behaviour, mischief, misconduct, naughtiness, rudeness; (*Inf*) acting up, carrying on, monkey business.
miscellaneous *adj* assorted, diverse, jumbled, mixed, motley, sundry, varied, various.
misconduct *n* misbehaviour, naughtiness, rudeness, transgression, wrong doing.

How are mirrors made?

Mirrors are made by coating the back of a sheet of glass with an alloy of mercury and another metal. Light does not pass through the glass, but is bounced back to give a reflection.

miserable *adj* **1** broken-hearted, depressed, distressed, down, downcast, forlorn, gloomy, heartbroken, unhappy; (*Inf*) down in the mouth. **2** destitute, impoverished, needy, penniless, poor, poverty-stricken. **3** bad, despicable, disgraceful, low, mean, pitiful, shabby, shameful, sordid, sorry, squalid, vile, worthless, wretched.
miserly *adj* mean, stingy, tight-fisted, ungenerous.
misery *n* **1** agony, depression, despair, distress, grief, sadness, sorrow, torment, unhappiness. **2** affliction, catastrophe, curse, disaster, misfortune, ordeal, sorrow, tribulation, trouble, woe.
misfire *v* fail, fail to go off, fall through, go wrong; (*Inf*) bite the dust, go phut, go up in smoke.
misfit *n* eccentric, fish out of water, square peg in a round hole; (*Inf*) oddball, weirdo.
misfortune *n* **1** bad luck, hard luck, ill luck. **2** accident, blow, calamity, disaster, failure, hardship, misadventure, mishap, setback, stroke of bad luck, tragedy, tribulation, trouble.
misguided *adj* foolish, mistaken, uncalled-for, unreasonable, unwarranted, unwise.
mishap *n* accident, adversity, bad luck, calamity, disaster, hard luck, ill fortune, ill luck, misadventure, misfortune.
mislead *n* deceive, delude, fool, hoodwink, lead astray, misguide, pull the wool over someone's eyes; (*Inf*) lead up the garden path, take for a ride.
miss *v* **1** avoid, be late for, evade, fail to notice, leave out,

let go, lose, miscarry, mistake, overlook, pass up, skip, slip, trip. **2** feel the loss of, long for, need, pine for, wish, yearn for.
miss *n* **1** blunder, error, failure, fault, loss. **2** damsel, girl, lass, maid, maiden, schoolgirl, spinster, young lady.
missile *n* projectile, rocket.
missing *adj* absent, astray, gone, lacking, left behind, left out, lost, mislaid, misplaced, not present, nowhere to be found, wanting.
mission *n* **1** aim, goal, job, office, purpose, pursuit, quest, task. **2** delegation, deputation, embassy, ministry, task force.
mist *n* cloud, condensation, dew, drizzle, film, fog, haar, haze, smog, spray, steam, vapour.
mistake *n* blunder, error, *faux pas*, gaffe, inaccuracy, over-sight, slip, misunderstand; (*Inf*) boob, clanger, goof, howler, slip up.
misty *adj* blurred, cloudy, dim, foggy, hazy, murky, obscure, overcast, unclear, vague.
misunderstand *v* **1** get the wrong idea about, misconstrue, misinterpret, missread, mistake. **2** the wrong end of the stick.
mix *v* **1** alloy, blend, combine, fuse, incorporate, join, merge, mingle, put together, unite. **2** associate, come together, mingle, socialize; (*Inf*) hang out.
mixture *n* assortment, blend, brew, compound, concoction, fusion, hotchpotch, jumble, mix, pot-pourri, variety.
mix-up *n* confusion, jumble, mess, mistake, muddle, tangle.
mob *n* crowd, flock, gang, herd, horde, host, mass, multitude, pack, press, swarm, throng.
mob *v* crowd around, jostle, overrun, set upon, surround, swarm around.
model *n* **1** dummy, facsimile, imitation, mock-up, replica. **2** example, mould, prototype, type. **3** poser, sitter, subject. **4** mannequin.
model *v* **1** base, carve, design, fashion, form, mould, pattern, plan, sculpt, shape. **2** display, show off, sport, wear.
model *adj* **1** standard, typical. **2** ideal, perfect.
moderate *adj* calm, controlled, cool, gentle, mild, reasonable, restrained, sober, steady.
moderate *v* calm, control, curb, decrease, diminish, lessen, play down, restrain, soften, subdue, tone down.
modern *adj* current, fresh, latest, newest, present-day, recent, twenty-first century, up-to-date, up-to-the-minute, with-it; (*Inf*) latest gizmo.
modernize *v* bring up to date, rejuvenate, remodel, renovate, update.
modest *adj* **1** blushing, coy, quiet, shy, unassuming. **2** fair, limited, moderate, ordinary, small, unexceptional.
modification *n* adjustment, alteration, change, refinement, revision, variation.
modify *v* adapt, adjust, alter, change, convert, redo, remodel, revise, transform, vary.
moist *adj* clammy, damp, dank, dripping, drizzly, humid, rainy, soggy, wet, wettish.
moisten *v* dampen, humidify, moisturize, soak, water, wet.

Cloisters are a covered walkway, usually around a quadrangle in a religious institution, having an open pillared area on the inside.

moisture *n* damp, dampness, dankness, dew, humidity, liquid, perspiration, sweat, water, wateriness, wetness.
molest *v* abuse, bother, disturb, harass, irritate, persecute, pester, plague, torment, upset, vex, worry; (*Inf*) bug.
moment *n* **1** flash, instant, minute, split second, twinkling; (*Inf*) jiffy, shake, tick. **2** hour, instant, juncture, point, stage, time, two shakes of a lamb's tail.
momentous *adj* critical, crucial, decisive, historic, important, pivotal, serious, significant, vital, weighty.
momentum *n* drive, energy, force, power, propulsion, push,

strength, thrust.
monarch *n* crowned head, emperor, empress, king, prince, princess, queen, ruler, sovereign.
monastery *n* abbey, cloister, convent, friary, house, nunnery, priory, religious community.
money *n* banknotes, capital, cash, coin, currency, funds, hard cash, legal tender, riches, the wherewithal, wealth; (*Inf*) bread, dosh, dough, loot, lolly, mazuma, moolah, readies, the ready, spondulix.
monitor *n* guide, invigilator, prefect, supervisor, watchdog.
monitor *v* check, follow, keep an eye on, keep track of, observe, oversee, record, scan, supervise, survey, watch.
monk *n* abbot, brother, friar, monastic, prior, religious.
monkey *n* **1** primate, simian. **2** devil, imp, mischief maker, rascal, rogue, scamp.
monster *adj* colossal, enormous, gigantic, ginormous, huge, mammoth, massive, stupendous, titanic, tremendous, vast; (*Inf*) jumbo, mega, whopping.
monument *n* cairn, cenotaph, commemoration, gravestone, headstone, marker, mausoleum, memorial, obelisk, pillar, shrine, statue, tombstone.
moon *n* satellite.
moon *v* daydream, idle, mooch, mope, waste time.
moor *n* fell, grouse moor, heath, moorland, muir.
moor *v* anchor, berth, dock, fix, lash, make fast, secure, tie up.
more *adj* added, additional, extra, fresh, further, new, other, spare, supplementary.
more *adv* better, further, longer, to a greater extent.
morsel *n* bite, crumb, fragment, grain, mouthful, nibble, scrap, snack, soupçon, taste, titbit.
mortified *v* annoyed, ashamed, embarrassed, humiliated, put to shame, rendered speechless, shamed, vexed; (*Inf*) made to eat humblepie, put out.
motion *n* **1** action, change, flow, locomotion, mobility, move, movement, passage, passing, progress, travel. **2** proposal, proposition, recommendation, submission, suggestion.
motion *v* beckon, direct, gesture, nod, signal, wave.
motivate *v* drive, give incentive to, impel, inspire, instigate, lead, move, persuade, prompt, provoke, stimulate, stir.
motive *n* cause, design, grounds, incentive, inducement, influence, inspiration, motivation, reason.
motley *adj* assorted, diversified, miscellaneous, mixed, varied.
motto *n* formula, proverb, rule, saying, slogan, watchword.
mould *n* **1** cast, die, form, matrix, pattern, shape. **2** brand, build, configuration, construction, cut, design, fashion, form, format, frame, kind, line, make, pattern, shape, structure, style.
mould *v* carve, cast, construct, create, fashion, forge, form, make, model, sculpt, shape, stamp, work.
mouldy *adj* bad, decaying, fusty, mildewed, musty, rotten, rotting, spoiled, stale.
mound *n* **1** barrow, drift, heap, pile, stack. **2** bank, dune, embankment, hill, hillock, hummock, knoll, rise.
mount *v* **1** ascend, climb, go up, scale. **2** climb onto, get astride, get up on, jump on. **3** ascend, rise, soar, tower. **4** accumulate, build, escalate, row, increase, intensify, multiply, pile up, swell. **5** display, frame, set, set off. **6** exhibit, prepare, produce, put on stage.

Monkeys are primates

Most primates live in family groups, except orang-utans who often live alone, joining other orang-utans only to mate.

Gorillas are the largest of the primates and a male can weigh up to 275kg (605lb).

The smallest primates are mouse lemurs which are only 12.5cm (6 inches) in length.

mount *n* **1** backing, base, fixture, foil, frame, mounting, setting, stand, support. **2** horse, steed.
mountain *n* alp, ben, elevation, fell, height, mount, Munro, peak, pinnacle. **3** mound, stack; (*Inf*) ton. **4** excess, surplus.
mountainous *adj* alpine, high, highland, hilly, lofty, rocky, steep, towering, upland.
mouth *n* **1** jaws, lips, muzzle. **2** crevice, door, entrance, gateway, inlet, opening, rim. **3 down in the mouth** blue, depressed, miserable, sad, unhappy; (*Inf*) down in the dumps.
move *v* **1** budge, proceed, progress, shift, stir, walk. **2** carry, shift, switch, transfer, transport. **3** change residence, leave, move house, quit, relocate. **4** activate, drive, propel, push, set going, shift, shove, start, turn. **5** inspire, motivate, persuade, stimulate. **6** advocate, propose, suggest.
move *n* act, action, deed, manoeuvre,measure, motion, ploy, shift, step, turn.
movement *n* **1** action, activity, development, exercise, manoeuvre, motion, move, operation, progress, shift, transfer. **2** campaign, crusade, drive, faction, front, group, grouping, organization, party. **3** division, part, passage, section. **4** beat, cadence, measure, metre, pace, rhythm, swing, tempo.
moving *adj* affecting, arousing, emotional, emotive, exciting, impelling, impressive, inspiring, pathetic, persuasive, poignant, stirring, touching.
mud *n* clay, dirt, silt, sludge.
muddle *v* **1** confuse, disorder, disorganize, jumble, make a mess of, mess, mix up, scramble, spoil, tangle. **2** bewilder, confuse, daze, perplex, stupefy.
muddle *n* chaos, disarray, disorganization, jumble, mess, mix-up, plight, predicament, tangle.
mug *n* beaker, cup, flagon, jug, pot, tankard, toby jug.
mull *v* consider, contemplate, deliberate on, examine, ponder, reflect, study, think about, view.
multiple *adj* collective, many, numerous, several, various.
multiply *v* accumulate, breed, build up, increase, proliferate, propagate, reproduce, spread.
mundane *adj* ordinary, routine.
murky *adj* dark, dim, dismal, dreary, dull, dusky, foggy, gloomy, grey, misty, nebulous, obscure, overcast.
murmur *n* babble, drone, humming, mumble, purr, rumble, undertone, whisper, whispering.
murmur *v* babble, buzz, drone, hum, mumble, mutter, purr, rumble, whisper.
muscle *n* **1** muscle tissue, sinew, tendon, threw. **2** brawn, force, forcefulness, might, potency, power, stamina, strength, sturdiness, weight; (*Inf*) clout.
muscular *adj* athletic, brawny, lusty, powerful, powerfully built, robust, strapping, strong, sturdy, vigorous, well-knit; (*Inf*) beefy, husky.
mushroom *n* chanterelle, fungus, ink-cap, morel.
mushroom *v* boom, burgeon, burst forth, flourish, prosper, spring up, sprout, thrive.
music *n* melody, rhythm, tune.
must *n* **1** essential, fundamental, necessity, prerequisite, requirement, requisite. **2** fungus, mildew, mould.
mute *adj* dumb, mum, silent, speechless, unexpressed, unspeaking, unspoken, voiceless, wordless.
mute *v* dampen, deaden, lower, moderate, muffle, soften, tone down, turn down.
mutilate *v* disfigure, dismember, hack, injure, lacerate, maim.
mutual *adj* common, joint, reciprocated, returned, share.
mystery *n* conundrum, enigma, puzzle, question, riddle, secret.
mystify *v* baffle, bewilder, confuse, perplex, puzzle, stump; (*Inf*) bamboozle, beat.
myth *n* fable, fairy story, fiction, folk tale, legend, parable, saga, story, tradition.
mythical *adj* **1** fabled, fairy-tale, legendary, mythological, storied. **2** fantasy, fictitious, imaginary, invented, make-believe, unreal, untrue; (*Inf*) pretend.
mythology *n* folklore, folk tales, legend, lore, mythos, myths, stories, tradition.

Some mushrooms are found on dying birch trees and an also live for a while on the wood after the tree has died.

Nn

nadir *n* bottom, lowest level, rock-bottom, zero; (*Inf*) the pits.
nag *v* annoy, badger, harass, irritate, pester, plague, provoke, scold, torment.
nail *v* attach, beat, fasten, fix, hammer, join, pin, secure, tack.
naive *adj* innocent, trusting, unworldly.
naked *adj* **1** bare, exposed, nude, stripped, unclothed, undressed. **2** helpless, insecure, vulnerable; (*Inf*) in one's birthday suit, in the buff, starkers.
name *n* **1** alias, Christian name, family name, label, nickname, pet name, pseudonym, stage name, style, surname, tag, title; (*Inf*) handle, moniker. **2** big name, celebrity, dignitary, megastar, star, VIP; (*Inf*) big shot, bigwig. **3** fame, honour, note, praise, prestige, renown, repute, reputation.
name *v* **1** baptize, call, christen, entitle, label, style, term, title. **2** appoint, choose, cite, give, identify, mention, nominate, pick, select, specify.
named *adj* baptized, called, christened, denominated, dubbed, entitled, known as, labelled, styled, termed.
nameless *adj* **1** anonymous, unnamed, untitled. **2** incognito, unknown.
namely *adv* i.e., specifically, that is to say, to wit, viz.
narrate *v* chronicle, describe, detail, recount, relate, repeat, report, set forth, tell, unfold.

The nations of the world are represented in the Olympic flag. There are five Olympic rings to represent the five continents of the world. The colours – blue, black, red, yellow, green – were chosen because every national flag in the world includes at least one of these colours.

narration *n* description, explanation, recital, rehearsal, story telling, voice-over in film or tape.
narrative *n* account, chronicle, detail, history, report, statement, story, tale.
narrator *n* author, chronicler, commentator, reporter, story-teller, writer.
narrow *adj* **1** close, constricted, cramped, limited, meagre, near, restricted, tight. **2** intolerant, narrow-minded, prejudiced, small-minded.
narrow *v* circumscribe, constrict, diminish, limit, reduce, simplify, straiten, tighten.
narrow-minded *adj* biased, bigoted, conservative, hidebound, illiberal, insular, intolerant, opinionated, parochial, petty, prejudiced, provincial, short-sighted, small-minded.
nasty *adj* **1** dirty, disagreeable, disgusting, filthy, foul, horrible, nauseating, objectionable, obnoxious, offensive, repugnant, sickening, unpleasant, vile; (*Inf*) grotty. **2** abusive, annoying, bad-tempered, despicable, disagreeable, distasteful, malicious, mean, spiteful, unpleasant, vicious, vile.
nation *n* commonwealth, community, country, people, population, race, society, state, tribe.
national *adj* **1** countrywide, nationwide, public, state, widespread. **2** domestic, internal, social.
nationality *n* birth, ethnic group, nation, race.
native *adj* **1** built-in, congenital, hereditary, inbred, instinctive, intrinsic, natural. **2** genuine, original, real. **3** domestic, home, home-grown, home-made, indigenous, local. **4** mother.
native *n* aborigine, citizen, countryman, dweller, inhabitant, national, resident.
natural *adj* **1** common, everyday, legitimate, logical, normal, ordinary, regular, typical, usual. **2** characteristic, congenital, essential, inborn, indigenous,

inherent, native. **3** genuine, relaxed, simple, spontaneous, unpretentious, unsophisticated, **4** additive-free, chemical-free, plain, pure, organic, real, whole.
nature *n* **1** attributes, character, complexion, constitution, essence, features, make-up, quality, traits. **2** category, description, kind, sort, species, style, type, variety. **3** cosmos, creation, earth, environment, universe, world. **4** disposition, humour, mood, outlook, temper, temperament. **5** country, countryside, landscape, natural history, scenery.
naughty *adj* bad, defiant, delinquent, disobedient, misbehaved, mischievous, perverse, playful, refractory, roguish, sinful, teasing, wayward, wicked, worthless.
nausea *n* **1** airsickness, biliousness, carsickness, gagging, morning sickness, motion sickness, queasiness, retching, seasickness, sickness, squeamishness, vomiting; (*Inf*) throwing up. **2** disgust, loathing, repugnance, revulsion.
nauseate *v* disgust, horrify, offend, repel, repulse, revolt, sicken, turn one's stomach.
nautical *adj* marine, maritime, naval, oceanic, seafaring, sea going, yachting.
naval *adj* marine, maritime, nautical, oceanic.
navigate *v* cross, cruise, direct, drive, guide, handle, journey, manoeuvre, pilot, plan, plot, sail, skipper, steer, voyage.
navigation *n* **1** cruising, directing, pilotage, steering. **2** helmsmanship, sailing, seamanship, voyaging.
navvy *n* labourer, workman.
navy *n* armada, fleet, flotilla.
near *adj* **1** adjacent, adjoining, alongside, beside, bordering, close by, nearby, neighbouring, touching. **2** approaching, impending, in the offing, looming, near-at-hand, next; (*Inf*) on the cards. **3** allied, attached, connected, familiar, intimate.
nearby *adj* adjacent, adjoining, convenient, neighbouring.
nearly *adv* about, all but, almost, as good as, closely, just about, not quite, practically, roughly, virtually, well-nigh.
nearness *n* **1** accessibility, availability, closeness, handiness, proximity, vicinity. **2** immediacy.
neat *adj* **1** accurate, dainty, nice, orderly, ship-shape, smart, spick-and-span, spruce, straight, systematic, tidy, trim, uncluttered. **2** adept, agile, apt, clever, deft, dexterous, efficient, elegant, expert, graceful, handy, nimble, precise, skilful, stylish, well-judged. **3** pure, straight, diluted.
neatness *n* **1** accuracy, daintiness, orderliness, simplicity, smartness, spruceness, tidiness. **2** agility, cleverness, dexterity, elegance, grace, nimbleness, precision, skilfulness, skill, style, stylishness, wit.
necessarily *adv* accordingly, automatically, certainly, consequently, inevitably.
neuter *v* castrate, dress, emasculate, geld, spay; (*Inf*) doctor, fix.
neutral *adj* disinterested, even-handed, impartial, indifferent, unbiased, undecided.
neutralize *v* cancel, compensate for, counteract, counterbalance, invalidate, negate, undo.
never-ending *adj* continual, eternal, everlasting, nonstop, perpetual, relentless, unbroken, unchanging, uninterrupted.

By navigating a zig zag course, called tacking, sailors are able to sail in the direction they require. It is important that the navigator keeps an accurate check on the boat's position so that it does not travel too far off course.

nevertheless *adv* but, even so, however, nonetheless, notwithstanding, regardless, still, yet.
new *adj* **1** advanced, current, latest, modern, new-fangled, novel, recent, state-of-the-art, ultramodern, up-to-date. **2** added, extra, supplementary. **3** altered, changed, improved, modernized, redesigned.
newcomer *n* arrival, beginner, foreigner, immigrant, novice, outsider, settler; (*Inf*) Johnny-come-lately.
newly *adv* anew, freshly, just, lately, latterly, recently.
news *n* account, advice, bulletin, communiqué, disclosure, exposé, gossip, hearsay, information, intelligence, leak, news-flash, report, rumour, scandal, statement, story.
next *adj* **1** ensuing, following, later, subsequent, succeeding. **2** adjacent, adjoining, closest, nearest, neighbouring.
next *adv* afterwards, closely, following, later, subsequently.
nice *adj* **1** amiable, attractive, charming, delightful, friendly, kind, pleasant, pleasurable, polite, well-mannered. **2** dainty, fine, neat, tidy, trim. **3** accurate, careful, delicate, discriminating, exacting, meticulous, precise, scrupulous, strict, subtle.
niche *v* **1** alcove, corner, hollow, nook, opening, recess. **2** calling, job, place, position, vocation; (*Inf*) slot.
nick *v* chip, cut, damage, dent, mark, notch, scar, score, scratch, snick.
nickname *n* familiar name, label, pet name; (*Inf*) handle, moniker.
night *n* dark, darkness, dead of night, hours of darkness, night-time.

The red-eyed tree frog lives in the rainforests of South America. It is nocturnal only coming out at night among the leaves of the trees where there are plentiful insects for food. The tree frog's toes have sticky pads that provide better grip for climbing.

nightfall *n* dusk, evening, eventide, gloaming, sun-down, sunset, twilight.
nightmare *n* **1** bad dream, hallucination. **2** horror, ordeal, torment.
nil *n* duck, love, naught, nihil, none, nothing, zero; (*Inf*) zilch.
nimble *adj* agile, deft, dexterous, prompt, quick, quick-witted, smart, swift; (*Inf*) nippy.
nip *v* **1** bite, catch, compress, grip, nibble, pinch, snag, snap, squeeze, sting, tweak, twitch. **2** cut off, dock, lop, snip. **3** dart, dash, hurry, rush.
nip *n* dram, drop, finger, mouthful, portion, sip, sup, taste; (*Inf*) peg, shot.
nippy *adj* biting, chilly, nipping, sharp, stinging.
nirvana *n* **1** bliss, joy, peace, serenity, **2** heaven, paradise. **3** enlightenment, oblivion.
noble *n* aristocrat, lady, lord, nobleman, noblewoman, peer.
nocturnal *adj* night, nightly, night-time, of the night.
nod *v* **1** acknowledge, bob, bow, dip, duck, gesture, indicate, salute, signal. **2** agree, assent, concur, show, agreement. **3** be sleepy, doze, droop, drowse, nap, sleep, slump.
node *n* bulge, bump, growth, lump, nodule, protuberance, swelling,
noise *n* babble, blare, clamour, clatter, commotion, cry, din, fracas, hubbub, loud sound, outcry, racket, row, sound, talk, tumult, uproar.
noisy *adj* blaring, blasting, boisterous, chattering,

clamourous, deafening, ear-splitting, loud, obstreperous, piercing, riotous, rowdy, strident, tumultuous, turbulent, uproarious, vociferous.

nomad *n* drifter, itinerant, migrant, rambler, rover, vagabond, wanderer

nominal *adj* **1** formal, ostensible, pretended, professed, puppet, purported, self-styled, so-called, supposed, theoretical, titular. **2** symbolic, token. **3** minimal, trivial.

nominate *v* appoint, assign, choose, commission, designate, elect, elevate, empower, name, present, propose, recommend, select, submit, suggest, term.

nomination *n* appointment, choice, designation, election, proposal, recommendation, selection, suggestion.

nominee *n* aspirant, candidate, contestant, entrant, favourite, protégé, runner.

nondescript *adj* characterless, dull, featureless, ordinary, unexceptional, uninspiring, uninteresting, unremarkable; (*Inf*) common or-garden.

none *pro* nil, nobody, no-one, no part, not a bit, not any, nothing, not one, zero.

non-essential *adj* dispensable, expendable, superfluous, unimportant, unnecessary.

nonetheless *adv* despite that, even so, however, in spite of that, nevertheless, yet.

non-existent *adj* fictional, ficticious, hypothetical, illusory, imaginary, imagined, missing, mythical, unreal.

nonsense *n* absurdity, balderdash, drivel, folly, foolishness, gibberish, jest, ludicrousness, ridiculousness, rot, rubbish, senselessness, silliness, stuff, stupidity, trash, twaddle, waffle; (*Inf*) bull, bunk, bunkum, claptrap, double Dutch, flannel, gobbledegook, mumbo-jumbo, poppycock, tosh, tripe.

Some nomad tribesmen live within the Arctic circle and are constantly moving from place to place to find fresh pasture and food.

nonstop *adj* ceaseless, constant, continuous, direct, endless, incessant, relentless, steady, unbroken, unending, unfaltering, uninterrupted.

nonstop *adv* ceaselessly, continuously, endlessly, incessantly, relentlessly, without stopping.

nook *n* **1** alcove, cavity, corner, cranny, crevice, cubbyhole, gap, hide-out, inglenook, niche, opening, recess, retreat. **2** den, hideaway, refuge, retreat, shelter.

norm *n* average, benchmark, criterion, mean, measure, model, pattern, rule, standard, type, yardstick.

normal *adj* accustomed, acknowledged, average, common, conventional, habitual, natural, ordinary, popular, regular, routine, run-of-the-mill, standard, typical, usual.

nosedive *v* dive, drop, fall, plunge.

nosedive *n* dive, get worse, go down, plunge, plummet, worsen.

nostalgia *n* homesickness, longing, pining, regret, regretfulness, remembrance, reminiscence, wistfulness, yearning.

nostalgic *adj* emotional, homesick, longing, regretful, sentimental, wistful.

nosy *adj* curious, eavesdropping, intrusive, meddlesome, prying.

nothing *n* emptiness, nobody, nonexistence, nothingness, nought, trifle, void, zero.

notice *v* detect, discern, mark, mind, note, observe, perceive, remark, see, spot.

notice *n* **1** consideration, note, observation, regard. **2** advice, announcement, instruction, intelligence, news, notification, order, warning. **3** advertisement, comment, criticism, poster, review, sign.

notion *n* **1** apprehension, belief, concept, conception, idea, impression, inkling, judgment, knowledge, opinion, sentiment, understanding, view. **2** caprice, desire, fancy, impulse, inclination, whim, wish.

notorious *adj* **1** dishonourable, disreputable, infamous, scandalous. **2** blatant, flagrant, glaring, obvious, open, overt, patent, undisputed.

nought *n* naught, nil, nothing, nothingness, zero.

nourish *v* attend, feed, furnish, nurse, nurture, supply, sustain, tend.

nourishing *adj* beneficial, healthful, health-giving, nutritious, wholesome.

nourishment *n* diet, food, nutrition, sustenance.

novel *adj* different, innovative, new, original, rare, singular, strange, uncommon, unfamiliar, unusual.

novel *n* fiction, narrative, romance, story, tale.

novelty *n* **1** freshness, innovation, originality, surprise, unfamiliarity. **2** bagatelle, bauble, curiosity, gadget, gimmick, knick-knack, memento, souvenir, trinket.

novice *n* amateur, apprentice, beginner, convert, greenhorn, learner, neophyte, newcomer, novitiate, probationer, pupil; (*Inf*) rookie.

now *adv* at once, immediately, instantly, presently, promptly, straightaway, without delay

nucleus *n* basis, centre, core, focus, heart, kernel, marrow, nub, pith, pivot.

nude *adj au naturel*, bare, disrobed, exposed, naked, stark-naked, stripped, unclad, unclothed, uncovered, undressed; (*Inf*) in one's birth-day suit, in the buff, in the raw, naked as the day one was born, mother naked, starkers, without a stitch on.

nudge *v* bump, dig, elbow, jog, poke, prod, push, shove, touch.

Nourishment is required immediately when baby birds first hatch. At this stage many of them have no feathers. Blind and helpless they are completely dependent on their parents for food and protection. As they grow, they become fledglings, with open eyes and healthy appetites.

nudity *n* bareness, nakedness, nudism, undress.

nugget *n* chunk, clump, hunk, lump, mass, piece.

nuisance *n* bore, bother, inconvenience, irritation, pest, plague, trouble, vexation.

numb *adj* dead, frozen, insensitive, paralysed, unfeeling.

numb *v* deaden, dull, freeze, immobilize, paralyse, stun.

number *n* **1** character, count, digit, figure, integer, numeral, sum, total, unit. **2** aggregate, amount, collection, company, crowd, horde, many, multitude, quantity, throng. **3** copy, edition, imprint, issue, printing.

number *v* account, add, calculate, compute, count, enumerate, include, reckon, tell, total.

numbness *n* deadness, insensitivity, paralysis.

numeral *n* character, digit, figure, integer, number, symbol.

numerous *adj* abundant, many, plentiful, profuse, several.

nunnery *n* abbey, cloister, convent, house, monastery.

nurse *v* **1** care for, look after, tend, treat. **2** breast-feed, feed, nourish, nurture, suckle, wet-nurse. **3** cherish. **4** cultivate, encourage, foster, harbour, keep alive, preserve, promote.

nurture *n* diet, food, nourishment.

nurture *v* **1** feed, nourish, nurse, support, sustain, tend. **2** bring up, cultivate, develop, educate, instruct, rear, school, train.

nutritious *adj* beneficial, health-giving, nourishing, wholesome.

nuts and bolts *pl n* basics, essentials, fundamentals, practicalities; (*Inf*) nitty-gritty.

Oo

oar *n* paddle.
oasis *n* haven, island, refuge, retreat, sanctuary, sanctum.
oath *n* **1** pledge, promise, sworn, statement, vow, word. **2** curse, profanity, strong language, swear-word; (*Inf*) cuss.
obedience *n* agreement, compliance, duty, observance, respect, submissiveness.
obedient *adj* compliant, docile, dutiful, law-abiding, observant, respectful, subservient, under control, well-trained.
obese *adj* fat, gross, heavy, overweight, plump, podgy, portly, roly-poly, rotund, stout, tubby; (*Inf*) well-upholstered.
obey *v* **1** act upon, adhere to, be ruled by, carry out, comply, conform, execute, follow, keep, observe, serve. **2** bow to, come to heel, do what one is told, get into line, give in, give way, submit, surrender to, toe the line, yield; (*Inf*) knuckle under.
object *n* **1** article, item, thing. **2** aim, focus, target, victim. **3** design, end purpose, goal, idea, intention, objective, point, purpose, reason.
object *v* argue, against, demur, expostulate, oppose, protest, raise objections, take exception.
objection *n* censure, doubt, exception, opposition, protest; (*Inf*) niggle.
objectionable *adj* distasteful, offensive, unpleasant.
objective *adj* detached, even-handed, fair, impartial, impersonal, just, open-minded, unbiased, unprejudiced.
objective *n* aim, ambition, aspiration, design, end, end in view, goal, intention, mark, object, purpose, target.
obligation *n* accountability, burden, compulsion, duty, liability, must, onus, requirement, responsibility, trust.
obligatory *adj* binding, coercive, compulsory, *de rigueur*, enforced, essential, imperative, mandatory, necessary, required, requisite, unavoidable.
oblige *v* **1** bind, coerce, compel, constrain, force, impel, make, necessitate, obligate, require. **2** accommodate, benefit, do someone a favour, gratify, indulge, please, put oneself out for, serve.
obliging *adj* accommodating, agreeable, considerate, cooperative, courteous, eager to please, friendly, helpful, polite, willing.
oblique *n* angled, at an angle, back slash, inclined, slanted, slanting line, sloping, tilted.
obliterate *v* annihilate, cancel, delete, destroy, eradicate, erase, wipe out.
oblivion *n* **1** disuse, neglect, suspension. **2** blackness, blankness, coma, darkness, eclipse, senseless. **3** amnesia, disregard, forgetfullness, preoccupation.
oblivious *adj* blind, careless, deaf, disregardful, forgetful, heedless, ignorant, inattentive, insensible, neglectful, negligent, regardless, unaware, unconcerned, unconscious, unmindful, unobservant.
obscure *adj* **1** ambiguous, deep, doubtful, hazy, hidden, indefinite, involved, mysterious, vague. **2** blurred, clouded, dim, faint, indistinct, murky, shadowy, shady, unlit, veiled.

An oasis is a fertile patch in a desert where water reaches ground level. No plants or animals can survive with no water at all for a prolonged period, but in desert regions many living things have adapted to thrive with very little water.

An observatory is an institution or building specially designed and equipped with powerful telescopes to observe meteorological and astronomical phenomena.

obscure *v* **1** conceal, disguise, hide, muddy, screen, throw a veil over, veil. **2** block, block out, blur, cloak, cloud, darken, dim, dull, eclipse, mask, overshadow, shade, shroud.

observance *n* **1** carrying out, compliance, honouring, notice, observation. **2** ceremony, custom, fashion, form, practice, rite, ritual, service, tradition.

observant *adj* alert, attentive, eagle-eyed, mindful, obedient, quick, sharp-eyed, vigilant, watchful, wide-awake.

observation *n* attention, consideration, experience, inspection, monitoring, notice, review scrutiny, study, surveillance.

observe *v* **1** detect, discern, discover, notice, see, spot, witness. **2** contemplate, keep under observation, look at, monitor, scrutinize, study, survey, view, watch; (*Inf*) keep an eye on. **3** comment, declare, mention, remark, say, state. **4** comply, conform to, follow, honour, keep, obey, perform, respect. **5** celebrate, commemorate, keep, remember.

observer *n* bystander, eye-witness, onlooker, spectator, spotter, viewer, watcher, witness.

obsessive *adj* compulsive, consuming, gripping, haunting, tormenting, unforgettable.

obsolescent *adj* declining, disappearing, dying out, going out of fashion, on the decline, on the way out, past its prime, waning; (I*nf*) not with it.

obsolete *adj* ancient, antiquated, archaic, dated, disused, extinct, musty, old, old-fashioned, out of date, out of fashion, passé; (*Inf*) out of the ark.

obstacle *n* bar, barrier, check, difficulty, hitch, obstruction, snag, stumbling block.

obstinate *adj* determined, dogged, firm, inflexible, intransigent, persistent, pig-headed, strong minded, stubborn, tenacious, unyielding, wilful.

obstruct *v* bar, barricade, block, bring to a standstill, check, curb, cut off, frustrate, get in the way of, hamper, hinder, hold up, impede, inhibit, interfere with, interrupt, obscure, prevent, restrict, retard, shield, shut off, slow down, stop, thwart. hindrance, snag, stop, stoppage.

obstructive *adj* awkward, blocking, delaying, hindering, inhibiting, preventative, restrictive, stalling, unhelpful.

obtain *v* achieve, acquire, attain, come by, earn, gain, get hold of, get ones hands on, procure, secure.

obtrusive *adj* forward, interfering, intrusive, meddling, nosy, prying; (*Inf*) pushy.

obvious *adj* apparent, clear, clear as a bell, distinct, evident, noticeable, open, overt, patent, pronounced, self-evident, straightforward, transparent, unconcealed, unmistakable, visible; (*Inf*) plain as the nose on your face, right under one's nose, staring one in the face, sticking out a mile.

occasion *n* **1** chance, convenience, incident, moment, occurrence,opportunity, time. **2** affair, celebration, event, experience, happening. **3** call, cause, excuse, grounds, inducement, influence, justification, motive, prompting, provocation, reason.

occasional *adj* casual, desultory,

The occupants of the rain forest live in four overlapping layers.
(1) The emergent layer – free flying birds and bats. (2) tree canopy – birds, fruit bats, monkeys and squirrels. (3) the mid zone – monkeys, squirrels, birds plus snakes and tree frogs. (4) forest floor – deer, elephants, jaguars and bush pigs.

incidental, infrequent, intermittent, irregular, odd, rare.

occasionally *adv* at intervals, at times, every now and then, every so often, from time to time, now and again, off and on, on and off, once in a while, periodically, sometimes.

occupant *n* addressee, dweller, householder, incumbent, indweller, inhabitant, inmate, lease-holder, occupier, owner-occupier, resident, tenant, user.

occupation *n* **1** activity, business, calling, craft, employment, job, line of work, post, profession, pursuit, trade. **2** control, holding, occupancy, possession, residence, tenancy, tenure, use. **3** conquest, foreign rule, invasion, seizure, subjugation.

occupied *adj* **1** busy, employed, engaged, working; (*Inf*) hard at it, tied up. **2** full, in use, taken, unavailable. **3** inhabited, lived-in, settled, tenanted.

occupy *v* **1** absorb, amuse, busy, divert, employ, engage, engross, entertain, hold the attention of, immerse, interest, involve, keep busy or occupied, monopolize, pre-occupy, take up, tie up. **2** capture, garrison, hold, invade, keep, overrun, seize, take over, take possession of.

occur *v* arise, befall, betide, chance, come about, eventuate, happen, materialize, result, take place; (*Inf*) crop up, turn up.

occurrence *n* adventure, afar, circumstance, episode, event, happening, incident, instance, proceeding, transaction.

odd *adj* **1** abnormal, atypical, bizarre, curious, deviant, different, eccentric, exceptional, extraordinary, fantastic, freak, freakish, funny, irregular, outlandish, out of the ordinary, peculiar, quaint, queer, rare, remarkable, singular, strange, uncanny, uncommon, unconventional, unusual, weird, whimsical. **2** leftover, lone, remaining, single, solitary, spare, surplus, unconsumed, uneven, unmatched; (*Inf*) freaky, kinky.

oddity *n* abnormality, anomaly, eccentricity, freak, idiosyncrasy, irregularity, peculiarity, phenomenon, quirk, rarity; (*Inf*) kink.

odds *pl n* **1** advantage, edge, lead, superiority. **2** balance, chances, likelihood, probability. **3** difference, disparity, dissimilarity, distinction.

odour *n* aroma, bouquet, essence, fragrance, perfume redolence, scent, smell, stench, stink.

off *adj* **1** absent, cancelled, finished, gone, inoperative, postponed, unavailable. **2** bad, below par, disappointing, disheartening, displeasing, low-quality, mortifying, poor, quiet, slack, substandard, unrewarding, unsatisfactory. **3** bad, decomposed, high, mouldy, rancid, rotten, sour.

off and on *adv* every now and again, every once in a while, from time to time, intermittently, now and then, occasionally, on and off, sometimes, sporadically.

offbeat *adj* bizarre, Bohemian, eccentric, hippy, idiosyncratic, novel,strange, uncommon, unconventional, unorthodox, unusual, weird; (*Inf*) far-out, freaky, kinky, oddball, wayout.

offence *n* **1** breach of conduct, crime, delinquency, fault lapse, misdeed, misdemeanour, eccadillo, sin, transgression, respass, wrong, wrongdoing. **2** anger, annoyance, displeasure, hard feelings, huff, indignation, needle, pique, resentment, wounded, feelings, wrath.

offend *v* **1** affront, annoy, disgruntle, displease, fret, gall, give offence, hurt someone's feelings, insult, irritate, outrage, pain, pique, provoke, rile, slight, snub, upset, vex, wound; (*Inf*) miff, put someone's back up, tread on someone's toes. **2** be disagreeable to, disgust, nauseate, repel, repulse, sicken; (*Inf*) turn someone off.

offender *n* criminal, crook, culprit, delinquent, lawbreaker, malefactor, miscreant, sinner, transgressor, wrongdoer

offensive *adj* **1** abusive, annoying, disrespectful, insulting, objectionable, rude, uncivil. **2** detestable, disgusting, nasty, obnoxious, revolting, sickening, unpleasant, vile. **3** aggressive, attacking, invading.

offensive *v* attack, drive, onslaught; (*Inf*) push.

offer *v* **1** bid, extend, give, hold out, put on the market, put up for sale, tender. **2** afford, furnish, make available, place at someone's disposal, present, provide, show. **3** advance, extend, move, propose, put forward, submit, suggest. **4** be at someone's service, come forward, offer one's services, volunteer.

offer *n* attempt, bid, endeavour, essay, overture, proposal, proposition, submission, suggestion, tender.

offering *n* contribution, donation, gift, oblation, present, sacrifice, subscription.

Police officer.

offhand *adj* abrupt, aloof, brusque, careless, casual, cavalier, couldn't care less, curt, glib, informal, off-handed, unconcerned, uninterested; (*Inf*) take it or leave it.

office *n* appointment, business, capacity, charge, commission, duty, employment, function, obligation, occupation, place, post, responsibility, role, service, situation, station, trust, work.

officer *n* agent, appointee, dignitary, executive, official, public servant, representative.

official *adj* accredited, authentic, authoritative, authorized, bona fide, certified, endorsed, formal, legitimate, licensed, proper, sanctioned; (*Inf*) straight from the horses mouth.

official *n* agent, bureaucrat, executive, functionary, office bearer, officer, representative.

officiate *v* chair, conduct, manage, oversee, preside, serve, superintend.

off-load *v* discharge, dump, get rid of, jettison, shift, transfer, unburden, unload.
off-putting *adj* daunting, disconcerting, discouraging, dismaying, dispiriting, disturbing, formidable, frustrating, intimidating, unnerving, unsettling, upsetting.
offset *v* balance out, cancel out, compensate for, counteract, counterbalance, counterpoise, countervail, make up for, neutralize.
offshoot *n* adjunct, appendage, branch, by-product, development, limb, outgrowth, spin-off, sprout.
often *adv* again and again, frequently, generally, many a time, over and over again, repeatedly, time after time, time and again.
oil *v* grease, lubricate.
old *adj* **1** advanced in years, aged, ancient, decrepit, elderly, grey-haired, grizzled, mature, past one's prime, senile; (*Inf*) getting on, over the hill. **2** antiquated, antique, dated, decayed, obsolete, out of date, passé, stale. **3** aboriginal, antique, archaic, bygone, early, of old, original, primitive, remote. **4** age-old, experienced, familiar, hardened, long-established, practised, skilled, time-honoured, traditional, versed, veteran, vintage.
old-fashioned *adj* ancient, archaic, behind the times, dated, dead, obsolete, oldfangled, old hat, out-dated, outmoded, out of date, out of style, passé, past, unfashionable; (*Inf*) not with it, out of the ark, square.

This old-fashioned car, driven by its manufacturer Mr Walter Arnold, is competing in the first London to Brighton race in 1896. Cars built from 1896 to 1914 are known as veteran cars, those built from 1919 to 1930 are known as vintage cars.

omen *n* indication, premonition, prognostication, sign, warning, writing on the wall.
ominous *adj* dark, fateful, foreboding, menacing, sinister, threatening, unpromising.
omission *n* default, exclusion, failure, gap, lack, leaving out, neglect, oversight.
omit *v* disregard, drop, eliminate, exclude, fail, forget, give something a miss, leave out, leave something undone, miss out, neglect, overlook, pass over, skip.
once *adv* **1** at one time, formerly, in the old days, in the past, in times gone by, long ago, once upon a time, previously. **2** at once, directly, forthwith, immediately, instantly, now, right-away, straightaway, this very minute, without delay, without hesitation. **3** at the same time, simultaneously, together.
one-sided *adj* biased, coloured, discriminatory, inequitable, lopsided, partial, partisan, prejudiced, unequal, unfair, unjust.
onlooker *n* bystander, eye-witness, observer, spectator, viewer, watcher, witness.
only *adv* at most, barely, exclusively, just, merely, purely, simply.
only *adj* exclusive, individual, lone, one and only, single, sole, solitary, unique.
onslaught *n* assault, attack, blitz, charge, offensive, onrush, onset.
ooze *v* bleed, discharge, drain, dribble, drip, drop, emit, escape, exude, filter, leach, leak, overflow with, percolate, seep strain, sweat, weep.

opaque *adj* clouded, cloudy, dim, dull, hazy, muddy, murky.
open *adj* **1** expanded, extended, gaping, uncovered, unlocked, unsealed, yawning. **2** airy, bare, clear, exposed, extensive, free, navigable, passable, rolling, spacious, sweeping, uncrowded, wide-open. **3** accessible, free, public, unrestricted, vacant. **4** apparent, clear, evident, frank, obvious, undisguised, visible. **5** debatable, unsettled, up in the air. **6** candid, fair, frank, honest, innocent, sincere, transparent. **7** exposed, unprotected.
open *v* **1** begin, commence, get the ball rolling, initiate, launch, set in motion, set up shop, start; (*Inf*) kickoff. **2** crack, throw wide, unblock, uncork, uncover, undo, unfasten, unlock, untie, unwrap. **3** expand, spread out, unfold, unfurl, unroll.
open-air *adj* alfresco, outdoor.
opening *n* **1** aperture, break, crack, fissure, gap, hole, slot, space. **2** chance, opportunity, place, vacancy. **3** beginning, birth, dawn, inauguration, inception, launch, onset, outset, start; (*Inf*) break, kickoff, look-in. **4** beginning, commencing, early, first, inaugural, initial, initiatory, introductory, maiden, primary.
open-minded *adj* broad minded, enlightened, impartial, liberal, reasonable, receptive, tolerant, unbiased, unprejudiced.
operate *v* act, function, perform, run, work.
operation *n* **1** action, campaign, course, exercise, manoeuvre, movement, performance, procedure, process, running, use, working. **2** activity, agency, effect, effort, force, influence, instrumentality, manipulation. **3** affair, business, deal, enterprise, proceeding, transaction, undertaking. **4 in operation** effective, functioning, going, in action, in force, operative.
operational *adj* functional, in working order, operative, prepared, ready, useable, viable, workable, working.
operator *n* conductor, driver, handler, mechanic, operative, practitioner, skilled employee, technician, worker.
opinion *n* assessment, belief, estimation, feeling, impression,

Operation Overlord. The miltary invasion of Normandy by the US and British Armed Forces in 1944 during World War II was known as Operation Overlord. Troops are seen here assembling at Weymouth ready for the attack which took place on the night of June 5/6 on Utah, Omaha, Gold, Juno and Sword beaches. The landings proved to be a turning point in the war with Germany, eventually leading to peace in 1945.

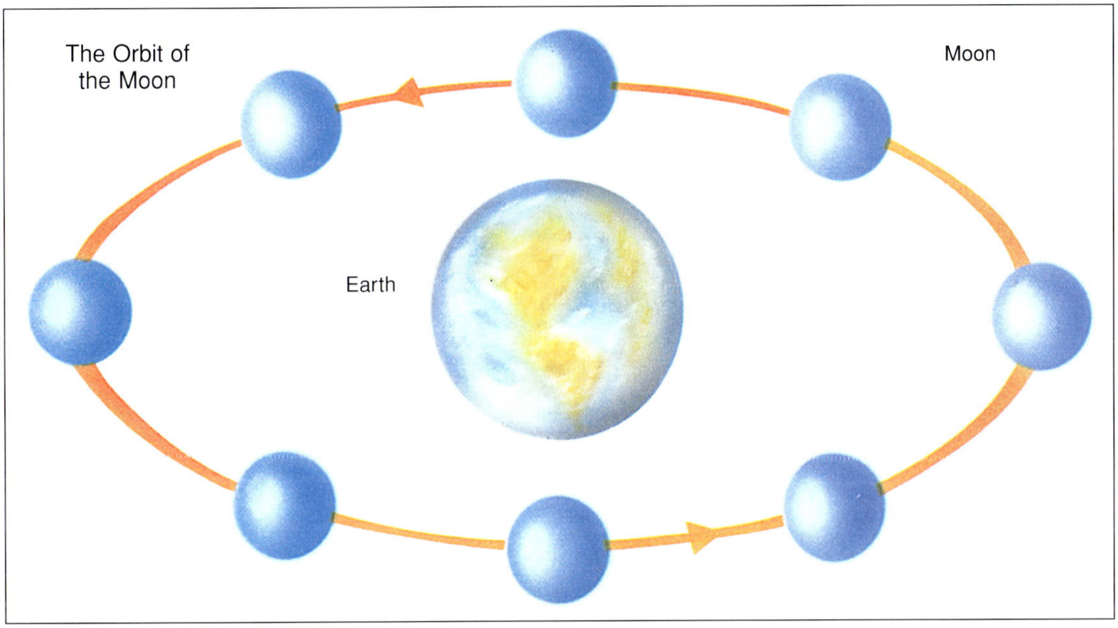

The Moon orbits the Earth once every 27.3 days and is lit by the Sun as it moves around. The Moon doesn't actually change shape although it appears to. Only the part of the Moon that is turned towards the Earth and is lit by the Sun is visible on Earth. The amount of the Moon's surface that can be seen changes with the position of the Moon.

judgment, persuasion, point of view, theory.

opinionated *adj* adamant, biased, bull-headed, dogmatic, inflexible, obstinate, pig-headed, single-minded, stubborn.

opponent *n* adversary, antagonist, challenger, competitor, contender, contestant, enemy, foe, opposer, rival, the opposition.

opportune *adj* advantageous, appropriate, apt, auspicious, convenient, favourable, felicitous, fit, fitting, fortunate, happy, lucky, proper, suitable, timely, well-timed.

opportunity *n* chance, moment, occasion, opening, scope, time; (*Inf*) break, look-in.

oppose *v* bar, check, combat, confront, contradict, counter, counterattack, defy, face, fight, fly in the face of, hinder, obstruct, take on, withstand.

opposed *v* against, antagonistic, conflicting, incompatible, in opposition, opposing, opposite.

opposite *adj* **1** corresponding, facing. **2** adverse, conflicting, contradictory, contrasted, different, diverse, hostile, inconsistent, reverse, unlike.

opposite *n* contradiction, converse, reverse; (*Inf*) the other side of the coin.

opposition *n* **1** antagonism, competition, disapproval, hostility, resistance. **2** antagonist, competition, foe, opponent, other side, rival

oppress *v* **1** burden, depress, harass, sadden, take the heart out of, torment. **2** abuse, crush, maltreat, overpower, persecute.

oppressive *adj* **1** brutal, cruel, harsh, inhuman, overbearing, repressive, severe, tyrannical, unjust. **2** airless, close, heavy, muggy, overpowering, stifling, suffocating, sultry.

oppressor *n* bully, tyrant.

opt for *v* choose, decide on, elect, make a selection, prefer; (*Inf*) go for.

optimistic *adj* bright, buoyant, buoyed up, cheerful, confident, encouraged, hopeful, positive.

option *n* alternative, choice, preference, selection.

optional *adj* discretionary, elective, extra, possible, up to the individual, voluntary.

oral *adj* spoken, verbal, vocal.

orator *n* lecturer, public speaker, speaker.

orbit *n* **1** circle, circumgyration, course, cycle, ellipse, path, revolution, rotation,trajectory.

2 compass, course, domain, range, reach, scope, sphere, sweep.
orbit *v* circle, circumnavigate, encircle, revolve around.
ordain *v* **1** anoint, appoint, call, consecrate, destine, elect, invest, nominate. **2** fate, intend, predetermine. **3** decree, dictate, enjoin, fix, lay down, legislate, order, prescribe, pronounce, rule, set, will.

Ornithology

Ornithology is the study of birds. Different species of birds have different diets and the shape of their beaks are adapted to the foods they eat:(1) A short beak for cracking seeds or nuts; (2) a sharp hooked beak for tearing meat; (3) a long thin beak to get shellfish out of their shells; (4) a scooped beak for digging through mud at the bottom of ponds.

ordeal *n* affliction, agony, anguish, nightmare, suffering, teat torture, trial, tribulations, troubles.
order *n* **1** arrangement, method, neatness, organization, pattern, plan, sequence, series. **2** calm, control, discipline, law and order, peace, quiet, rule. **3** caste, class, degree, grade, hierarchy, position, rank, status. **4** family, kind, sort, species, tribe, type; (*Inf*) pecking order. **5** command, decree, dictate, instruction, law, mandate, rule; (*Inf*) say-so. **6** application, booking, request, reservation. **7** association, community, company, fraternity, guild, league, lodge, organization, sect, society, union.
order *v* **1** bid, charge, command, direct, instruct, ordain, prescribe, require. **2** apply for, book, call for, request, send away for. **3** arrange, catalogue, classify, conduct, control, dispose, group, lay out, manage, organize, set in order, sort out, systematize.
ordinary *adj* **1** common, everyday, normal, regular, routine, standard, typical. (*Inf*) common. **2** conventional, familiar, modest, plain, run-of-the-mill, simple. **3** average, fair, mediocre, second-rate, stereotyped, unremarkable.
organ *n* **1** device, implement, instrument, tool. **2** element, member, part, process, structure, unit. **3** agency, channel, forum, journal, means, medium, mouthpiece, newspaper, paper, periodical, publication, voice.
organism *n* animal, being, body, creature, entity, living thing.
organization *n* **1** arrangement, coordination, management, planning, structuring. **2** alliance, association, body, business, club, combine, company, concern, confederation, consortium, corporation, federation, group, institution, league, syndicate; (*Inf*) outfit.
origin *n* **1** basis, beginning, birth, creation, dawning, early stages, fountain, genesis, inauguration, inception, launch, origination, outset, start. **2** background, descent, extraction, family, parentage, pedigree, roots, source, stock.
original *adj* **1** aboriginal, earliest, first, initial, primary, primitive. **2** creative, fresh, imaginative, ingenious, innovative, inventive, new, novel, resourceful, thoughtful, unusual. **3** authentic, genuine, real.
originate *v* **1** begin, emerge, flow, issue, proceed, result, rise, spring, start, stem. **2** bring about, conceive, create, develop, evolve, institute, invent, launch, pioneer, produce, set in motion.
ornament *n* **1** accessory, adornment, bauble, decoration, embellishment, frill, garnish, knick-knack, trimming, trinket.
ornithology *n* bird watching.
orphan *n* foundling, stray, waif.
orthodox *adj* accepted, approved, conformist, conventional, customary, established, mainstream, normal, official, ordinary, regular, traditional, usual; (*Inf*) kosher.
ostensible *adj* alleged, apparent, avowed, exhibited, outward, plausible, pretended, professed, superficial, supposed, visible; (*Inf*) put on.
other *adj* **1** additional, alternative, auxiliary, extra, further, more, spare,

supplementary. **2** contrasting, different, distinct, diverse, remaining, separate, unrelated.
otherwise *adv* differently, if not, in other respects, in other ways, or else, or then.
out *adj* **1** impossible, not allowed, ruled out, unacceptable; (*Inf*) not on. **2** abroad, absent, away, elsewhere, gone, not at home, outside.
outbreak *n* burst, epidemic, eruption, explosion, flare-up, flash, outburst, rash, spasm, upsurge.
outcast *n* castaway, derelict, displaced person, exile, leper, pariah, *persona non grata,* refugee, untouchable, vagabond.
outcome *n* after-effect, aftermath, conclusion, consequence, end result, issue, result, upshot; (*Inf*) payoff.
outcry *n* clamour, commotion, complaint, exclamation, howl, hue and cry, hullabaloo, noise, outburst, protest, scream, uproar.
outdated *adj* antiquated, antique, archaic, démodé, obsolete, old-fashioned, outmoded, out of date, out of fashion, passé, unfashionable; (*Inf*) behind the times.
outdoor *adj* alfresco, open-air, out-of-doors, outside.
outer *adj* exposed, exterior, external, outlying, outside, outward, peripheral, remote, superficial, surface.
outfit *n* accoutrements, clothes, costume, garb, gear, kit, suit; (*Inf*) get-up, rigout, togs.
outfit *v* appoint, equip, fit out, furnish, kit out, provision, stock, supply, turn out.
outgoing *adj* **1** departing, ex-, former, late, leaving, retiring, with-drawing. **2** affectionate, communicative, demonstrative, easygoing, extrovert, friendly, genial, sociable, talkative.
outgoings *pl n* costs, expenses, outlay, overheads.
outing *n* excursion, expedition, jaunt, pleasure trip, trip; (*Inf*) spin.
outlandish *adj* alien, barbarous, bizarre, eccentric, exotic, fantastic, foreign, freakish, grotesque, outré, preposterous, queer, strange, unheard-of, weird; (*Inf*) far-out.
outlaw *n* bandit, brigand, desperado, fugitive, highwayman, marauder, outcast, pariah, robber.
outlaw *v* ban, banish, bar, condemn,embargo, exclude, forbid, prohibit, proscribe, put a price on someone's head.
outlay *n* charge, cost, disbursement, expenditure, expenses, investment, money spent, outgoings, payment, price, spending.

Outlaws of the wild west between1860 and 1890 were legendary for their ruthless use of the gun. Jesse James killed and robbed his way into the folklore of the west, but was finally shot in the back by Robert Ford a member of his own gang in 1882. However Butch Cassidy, real name Robert Leroy Parker, was never known to kill anyone leaving the "dirty work" to his gunfighter partner The Sundance Kid (Harry Longabaugh). Butch and Sundance are pictured with other members of their notorious Wild Bunch gang in the 1890s towards the end of the age of the gun-fighting outlaw (Butch far right; Sundance left).

JESSE JAMES

BUTCH CASSIDY

Sporting activity and exercise in general is a good outlet for aggression and human energy. It allows sportsmen and women to express themselves physically and in a way in which many would otherwise find difficult to articulate.

outlet *n* avenue, channel, duct, egress, exit, means of expression, opening, orifice, release, safety, valve, vent, way out.
outline *n* **1** draft, framework, layout, plan, rough, skeleton, sketch. **2** bare facts, résumé, rough idea, summary, synopsis. **3** configuration, contour, form, profile, shape, silhouette.
outline *v* draft, plan, rough out, sketch in, summarize, trace.
outlook *n* **1** angle, attitude, frame of mind, perspective, point of view, slant, standpoint, viewpoint, views. **2** expectations, forecast, future, prospect.
output *n* manufacture, product, production, productivity, yield.
outrage *n* **1** atrocity, barbarism, evil. **2** abuse, affront, injury, insult, offence, shock, violation. **3** anger, fury, hurt, resentment.
outrage *v* incense, infuriate, madden, make one's blood boil, offend, shock.
outrageous *adj* **1** abominable, atrocious, beastly, horrible, inhuman, scandalous, shocking, violent, wicked. **2** disgraceful, excessive, exorbitant, unreasonable; (*Inf*) steep.
outright *adj* **1** absolute, complete, downright, out-and-out, perfect pure, thorough, total, utter, wholesale. **2** definite, direct, flat, straightforward.
outright *adv* **1** completely. **2** at once, cleanly, immediately, instantaneously, instantly, on the spot, straight away, there and then, without more ado.
outset *n* beginning, early days, inception, onset, opening, start, starting point; (*Inf*) kickoff.
outside *adj* **1** exterior, external, outdoor, outer, outward, surface. **2** distant, faint, marginal, negligible, remote, slight, slim, small.
outside *n* exterior, façade, face, front, skin, surface, topside.
outskirts *pl n* borders, boundary, edge, periphery, suburbs, vicinity.
outspoken *adj* abrupt, blunt, candid, direct, explicit, forthright, frank, plain-spoken, unreserved.
outstanding *adj* **1** celebrated, distinguished, eminent, excellent, exceptional, great, important, impressive, special, well-known. **2** conspicuous, eye-catching, marked, memorable, notable, prominent, striking. **3** due, owing, payable, pending, remaining, uncollected, unpaid, unresolved, unsettled.
outward *adj* apparent, evident, noticeable, obvious, visible.
outweigh *v* compensate for, eclipse, make up for, outbalance, overcome, override, predominate, prevail over, take precedence over, tip the scales.
outwit *v* cheat, deceive, defraud, dupe, get the better of, make a fool of, outfox, outmanoeuvre, swindle; (*Inf*) outsmart, put one over on, run rings round, take in.
ovation *n* acclaim, applause, cheering, clapping, tribute.
over *adv* **1** ancient history, closed, completed, concluded,

done with, ended, finished, gone, no more, past, terminated. **2** extra, in addition, in excess, left over, remaining, superfluous, surplus, unused.
over *prep* **1** above, on, on top of, superior to, upon. **2** above, exceeding, in excess of, more than. **3** around, everywhere, throughout.
overall *adj* all-embracing, blanket, complete, comprehensive, general, global, inclusive, long-range, long-term, total, umbrella
overbalance *v* capsize, keel over, lose one's balance, lose one's footing, overturn, slip, take a tumble, topple over, tumble, upset.
overbearing *v* arrogant, autocratic, cavalier, dictatorial, superior, tyrannical; (*Inf*) bossy.
overcast *adj* cloudy, darkened, dismal, dreary, dull, grey, hazy, murky, sombre, threatening.
overcharge *v* cheat, fleece, shortchange, surcharge; (*Inf*) diddle, do, rip off.
overcome *v* beat, conquer, crush, defeat, get the better of, master, overpower, overwhelm, prevail, rise above, subdue, survive, triumph over.
overcrowded *adj* choked, congested, crammed full, jam-packed, overloaded, packed out, swarming; (*Inf*) chock-a-block.
overdo *v* exaggerate, go to extremes, not know when to stop, overindulge, overplay, overstate, overwork, run, riot; (*Inf*) do to death, go overboard, lay it on thick.
overdone *adj* **1** excessive, over-elaborate, too much, undue, unnecessary. **2** burnt, burnt to a cinder, charred, dried up, over-cooked, spoiled.
overdue *adj* behind schedule, behind time, late, long delayed, owing, unpunctual; (*Inf*) not before time.
overemphasize *v* **1** blow up out of all proportion, lay too much stress on, make something out of nothing, make too much of, overdramatize, overstress; (*Inf*) make a big thing of, make a mountain out of a molehill.
overflow *v* cover, deluge, drown, flood, inundate, soak, submerge, swamp.
overflow *n* discharge, flash flood, flood, flooding,

Overcrowded cities result in tall skyscraper buildings. In confined spaces such as New York or Tokyo, the inhabitants have to build upwards rather than spread out. In Tokyo (top picture) the buildings are all specially designed to resist earthquake tremors. New York is a city built on water. Of its five boroughs, Manhattan (seen above) and Staten Island are islands, Brooklyn and Queens are on the western end of a large island called Long Island and the Bronx is a peninsula surrounded on three sides by water.

inundation, spilling over, surplus.
overflowing *adj* brimful, copious, plentiful, profuse, rife, teeming.
overhaul *v* **1** check, examine, inspect, recondition, repair, restore, service; (*Inf*) do up. **2** catch up with, get ahead of, overtake, pass.
overhaul *n* check, checkup, examination, going-over, inspection, reconditioning, service; (*Inf*) going-over.
overhead *adv* above, aloft, atop, in the sky, on high, skyward, up above, upward.
overhead *adj* aerial, overhanging, roof, upper.
overheads *pl n* disbursement, expenditure, expenses, operating costs, running costs.
overjoyed *adj* delightful, deliriously happy, elated, euphoric, happy as a lark, happy as a sandboy, in raptures, joyful, jubilant, thrilled, tickled pink; (*Inf*) on cloud nine, rapt.
overlook *v* **1** disregard, fail to notice, forget, ignore, leave undone, miss, neglect, omit, pass, slight, slip up on. **2** condone, disregard, excuse, forgive, let bygones be bygones, let pass, make allowances for, pardon, turn a blind eye to.
overpower *v* beat, conquer, crush, defeat, get the upper hand over, immobilize, knock out, master, overcome, overthrow, overwhelm, quell, subdue.
overrate *v* assess too highly, exaggerate, make too much of, overestimate, overpraise, rate too highly, think or expect too much of, think too highly of.
overriding *adj* central, chief, compelling, dominant, final, focal, major, number one, overruling, paramount, pivotal, predominant, prevailing, primary, prime, principal, ruling, supreme, ultimate.
overrule *v* alter, annul, cancel, countermand, make null and void, overturn, recall, repeal, reverse, revoke, rule against, set aside, veto.
overseer *n* chief, foreman, manager, master, superintendent, superior, supervisor; (*Inf*) boss, gaffer, super.

Overhead cables carrying electrical power between pylons are such a familiar sight these days that is hard to remember that 200 hundred years ago no one had any electrical appliances, lighting or heating.

overshadow *v* **1** dominate, dwarf, eclipse, excel, leave in the shade, outshine, outweigh, put in the shade, render insignificant, by comparison, rise above, steal the limelight from, surpass, take the precedence over, tower above, transcend, upstage. **3** cloud, darken, dim, obscure, veil.
oversight *n* **1** blunder, carelessness, delinquency, error, fault, inattention, lapse, laxity, mistake, neglect, omission, slip. **2** administration, care, charge, control, custody, direction, handling, inspection, keeping, management, superintendence, supervision, surveillance.
overtake *v* catch up with, do better than, draw level with, get past, leave behind, outdistance, outdo, outstrip, overhaul, pass.
overthrow *v* **1** abolish, beat, bring down, conquer, crush, defeat, depose, dethrone, do away with master, oust, overcome overpower, overwhelm, subdue, topple, unseat. **2** bring to ruin, demolish, destroy, knock down level, overturn, put an end to, raze, ruin, subvert, upend, upset.
overthrow *n* defeat, deposition, destruction, dethronement, dispossession, downfall, end, fall, ruin, subversion, suppression, undoing unseating.
overturn *v* **1** capsize, keel over, knock over, overbalance, reverse, spill, tipover, topple, tumble, upend, upset, upturn. **2** abolish, bring down, depose, destroy,

The overwhelming influence of Greek architecture on the appearance of buildings around the world can still be seen today as new buildings combine recent ideas with traditonal motifs such as the Doric columns used on the classical proportioned Parthenon (above) built in ancient Athens at the height of the Greek civilization.

invalidate, overthrow, repeal, rescind, reverse, unseat.

overwhelm *v* **1** bury, crush, deluge, engulf, flood, inundate, snow under, submerge, swamp. **2** confuse, devastate, overcome, overpower, prostrate, render speechless, stagger; (*Inf*) bowl over, knock someone for six.

overwhelming *adj* breathtaking, crushing, devastating, invincible, irresistible, overpowering, shattering, stunning, towering, uncontrollable, vastly superior.

overwork *v* be a slave driver, be a hard taskmaster to, burden, burn the midnight oil, drive into the ground, exhaust, exploit, oppress, overstrain, overtax, overuse, prostrate, strain, wear out, weary, work one's fingers to the bone.

owing *adj* due, outstanding, overdue, owed, payable, unpaid, unsettled.

own *adj* individual, particular.

on one's own *pron* alone, by oneself, by one's own efforts, independently, isolated, left to one's own devices, off one's own bat, standing on one's own two feet, unaided, unassisted.

own *v* be in possession of, be responsible for, enjoy, have, hold, keep, possess, retain.

own up to *v* **1** to admit, confess, make a clean breast of, tell the truth about; (*Inf*) come clean about. **2** acknowledge, admit, allow, concede, confess, disclose, recognize; (*Inf*) go along with.

owner *n* holder, landlord, lord, master, mistress, possessor, proprietor, proprietress, proprietrix.

ownership *n* dominion, possession, proprietary rights, right of possession, title.

Pp

pace *n* **1** measure, step, stride, tread, walk. **2** momentum, motion, movement, progress, rate, speed, tempo, velocity.
pace *v* **1** march, patrol, pound, stride, walk back and forth, walk up and down. **2** count, mark out, measure, step.
pack *n* **1** back-pack, bale, bundle, burden, kit, kitbag, knapsack, load, package, packet, parcel, rucksack, truss. **2** band, bunch, collection, company, crew, crowd, deck, flock, gang, group, herd, lot, mob, set, troop.
pack *v* **1** batch, bundle, burden, load, package, packet, store, stow. **2** charge, compact, compress, cram, crowd, fill, jam, mob, press, ram, stuff, tamp, throng, wedge.
packaging *n* container, covering, packet, wrapping.
packet *n* bag, carton, container, package, wrapper, wrapping.
pact *n* agreement, alliance, arrangement, contract, deal, treaty.
padding *n* filling, packing, stuffing, wadding.
paddle *n* oar, scull, sweep.
paddle *v* **1** oar, propel, pull, punt, row, scull. **2** dabble, plash, plunge, slop, splash about, stir, wade.
paddock *n* corral, enclosure, field, meadow, pen, yard.
page *n* **1** folio, leaf, recto, sheet, side, verso. **2** episode, epoch, era, event, incident, stage, time. **3** attendant, bellboy, bellhop, footboy, page-boy, servant.
page *v* **1** announce, call out, send for, summon. **2** paginate.
pain *n* **1** ache, cramp, hurt, irritation, soreness, spasm, throb, twinge. **2** agony, distress, grief, heartache, misery, suffering, torment, torture.
pain *v* **1** ache, chafe, discomfort, harm, hurt, inflame, injure, smart, sting, throb. **2** afflict, agonize, distress, hurt, sadden, torment, torture, worry, wound.
painful *adj* **1** afflictive, disagreeable, distasteful, distressing, grievous, unpleasant. **2** agonizing, excruciating, hurting, inflamed, raw, smarting, sore, tender, throbbing. **3** arduous, difficult, hard, laborious, severe, tedious, trying.
painless *adj* easy, effortless, fast, pain-free, quick, simple, thorough.
paint *n* **1** colour, colouring, decorate, distemper, dye, emulsion, gloss, pigment, stain, tint, whitewash. **2** oil, oil-paint, water-colour. **3** greasepaint, make-up.
paint *v* **1** depict, describe, draw, evoke, figure, picture, portray, recount, represent, sketch. **2** apply, coat, colour, cover, daub, decorate, slap on.
pair *n* brace, couple, doublet, duo, match, matched set, span, twins, two of a kind, twosome, yoke.
pair *v* bracket, couple, join, marry, match, match up, mate, par off, put together, team, twin, wed, yoke.
pale *adj* **1** anaemic, ashen, bloodless, colourless, faded, light, pallid, pasty, sallow, washed-out, whitish. **2** dim, faint, feeble, inadequate, poor, thin, weak.
pamper *v* baby, cater to one's every whim, coddle, cosset, indulge, spoil.
pamphlet *n* booklet, brochure, circular, folder, leaflet.

How does packaging help to preserve food?

Packaging preserves food by preventing bacteria from contaminating the contents. Modern packaging is very sophisticated. Some foods are vacuum packed, so that the plastic wrappings exclude any air from the product. Other kinds of packaging trap gases to help to preserve different foods. Packaging also contains important nutritional information and a date by which the food should be eaten, while it is still fresh.

pan *n* casserole, fish-kettle, frying pan, pot, pressure cooker, saucepan, skillet, vessel, wok.
pan *v* **1** censure, criticize, knock, roast; (*Inf*) knock, rubbish, slag off, slam, slate. **2** search for, sift for. **3** follow, scan, sweep, track.
pancake *n* blini, crêpe, drop scone, tortilla.
panic *n* agitation, alarm, consternation, dismay, fear, fright, horror, hysteria, scare, terror.
pant *v* blow, breathe, gasp, heave, huff, palpitate, puff, throb, wheeze.
paper *n* **1** assignment, certificate, deed, document, instrument, record. **2** archive, diaries, documents, dossier, file, record. **3** daily, gazette, journal, news, newspaper, organ, weekly; (*Inf*) rag. **4** article, dissertation, essay, report, study, thesis.
paper *v* **1** decorate, hang, line, paste up, wallpaper. **2 paper over** camouflage, conceal, disguise, gloss over, hide, whitewash.
parade *n* **1** array, cavalcade, ceremony, column, march, pageant, procession, review, spectacle, train. **2** array, display, exhibition, flaunting, ostentation, pomp, show, spectacle.
parade *v* **1** defile, march. **2** air, brandish, display, exhibit, flaunt, make a show of, show; (*Inf*) show off, strut, swagger.
parallel *adj* **1** aligned, alongside, side by side. **2** like, matching, resembling, similar, uniform.
parallel *n* **1** duplicate, equal, likeness, match, twin. **2** analogy, comparison, likeness, parallelism, resemblance, similarity.
paralyse *v* **1** cripple, disable, incapacitate. **2** anaesthetize, freeze, immobilize, numb, stop dead, stun, transfix.
paralysis *adj* **1** immobility, incapacity, palsy. **2** breakdown, halt, shutdown, standstill.
parcel *n* **1** bundle, carton, pack, package, packet. **2 parcel up** do up, pack, package, tie up, wrap.
parched *adj* arid, dehydrated, dried up, scorched, shrivelled, thirsty, waterless, withered.
pardon *v* absolve, acquit, excuse, forgive, free, liberate, release, reprieve; (*Inf*) let off.
pardon *n* absolution, acquittal, discharge, forgiveness, mercy, release, remission, reprieve.
parent *v* father, guardian, mother, procreator, sire.
parish *n* church, churchgoers, community, congregation, flock, fold, parishioners.
park *n* estate, garden, grounds, parkland, pleasure garden, recreation ground, woodland.
parliament *n* assembly, congress, legislature, senate.
part *n* **1** bit, fraction, fragment, lot, particle, piece, portion, scrap, section, sector, segment, share, slice. **2** branch, component, constituent, department, division, element, ingredient, limb, member, module, organ, piece, unit. **3** behalf, concern, faction, interest, party, side. **4** bit, business, capacity, charge, duty, function, involvement, office, pace, responsibility, role, say, share, task, work. **5** character, lines, role. **6 in good part** cheerfully, cordially, good-naturedly, well, without offence. **7 in part** a little, partly, slightly, to a certain extent, to some degree.
part *v* **1** break, come apart, detach, disconnect, dismantle,

The Houses of Parliament, located on the left bank of the River Thames in London, is also known as Westminster Palace. Built in the 11th century by Edward the Confessor and enlarged by William the Conqueror, the palace has suffered numerous fires and was targeted in air raids during World War II.

The particles in an atom

Although there may be many subatomic particles within an atom, most of the atom is empty space.

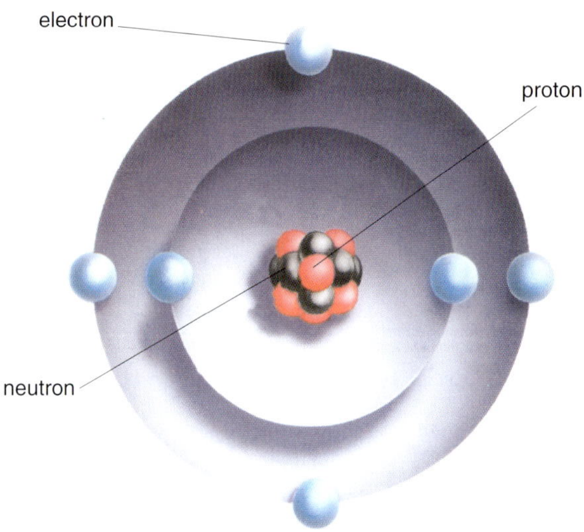

divide, separate, split, tear. **2** come apart, detach, disconnect, disjoin, dismantle, disunite, divide, rend, separate, sever, split, tear. **3** break up, depart, go, go away, go their separate ways, leave, part company, quit, separate, split up.

partial *adj* **1** incomplete, limited, uncompleted, unfinished. **2** biased, influenced, interested, one-sided, partisan, prejudiced, unfair, unjust.

participate *v* be a participant, engage in, enter into, get in on the act, have a hand in, join in, perform, share, take part.

particle *n* atom, bit, crumb, grain, iota, jot, mite, molecule, mote, piece, scrap, shred, speck.

particular *adj* **1** distinct, exact, precise, specific. **2** exceptional, marked, notable, noteworthy, remarkable, unusual. **3** critical, demanding, discriminating, exacting, fastidious, finicky, fussy, meticulous, overnice; (*Inf*) choosy, pernickety, picky.

parting *n* **1** adieu, departure, farewell, going, goodbye, leave-taking, valediction. **2** breaking, detachment, divergence, division, partition, rift, rupture, separation, split.

partition *n* **1** breaking up, dividing, division, segregation, separation, splitting up, sub-division. **2** barrier, divider, room divider, fence, screen.

partition *v* apportion, cut up, divide, portion, section, segment, separate, share, split up, subdivide.

partnership *n* alliance, combine, company, conglomerate, cooperative, corporation, union.

party *n* **1** at-home, celebration, festivity, function, gathering, reception, social gathering. (*Inf*) bash, do, get-together, knees-up, rave-up, shindig. **2** band, body, company, crew, detachment, gang, gathering, group, squad, team, unit. **3** alliance, association, cabal, coalition, confederacy, faction, league, side. **4** individual, person, somebody, someone.

pass *v* **1** depart, elapse, flow, go, go by, lapse, leave, move, move onwards, proceed, roll, run. **2** beat, exceed, excel, go beyond, outdistance, outdo, outstrip, surpass, transcend. **3** answer, do, get through, graduate, qualify, succeed; (*Inf*) come up to scratch. **4** develop, happen, occur, take place. **5** convey, deliver, exchange, give, hand, let have, reach, send, throw, transfer, transmit. **6** accept, adopt, approve, authorize, decree, enact, establish, legislate, ordain, ratify, sanction, validate.

pass *n* **1** canyon, col, defile, gap, gorge, narow road, ravine. **2** authorization, licence, passport, permission, permit, safe-conduct, ticket, warrant.

passable *adj* acceptable, adequate, admissible, allowable, all right, average, fair, mediocre, middling, moderate, not too bad, ordinary, presentable, tolerable; (*Inf*) so-so.

passage *n* **1** avenue, channel, course, lane, opening, path, road, route, thoroughfare, way. **2** corridor, door-way, entrance, entrance hall, exit, hall, hallway, lobby, passageway, vestibule. **3** clause, excerpt, extract, paragraph, piece, quotation, reading, section, sentence, text, verse. **4** crossing, journey, your,

trek, trip, voyage. **5** allowance, authorization, freedom, permission, right, safe-conduct, visa, warrant.
passing *adj* **1** brief, fleeting, momentary, short, short-lived, temporary, transient, transitory. **2** casual, cursory, glancing, hasty, quick, shallow, short, slight, superficial.
passive *adj* complaint, docile, inert, lifeless, long-suffering, patient, receptive, resigned, submissive, unassertive.
past *adj* **1** completed, done, ended, extinct, finished, gone, over, over and done with, spent. **2** ancient, bygone, early, former, late, previous, prior, recent.
past *n* background, experience, history, life, past life.
past *adv* across, beyond, by, on, over.
pasta *n* types of: cannelloni, fettuccine, fusilli, macaroni, penne, ravioli, rigatoni, spaghetti, tortellini, vermicelli.
pastime *n* activity, amusement, distraction, diversion, entertainment, game, hobby, leisure, play, recreation, relaxation, sport.
pastry *n* pie, pasty, patty, quiche, tart, vol-au-vent.
pasture *n* grass, grassland, grazing, grazing land, meadow.
pat *v* caress, dab, fondle, pet, slap, stroke, tap, touch.
pat *n* dab, light blow, slap, stroke, tap.
patch *n* **1** piece of material, reinforcement. **2** bit, scrap, shred, small piece, spot, stretch. **3** area, ground, land, plot, tract.
patchy *adj* bitty, erratic, fitful, irregular, random, sketchy, spotty, uneven, varying.
patent *adj* apparent, blatant, clear, conspicuous, downright, evident, flagrant, glaring, indisputable, manifest, obvious, open, palpable, transparent, unconcealed, unequivocal, unmistakable.
patent *n* copyright, invention, licence.
path *n* **1** footpath, footway, pathway, towpath, track, trail, walkway. **2** direction, passage, procedure, road, route, track.
pathetic *adj* affecting, distressing, heartbreaking, moving, poignant, sad, tender, touching.
patience *n* **1** calmness, composure, even temper, restraint, serenity, tolerance; (*Inf*) cool. **2** diligence, endurance, long-suffering, persistence, stoicism, submission.
patient *adj* **1** calm, composed, enduring, persevering, persistent, philosophical, quiet, resigned, self-possessed, serene, submissive, uncomplaining, untiring. **2** even-tempered, forgiving, lenient, mild, tolerant.
patient *n* case, invalid, sick person, sufferer.
patriotic *adj* chauvinistic, flag-waving, loyal, nationalistic.
patrol *n* **1** guarding, policing, protecting, rounds, safeguarding, vigilance, watching. **2** garrison, guard, patrolman, sentinel, watch, watchman.
patrol *v* cruise, guard, inspect, keep watch, make the rounds, police, pound, range, safeguard, walk the beat.
patron *n* **1** advocate, backer, benefactor, champion, defender, friend, guardian, helper, philanthropist, protector, sponsor, supporter; (*Inf*) angel. **2** buyer, client, customer, shopper. promotion, sponsorship, support. **3** business, clientele, commerce, custom, trade.
pattern *n* **1** arrangement, design, figure, motif. **2** method, order, plan, sequence, system. **3** kind, shape, sort, style, type, variety. **4** diagram, guide, instructions, stencil, template. **5** criterion, example, model, norm, original, prototype, sample, specimen.
pattern *v* copy, emulate, follow, form, imitate, model, mould, order, shape, style.
pause *v* break, cease, delay, deliberate, desist, discontinue, halt, hesitate, interrupt, rest, stop briefly, take a break, wait, waver; (*Inf*) have a breather.
pause *n* break, cessation, delay, gap, halt, hesitation, interlude, intermission, interruption, interval, lull, respite, rest, stay, stoppage, wait; (*Inf*) breather, let-up.
pay *v* **1** compensate, meet, offer, recompense, reimburse, reward,

Pasta is made from a mixture of flour and eggs. It is shaped when damp and then dried. In this form, it will keep for months. When it is boiled in water, pasta takes in water molecules and becomes soft.

settle, square up. **2** benefit, be worthwhile, serve. **3** bestow, extend, give, grant, present, proffer, render. **4** bring in, produce, profit, return, yield; (*Inf*) cough up.
pay *n* allowance, compensation, earnings, fee, hire, income, payment, recompense, reimbursement, remuneration, reward, salary, stipend, takings, wages.
payable *v* **1** compensate, foot,

There are two main ways of patterning fabrics. By using coloured threads in the knitting or weaving, patterns can be made in the fabric itself. This is an easy way to create stripes and checks. Another method is to print it, using special dyes. This can be done by using big rollers or by squeezing dye through patterned screens.

give, honour, meet, reimburse, settle, square up; (*Inf*) cough up. **2** benefit, be worthwhile, repay, serve. **3** give, grant, present, render. **4** bring in, produce, profit, return, yield.
payable *n* compensation, earnings, fee, hire, income, payment, renumeration, reward, salary, stipend, takings, wages.
payable *adj* due, obligatory, outstanding, owing, to be paid.
pay back *v* get one's own back, recompense, retaliate, settle a score; (*Inf*) get even with.
payment *n* **1** outlay, remittance, settlement. **2** earnings, fee, hire, remuneration, reward, wage.
pay off *v* **1** discharge, dismiss, fire, lay off, let go; (*Inf*) sack. **2** clear, liquidate, pay in full, settle, square. **3** succeed, work.
pay out *v* disburse, spend; (*Inf*) cough up, fork out, shell out.
peace *n* **1** accord, agreement, harmony. **2** armistice, cessation of hostilities, truce. **3** calm, composure, relaxation, serenity. **4** quiet, rest, silence, stillness, tranquillity.
peaceful *adj* **1** amicable, at peace, friendly, harmonious, on good terms, without hostility. **2** calm, placid, quiet, serene, still, tranquil.
peak *n* **1** apex, brow, crest, pinnacle, point, summit, tip, top. **2** acme, climax, culmination, highest point, zenith.
peak *v* climax, come to a head, culminate, reach its highest point, reach the pinnacle.
peculiar *adj* abnormal, bizarre, curious, eccentric, exceptional, extraordinary, far-out, freakish, funny, odd, quaint, strange, uncommon, unconventional, unusual, weird; (*Inf*) far-out.
pedestal *n* base, dado, foot, foundation, mounting, pier, plinth, stand, support.
pedigree *n* ancestry, blood, breed, decent, extraction, family, family tree, genealogy, heritage, line, lineage, race, stock.
peek *v* glance, look, peep, peer, snatch a glimpse, sneak a look, spy, squint, take a gander at; (*Inf*) take a look.
peel *v* flake off, pare, scale, skin, strip off.
peer *v* look closely, squint.
peer *n* **1** aristocrat, baron, count, duke, earl, lord, marquess, marquis, noble, nobleman, viscount; (*Inf*) aristo. **2** coequal, compeer, confrère, equal, fellow, like, match.
pelt *v* batter, beat, bombard, cast, hurl, pepper, pummel, shower, sling, strike, thrash, throw; (*Inf*) wallop.
pen *n* **1** ball-point, felt-tip, fountain pen, marker. **2** coop, corral, enclosure, fold, hutch, sty.
pen *v* **1** commit to paper, compose, draft, jot down, write. **2** cage, confine, coop up, enclose, fence in, hedge, hem in, hurdle, shut in.
penalize *v* castigate, correct, discipline, handicap, impose a penalty on, inflict a handicap on, punish, put at a disadvantage.
penalty *n* **1** disadvantage, fine, forfeit, handicap, punishment, retribution. **2** drawback, handicap, obstacle, snag.
pencil *v* **1** compose, draft, jot down, pen, scribble down. **2** draw, outline, sketch, trace.
pendent *adj* dangling, hanging, suspended.
pending *prep* **1** awaiting, until, waiting for. **2** during, in the course of, throughout.
pending *adj* **1** awaiting action, uncertain, unresolved, unsettled, up in the air; (*Inf*) on the back burner. **2** approaching, coming, forthcoming, imminent, impending, in the balance, in the offing.
penetrate *v* **1** bore, enter, go through, perforate, pierce, prick, probe, stab. **2** diffuse, get in,

infiltrate, permeate, pervade, seep, suffuse.
penetration *n* **1** entrance, entry, inroad, invasion, perforation, piercing, puncturing. **2** cuteness, astuteness, discernment, insight, keenness, perception, perspicacity, sharpness, shrewdness, wit.
penniless *adj* bankrupt, destitute, needy, poor, poverty-stricken, without a penny to one's name; (*Inf*) broke, cleaned out, skint, stonybroke, strapped for cash.
pension *n* **1** allowance,old-age pension, retirement pension, superannuation. **2** allowance, benefit, support, welfare.
people *n* **1** human beings, humanity, humans, mankind, men and women, mortals, persons. **2** citizens, clan, family, folk, inhabitants, nation, population, public, race, tribe. **3** crowd, general public, grass roots, masses, mob, multitude, populace, rabble, rank and file, the herd.
people *v* colonize, inhabit, occupy, populate, settle.
perceive *v* be aware of, behold, descry, discern, discover, distin-guish, espy, make out, note, notice, observe, recognize, remark, see, spot.
perch *n* branch, pole, post, resting place, roost.
perch *v* alight, balance, land, rest, roost, settle, sit on.
percolate *v* **1** drain, drip, filter, seep. **2** filtrate, sieve, strain.
perennial *adj* chronic, constant, continual, continuing, enduring, lasting, lifelong, persistent, recurrent, unchanging.
perfect *adj* **1** absolute, complete, entire, finished, full, out-and-out, sheer, unadulterated, whole. **2** excellent, faultless, flawless, ideal, immaculate, impeccable, pure, splendid, spotless, superb, superlative, supreme, unblem-ished, unmarred, untarnished.
perfect *v* achieve, carry out, complete, consummate, effect, finish, fulfil, perform, realize.
perform *v* **1** accomplish, act, bring about, carry out, complete, do, execute, function, observe, pull off, satisfy, work. **2** appear as, depict, enact, play, present, produce, put on, render, repre-sent, stage.
performance *n* **1** achievement, act, carrying out, completion, conduct, execution, exploit, feat, fulfilment, work. **2** acting, appearance, exhibition, interpretation, play, portrayal, presentation, production, representation, show; (*Inf*) gig.
perfume *n* aroma, bouquet, cologne, essence, fragrance, incense, odour, redolence, scent, smell, sweetness.
peril *n* danger, hazard, jeopardy, menace, pitfall, risk, uncertainty.
perimeter *n* border, borderline, boundary, circumference, edge, fringe, frontier, limits, margin, outer limits, periphery.
period *n* **1** interval, season, space, span, spell, stretch, term, time, while. **2** aeon, age, days, epoch, era. **3** conclusion, end, finis, finish, halt, stop. **4** full

How are characteristics passed from one generation to the next?

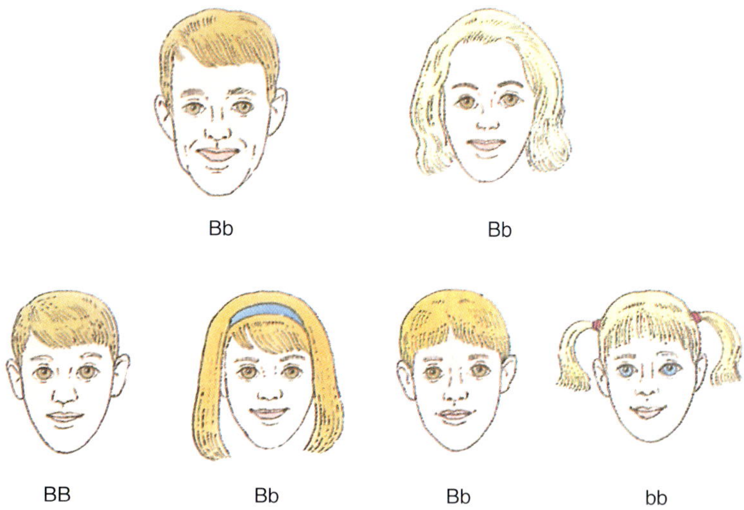

In this diagram, **B** stands for brown eyes and **b** stands for blue eyes. If a child inherits one brown-eyes gene and one blue-eyes gene, she will have brown eyes, but she still has a blue-eyes gene to pass on to half of her own children. If her children's father also has brown eyes but a recessive blue-eyes gene, on average one in four of her children will inherit two blue-eyes genes and therefore have blue eyes.

stop, point, stop.

periodical *n* journal, magazine, monthly, paper, publication, quarterly, review, serial, weekly.

perish *v* **1** be killed, be lost, decease, die, expire, lose ones life, pass away. **2** be destroyed, collapse, decline, disappear, fall, go under, vanish. **3** decay, decompose, disintegrate, moulder, rot, waste, wither.

perishable *adj* decaying, destructible, easily, spoilt, liable to rot, short-lived, unstable.

perjury *n* bearing false witness, false statement, giving false testimony, lying under oath, oath breaking, violation of an oath, wilful falsehood.

permanent *adj* constant, durable, enduring, everlasting, fixed, indestructible, lasting, long-lasting, perennial, perpetual, persistent, stable, steadfast, unchanging, unfading.

permeate *v* charge, diffuse, throughout, fill, filter through, imbue, impregnate, infiltrate, pass through, penetrate, percolate, pervade, saturate, seep, through, soak through, spread throughout.

permissible *adj* acceptable, allowable, all right, authorized, lawful, legal, legitimate, permitted, proper, sanctioned; (*Inf*) kosher, legit, OK.

permission *n* approval, consent, green light, leave, licence, permit, sanction; (*Inf*) go-ahead.

permit *v* admit, agree, allow, authorize, consent, empower, enable, endorse, endure, give leave, grant, let, license, sanction, suffer, tolerate, warrant.

permit *n* authorization, licence, pass, passport, permission, sanction.

perpendicular *adj* at right angles to, on end, plumb, straight, upright, vertical.

perpetrate *v* bring about, carry out, commit, do, effect, enact, execute, inflict, perform, wreak.

perpetual *adj* abiding, endless, enduring, eternal, everlasting, immortal, infinite, lasting, never-ending, perennial, permanent, unchanging, undying, unending.

Perennials are flowers that die down in the autumn and spend winter as underground roots, reappearing each spring.

perplex *v* **1** baffle, befuddle, beset, bewilder, confound, confuse, dumbfound, mix up, muddle, mystify, puzzle, stump. **2** complicate, encumber, entangle, involve, jumble, mix up, snarl up, tangle, thicken.

persecute *v* afflict, distress, harass, hound, hunt, illtreat, injure, maltreat, martyr, molest, oppress, torment, torture, pester, tease, vex, worry.

persevere *v* be determined, continue, endure, go on, keep going, maintain, persist, pursue, remain, stand firm, stick at; (*Inf*) hold on, plug away.

persist *v* **1** continue, insist, persevere, stand firm. **2** abide, carry on, continue, endure, last, linger, remain; (*Inf*) hold on.

person *n* being, body, human, human being, individual, living soul, soul.

personal *adj* **1** confidential, private, secret. **2** individual, special, unique. **3 personal remarks** critical, derogatory, insulting, offensive.

personality *n* **1** character, identity, individuality, make-up, nature, psyche, temper, temperament, traits. **2** celebrity, famous-name, household name, notable, personage, star, well-known face, well-known person.

personally *adv* **1** alone, by oneself, in person, on one's own, solely. **2** individually, privately, specially, subjectively.

personify *v* body forth, embody, epitomize, exemplify, express, incarnate, mirror, represent, symbolize, typify.

personnel *n* employees, helpers, human resources, members, men and women, people, staff, workers, workforce.

perspective *n* **1** angle, attitude, context, objectivity, outlook, overview, proportion, relation, relative importance, relativity, way of looking. **2** outlook, panorama, prospect, scene, view.

perspire *v* be damp, be wet, drip, exude, glow, pour with sweat, secrete, sweat, swelter.

persuasive *adj* compelling, convincing, credible, effective, eloquent, forceful, impelling, impressive, inducing influential, moving, plausible, sound, telling, touching, valid, weighty, winning.
pessimistic *adj* bleak, cynical, dark, dejected, depressed, despairing, despondent, downhearted, fatalistic, gloomy, glum, hopeless, sad.
pest *n* **1** annoyance, bother, irritation, nuisance, thorn in one's side, trial; (*Inf*) pain, pain in the neck. **2** blight, bug, curse, epidemic, infection, plague, scourge.
pester *v* annoy, badger, bother, disturb, fret, get on someone's nerves, harass, nag, pick on, plague, torment, worry; (*Inf*) bug, drive one up the wall, hassle, rile.
peter out *v* come to nothing, die out, dwindle, ebb, fade, give out, run out, stop, taper off, wane.
petition *n* address, appeal, plea, prayer, request.
petition *v* appeal, ask, beg, call, upon, crave, plead, pray, press, solicit, sue, urge.
petty *adj* **1** insignificant, little, negligible, paltry, slight, small, trifling, trivial, unimportant; (*Inf*) measly, piddling. **2** cheap, grudging, mean, spiteful, stingy.
phantom *n* apparition, chimera, ghost, spirit; (*Inf*) spook.
phase *n* aspect, chapter, condition, development, juncture, period, point, position, stage, state, step, time.
phase out *v* close, dispose of gradually, ease off, eliminate, pull out, remove, replace, run down, taper off, terminate, wind down, withdraw; (*Inf*) wind up.

How are photographs developed?

The film is immersed in a chemical solution that develops the image.

It is then bathed in more chemicals to fix the image onto the film.

The dried film image is negative: dark areas look light and vice versa.

phenomenal *adj* amazing, extraordinary, exceptional, fantastic, marvellous, miraculous, outstanding, remarkable, sensational, unheard of, unique, unusual, wondrous; (*Inf*) fabulous, mind-blowing, mind-boggling.
phobia *n* aversion, dislike, distaste, dread, fear, hatred, horror, irrational fear, loathing, obsession, overwhelming anxiety, repulsion, terror; (*Inf*) hang-up, thing.
phone *n* **1** car phone, mobile phone, telephone; (*Inf*) blower. **2** call, give someone a call, give someone a ring, make a call, ring, ring up, telephone; (*Inf*) get on the blower, give someone a bell, give someone a buzz, give someone a tinkle.
photograph *n* image, likeness, picture, print, shot, slide, snapshot, transparency; (*Inf*) photo, snap.
photograph *v* capture on film, film, get a shot of, record, shoot, take, take a picture of; (*Inf*) snap.
phrase *n* expression, group of words, motto, remark, saying, tag, utterance, way of speaking.
phrase *v* express, formulate, frame, present, put into words, say, term, utter, voice, word.
physical *adj* **1** bodily, earthly, fleshly, mortal, unspiritual. **2** material, natural, palpable, real, sensible, solid, substantial, tangible, visible.
physique *n* body, build, figure, form, frame, shape, structure.
pick *v* **1** choose, decide upon, elect, fix upon, hand-pick, mark out, opt for, select, settle upon, sift out, sort out. **2** collected, cull, cut, gather, harvest, pluck, pull.
pick up **1** gather, grasp, hoist, lift, raise, take up, uplift. **2** buy, come across, find, garner, happen upon, obtain, purchase. **3** gain, gain ground, improve, mend, perk up, rally, recover, take a turn for the better; (*Inf*) get better. **4** call for, collect, get, give someone a lift, go to get, uplift. **5** acquire, learn,

Brighton's West Pier was one of England's finest seaside piers and opened in 1866. It is now a shell of its former glory as after two fires, one in March and another in May 2003, it was virtually destroyed.

master; (*Inf*) get the hang of.
pick *n* **1** choice, choosing, decision, option, preference, selection. **2** choicest, *créme de la créme*, elect, elite, flower, pride, prize, the best, the cream.
picnic *n* alfresco meal, excursion, outdoor meal, outing.
picture *n* **1** drawing, effigy, engraving, illustration, image, likeness, painting, photograph, portrait, portrayal, print, representation, sketch. **2** account, depiction, description, image, impression, re-creation, report. **3** carbon copy, copy, double, duplicate, image, likeness, living image, lookalike, replica, twin; (*Inf*) dead ringer, ringer, spitting image. **4** film, motion picture, movie; (*Inf*) flick.
picture *v* conceive of, envision, image, see, see in the mind's eye, visualize.
picturesque *adj* attractive, beautiful, charming, colourful, delightful, graphic, pretty, scenic, striking, vivid.
pie *n* pastry, quiche, tart.
piece *n* **1** allotment, bit, chunk, division, fraction, fragment, length, morsel, mouthful, part, portion, quantity, scrap, section, segment, share, shred, slice. **2** article, composition, creation, item,production, study, work, work of art; (*Inf*) bit.
piecemeal *adv* bit by bit, by degrees, in fits and starts, in stages, in steps, little by little, piece by piece.
pier *n* **1** dock, jetty, landing-place, promenade, quay, wharf. **2** buttress, column, pile, piling, pillar, post, support, upright.
pierce *v* bore, drill, enter, penetrate, perforate, prick, probe, puncture, run through, spike, stab, stick into, transfix.
pig *n* boar, grunter, hog, piglet, porker, sow, swine; (*Inf*) piggy.
pile *n* **1** assortment, collection, heap, hoard, mass, mound mountain, stack, stockpile. **2** building, edifice, erection, structure.
pile *v* accumulate, collect, gather, heap, hoard, load up mass, stack, store.
pile-up *n* accident, collision, crash, multiple collision, smash; (*Inf*) smash-up.
pilgrim *n* crusader, hajji, traveller, wanderer, wayfarer.
pilgrimage *n* crusade, excursion, expedition, hajj, journey, mission, tour, trip.
pillar *n* **1** column, pier, pilaster, post, prop, shaft, support, upright. **2** leader, mainstay, rock, supporter, tower of strength, upholder; (*Inf*) leading light.
pilot *n* airman, aviator, captain, conductor, coxswain, director, flier, guide, helmsman, leader, navigator, steersman.
pilot *v* conduct, control, direct, drive, fly, guide, handle, lead, manage, navigate, operate, shepherd, steer.
pilot *adj* experimental, model, test, trial.
pin *v* **1** affix, attach, fasten, fix, join, secure. **2** fix, hold down, immobilize, press, restrain.
pinch *v* **1** compress, grasp, nip, press, squeeze, tweak. **2** confine, cramp, crush, hurt, pain.
pinch *n* **1** nip, squeeze, tweak. **2** bit, dash, jot, mite, small, quantity, speck, taste. **3** crisis, difficulty, emergency, hardship, necessity, oppression, pass, plight, predicament, pressure, strait, stress.
pin down *v* **1** compel, constrain, force, make, press, pressurize. **2** bind, confine, constrain, fix, hold, hold down, immobilize, nail down, tie down.
pink *adj* flesh, flushed, reddish,

rose, rosy, salmon.
pinnacle *n* acme, apex, crest, crown, eminence, height, meridian, peak, summit, top, vertex, zenith.
pinpoint *v* define, distinguish, get a fix on, home in on, identify, locate, spot.
pioneer *n* **1** explorer, frontiersman, settler. **2** developer, founder, founding, father, innovator, leader, trailblazer.
pioneer *v* create, develop, discover, establish, initiate, instigate, institute, invent, launch, lay the ground-work, map out, open up, originate, prepare, show the way, start, take the lead.
pipe *n* **1** conduit, conveyor, duct, hose, line, main, passage, pipeline, tube. **2** briar, clay, meerschaum. **3** fife, horn, tooter, whistle, wind instrument.
pipe *v* cheep, peep, play, sing, sound, tootle, trill, tweet, twitter, warble, whistle.
piracy *n* hijacking, infringement, plagiarism, robbery at sea, stealing, theft.
pirate *n* **1** buccaneer, corsair, filibuster, freebooter, marauder, raider, rover, sea, robber, sea rover, sea-wolf. **2** infringer, plagiarist, (*Inf*) cribber.
pirate *v* appropriate, borrow, copy, plagiarize, poach, reproduce, steal; (*Inf*) crib, lift.
pit *n* abyss, cavity, chasm, coal-mine, crater, dent, depression, dimple, gulf, hole, hollow, indentation, mine, pothole, trench.
pitch *v* **1** cast, fling, heave, hurl, launch, sling, throw, toss; (*Inf*) bung, chuck, lob. **2** erect, fix, locate, place, plant, put up, raise, settle, set up, station.
pitch *n* **1** angle, gradient, incline, slope, steepness, tilt. **2** degree, height, highest point, level, point, summit. **3** harmonic, modulation, sound, timbre, tone. **4** line, patter, sales talk; (*Inf*) spiel. **5** field of play, ground, sports field; (*Inf*) park.
pitfall *n* catch, danger, difficulty, drawback, hazard, snag, trap.
pitiful *adj* **1** deplorable, distressing, grievous, heartbreaking, miserable, pathetic, sad, woeful, wretched. **2** contemptible, despicable, insignificant, low, mean, miserable, paltry, shabby, sorry, vile, worthless.
pitiless *adj* brutal, callous, cold-blooded, cruel, harsh, heartless, inhuman, merciless, ruthless, uncaring, unfeeling, unmerciful, unsympathetic.
pittance *n* allowance, drop, mite, portion, ration, slave wages, trifle; (*Inf*) chicken feed, peanuts.
pity *n* charity, clemency, compassion, condolence, kindness, mercy, sympathy, tenderness, understanding.
pity *v* bleed for, commiserate with, condole with, feel for, feel sorry for, grieve for, have compassion for, sympathize with, weep for.
pivot *n* **1** axis, axle, fulcrum, spindle, swivel. **2** centre, focal point, heart, hinge, hub, kingpin.
pivot *v* **1** revolve, rotate, spin, swivel, turn. **2** be contingent, depend, hang, hinge, rely, revolve round, turn.
placard *n* advertisement, bill, poster, public notice, sticker.
placate *v* calm, humour, pacify, soothe, win over.
place *n* **1** area, location, point, position, site, situation, spot, station, venue, whereabouts. **2** city, district, hamlet, locality, neighbourhood, quarter, region, town, village. **3** grade, position, rank, station, status. **4** appointment, employment, job, position, post. **5** accommodation, berth, billet, room, space, stead. **6** affair, charge, concern, duty, function, prerogative, responsibility, right, role. **7** take place. **8** befall, betide, come about, come to go on, happen, occur, transpire.
place *v* **1** deposit, dispose, establish, fix, install, lay, locate, plant, position, put, rest, set,

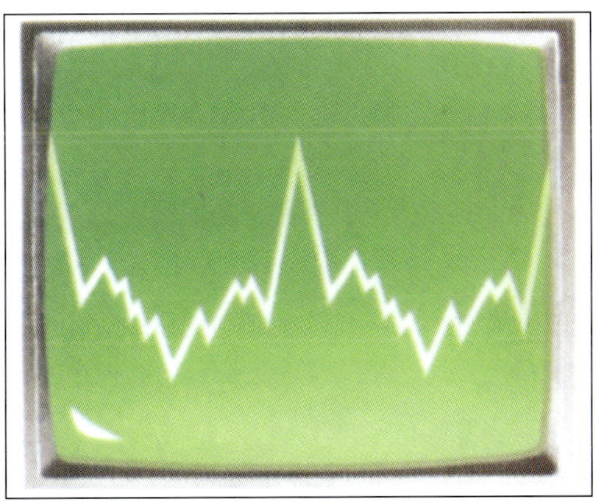

Most sound waves are not pure sounds of a single wavelength and frequency. Complex sounds produce distinctive sound wave patterns when viewed on a screen. These are so individual that the sound of a person's voice can be recognized from the wave patterns it makes.

settle, stand. **2** arrange, class, classify, grade, group, order, rank, sort. **3** allocate, appoint, assign, charge, commission, entrust, give.
placid *adj* calm, collected, compose, cool, even-tempered, gentle, halcyon, mild, peaceful, quiet, serene, still, tranquil, undisturbed, unexcitable, unmoved, untroubled.
plagiarize *v* borrow, copy, imitate, pirate; (*Inf*) crib, lift.
plague *n* **1** disease, epidemic, infection, pandemic, pestilence. **2** affliction, bane, blight, calamity, cancer, curse, evil, torment, trial. **3** annoyance, bother, irritant, nuisance, pest, problem, thorn in one's flesh, vexation; (*Inf*) aggravation, pain.
plague *v* afflict, annoy, badger, bedevil, bother, disturb, fret, harass, harry, haunt, molest, pain, persecute, pester, tease, torment, torture, trouble, vex; (*Inf*) hassle.
plain *adj* **1** apparent, clear, distinct, evident, legible, lucid, obvious, transparent, understandable, visible. **2** blunt, candid, direct, forthright, frank, honest, open, outspoken, sincere, straightforward. **3** commonplace, everyday, homely, modest, ordinary, simple, unpretentious, **4** austere, basic, discreet, modest, muted, pure, restrained, severe, simple, Spartan, stark. **5** even, flat, level, plane, smooth.
plain *n* flatland, grassland, lowland, open country, plateau, prairie, steppe.
plan *n* **1** design, device, idea, method, programme, project, proposal, proposition, scenario, scheme, strategy, suggestion, system. **2** blueprint, chart, diagram, drawing, illustration, layout, map, representation, scale drawing, sketch.
plan *v* **1** arrange, design, devise, formulate, invent, line up, organize, outline, plot, prepare, represent, scheme, schedule, think out. **2** aim, contemplate, foresee, intend, mean, purpose.
plane *n* **1** flat surface, level surface. **2** condition, degree, level, position, rank, stage. **3** aircraft, jet jumbo jet. **4** airplane.
plane *adj* even, flat, flush, horizontal, level, plain, regular, smooth, uniform.
plant *n* **1** bush, flower, greenery, herb, shrub, vegetable, weed. **2** factory, foundry, mill, shop, works, yard. **3** apparatus, equipment, gear, machinery.
plant *v* **1** implant, put in the ground, scatter, seed, set out, sow, transplant. **2** position, set, situate. **3** establish, fix, insert, lodge, place. **4** conceal, hide, place secretly, secrete.
plaster *n* **1** gypsum, mortar, plaster of Paris, stucco. **2** adhesive plaster, bandage, dressing, Elastoplast (Trademark), sticking plaster.
plaster *v* coat, cover, daub, overlay, smear, spread.
plastic *adj* ductile, flexible, mouldable, pliable, pliant, soft, supple.
plate *n* **1** dish, platter. **2** course, dish, helping, portion, serving. **3** layer, panel, sheet, slab.
plateau *n* highland, plain, table, tableland, upland.
platform *n* dais, podium, rostrum, stage, stand.
plausible *adj* believable, colourable, conceivable, credible, likely, possible, probable, reasonable, smooth, smooth-talking, smooth-tongued, tenable.
play *v* **1** amuse oneself, caper, engage in games, frisk, frolic, gambol, have fun, revel, romp, sport. **2** be in a team, challenge, compete, contend against, participate rival, take on, take part, view with. **3** act on the part of, execute, impersonate,

Aircraft travelling faster than the speed of sound are said to be moving at supersonic speeds. The speed of sound is described as Mach 1. Concorde, which can travel at twice the speed of sound, reaches Mach 2.

perform, personate, portray, represent, take the part of. **4 play by ear** ad lib, extemporize, improvise, rise to the occasion, take it as it. comes. **5 play for time** delay, hang fire, procrastinate, stall, temporize; (*Inf*) drag one's feet.

play *n* **1** comedy, drama, performance, piece, radio play, show, soap opera, stage show, television drama, tragedy. **2** amusement, caper, diversion, entertainment, frolic, fun, gambol, game, pastime, prank, recreation, romp, sorry. **3** foolery, fun, humour, jest, joking, prank, sport, teasing; (*Inf*) lark.

player *n* **1** competitor, contestant, participant, sportsman, sportswoman, team member. **2** actor, actress, entertainer, performer, Thespian, trouper. **3** artist, instrumentalist, musician, music maker, performer, virtuoso.

plea *n* appeal begging, entreaty, overture, petition, prayer, request.

plead *v* **1** appeal to, ask, beg, crave, implore, petition, request. **2** allege, argue, assert, maintain, put forward, use as an excuse.

pleasant *adj* **1** acceptable, agreeable, amusing, delightful, enjoyable, fine, lovely, nice, pleasing, pleasurable, satisfying, welcome. **2** agreeable, amiable, charming, cheerful, cheery, friendly, genial, good-humour, likable, nice.

please *v* amuse, charm, cheer, content, delight, entertain, give pleasure to, gladden, gratify, humour, indulge, rejoice, satisfy, suit, tickle, tickle pink.

pledge *n* **1** assurance, covenant, oath, promise, undertaking, vow, warrant, word, word of honour. **2** bail, bond, collateral, deposit, earnest, gage, guarantee, security, surety. **3** health, toast.

There are still many parts of the world where traditional ploughing methods are used, but the use of machinery is increasing year by year.

pledge *v* contract, engage, give one's word, promise, swear, undertake, vouch.

plenty *n* **1** abundance, enough, fund, good deal, great deal, masses, mine, mountains, plethor, quantities, quantity, store, sufficiency, volume; (*Inf*) heaps, lots, oodles, piles, stacks. **2** affluence, copiousness, fertility, fruitfulness, luxury, opulence, plenitude, plenteousness, plentifulness, profusion, prosperity, wealth.

pliable *adj* **1** bendable, bendy, ductile, flexible, limber, lithe, malleable, plastic, pliant, supple. **2** adaptable, compliant, docile, easily led, impressionable, influenceable, persuadable, receptive, responsive.

plot *n* **1** cabal, conspiracy, intrigue, machination, plan, scheme. **2** action, narrative, outline, scenario, story, story line, subject, theme, thread.

plot *v* **1** collude, conspire, contrive, hatch, plan, scheme. **2** calculate, chart, compute, draft, draw, locate, map, mark, outline. **3** brew, conceive, concoct, contrive, design, devise, frame, hatch, imagine, lay, project; (*Inf*) cook up.

plot *n* allotment, area, ground, lot, parcel, patch, tract.

plough *v* cultivate, dig, furrow, ridge, till, turn over.

plug *n* **1** bung, cork, spigot, stopper. **2** advertisement, good word, mention, publicity, puff, push; (*Inf*) advert, hype.

plug *v* **1** block, bun, choke, close, cork, cover, fill, pack, seal, stop, stopper, stopple, stop up, stuff. **2** build up, mention, promote, publicize, puff, push, write up; (*Inf*) advertise, hype.

plumb *n* lead, plumb bob, plummet, weight.

plump *adj* burly, buxom, chubby,

corpulent, dumpy, fat, fleshy, full, obese, podgy, portly, roly-poly, rotund, round, stout, tubby, wellcovered; (*Inf*) beefy, well-upholstered.

plunder *v* devastate, loot, pillage, raid, ransack, ravage, rifle, rob, sack, spoil, steal, strip.

plunder *n* booty, ill-gotten gains, loot, pillage, prey, prize, rapine, spoils; (*Inf*) swag.

plunge *v* cast, descend, dip, dive, douse, drop, fall, go down, immerse, jump, nosedive, pitch, plumet, sink, sumerge, swoop, throw, tumble.

plunge *n* descent, dive, drop, fall, immersion, submersion.

plus *adj* added, additional, extra, positive, supplementary.

poach *v* appropriate, encroach, hunt illegally, plunder, rob, steal game, trespass.

pocket *n* bag, compartment, hollow, pouch, receptacle, sack.

pocket *adj* compact, concise, little, miniature, portable, small; (*Inf*) pint-sized, potted.

poem *n* lyric, ode, rhyme, song, sonnet, verse.

poetry *n* metrical composition, poems, rhyme, rhyming, verse.

point *n* **1** dot, full stop, mark, period, speck, stop. **2** location, place, position, site, spot, stage. **3** apex, end, prong, spike, spur, summit, tip, top. **4** bluff, cape, headland, ness, promontory. **5** circumstance, condition, degree, extent, position, stage.

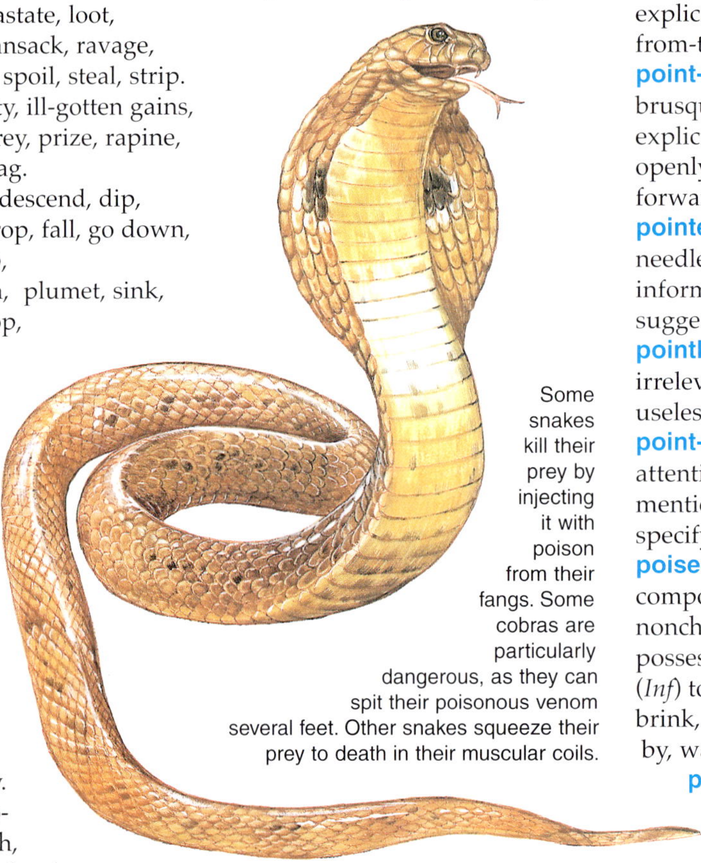

Some snakes kill their prey by injecting it with poison from their fangs. Some cobras are particularly dangerous, as they can spit their poisonous venom several feet. Other snakes squeeze their prey to death in their muscular coils.

6 instant, moment, time, very minute. **7** aim, design, goal, intention, motive, purpose, reason, use. **8** core, crux, drift, essence, gist, heart, meaning, subject, theme, thrust. **9** score, tally, unit. **10 beside the point** incidental, irrelevant, out of the way, pointless, unimportant, without connection. **11 to the point** applicable, appropriate, apropos, apt, brief, fitting, relevant, short, suitable, terse.

point *v* designate, direct, indicate, show, signify.

point-blank *adj* abrupt, blunt, categorical, direct, downright, explicit, express, plain, straight-from-the-shoulder, unreserved.

point-blank *adv* bluntly, brusquely, candidly, directly, explicitly, forthrightly, frankly, openly, plainly, straight, straight-forwardly.

pointer *n* **1** guide, indicator, needle. **2** advice, caution, hint, information, recommendation, suggestion, tip, warning.

pointless *adj* absurd, futile, irrelevant, senseless, stupid, useless, vain, worthless.

point-out *v* bring up, call attention to, identify, indicate, mention, remind, reveal, show, specify.

poised *adj* **1** calm, collected, composed, dignified, graceful, nonchalant, self-confident, self-possessed, serene, unruffled; (*Inf*) together. **2** all set, on the brink, prepared, ready, standing by, waiting.

poisonous *adj* **1** deadly, fatal, lethal, mortal, toxic, venomous, virulent. **2** evil, noxious, vicious.

poke *v* **1** butt, dig, elbow, hit, jab, nudge, prod, punch, push, shove, stab stick, thrust. **2 poke fun at** chaff, jeer, make a mock of, make fun of, mock, ridicule, tease; (*Inf*) rib, send up, take the mickey.

poke *n* butt, dig, hit, jab, nudge, prod, punch, thrust.

pole *n* bar, mast, pillar, post, rod, shaft, spar, staff, stanchion, standard, stick, support, upright.

police *n* constabulary, law enforcement agency, police force; (*Inf*) boys in blue, fuzz, the law, the Old Bill.
police *v* control, guard, keep in order, keep the peace, patrol, protect, regulate, watch.
policeman, policewoman *n* constable, PC, police officer, WPC; (*Inf*) bobby, cop, copper.
policy *n* action, approach, code, course, custom, guideline, plan, practice, procedure, programme, protocol, rule, theory.
polish *v* **1** buff, burnish, clean, rub, shine, smooth, wax. **2** brush up, correct, finish, improve, perfect, refine, touch up.
polish *n* **1** brightness, brilliance, finish, glaze, gloss, lustre, sheen, smoothness, sparkle, veneer. **2** varnish, wax. **3** elegance, finesse, finish, grace, politeness, refinement, style; (*Inf*) class.
polite *adj* civil, courteous, gracious, mannerly, respectful, well-behaved, well-mannered.
politician *n* legislator, Member of Parliament, MP, office bearer, public servant, statesman; (*Inf*) politico.
poll *n* **1** figures, returns, tally, vote, voting. **2** ballot, canvass, census, count, public opinion poll, sampling, survey.
pollute *v* **1** contaminate, dirty, foul, infect, poison, spoil, stain, taint. **2** corrupt, defile, deprave, dishonour, violate.
pompous *v* **1** arrogant, bloated, grandiose, ostentatious, pretentious, self important, showy. **2** boastful, inflated, overblown.
pool *n* **1** fish pool, lake, mere, pond, puddle, splash, tarn, water hole. **2** swimming bath, swimming pool. **3** collective, combine, consortium, group, syndicate, team. **4** bank, funds, jackpot, kitty, pot, stakes.
pool *v* amalgamate, combine, join forces, merge, share.
poor *adj* **1** destitute, needy, penniless, poverty stricken; (*Inf*) broke, hard up, skint, stony-broke. **2** deficient, inadequate, lacking, meagre, scanty, sparse. **3** below par, inferior, mediocre, second-rate, shoddy, substandard, unsatisfactory, worthless; (*Inf*) rotten. **4** barren, exhausted, fruitless, infertile, unproductive. **5** ill-fated, pathetic, unfortunate, unlucky. **6** humble, lowly, mean, modest, paltry, plain, trivial.
popular *adj* **1** accepted, famous, fashionable, in, in favour, liked. **2** common, general, prevailing, public, standard, universal, widespread.
populate *v* colonize, inhabit, live in, occupy, people, settle.
port *n* anchorage, harbour, haven, roads, roadstead, seaport.
portable *adj* compact, convenient, easily carried, handy, light, manageable, movable, portative.warn of.
porter *n* **1** baggage attendant, bearer, carrier. **2** caretaker, concierge, doorman, gatekeeper, janitor.
portion *n* **1** bit, fragment, morsel, part, piece, section, segment. **2** allowance, measure, quota, ration, share. **3** helping, piece, serving.
portrait *n* image, likeness, painting, photograph, picture, portraiture, representation, sketch.
portray *v* **1** depict, draw, figure, illustrate, paint, picture, sketch. **2** charcterize, depict, describe.
pose *v* **1** arrange, model,

How does pollution cause acid rain?

When fossil fuels are burnt, nitrogen oxide, and sulphur dioxide dissolve into the moisture in the air and rise into the clouds. These are blown along by the wind and fall as rain, sometimes hundreds of kilometres away. This “acid rain” kills vegetation and the living things that feed on it. It can be difficult to find the source of the problem because of its distance fom the damage being done.

position, sit for. **2 pose as**, feign, impersonate, pass oneself off as, pretend to be; (*Inf*) show off.
position *n* **1** area, bearings, location, place, site, situation, spot, whereabouts. **2** attitude, pose, stance. **3** standpoint, view. **4** plight, situation, state. **5** caste, class, place, rank, standing, stature, status. **6** capacity, duty, job, occupation, place, post, role, situation; (*Inf*) berth, billet.
position *v* arrange, lay out, place, put, settle; (*Inf*) stick.
positive *adj* **1** absolute, certain, clear, conclusive, decisive, definite, direct, explicit, express, firm, unmistakable. **2** assured, confident, convinced, sure. **3** assertive, dogmatic, emphatic, firm, forceful, resolute, stubborn. **4** beneficial, constructive, effective, forward looking, helpful, practical, productive, progressive, useful. **5** absolute, complete, perfect, thorough.
possess *v* **1** be born with, be endowed with, enjoy, have, hold, own. **2** acquire, control, occupy, seize, take possession of.
possession *n* **1** control, custody, hold, ownership, proprietorship, tenure, title. **2** assets, belongings, chattels, effects, estate, goods and chattels, property, things.
possibility *n* **1** feasibility, likelihood. **2** chance, likelihood, odds, probability, prospect, risk.
possible *adj* **1** conceivable, credible, likely. **2** feasible, viable, within reach, workable; (*Inf*) on. **3** hopeful, likely, potential, probable, promising.
post *n* **1** column, newel, pillar, pole, shaft, support, upright. **2** appointment, assignment, employment, job, office, place, position, situation; (*Inf*) berth, billet. **3** collection, delivery, mail, postal service.

How does a dry cell battery store power?

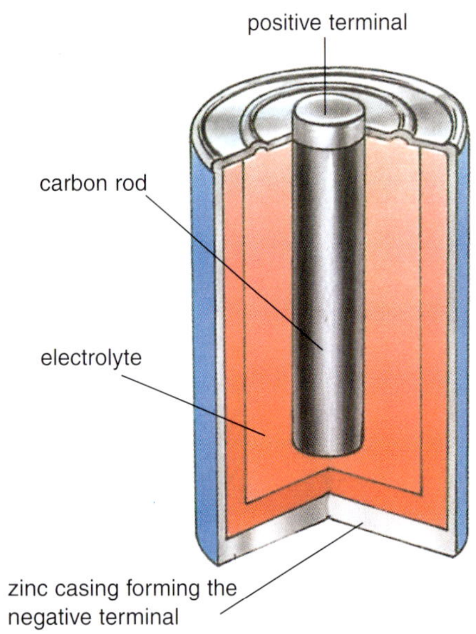

Electrical energy can be stored in batteries. Inside a dry cell battery there is a chemical paste called an electrolyte, a positive terminal and a negative terminal. When the battery is put into an electrical circuit, chemical reactions cause electrons to flow out through the negative terminal, through the circuit, and back through the postive terminal. The illustration shows a single cell battery, In larger batteries there can be several single cells.

post *v* **1** advertise, announce, display, pin up, proclaim, publicize, publish, put up, stick up. **2** assign, establish, locate, place, position, put, situate, station. **3** dispatch, mail, send, transmit.
poster *n* advertisement, notice, placard, public notice, sticker; (*Inf*) advert.
postpone *v* adjourn, defer, delay, hold over, put back, put off, shelve, suspend, table.
posture *v* make a show, pose, put on airs, try to attract attention; (*Inf*) show off.
potent *adj* forceful, mighty, powerful, strong, vigorous.
potential *adj* budding, future, hidden, likely, possible, promising, undeveloped, unrealized.
potential *n* ability, aptitude, capability, power, wherewithal; (*Inf*) what it takes.
pouch *n* bag, container, pocket, purse, sack.
pounce *v* ambush, attack, dash at, drop, fall upon, jump, leap at, snatch, spring, strike, swoop, take by surprise, take unaware.
pounce *n* assault, attack, bound, jump, leap, spring.
pour *v* **1** decant, let flow, spill, splash. **2** course, emit, flow, gush, jet, run, rush, spew, spout, spurt, stream. **3** come down in torrents, rain, rain heavily, sheet, teem; (*Inf*) bucket down, rain cats and dogs. **4** crowd, flood, stream, swarm, throng.
powder *n* dust, fine, grains, loose particles, pounce, talc.
powder *v* **1** crush, granulate, grind, pestle, pound, pulverize. **2** dredge, dust, scatter, sprinkle.
power *n* **1** ability, capability, capacity, competence, potential.

2 energy, force, intensity, might, muscle, potency, strength. 3 command, control, influence, mastery, rule, sovereignty, supremacy, sway. 4 authority, licence, right, warrant.
powerful *adj* **1** energetic, mighty, robust, strong, sturdy, vigorous. **2** commanding, controlling, influential. **3** compelling, effective, impressive, persuasive.
powerless *adj* **1** disabled, feeble, frail, helpless, incapacitated, paralysed, weak. **2** defenceless, dependent, ineffective, unarmed, vulnerable.
practical *adj* **1** efficient, functional, realistic, utilitarian. **2** mundane, ordinary, realistic. **3** efficient, experience, proficient, qualified, skilled, trained.
practice *n* custom, habit, mode, routine, system, tradition, use, usual, procedure, way. **3** discipline, drill, exercise, preparation, rehearsal, repetition, study, training, work-out. **4** business, career, profession, vocation, work.
practise *v* **1** go over, go through, polish, prepare, rehearse, repeat, study, train, warm up, work out. **2** apply, carry out, do, follow, live up to, observe, perform, put into practice. **3** carry on, pursue, specialize in, undertake, work at.
precarious *adj* dangerous, dubious, hazardous, risky, shaky, touch and go, tricky, uncertain, unsafe, unstable, unsteady, unsure; (*Inf*) chancy, dicey, dodgy, hairy.
precede *v* come first, go ahead of, go before, head, lead, pave the way, preface, take precedence.
precious *adj* **1** adored, beloved,

Bordering Zimbabwe and Zambia, the Victoria Falls are located midway along the Zambezi River. The waterfall is spectacular as the river plunges over a sheer precipice to a maximum drop of 108m (355 ft).

favourite, loved, treasured, valued. **2** choice, costly, dear, expensive, fine, high-priced, priceless, prized, rare, valuable.
precipice *n* bluff, brink, cliff, cliff face, crag, height, rock face, sheer drop, steep.
precisely *adv* absolutely, accurately, correctly, exactly, just so, literally, neither more nor less, square, squarely; (*Inf*) bang on, plumb, slap, smack.
precision *n* accuracy, care, correctness, preciseness.
prediction *n* forecast, prognosis, prophecy, soothsaying.
prefer *v* adopt, be partial to, choose, desire, elect, fancy, favour, go for, incline towards, like better, opt for, pick, plump for, select, single out, wish.
preference *n* **1** choice, desire, election, favourite, first choice, option, partiality, pick, selection, top of the list. **2** advantage, favoured treatment, favouritism, first place, precedence, pride of place, priority.
prejudice *n* **1** bias, preconceived notion. **2** bigotry, chauvinism, discrimination, intolerance, narrow-mindedness, racism, sexism. **3** damage, harm, hurt, loss, mischief.
prejudice *v* **1** bias, colour, influence, jaundice, poison, predispose, prepossess, slant, sway, warp. **2** damage, harm, hinder, hurt, impair, injure, mar, spoil, undermine.
preliminary *adj* exploratory, first, initial, introductory, opening, preparatory, prior, qualifying, test, trial.
preliminary *n* beginning, first round, foundation, groundwork, initiation, introduction, opening, prelims, prelude, start.
premature *adj* **1** early, forward, green, immature, incomplete, undeveloped, unripe. **2** hasty, ill-timed, impulsive, overhasty, rash, too soon; (*Inf*) previous.
premeditated *adj* calculated, conscious, contrived, deliberate, intended, intentional, planned, prepense, studied, wilful.
premier *n* chancellor, head of government, PM, prime minister.
premier *adj* **1** chief, first, foremost, head, highest, leading, main, primary, prime, principal, top. **2** earliest, first, inaugural,

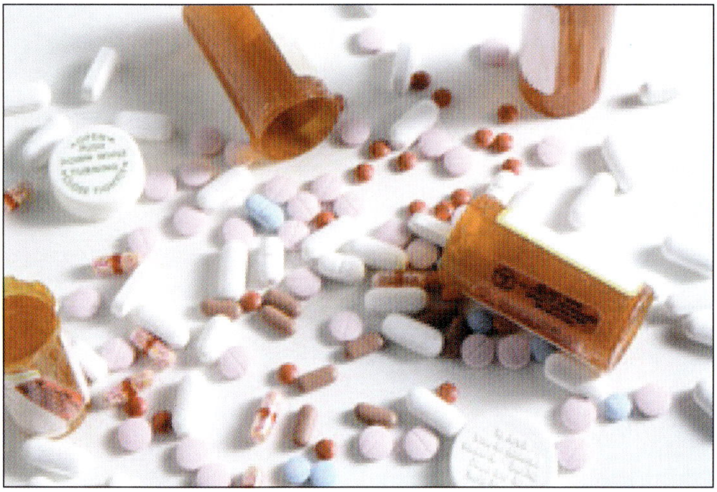

Prescription drugs in powder form may be pressed into tablets or contained in capsules that dissolve in the stomach. To help pharmacists and patients to distinguish between drugs, they are shaped and coloured in different ways.

initial, original.
première *n* debut, first night, first performance, first showing, opening.
premonition *n* apprehension, feeling, feeling in one's bones, foreboding, forewarning, hunch, idea, intuition, omen, sign, warning; (*Inf*) funny feeling.
preparation *n* **1** development, getting ready, groundwork, preparing. **2** anticipation, foresight, provision, readiness. **3** composition, compound, concoction, medicine, mixture, tincture. **4** homework, revision, schoolwork, study; (*Inf*) prep, swotting.
prepare *v* **1** adjust, arrange, coach, dispose, form, groom, make ready, plan, practise, train, warm up. **2** fortify, strengthen. **3** assemble, concoct, construct, contrive, draw up, fashion, fix up, make, produce, put together, turn out; (*Inf*) get up.
prepared *adj* **1** all set, arranged, planned, primed, ready, set. **2** able, disposed, inclined, predisposed, willing.
preposterous *adj* absurd, bizarre, crazy, extreme, foolish, incredible, ludicrous, monstrous, out of the question, outrageous, ridiculous, senseless, shocking, unreasonable, unthinkable.
prescription *n* drug, medicine, mixture, preparation, remedy.
present *adj* **1** contemporary, current, existent, existing, extant, immediate, instant, present-day. **2** accounted for, available, here, nearby, ready, there, to hand.
present *v* **1** introduce, made known. **2** demonstrate, display, exhibit, give, mount, put before the public, put on show, stage. **3** advance, declare, introduce, offer, produce, put forward, raise, recount, relate, state, submit, suggest, tender.
present *n* award, benefaction, donation, favour, gift, grant, gratuity, offering; (*Inf*) prezzie.
presentation *n* **1** award, donation, investiture, offering. **2** appearance, arrangement, delivery, production, staging, submission. **3** demonstration, display, exhibition, performance, production, show.
preservation *n* conservation, defence, keeping, maintenance, perpetuation, protection, safe-guarding, safekeeping, safety, security, storage, support.
preserve *v* care for, conserve, defend, guard, keep, protect, safeguard, save, shelter, shield.
preserve *n* area, domain, field, realm, sphere.
press *v* **1** bear down on, compress, crush, force down, reduce, squeeze, stuff. **2** calender, finish, flatten, iron, put the creases in, smooth, steam. **3** clasp, crush, embrace, encircle, enfold, fold in one's arms, hold close, hug, squeeze. **4** compel, constrain, demand, enforce, enjoin, force, insist on. **5** beg, entreat, exhort, implore, importune, petition, plead, pressurize, sue. **6** cluster, crowd, flock, gather, hasten, herd, hurry, mill, push, rush, seethe, surge, swarm, throng.
press *n* **1** the press, Fleet Street, fourth estate, journalism, news, media, newspapers, the papers. **2** columnists, correspondents, journalists, newsmen, photographers, pressmen, reporters.
pressure *n* **1** compression, crushing, force, heaviness, weight. **2** compulsion, force, influence, power, sway.
prestige *n* authority, cachet, celebrity, distinction, eminence, fame, honour, influence, kudos, renown, reputation, standing, stature, status, weight.

presume *v* assume, believe, conjecture, infer, posit, postulate, presuppose, suppose, surmise, take for granted, take it, think
presumption *n* assurance, audacity, boldness, effrontery, forwardness, impudence, insolence, presumptuousness, temerity; (*Inf*) brassneck, cheek, gall, nerve.
pretence *n* **1** acting, charade, deception, fabrication, feigning, invention, make-believe, sham, simulation, subterfuge, trickery. **2** affection, appearance, artifice, display, façade, pretentiousness, show, veneer.
pretend *v* **1** assume, counterfeit, fake, falsify, feign, impersonate, make out, pass oneself off as, profess, put on, simulate. **2** act, make up, play, play the part of, suppose.
pretty *adj* appealing, attractive, beautiful, bonny, charming, cute, fair, good-looking, graceful, lovely, personable.
pretty *adv* moderately, quite, rather, reasonably, somewhat; (*Inf*) fairly, kind of.
prevail *v* **1** overcome, overrule, succeed, triumph, win. **2** abound, be prevalent, be widespread, predominate. **3 prevail upon** bring round, convince, induce, influence, persuade, prompt, sway, talk into, win over. usual, widespread.
prevention *n* **1** anticipation, avoidance, elimination, safeguard, thwarting. **2** bar, check, hindrance, impediment, obstacle, obstruction, stoppage.
previous *adj* earlier, former, one-time, past, preceding, prior.
previously *adv* at one time, a while ago, before, earlier, formerly, in days gone by, in the past, once, then, until now.
prey *n* **1** game, kill, quarry. **2** dupe, fall, guy, mark, victim. **3** target; (*Inf*) mug.
price *n* **1** amount, asking price, assessment, bill, charge, cost, estimate, expenditure, expense, face value, fee, figure, outlay, payment, rate, valuation, value, worth. **2** consequences, cost, penalty, sacrifice. (*Inf*) damage.
price *v* cost, estimate, evaluate, put a price on, rate, value.
priceless *adj* beyond price, dear, expensive, incalculable, invaluable, irreplaceable, precious, prized, rare, rich, treasured.
prick *v* **1** bore, jab, lance, perforate, pierce, pink, punch, puncture, stab. **2** bite, itch, prickle, smart, sting, tingle.
prick *n* cut, gash, hole, perforation, pinhole, puncture, wound.
prickly *adj* **1** barbed, brambly, briery, bristly, spiny, thorny. **2** crawling, itchy, prickling, scratchy, smarting, stinging, tingling.
primarily *adv* basically, chiefly, essentially, for the most part, generally, mainly, mostly, on the whole, principally.
primary *adj* **1** best, cardinal, chief, dominant, first, greatest, highest, leading, main, principal, top. **2** basic, beginning, essential, fundamental, radical, ultimate, underlying.
prime *adj* **1** best, capital, choice, excellent, first-class, first-rate, grade A, highest, quality, select, selected, superior, top. **2** basic, earliest, fundamental, original, primary, underlying. **3** chief, leading, main, predominant, pre-eminent, primary, principal, ruling, senior.
prime *n* best days, bloom, flower, full flowering, height, heyday, maturity, peak, zenith.
prime *v* **1** break in, coach, fit, get ready, groom, make ready, prepare, train. **2** brief, clue up, give someone the lowdown, inform, notify, tell; (*Inf*) fill in.

Primary colours

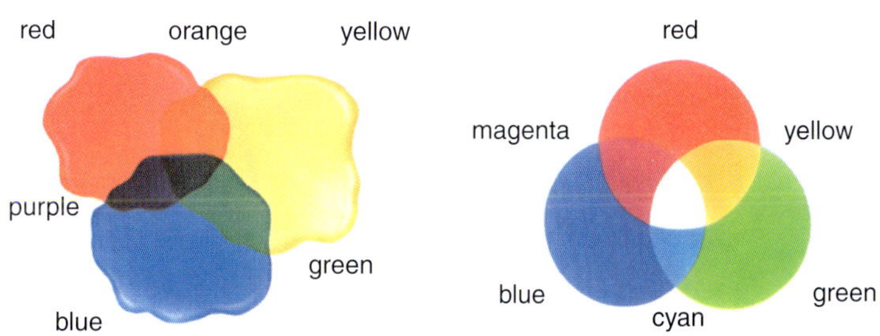

There are three primary colours of paint – red, yellow and blue. When each of these colours is mixed with one or both other colours, a new colour is produced.

The three primary colours of light are red, green and blue. Mixed in pairs, they create the secondary colours of cyan, magenta and yellow. White light occurs when all three colours are mixed in equal amounts.

Primitive life in prehistoric times is depicted in cave paintings found in several parts of the world.Hidden from sight for thousands of years, the images appear to move when viewed by torch light.

primitive *adj* **1** earliest, early, elementary, first, original, primary, primeval, pristine. **2** barbaric, crude, rough, rude, savage, simple, uncivilized.
prince *n* lord, monarch, ruler, sovereign.
principal *adj* capital, cardinal, chief, controlling, dominate, essential, foremost, highest, key, leading, main, most important, paramount, primary, strongest.
principal *n* **1** chief, director, head, leader, master, ruler, superintendent. **2** dean, head-master, head-mistress, head-teacher, master, rector. **3** assets, capital, capital funds, money; (*Inf*) boss, head.
priority *n* first concern, greater importance, precedence, preference, rank, right of way, seniority, superiority, supremacy, the lead.
prison *n* confinement, dungeon, gaol, glasshouse, jail, peniten-tiary; (*Inf*) can, clink, cooler, glasshouse, jug, slammer, stir.
prisoner *n* **1** convict, jailbird. **2** captive, detainee, hostage, internee; (*Inf*) con, lag.
privacy *n* isolation, retirement, retreat, seclusion, separateness, sequestration, solitude.
private *adj* **1** clandestine, closet, confidential, in camera, inside, off the record, secret, unofficial; (*Inf*) hush-hush. **2** exclusive, individual, intimate, personal, reserved, special. **3** concealed, isolated, secluded, solitary.
privilege *n* advantage, benefit, birthright, claim, entitlement, franchise, freedom, prerogative, right, sanction.
prize *n* **1** accolade, award, honour, premium, reward, trophy. **2** windfall, winnings. **3** aim, ambition, conquest, goal, hope. **4** booty, capture, loot, pickings, pillage, plunder, spoils, trophy.
prize *adj* award-winning, best, champion, first-rate, outstand-ing, top, winning; (*Inf*) topnotch.
prize *v* appreciate, cherish, esteem, hold dear, regard highly, set store by, treasure, value.
probability *n* chances, expectation, liability, likelihood, odds, presumption, prospect.
probe *v* **1** examine, explore, go into, investigate, look into, query, scrutinize, search, sift, sound, test, verify. **2** feel around, poke, prod.
probe *n* detection, examination, exploration, inquest, inquiry, investigation, scrutiny, study.
problem *n* **1** complication, difficulty, dilemma, disagreement, disputed point, doubt, point at issue, predicament, quandary, trouble; (*Inf*) can of worms, hard nut to crack. **2** conundrum, enigma, poser, puzzle, question, riddle.
problem *adj* delinquent, uncontrollable, unmanageable, unruly; (*Inf*) brain-teaser.
procedure *n* action, conduct, course, custom, form, formula, method, *modus operandi*, operation, performance, plan of action, policy, practice, process, routine, scheme, step, strategy, system, transaction.
proceed *v* **1** advance, carry on, continue, get going, get on with, get under way with, go ahead, go on, progress, set in motion. **2** arise, come, derive, emanate, ensue, flow, follow, issue, originate, result, spring, stem.
proceeding *n* **1** action, course of action, deed, measure, move, procedure, process, step, under-taking, venture. **2** account, affairs, archives, business, dealings, matters, minutes, records, report, transactions.
proceeds *pl n* earnings, gain, income, produce, products, profit, receipts, returns, revenue, takings, yield.
process *n* **1** course, course of action, means, method, mode, operation, practice, procedure, system. **2** advance, course, development, evolution, formation, growth, progress.
process *v* **1** deal with, dispose of, fulfil, handle, take care of. **2** alter, convert, prepare, refine, transform, treat.

procession *n* cavalcade, column, cortege, file, march, motorcade, parade, train.

prod *v* **1** dig, elbow, jab, nudge, poke, prick, propel, push, shove. **2** egg on, incite, motivate, move, prompt, rouse, spur, stimulate, stir up, urge.

prod *n* **1** boost, dig, elbow, jab, nudge, poke, push shove. **2** poker, spur, stick. **3** boost, cue, prompt, reminder, signal.

produce *v* **1** compose, construct, create, develop, fabricate, invent, make, manufacture, originate, put together, turn out. **2** afford, bear, breed, deliver, give, render, supply, yield. **3** bring about, cause, effect, generate, give rise to, provoke, set off. **4** advance, bring forward, bring to light, demonstrate, exhibit, present, put forward, show. **5** direct, do, exhibit, mount, present, put on show, stage. **6** extend, lengthen, prolong, protract.

produce *n* crop, fruit and vegetables, greengrocery, greens, harvest, product, yield.

profession *n* **1** business, career, employment, occupation, office, position, vocation. **2** claim, confession, declaration, statement, testimony, vow.

profile *n* **1** contour, drawing, figure, form, outline, portrait, side view, silhouette, sketch. **2** biography, characterization. **3** analysis, examination, graph, review, study, survey, table.

prolong *v* carry on, continue, delay, drag out, draw out, extend, lengthen, make longer, perpetuate, protract, spin out, stretch.

promise *v* **1** assure, contract, cross one's heart, give one's word, guarantee, pledge, plight, stipulate, swear, take an oath, undertake, vouch, vow, warrant. **2** denote, hint at, hold out hopes of, indicate, lead one to expect, look like, seem likely to, show signs of, suggest.

prompt *adj* **1** immediate, punctual, quick, rapid, speedy, swift. **2** alert, brisk, eager, efficient, expeditious, quick, ready, responsive, smart, willing.

propel *v* drive, force, launch, push, send, set in motion, shoot, shove, start, thrust.

proposal *n* bid, design, offer, plan, presentation, programme, project, proposition, scheme, suggestion, tender, terms.

proposition *n* motion, plan, programme, project, proposal, recommendation, scheme, suggestion.

prosperous *adj* **1** blooming, booming, doing well, flourishing, fortunate, lucky, prospering, successful, thriving; (*Inf*) on the up and up. **2** affluent, moneyed, opulent, rich, wealthy, well-off, well-to-do; (*Inf*) in clover, in the money, well-heeled.

protect *v* care for, chaperon, cover, cover up for, defend, foster, give sanctuary, guard, harbour, keep safe, look after, mount guard over, preserve, safeguard, save, screen, secure, shelter, shield, support, take under one's wing, watch over.

protest *n* dissent, formal complaint, objection, outcry, protestation.

protest *v* complain, cry out, demonstrate, disapprove, express disapproval, object, oppose, remonstrate, say no to, take exception; (*Inf*) kick against.

prototype *n* example, first, mock-up, model, original, pattern, precedent, standard.

proud *adj* **1** gratified, honoured, pleased, satisfied. **2** arrogant, conceited, presumptuous, self-important, snobbish, vain; (*Inf*) high and mighty, stuck-up, toffee-nosed.

Parades and processions are a common sight in towns and cities all over the world as people celebrate special days of the year, in their particular country.

prove *v* **1** acertain, authenticate, bear out, confirm, corroborate, demonstrate, evidence, justify, show, substantiate, verify. **2** analyse, check, examine, to trial, test, try. **3** end up, result, turn out.

province *n* **1** colony, county, department, district, domain, region, section, territory, tract, zone. **2** area, business, capacity, concern, duty, employment, field, function, line, part, post, responsibility, role, sphere.

provisional *adj* conditional, interim, limited, provisory, stopgap, temporary, tentative.

prune *v* clip, cut, cut back, dock, lop, pare down, reduce, shape, shorten, snip, trim.

publication *n* book, booklet, brochure, handbill, issue, leaflet, magazine, newspaper, pamphlet, periodical.

publicity *n* advertising, press, promotion, public notice. (*Inf*) ballyhoo, hype, plug.

publish *v* **1** issue, print, produce. **2** advertise, broadcast, circulate, declare, distribute, divulge, leak, reveal, spread.

pull out *v* abandon, depart, evacuate, leave, retreat, stop participating, withdraw.

pull through *v* come through, get better, get over, pull round, rally, recover, survive, weather.

pump *v* **1** drive, force, inject, pour, push send, supply. **2** cross-examine, give someone the third degree, interrogate, probe, question closely, quiz; (*Inf*) grill.

punctual *adj* early, exact, in good time, on the dot, on time, precise, prompt, punctilious, seasonable, strict, timely.

purchase *v* acquire, buy, come by, gain, get hold of, invest in. **2** obtain, pay for, put money into, secure, shop for. **3** achieve, earn, gain, realize, win.

pursuit *n* **1** chase, hunt, hunting, inquiry, quest, search, seeking, tracking, trail, trailing. **2** activity, hobby, interest, line, occupation, pastime, pleasure, vocation.

pushy *adj* **1** ambitious, determined, dynamic, enterprising, go-ahead, on the go, purposeful, resourceful. **2** assertive, bold, brash, forward, intrusive, self-assertive; (*Inf*) pushy.

put *v* **1** bring, deposit, establish, fix, lay, place, position, rest, set, settle, situate. **2** assign, constrain, employ, force, induce, make, oblige, require, set, subject to. **3** advance, bring forward, forward, offer, present, propose, set before, submit, tender. **4** cast, fling, heave, hurl, lob, pitch, throw, toss.

put off *v* **1** defer, delay, hold over, postpone, put back, reschedule. **2** confuse, dismay, distress, perturb, unsettle; (*Inf*) rattle, throw. **3** discourage, dishearten, dissuade.

put out *v* **1** annoy, disturb, exasperate, harass, irritate, perturb, provoke. **2** blow out, douse, extinguish, quench, smother, snuff out. **3** bother, disturb, embarrass, impose upon, inconvenience, put on the spot, trouble, upset.

put up *v* **1** build, construct, erect, fabricate, raise. **2** accommodate, board, entertain, house, lodge, take in. **3** float, nominate, offer, present, propose, put forward, recommend, submit. **4** advance, give, invest, pay, pledge, provide, supply; **put up with** bear, endure, pocket, stand for, stomach, suffer, swallow, take, tolerate.

puzzle *v* **1** baffle, beat, bewilder, confound, confuse, flumox, mystify, nonplus, perplex, stump. **2** ask oneself, brood, mull over, muse, ponder, rack one's brains, study, think about, think hard. **3 puzzle out** clear up, crack the code, decipher, find the key, get the answer, resolve, see, solve, sort out, unravel, work out.

puzzle *n* **1** conundrum, enigma, mystery, problem, riddle. **2** difficulty, dilemma, quandary; (*Inf*) brain-teaser.

puzzling *adj* above one's head, baffling, bewildering, beyond one, full of surprises, hard, mystifying, perplexing.

pyromaniac *n* arsonist, fire-raiser, incendiary.

On land, oil is brought up to the surface by a pump called a nodding donkey. It gets its name from the upward and downward motion of its 'head'.

Qq

quagmire *n* **1** bog, fen, marsh, mire, quicksand, swamp. **2** difficulty, dilemma, muddle, predicament, quandary; (*Inf*) fix, jam, pickle, scrape.
quaint *adj* curious, eccentric, odd, old-fashioned, original, peculiar, strange, unusual.
quake *v* move, quiver, rock, shake, shiver, tremble, vibrate, waver, wobble.
qualified *adj* **1** adept, capable, competent, experienced, expert, knowledgeable, proficient, skilful, trained. **2** confined, guarded, limited, reserved.
quality *n* **1** condition, feature, mark, peculiarity, property, trait. **2** character, description, kind, make, nature, sort. **3** calibre, distinction, excellence, grade, merit, position, rank, status, value, worth.
quantity *n* aggregate, allotment, amount, lot, number, part, portion, quota, sum, total.
quarrel *n* argument, brawl, breach, broil, commotion, controversy, difference of opinion, disagreement, discord, disputation, dispute, dissension, dissidence, disturbance, feud, fight, fracas, fray, misunderstanding, row, spat, squabble, strife, tiff, tumult, vendetta, wrangle; (*Inf*) scrap.
quarrel *v* argue, bicker, brawl, clash, differ, disagree, dispute, fight, row, spar, squabble, wrangle; (*Inf*) fall out.
quarry *n* aim, game, goal, objective, prey, prize, victim.
quarter *n* area, direction, district, locality, neighbourhood, part, place, point position, province, region, side, spot, station, territory, zone.
quarter *v* accommodate, billet, board, house, install, lodge, place, post, put up, station.
quarters *pl n* accommodation, barracks, billet, chambers, digs, domicile, dwelling, habitation, lodging, lodgings, post, residence, rooms, shelter, station; (*Inf*) digs.
quash *v* annul, cancel, declare null and void, invalidate, nullify, over-rule, overthrow, rescind, reverse, revoke, set aside, void.
queen *n* consort, monarch, ruler, sovereign.
queer *adj* **1** abnormal, curious, eerie, erratic, extraordinary, funny, odd, peculiar, remarkable, singular, strange, uncanny, uncommon, unnatural, unusual, weird. **2** doubtful, dubious, irregular, mysterious, puzzling, questionable, suspicious; (*Inf*) fishy, shady. **3** crazy, demented, eccentric, irrational, mad, odd, touched, unbalanced, unhinged.
quench *v* check, crush, destroy, douse, end, extinguish, put out, smother, snuff out, squelch, stifle, suppress.
query *v* **1** ask, enquire, question. **2** challenge, disbelieve, dispute, doubt, mistrust, suspect.
query *n* demand, doubt, hesitation, inquiry, objection, problem, question, reservation, scepticism, suspicion.
question *v* **1** ask, cross-examine, enquire, examine, interrogate, interview, investigate, probe, quiz, sound out; (*Inf*) grill, pump. **2** challenge, disbelieve, dispute, distrust, doubt, query, suspect.
question *n* **1** examination, inquiry, interrogation, investigation. **2** argument, confusion, contention, controversy, debate, difficulty, dispute, doubt, misgiving, problem, query, uncertainty. **3** issue, motion, point, point at issue, proposal, proposition, subject, theme, topic.
questionable *adj* arguable, controversial, controvertible, debatable, disputable, doubtful, dubious, suspect, suspicious, uncertain, unproven, unreliable; (*Inf*) fishy, shady.
queue *n* chain, file, line, order, progression, sequence, series, string, succession, train.

Queen Elizabeth II, who has reigned since 1952, is the most widely travelled Head of State in the world. She will celebrate her golden jubilee in 2002.

quibble *v* carp, equivocate, evade, pretend, prevaricate, shift, split hairs.
quibble *n* artifice, complaint, criticism, equivocation, evasion, nicety, niggle, objection, pretence, prevarication, protest, quirk, shift, sophism, subterfuge, subtlety.
quick *adj* **1** active, brief, brisk, cursory, expeditious, express, fast, fleet, hasty, headlong, hurried, prompt, rapid, speedy, sudden, swift. **2** agile, alert, energetic, flying, keen, lively, nimble, spirited, sprightly, spry, vivacious. **3** able, acute, adept, apt, astute, bright, clever, deft, intelligent, nimble-witted, quick-witted, sharp, shrewd, skilful, smart; (*Inf*) all there, quick on the uptake.
quick-tempered *adj* fiery, hasty, hot-tempered, impatient, irritable, petulant, quarrelsome, snappish, touchy.
quick-witted *adj* alert, bright, discerning, intelligent, lively, quick, sharp-witted, shrewd, smart; (*Inf*) quick on the uptake.
quicken *v* **1** accelerate, hurry, speed. **2** activate, animate, arouse, excite, galvanize, incite, inspire, invigorate, kindle, refresh, reinvigorate, resuscitate, revitalize, revive, rouse, stimulate, strengthen, vitalize, vivify.
quiet *adj* **1** hushed, inaudible, low, low-pitched, noiseless, peaceful, placid, restful, serene, smooth, tranquil, untroubled. **2** isolated, private, retired, secluded, secret, sequestered, undisturbed, unfrequented. **3** conservative, modest, plain, restrained, simple, subdued, unassuming, unobtrusive, unpretentious. **4** collected, docile, even-tempered, gentle, imperturbable, meek, mild, phlegmatic, reserved, retiring, sedate, shy, unexcitable.

In North America, it is common for quilts to be made up by groups of neighbours or family members to commemorate a special event such as the birth of a baby or wedding.

quiet *n* calmness, ease, hush, peace, quietness, repose, rest, serenity, silence, stillness, tranquillity; (*Inf*) shut up.
quieten *v* allay, alleviate, appease, assuage, blunt, calm, compose, deaden dull, hush, lull, mitigate, mollify, muffle, mute, palliate, quell, quiet, silence, soothe, stifle, still, stop, subdue, tranquilize; (*Inf*) shush.
quilt *n* continental quilt, duvet, eiderdown.
quip *n* jest, joke; (*Inf*) wisecrack.
quit *v* **1** abandon, abdicate, decamp, depart, desert, exit, forsake, go, leave, pull out, relinquish, renounce, resign, retire, surrender, withdraw; (*Inf*) take off. **2** abandon, cease, conclude, discontinue, drop, end, give up, halt, stop, suspend.
quite *adv* **1** completely, entirely, fully, precisely, totally, wholly, without reservation. **2** fairly, moderately, rather, reasonably, relatively, somewhat, to a certain extent, to some degree.
quiver *v* agitate, convulse, pulsate, quake, quaver, shake, shiver, shudder, tremble, vibrate.
quiz *n* examination, investigation, questioning, test.
quiz *v* ask, examine, interrogate, investigate, question; (*Inf*) grill, pump.
quota *n* allocation, allowance, assignment, part, portion, proportion, ration, share, slice; (*Inf*) cut, whack.
quotation *n* **1** citation, cutting, excerpt, extract, passage, reference, selection; (*Inf*) quote. **2** bid, price, charge, cost, estimate, figure, price, rate, tender.

Rr

race *n* **1** chase, competition, contest, dash, pursuit, rivalry. **2** blood, bloodline, breed, clan, ethnic group, family, folk, house, issue, kin, kindred, line, lineage, nation, offspring, people, stock, tribe, type.

race *v* career, compete, contest, dart, dash, fly, gallop, hasten, hurry, run, speed, tear, zoom; (*Inf*) hare, run like mad.

rack *n* **1** frame, framework, stand, structure. **2** agony, pain, suffering, torment, torture.

rack *v* afflict, agonize, distress, excruciate, harass, pain, torment, torture.

racket *n* **1** commotion, din, disturbance, fuss, hullabaloo, noise, outcry, pandemonium, row, shouting, uproar. **2** criminal activity, fraud, illegal enterprise, scheme.

radiant *adj* beaming, bright, brilliant, gleaming, glittering, glorious, glowing, incandescent, luminous, lustrous, shining, sparkling, sunny.

radiate *v* **1** diffuse, emit, give out, gleam, glitter, pour, scatter, send out, shed, shine, spread. **2** branch out, issue, spread out.

radical *adj* **1** basic, fundamental, native, natural, organic, profound, thoroughgoing. **2** complete, entire, excessive, extreme, extremist, fanatical, revolutionary, severe, sweeping, thorough, violent.

radical *n* extremist, fanatic, militant, revolutionary.

rage *n* agitation, anger, frenzy, fury, high dudgeon, ire, madness, mania, obsession, passion, rampage, raving, vehemence, violence, wrath.

rage *v* be furious, blow one's top, foam at the mouth, fume, rant and rave, seethe; (*Inf*) blow up, throw a fit.

ragged *adj* contemptible, down at the heel, frayed, in holes, in rags, in tatters, mean, poor, shabby, shaggy, tattered, tatty, threadbare, torn, unkempt, worn-out.

raid *n* attach, break-in, hit-and-run attack, incursion, invasion, irruption, onset, sally, seizure, sortie, surprise attack.

raid *v* assault, attack, break into, descend on, fall upon, forage foray, invade, pillage, plunder, rifle, sack, sally forth, swoop down upon.

rain *n* **1** cloudburst, deluge, downpour, drizzle, fall, precipitation, raindrops, rainfall, showers. **2** deluge, flood, hail, shower, spate, stream, torrent.

rain *v* drizzle, fall, shower, teem; (*Inf*) bucket down, come down in buckets, rain cats and dogs.

raise *v* **1** build, construct, elevate, erect, hoist, lift, move up, put up, rear. **2** advance, boost, enhance, enlarge, escalate, increase, inflate, intensify, jack up, magnify, reinforce, strengthen; (*Inf*) hike up. **3** elevate, promote, upgrade. **4** bring about, cause, create, originate, produce, start. **5** bring up, introduce, put forward, suggest. **6** assemble, collect, form, muster, rally, recruit. **7** breed, cultivate, grow, nurture, propagate.

rake *v* **1** collect, gather, remove, scrape up. **2** break up, harrow,

Rainwater is not neutral. It is slightly acidic because carbon dioxide from the air is dissolved in it. This reacts with limestone, made of alkaline calcium carbonate. Minerals dissolved in the water gradually build up into the strange rock formations. known as stalagmites (rising from the floor of caves) and stalactites.

A fort is an enclosure protected by ramparts and constructed in a location where it can be used to defend its inhabitants against enemy attack. In this example, the fort has very thick walls so they can withstand prolonged bombardment from ship's guns to deter invaders.

hoe, scrape, scratch.
rally *v* **1** bring to order, re-form, regroup, unite. **2** assemble, bond together, bring together, collect, convene, gather, get together, marshal, mobilize, muster, organize, round up, summon, unite. **3** come round, get better, improve, perk up, pick up, pull through, recover, recuperate, revive, take a turn for the better.
rally *n* **1** reorganization, reunion, stand. **2** assembly, conference, convention, mass meeting. **3** recovery, recuperation, revival. (*Inf*) comeback.
ram *v* butt, collide with, crash, dash, drive, force, hit, impact, run into, slam, smash, strike.
ramble *v* **1** drift, roam, saunter, straggle, stray, stroll, walk, wander; (*Inf*) traipse. **2** babble, chatter, rattle on, wander, witter on; (*Inf*) rabbit on.
ramble *n* excursion, hike, saunter, stroll, tour, trip, walk; (*Inf*) traipse.
rampage *v* go berserk, rage, run riot, run wild, storm, tear.
rampage *n* destruction, frenzy, fury, rage, storm, tempest, tumult, uproar, violence.
rampart *n* barricade, bastion, breastwork, bulwark, defence, earthwork, embankment, fence, fort, fortification, guard, parapet, security, stronghold, wall.
ramshackle *adj* broken-down, crumbling, decrepit, derelict, dilapidated, flimsy, jerry-built, rickety, shaky, tottering, tumble-down, unsafe, unsteady.
random *adj* arbitrary, casual, chance, haphazard, hit or miss, unplanned.
range *n* area, bounds, distance, extent, limits, radius, reach, span; (*Inf*) parameters.
range *v* **1** arrange, dispose, draw up, line up, order. **2** cruise, explore, ramble, roam, stroll, wander.
rank *n* **1** caste, class, degree, division, grade, level, order, sort, standing, status, type. **2** column, file, group, line, row, series, tier.
rank *v* align, arrange, array, class, grade, line up, marshal, order, position, range, sort.
ransack *v* **1** comb, explore, go through, rake, rummage, scour, search, turn inside out. **2** loot, pillage, plunder, raid, ravage, rifle, strip.
rant *v* cry, rave, roar, shout, yell; (*Inf*) spout.
rapid *adj* brisk, express, fast, fleet, flying, hasty, prompt, quick, speedy, swift.
rare *adj* **1** exceptional, scarce, uncommon, unusual. **2** infrequent, occasional.
rarely *adv* hardly ever, infrequently, once in a while, on rare occasions, scarcely ever, seldom.
rascal *n* devil, disgrace, imp, rogue, scamp, scoundrel, villain, wretch; (*Inf*) scallywag, varmint.
rash *adj* careless, foolhardy, hare-brained, hasty, headstrong, heedless, helter-skelter, hot-headed, ill-advised, impetuous, impulsive, indiscreet, reckless, thoughtless.
rash *n* eruption, outbreak, epidemic, flood, outbreak, plague, series, spate, wave.
rate *n* **1** degree, percentage, ratio, relation, scale. **2** charge, cost, duty, fee. **3** figure, hire, price, tariff, tax, toll. **4** measure, pace, speed, tempo, velocity. **5** class, degree, grade, position, quality, rank, rating, status, value, worth. **6** at any rate, anyhow, anyway, nevertheless.
rate *v* assess, classify, consider, count, estimate, evaluate, grade, measure, value, weigh.
rather *adv* **1** fairly, moderately, quite, slightly, somewhat, to some degree, to some extent; (*Inf*) kind of, pretty, sort of. **2** noticeably, significantly, very. **3** instead, preferably, sooner.
ration *n* **1** allowance, helping, measure, part, portion, quota, share. **2** food, provender,

provisions, stores, supplies.
ration *v* **1** allocate, allot, deal, distribute, issue, measure out. **2** budget, conserve, control, limit, restrict, save.
rational *adj* intelligent, judicious, logical, lucid, realistic, reasonable, sagacious, sane, sensible, sound, wise.
rattle *v* **1** bang, clatter, jangle. **2** bounce, jolt, shake, vibrate. **3** disturb, frighten, scare, upset; (*Inf*) discomfit, faze.
ravage *v* demolish, destroy, devastate, leave in ruins, loot, pillage, plunder, ransack, raze, ruin, shatter, spoil, wreck.
rave *v* babble, be delirious, fume, rage, rant, storm.
ravenous *adj* famished, starved, starving, very hungry.
ravine *n* abyss, canyon, chasm, defile, flume, gap, gorge, gulf, gully, pass.
raw *adj* **1** bloody, fresh, natural, uncooked, unprepared. **2** basic, natural, organic, unprocessed, untreated. **3** open, sensitive, skinned, sore, tender. **4** green, inexperienced, new, untrained. **5** biting, bitter, bleak, chilly, cold, damp, freezing, wet.
ray *n* bar, beam, flash, gleam, shaft.
reach *v* **1** arrive at, get as far as, get to, land at, make. **2** contact, get a hold of, grasp, stretch to, touch. **3** amount to, arrive at, attain, climb to, come to, drop, fall, move, rise, sink.
reach *n* capacity, command, compass, distance, extension, extent, grasp, influence, j urisdiction, mastery, power, range, scope, spread, sweep.
react *v* **1** acknowledge, answer, reply, respond. **2** act, behave, conduct oneself, function, operate, proceed, work.
read *v* **1** glance at, look at, pore over, refer to, scan, study. **2** announce, deliver, recite, speak, utter. **3** comprehend, decipher, interpret, see, understand. **4** display, indicate, record, register, show.
ready *adj* **1** all set, arranged, completed, fit, in readiness, organized, prepared, primed, ripe, set. **2** agreeable, eager, glad, happy, keen, willing; (*Inf*) game. **3** acute, alert, bright, clever, deft, expert, handy, prompt, quick, quick-witted, rapid, sharp, skilful, smart. **4** accessible, at the ready, available, close to hand, convenient, handy, near, on call, present; (*Inf*) on tap.
real *adj* actual, authentic, certain, essential, genuine, honest, intrinsic, legitimate, positive, rightful, sincere, true, valid.
realistic *adj* **1** businesslike, common-sense, down-to-earth, level-headed, practical, real, sensible, sober. **2** authentic, faithful, genuine, graphic, lifelike, naturalistic, true, true to life.
realize *v* **1** become aware of, imagine, recognize, take in, understand. (*Inf*) catch on, twig. **2** bring about, complete, do, make happen. **3** acquire, clear, earn, gain, make, obtain, produce, sell for.
reap *v* acquire, bring in, collect, cut, derive, gain, garner, gather, get, harvest, obtain, win.
rear *n* back, back end, end, rear guard, stern, tail, tail end.
rear *adj* aft, after, back, following, hind, hindmost, last, trailing.
rear *v* bring up, care for, cultivate, educate, foster, grow, nurse, nurture, raise, train. **2** build, construct, erect, fabricate, put up.
reason *n* **1** logic, reasoning, senses, understanding. **2** aim, basis, goal, impetus, intention, motive, object, occasion, purpose, target, warrant; (*Inf*) why and wherefore. **3** bounds,

The Grand Canyon is a famous ravine and an example of how erosion and climatic changes have altered the land mass and created stunning scenery.

limits, moderation, sense, wisdom.
reason *v* conclude, deduce, draw conclusions, infer, resolve, solve, think, work out.
reasonable *adj* **1** credible, fair, intelligent, logical, rational, reasoned, sensible, sound, well-thought-out. **2** acceptable, average, equitable, fair, fit, honest, inexpensive, just, moderate, modest, proper, right, tolerable, within reason; (*Inf*) OK.
reassure *v* bolster, buoy up, cheer up, comfort, encourage, hearten, inspirit, put or set one's mind at rest, relieve someone of anxiety, restore confidence to.
rebound *v* **1** bounce, recoil, resound, return, ricochet, spring back. **2** backfire, boomerang, misfire, recoil.
rebound *n* bounce, comeback, kickback, repercussion, return, ricochet.
rebuke *v* admonish, blame, castigate, censure, lecture, scold, take to task; (*Inf*) bawl out, carpet, dress down, haul someone over the coals, tear someone off a strip, tell off, tick off.
rebuke *n* blame, censure, lecture, reprimand; (*Inf*) dressing down, telling-off, ticking-off.
recall *v* **1** bring to mind, call up, recollect, remember, reminisce. **2** call back, call in, cancel, repeal, rescind, retract, revoke, take back, withdraw.
recede *v* **1** ebb, go back, retreat, subside, withdraw. **2** decline, diminish, dwindle, fade, lessen, shrink, sink, wane.
receipt *n* **1** acknowledgment, counterfoil, proof of purchase, sales slip, stub. **2** delivery, receiving, reception, recipient.
receive *v* **1** accept delivery of, acquire, be given, be in receipt of, collect, derive, get, obtain, pick up, take. **2** apprehend, be informed of, hear. **3** bear, experience, go through, meet with, suffer, sustain, undergo. **4** admit, entertain, greet, meet, take in, welcome.
recent *adj* contemporary, current, fresh, late, modern, new, novel, up-to-date, young.
reception *n* **1** acceptance, receipt. **2** acknowledgment, greeting, response, treatment, welcome. **3** entertainment, function, party; (*Inf*) do.
recess *n* **1** alcove, bay, cavity, corner, hollow, niche. **2** break, holiday, rest, vacation.
recession *n* decline, depression, downturn, slump.
reciprocate *v* exchange, return the compliment, swap, trade.
recite *v* describe, detail, narrate, perform, speak.
reckless *adj* careless, foolhardy, hare-brained, hasty, ill-advised, irresponsible, rash, wild.
reckon *v* **1** add up, calculate, compute, count, tally, total. **2** imagine, suppose, think; (*Inf*) guess.
reclaim *v* get back, recover, rescue, restore, retrieve, salvage.
recline *v* drape oneself over, lounge, sprawl, stretch out.
recognize *v* **1** identify, know, recall, remember, spot. **2** accept, admit, allow, concede, confess, realize, see, understand.
recoil *n* backlash, kick, reaction, rebound, repercussion.
recollect *v* recall, remember, reminisce.
reconsider *v* change one's mind, re-examine, review, take another look at, think twice.
reconstruct *v* **1** reassemble, rebuild, renovate, restore. **2** build up, piece together.
record *n* **1** account, chronicle, diary, file, log, report. **2** evidence, testimony, witness. **3** background, career, curriculum vitae, CV; (*Inf*) track record. **4** album, black disc, cassettes, CD, compact disc, disc, EP, forty-five, gramophone record, LP, mini-disc, platter, recording, release, single, vinyl. **5 off the record** confidential, in private, not for publication, private, unofficially.
record *v* chronicle, document, enrol, enter, log, note, report, write down; (*Inf*) chalk up.

How does a compact disc record music?

The plastic surface on the CD stores sounds in a binary code, as very small holes, called pits, and flat areas, called lands. A laser beam scans across the disc. When it falls on a land, it is reflected back to a light-sensitive detector. This causes a pulse of current to pass to a loud speaker, which converts it back to sound.

Amusements parks have a variety of rides which can include rollercoasters. These rides speed occupants in carriages around the track. The forward-acting force, known as centrifugal force, makes the ride constantly change direction and keeps the carriage on the track, even when it is upside down.

recount *v* describe, narrate, portray, recite, repeat, report, tell the story of.

recover *v* **1** get back, reclaim, regain, restore, retrieve, take back. **2** come round, convalesce, get better, heal, improve, mend, pull through, rally, recuperate.

recreation *n* amusement, fun, play, pleasure, sport.

recruit *n* apprentice, beginner, novice, trainee; (*Inf*) greenhorn, rookie.

rectify *v* correct, fix, improve, mend, repair.

recuperate *v* convalesce, get better, mend, pick up, recover, regain one's health.

recur *v* come again, happen again, reappear, repeat, return, revert.

reduce *v* **1** cut down, decrease, diminish, lessen, shorten, slow down. **2** discount, mark down, slash.

reel *v* **1** falter, lurch, stagger, stumble, sway, totter, wobble. **2** revolve, spin, swirl, twirl.

refer to *v* **1** comment on, mention. **2** consult on, turn to.

refined *adj* civilized, cultured, elegant, polite, well-mannered.

reflect *v* consider, mull over, ponder, think, wonder.

reform *v* change, improve, mend, rectify, renovate, repair.

refrain *v* abstain, avoid, cease, do without, give up, stop.

refresh *v* **1** breathe new life into, enliven, reinvigorate, revive. **2** jog, prod, prompt, renew, stimulate; (*Inf*) brush up.

refuge *n* asylum, bolt hole, haven, protection, retreat, sanctuary, security, shelter.

refugee *n* displaced person, escapee, exile, fugitive, runaway.

refund *v* give back, pay back, repay, return.

refuse *v* decline, deny, reject, repel, say no, spurn, turn down, withhold.

regain *v* get back, recapture, retrieve, take back, win back.

regard *v* **1** gaze at, look closely at, notice, observe, view, watch. **2** consider, look upon, view.

region *n* area, country, district, division, expanse, land, locality, part of the world, place, province, quarter, section, sector, territory, tract, zone.

register *n* annals, archives, catalogue, chronicle, diary, file, ledger, list, log, memorandum, record, roll, roster, schedule.

register *v* **1** check in, enrol, enter, inscribe, list, note, record, set down, sign up, take down. **2** display, exhibit, reflect, reveal, say, show.

regret *v* deplore, grieve, lament, miss, weep over.

regret *n* bitterness, disappointment, grief, sorrow.

regrettable *adj* deplorable, disappointing, unhappy, wrong.

regular *adj* daily, normal, routine, typical, usual.

regulate *v* control, direct, fit, handle, manage, monitor, order.

regulation *n* law, order, rule, standing order, statute.

rehearse *v* practise, prepare, recite, repeat, run through, study, train, try out.

reign *n* command, monarchy, power, rule, sovereignty.

reign *v* command, govern, rule, wear the crown.

reinforce *v* bolster, buttress, fortify, prop, shore up, support.

reinforcement *n* **1** brace, prop, support. **2** additional troops, auxiliaries, reserves, support.

reject *v* cast aside, decline, discard, eliminate, exclude, jettison, jilt, refuse, throw out, turn down, veto.

reject *n* castoff, discard, failure, flotsam, second.
rejoice *v* be glad, be happy, celebrate, delight, joy, jump for joy, revel, triumph.
relate *v* describe, detail, give an account of, recount, report, set forth, tell.
related *adj* associated, connected, joint, linked.
relationship *n* association, bond, connection, link, tie-up.
relative *n* connection, member of one's or the family, relation.
relax *v* **1** let up, loosen, slacken, weaken. **2** be at ease, put one's feet up, rest, unwind; (*Inf*) let one's hair down, take it easy.
relay *n* **1** relief, shift, turn. **2** communication, message, transmission.
relay *v* broadcast, communicate, pass on, send, transmit.
release *v* **1** drop, free, let go, set free, turn loose, untie. **2** acquit, excuse, let go. **3** break, circulate, disseminate, distribute, issue, launch, make known, make public, present, publish, put out, unveil.
release *n* acquittal, freedom, liberty, relief.
relent *v* change one's mind, come round, give in, give way, soften, yield.
relentless *adj* grim, harsh, ruthless, unstoppable.
relevant *adj* appropriate, apt, fitting, significant.
reliable *adj* dependable, faithful, predictable, regular, unfailing.
relief *n* **1** comfort, help, solace. **2** aid, support. **3** break, relaxation, respite, rest; (*Inf*) breather, let-up.
relieve *v* **1** ease, reduce, relax, soothe. **2** assist, help, support, take over from.

Old family photographs can be a great source of information when tracing your relatives for a family tree.

relish *v* appreciate, delight in, enjoy, fancy, like, look forward to, luxuriate in, prefer, revel in, savour, taste.
relish *n* savour, spice, tang.
reluctant *adj* disinclined, loath, unwilling.
rely *v* bank, be confident of, be sure of, bet, count, depend, have confidence in, lean, reckon, repose, trust in, swear by, trust
remain *v* continue, endure, linger, persist, stay, survive, wait; (*Inf*) stay put.
remainder *n* balance, remains, residue, surplus.
remark *v* **1** comment, mention, pass comment, state. **2** heed, note, notice, observe, see.
remark *n* comment, opinion, statement, thought, word.
remarkable *adj* extraordinary, famous, notable, outstanding, striking, unusual.
remedy *n* antidote, cure, medicine, panacea, treatment.
remedy *v* cure, ease, heal, help, relieve, soothe, treat.
remember *v* recall, recollect, reminisce, think back.
remind *v* jog one's memory, prompt, refresh one's memory.
remorse *n* grief, guilt, regret, shame, sorrow.
remote *adj* **1** distant, faraway, far-off, isolated, off the beaten track, outlying, secluded. **2** alien, foreign, removed, unrelated. **3** cold, detached, distant, indifferent, reserved, standoffish.
remove *v* **1** delete, erase, wipe out. **2** move, relocate, shift, transfer, vacate.
renew *v* breathe new life into, bring up to date, modernize, overhaul, renovate, revitalize.
renovate *v* modernize, overhaul, refurbish; (*Inf*) do up, fix up.
renowned *adj* eminent, famous, notable, noted, well-known.
rent *n* fee, hire, lease, payment, rental, tariff.
rent *v* charter, hire, lease, let.
repair *v* compensate for, fix, heal, mend, patch up, put back together, put right, rectify, renew, restore to working order.
repair *n* darn, mend, overhaul, patch, restoration.
repay *v* **1** compensate, pay back, refund, reimburse, square. **2** even the score with, retaliate, revenge; (*Inf*) get even with.
repeat *v* redo, replay, rerun.
repeat *n* duplicate.
repeatedly *adv* again and again,

frequently, over and over, time and time again.
repel *v* **1** drive off, fight, hold off, keep at arms length, resist. **2** ward off. **3** disgust, offend, revolt, sicken; (*Inf*) give one the creeps, turn one off.
repercussion *n* consequence, result, side effect.
repetition *n* duplication, echo, repeat, replication.
replace *v* put back, restore, substitute, supply, take over from, take the place of.
replica *n* carbon copy, duplicate, facsimile, imitation, model, reproduction.
reply *v* acknowledge, answer, respond, write back.
reply *n* acknowledgment, answer, response, retort, return; (*Inf*) come back.
report *n* **1** account, declaration, detail, note, record, statement, summary, version. **2** gossip, rumour, talk.
report *v* announce, broadcast, declare, document, give an account of, inform of, mention, narrate, notify, publish, recite, write up.
reporter *n* correspondent, hack, journalist, newscaster, pressman, writer; (*Inf*) newshound.
represent *v* **1** act for, be, speak for. **2** symbolize. **3** denote, depict, describe, illustrate, portray, render, reproduce, show, sketch. **4** act, appear as, assume the role of, enact, exhibit, perform, play the part of, produce, put on, show, stage.
reprieve *n* amnesty, pardon, postponement, remission, stay of execution.
reprimand *n* blame, censure, lecture, rebuke; (*Inf*) dressing-down, flea in one's ear, talking-to, telling-off, ticking-off.
reproduce *v* **1** copy, duplicate, imitate, mirror, replicate. **2** breed, generate, multiply, procreate, produce young, propagate, spawn.
reproduction *n* **1** breeding, procreation, propagation. **2** copy, duplicate, facsimile, imitation, print, replica.
repulsive *adj* disgusting, foul, hideous, horrid, obnoxious, offensive, revolting, sickening, ugly, vile.
reputation *n* estimation, fame, honour, name, opinion, renown, repute, standing, stature.
request *v* appeal for, apply for, ask for, beg, beseech, call for, demand, desire, entreat, petition, pray, put in for, requisition, seek, solicit, sue for, supplicate.
request *n* appeal, demand, entreaty, requisition, solicitation.
require *v* **1** crave, desire, need, want, wish. **2** ask, beg, demand, insist upon, instruct, oblige, order, request.
requirement *n* demand, essential, necessity, need, precondition, prerequisite, qualification, specification.
rescue *v* deliver, free, get out, liberate, recover, salvage, save, save the life of, set free.
research *n* analysis, delving, examination, experimentation, exploration, fact-finding, groundwork, inquiry, investigation, probe, scrutiny, study.
resemblance *n* likeness, parity, sameness, similarity.
resemble *v* be similar to, echo, look like, mirror, remind one of, take after; (*Inf*) favour.
resent *v* begrudge, dislike, feel bitter about, object to, take exception to, take offence at.
resentful *adj* angry, bitter, jealous, put out, wounded; (*Inf*) miffed, peeved.
resentment *n* anger, fury, hurt, ill feeling, malice, rage.

Helicopters are extremely useful for rescues at sea as they can fly close to cliff faces and hover over the sites of wrecks. They are able to hover due to the two sets of rotor blades which allow movement in any direction.

reserve *v* **1** conserve, hoard, hold, keep back, preserve, put by, save, set aside, stockpile, store, withhold. **2** book, order, retain. **3** defer, delay, keep back, postpone, put off, withhold.
reserve *n* **1** fund, hoard, reservoir, **2** game park, preserve, reservation, safari park, sanctuary, tract. **3** aloofness, coolness, modesty, shyness.
reserved *adj* aloof, bashful, cool, modest, restrained, retiring, shy, silent, undemonstrative, with-drawn.
reside *v* abide, dwell, have one's home, inhabit, live, lodge, remain, settle, sojourn, stay; (*Inf*) hang out.
residence *n* **1** abode, address, dwelling, home, house. **2** hall, manor, mansion, palace, seat, villa; (*Inf*) pad.
resident *n* citizen, inhabitant, lodger, occupant, tenant.
resign *v* abandon, give up, quit, surrender, vacate.
resist *v* avoid, counteract, defy, oppose, prevent, stand up to, withstand.
resolute *adj* adamant, bold, determined, firm, inflexible, strong-willed, stubborn, unshaken, unwavering.
resolve *v* **1** agree, con-clude, decide, design, determine, fix intend, make up one's mind, opt, settle, undertake. **2** answer, settlement, solution. **3** decision, motion, statement.
resolve *n* **1** conclusion, decision, design, intention, objective, project, purpose, resolution, undertaking. **2** boldness, courage, determination, earnest-ness, firmness, resoluteness, resolution, steadfastness, willpower.
resort *v* **1** employ, make use of, turn to, use, utilize.
resort *n* haunt, holiday centre, refuge, retreat, spa, spot, tourist centre, watering-place.
resound *v* echo, fill the air, re-echo, resonate, reverberate, ring.
resourceful *adj* able, bright, capable, clever, creative, imaginative, ingenious, inventive, quick-witted, sharp, talented.
resources *adj* assets, capital, funds, holdings, materials, means, money, property, reserves, riches, supplies, wealth, wherewithal.
respect *n* **1** admiration, honour, regard. **2** aspect, characteristic, detail, facet, feature, matter, particular, point, sense, way.
respect *v* admire, adore, appreciate, defer to, esteem, honour, look up to, revere, think highly of, value.
respectable *adj* decent, good, honest, reputable, respected.
respiration *n* breathing.
respite *n* break, breathing space, halt, hiatus, intermission, interruption, interval, let-up, lull, pause, recess, relaxation, relief, rest; (*Inf*) breather.
respond *v* acknowledge, answer, come-back, counter, feedback, reply.
response *n* acknowledgment answer, counterblast, feedback, reaction, rejoinder, reply.
responsibility *n* **1** accountability, care, charge, duty, liability, obligation, onus. **2** authority, importance, power. **3** blame, burden, fault, guilt.
responsible *adj* **1** answerable, in charge of. **2** blameworthy, dependable. **3** authoritative, decision-making, executive, high, important. **4** dependable, honest, trustworthy.
rest *n* **1** lie-down, nap, relax-ation, siesta, sleep; (*Inf*) forty winks, snooze. **2** break, breath-ing space, holiday, interlude, interval, lull, pause, respite,

Yellowstone National Park, Wyoming, is one of the best-known national parks in the United States. and has the greatest concentration of geothermal features in the world. There are more than 10,000 hot springs and it is home to one of the most famous geysers, Old Faithfull, which erupts which great regularly shooting steam and hot water up in the air to 52 metres (170 feet).

vacation; (*Inf*) breather. **3** balance, excess, leftovers, others, remainder, remains, remnants, residue, residuum, rump, surplus.

rest *v* **1** laze, nap, put one's feet up, relax, take a nap; (*Inf*) have a snooze, have forty winks, take it easy. **2** be supported, lay, lean, lie, prop, recline, repose, sit, stand, stretch out. **3** depend on, hang on, hinge, rely, turn.

restless *adj* **1** active, bustling, changeable, footloose, hurried, inconstant, irresolute, moving, nomadic, roving, transient, turbulent, unsettled, unstable, unsteady, wandering. **2** agitated, edgy, fidgety, ill at ease, jumpy, nervous, on edge, tossing and turning, unsettled, worried.

restore *v* **1** fix, mend, rebuild, recondition, reconstruct, recover, refurbish, rehabilitate, renew, renovate, repair, retouch, set to rights, touch up. **2** bring back to health, build up, reanimate, refresh, rejuvenate, revitalize, revive, revivify, strengthen. **3** bring back, give back, hand back, recover, re-establish, reinstate, replace, return, send back.

restrain *v* bridle, check, confine, constrain, contain, control, curb, curtail, debar, govern, hamper, handicap, harness, hold back, inhibit, keep under control, limit, restrict, suppress.

restrict *v* confine, handicap, hem in, inhibit, limit, restrain.

restriction *n* check, constraint, containment, control, curb, curfew, limitation, restraint, rule.

result *n* consequence, effect, outcome, product, upshot.

result *v* **1** appear, arise, emerge, follow, happen, occur, stem, take place, turn out. **2 result in** culminate, end, finish, terminate; (*Inf*) wind up.

resume *v* begin again, carry on, continue, proceed, restart, take up where one left off; (*Inf*) pick up the threads.

resurrect *v* breathe new life into, bring back, raise from the dead, restore to life, revive.

resurrection *n* rebirth, return, return from the dead, revival; (*Inf*) comeback.

retain *v* **1** hold back, keep, maintain, preserve, reserve, save; (*Inf*) hang on to. **2** bear in mind, recall, recollect, remember. **3** commission, employ, engage, hire, pay reserve.

retainer *n* **1** domestic, servant, supporter, valet. **2** advance, deposit, fee.

retaliate *v* even the score, give tit for tat, make reprisal, pay back, strike back, take revenge, wreak vengeance; (*Inf*) get back at, get even with, get one's own back, give as good as one gets.

retaliation *n* counter attack, reprisal, retribution, revenge, tit for tat, vengeance.

retire *v* **1** give up work, stop working. **2** depart, exit, go away, leave, remove, withdraw. **3** go to bed, go to one's room, go to sleep, turn in; (*Inf*) be put out to grass, hit the sack, kip down.

retract *v* **1** draw in, pull back, pull in. **2** cancel, deny, disown, recall, renounce, reverse, revoke, take back, withdraw.

retreat *v* draw back, fall back, give ground, go back, pull back, recede, recoil, retire, shrink, turn tail, withdraw.

retreat *n* **1** departure, escape, flight, retirement, withdrawal.

The Leaning Tower of Pisa, in Italy, has undergone many attempts at stabilizing its structure ever since it was first built. Restoration is an on going problem as engineers battle to prevent the structure from collapsing.

2 asylum, den, haven, hide-away, hide-out, refuge, sanctuary, seclusion, shelter.

retribution *n* compensation, retaliaiton, revenge.

retrieve *n* fetch back, get back, recall, recover, regain, rescue, salvage, win back.

return *v* **1** come back, reappear, recoil, re-enter, recur, retrace your steps, turn back. **2** give back, put back, re-establish, reinstate, replace, restore, send back, take back, transmit. **3** give back, pay back, recompense, refund, reimburse, repay. **4** bring in, earn, make, repay.

return *n* **1** come back, reappear. **2** re-establishment, reinstatement, replacement, restoration. **3** gain, income, interest, proceeds, profit, revenue, takings, yield. **4** refund, reimbursement, repay, repayment. **5** account, form, list, report, statement, summary. **6** answer, reply, response, retort; (*Inf*) comeback.
reveal *v* **1** bare, betray, communicate, confess, disclose, divulge, leak, make known, make public, proclaim, publish, tell. **2** bare, display, exhibit, expose to view, open, show, uncover, unfold, unearth, unmask, unveil.
revel in *v* crow, delight, enjoy, gloat, indulge, joy, lap up, love, luxuriate, rejoice, relish, savour, take pleasure in, wallow.
revenge *n* reprisal, retaliation, retribution, vengeance.
revenue *n* income, proceeds, profits, receipts, takings.
revere *v* adore, honour, idolize, look up to, put on a pedestal, respect, think highly of, worship.
reverse *v* **1** change, invert, transpose, turn over, turn round, turn upside down. **2** cancel, declare null and void, invalidate, negate, overturn, quash, retract, undo. **3** back, backtrack, move backwards, retreat.
reverse *n* **1** contrary, converse, opposite. **2** defeat, failure, hardship, misfortune, setback.
reverse *adj* back, backward, opposite, rear.
review *v* **1** assess, discuss, revise, run over, take another look at, think over. **2** recall, reflect on. **3** consider, evaluate, inspect, judge, read through, scrutinize, study.
review *n* **1** appraisal, examination, inspection, study, survey. **2** criticism, report.
revise *v* alter, correct, edit, emend, re-examine, review, rework, rewrite, update.
revival *n* recovery, upsurge.
revive *v* awaken, bring back to life, come round, comfort, rally, recover, refresh, renew, renovate, restore, spring up again.
revoke *v* abolish, cancel, declare null and void, quash, reverse, withdraw.

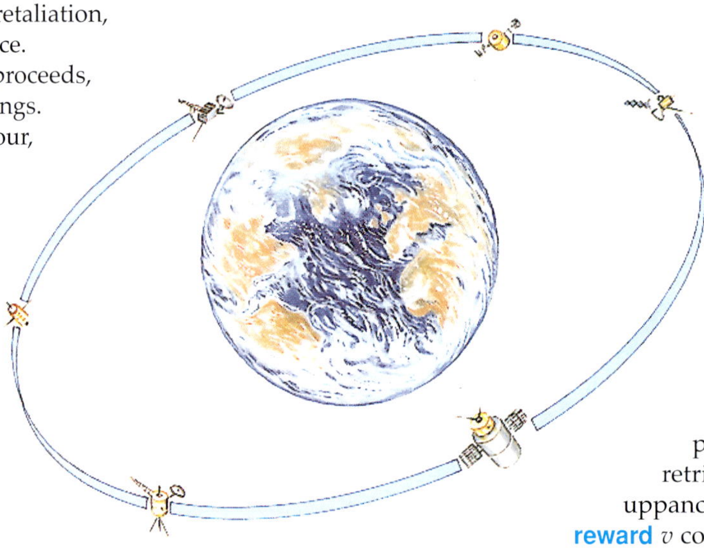

Communication satellites usually circle the Earth in what is called geostationary orbit. This means that the satellite is always above the same on the Earth's surface point.

revolt *n* defection, insurgency, insurrection, mutiny, putsch, rebellion, revolution, rising, sedition, uprising.
revolt *v* **1** disobey, mutiny, rebel, resist, rise, take to the streets, take up arms against. **2** disgust, make one's flesh creep, nauseate. offend, repel, repulse, shock, sicken, turn one's stomach; (*Inf*) give one the creeps, turn off.
revolting *adj* appalling, disgusting, foul, horrid, nasty, offensive, repulsive, shocking.
revolution *n* **1** coup, *coup d'état*, rebellion, revolt, uprising. **2** innovation, transformation. **3** circuit, cycle, gyration, lap, orbit, rotation, round, spin, turn, wheel, whirl.
revolutionary *adj* extremist, radical, rebel.
revolve *v* circle, go round, gyrate, orbit, rotate, spin, turn, twist, wheel, whirl.
reward *n* **1** benefit, honour, prize, return. **2** dessert, just desserts, punishment, requital, retribution; (*Inf*) comeuppance.
reward *v* compensate, honour, make it worth one's while, pay, recompense, remunerate, repay, requite.
rewarding *adj* beneficial, pleasing, productive, satisfying, valuable, worthwhile.
rhyme *n* ode, poem, poetry,

song, verse.
rhyme *v* chime, harmonize, sound like.
rhythm *n* accent, beat, metre, movement, tempo, time.
rich *adj* **1** affluent, opulent, prosperous, wealthy, well-off, well-to-do; (*Inf*) flush, loaded, made of money, rolling, well-heeled. **2** full, well-stocked. **3** ample, copious, lush, prolific. **4** costly, expensive, priceless, splendid, superb, valuable. **5** creamy, fatty, full-bodied, luscious, succulent.
riches *pl n* affluence, fortune, gold, money, opulence, property, treasure, wealth.
rid *v* **1** clear, free, make free, purge. **2 get rid of** dispose of, do away with, dump, eliminate, expel, jettison, remove, shake off, throw away, weed out.
riddle *n* Chinese puzzle, enigma, mystery, poser, problem, puzzle; (*Inf*) brain-teaser.
ride *n* drive, jaunt, journey, lift, outing, trip; (*Inf*) spin, whirl.
ridicule *v* laugh at, make fun of, mock, scorn, sneer, taunt. (*Inf*) send up, take the mickey out of.
ridiculous *adj* absurd, comical, foolish, hilarious, ludicrous, outrageous, preposterous, silly, stupid, unbelievable.
rift *n* **1** break, crack, fault, fracture, gap, opening, space, split. **2** difference, disagreement, quarrel; (*Inf*) falling out.
rig *n* apparatus, equipment, fittings, fixtures, gear, machinery, outfit, tackle.
right *adj* **1** fair, good, honest, just, lawful, moral, proper, true. **2** correct, exact, genuine, precise, valid; (*Inf*) spot-on. **3** becoming, convenient, fitting, ideal, proper, rightful, seemly. **4** balanced, in good health, in the pink, normal, rational, sane, sound. **5** conservative, right-wing, Tory; (*Inf*) all there.
right *n* **1** authority, business, licence, power, title. **2** goodness, honour, truth, virtue. **3** by rights, entitlement, freedom, liberty.

This unusual egg-shaped variety of tomato, turns the colour of cream when ripe.

right *v* correct, fix, put right, rectify, sort out, straighten.
rigid *adj* adamant, exact, fixed, harsh, inflexible, severe, stern, uncompromising, unrelenting.
rigorous *adj* **1** challenging, demanding, exacting, harsh, rigid, stern, tough. **2** bad, bleak, extreme, harsh, inhospitable, severe.
rim *n* border, brim, brink, circumference, edge, lip, margin, verge.
ring *n* **1** band, circle, circuit, halo, hoop, loop, round. **2** arena, circus, enclosure, rink. **3** chime, knell, peal. **4** call, phone call; (*Inf*) buzz. **5** association, band, cable, cartel, cell, circle, clique, gang, group, junta, mob, syndicate; (*Inf*) crew.
riot *n* **1** anarchy, disorder, fray, mob violence, quarrel, row, street fighting, turmoil, uproar. **2** display, show, splash. **3 run riot** be out of control, break loose, go wild, let oneself go, raise hell, rampage. **4** grow profusely, spread like wild fire.
riot *v* cut loose, frolic, go on a binge, make merry, revel, romp; (*Inf*) paint the town red.
ripe *adj* **1** fully grown, mature, ready, ripened. **2** favourable, ideal, opportune, right, suitable, timely.
rise *v* **1** arise, get up, rise and shine, stand up. **2** ascend, climb, go up, increase, intensify, lift, move up. **3** advance, climb the ladder, progress, work one's way up; (*Inf*) go places. **4** appear, emerge, occur. **5** mutiny, rebel, resist, revolt. **6** ascend, go uphill, mount, slope upwards.
rise *n* **1** advance, ascent, climb, increase, upturn. **2** advancement, progress, promotion. **3** ascent, elevation, hillock, incline, rising ground, upward slope.

Roads, particularly in the United States, commonly have multiple interchanges such as these above. They have evolved to cope with the ever-increasing number of motor cars on the roads today and are designed to allow the smooth transfer from one route to another.

4 increment, pay increase, raise.
risk *n* chance, danger, gamble, hazard, jeopardy.
risk *v* dare, endanger, expose to danger, jeopardize, take a chance on, venture.
rival *n* challenger, competitor, contender, contestant, opponent.
rival *v* be a match for, compare with, compete, match, measure up to, oppose, vie with.
rivalry *n* conflict, contest, duel, opposition.
road *n* avenue, course, direction, freeway. highway, lane, motorway, path, roadway, route, street, thoroughfare, track, way.
roam *v* drift, meander, prowl, ramble, range, rove, stray, stroll, travel, walk, wander.
roar *v* **1** bawl, bellow, cry, howl, rumble, shout, thunder, vociferate, yell. **2** hoot, laugh, heartily; (*Inf*) split one's sides.
roar *n* bellow, clamour, crash, cry, howl, outcry, rumble, shout, thunder, yell.
rob *v* burgle, cheat, defraud, hold up, loot, pillage, plunder, raid, ransack, rifle, sack, strip, swindle; (*Inf*) con, mug, rip off.
robber *n* bandit, burglar, fraud, highwayman, looter, swindler, thief; (*Inf*) con man, crook, mugger.
robbery *n* burglary, fraud, hold-up larceny, pillage, plunder, raid, stealing, swindle, theft; (*Inf*) mugging, rip-off, stick-up.
robe *n* costume, gown, habit, vestment.
robe *v* apparel, attire, clothe, drape, dress, garb.
robust *v* able-bodied, athletic, fit, healthy, strapping, strong, sturdy. (*Inf*) husky.
rock *n* **1** lurch, pitch, reel, roll, sway, wobble. **2** astound, daze, shock, stun, surprise.
rod *n* bar, baton, birch, cane, dowel, mace, pole, sceptre, shaft, staff, stick, switch, wand.
rogue *n* cheat, fraud, rascal, scoundrel, swindler, villain; (*Inf*) con man, crook.
role *n* **1** character, part, portrayal, representation. **2** capacity, duty, function, job, part, position, post, task.
roll *v* **1** elapse, flow, pass, pivot, reel, revolve, rotate, spin, swivel, trundle, turn, whirl. **2** bind, coil, curl, envelop, twist, wind, wrap. **3** flatten, level, press smooth,

spread. **4** boom, drum, echo, grumble, resound, reverberate, roar, rumble, thunder. **5** billow, lurch, reel, rock, sway, swing, toss, tumble, wallow. **6** lumber, reel, stagger, swagger, sway, waddle.

roll *n* **1** cycle, gyration, reel, revolution, rotation, run, spin, turn, twirl, undulation, wheel, whirl. **2** annals, catalogue, census, chronicle, directory, index, inventory, list, record, register, roster, schedule, scroll, table. **3** boom, drumming, growl, resonance, reverberation, roar, rumble, thunder.

romance *n* **1** affair, affair of the heart, liaison, love affair, relationship. **2** excitement, glamour, mystery. **3** fairy tale, fantasy, fiction, love story, story, tale; (*Inf*) tear-jerker.

romantic *n* dreamer, idealist, romancer, visionary.

room *n* **1** area, capacity, compass, expanse, margin, range, space. **2** apartment, chamber, office. **3** chance, occasion, opportunity, scope.

root *n* **1** rhizome, stem, tuber. **2** base, core, crux, foundation, heart, nucleus, origin, source, starting point. **3** birthplace, heritage, home, origins.

root *v* anchor, embed, entrench, establish, fasten, fix, ground, implant, set, stick, take root.

rope *n* cable, cord, halyard, hawser, line, strand.

rope *v* bind, fasten, hitch, lash, lasso, moor, tether, tie.

roster *n* agenda, catalogue, inventory, list, listing, register, roll, rota, schedule, table.

rosy *adj* **1** pink, red. **2** blushing, flushed. **3** bright, cheerful, encouraging, optimistic, promising, reassuring, sunny.

rot *v* **1** corrode, crumble, decay, decompose, degenerate, deteriorate, disintegrate, fester, perish. **2** decline, deteriorate, waste away, wither away.

rot *n* blight, corrosion, decay, mould.

rotate *v* **1** go round, pivot, reel, revolve, swivel, turn, wheel. **2** alternate, switch.

rotation *n* **1** gyration, orbit, pirouette, reel, revolution, spin, spinning, turn, turning, wheel. **2** cycle, interchanging, sequence, succession, switching.

rotten *adj* **1** bad, corroded, corrupt, crumbling, decaying, decomposing, disintegrating, festering, foul, perished, putrid, rank, sour, stinking. **2** corrupt, deceitful, degenerate, dishonest, disloyal, treacherous; (*Inf*) bent, crooked. **3** bad, deplorable, disappointing, regrettable, unfortunate, unlucky.

rough *adj* **1** broken, bumpy, craggy, irregular, jagged, rugged, stony, uneven. **2** bristly, bushy, coarse, dishevelled, fuzzy, hairy, tousled, unshaven. **3** agitated, choppy, stormy, turbulent, wild. **4** blunt, coarse, discourteous, ill-bred, ill-mannered, impolite, inconsiderate, rude, uncivil.

rough *n* bully boy, casual, lager lout, rowdy, ruffian, thug, tough; (*Inf*) bruiser, ned, roughneck.

round *adj* **1** ball-shaped, bowed, circular, curved, cylindrical, disc-shaped, ring-shaped, rotund, rounded, spherical. **2** ample, full-fleshed, plump, rounded. **3** full, rich.

round *n* **1** ball, band, circle, disc, globe, orb, ring, sphere. **2** bout, cycle, session. **3** division, lap, level, period, session, stage, turn. **4** beat, circuit, compass, course, routine, schedule, series, tour, turn. **5** bullet, cartridge, discharge, shell, shot.

round *v* bypass, circle, encircle,

Crop rotation

In the Middle Ages, the Agricultural Revolution led to a change in farming practice where ground was rested for a year, leaving it fallow. Crops were rotated so that the same crop was not grown year after year in the same plot. This was tested and found to improve harvests. A two-year rotation, and later three- and four-year rotation came to be widely used.

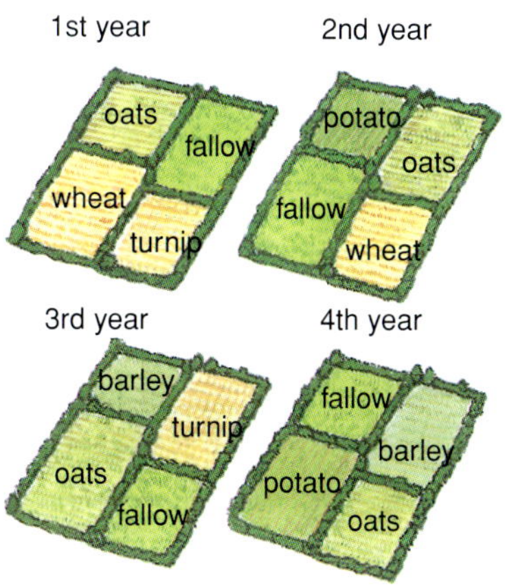

flank, go round, skirt, turn.
round off *v* bring to a close, cap, close, complete, conclude, crown, finish off, put the finishing touch to, settle.
rouse *v* **1** awaken, call, get up, rise, wake, wake up. **2** agitate, anger, animate, disturb, excite, exhilarate, galvanize, get going, incite, inflame, instigate, move, provoke, startle, stimulate.
rout *n* beating, debacle, defeat, disorderly, retreat, drubbing, headlong, flight, overthrow, overwhelming defeat, ruin, shambles, thrashing; (*Inf*) hiding, licking.
rout *v* beat, chase, conquer, crush, cut to pieces, defeat, destroy, dispel, drive off, overpower, over-throw, scatter, thrash, worst; (*Inf*) lick.
route *n* avenue, circuit, course, direction, itinerary, journey, path, road, round, run, way.
routine *n* custom, formula, groove, method, order, patter, practice, procedure, programme, usage, way; (*Inf*) grind.
routine *adj* **1** customary, everyday, familiar, normal, standard, typical, usual. **2** boring, dull, predictable, run-of-the-mill, tedious, tiresome, uninspired, unoriginal.
row *n* **1** bank, column, file, line, queue, range, rank, sequence, series, string, tier. **2** brawl, dispute, disturbance, fracas, fray, quarrel, racket, squabble, tiff, trouble, uproar; (*Inf*) falling-out, ruckus, ruction, scrap, shouting match, slanging match.
row *v* argue, brawl, dispute, fight, squabble; (*Inf*) scrap.
rowdy *adj* boisterous, loud, noisy, unruly, wild.
royal *adj* **1** imperial, kinglike, kingly, monarchical, princely, queenly, regal, sovereign. **2** grand, impressive, magnificent, majestic, splendid, stately, superb, superior.
rub *v* **1** caress, knead, massage, polish, scour, scrape, shine, smooth, stroke, wipe. **2** apply, put, smear, spread.
rub *n* caress, kneading, massage, polish, shine, stroke, wipe.
rubbish *n* debris, dregs, dross, flotsam and jetsam, garbage, junk, litter, lumber, offal, refuse, scrap, trash, waste; (*Inf*) drivel, garbage, nonsense, twaddle.
rub out *v* cancel, delete, efface, erase, expunge, obliterate, remove, wipe out.
rude *adj* **1** abrupt, abusive, blunt, ill-mannered, impolite, impudent, insulting, offhand, short. **2** coarse, crude, obscene, vulgar. **3** abrupt, harsh, sharp, sudden, violent.
rudiments *pl n* basics, essentials, first principles, foundation, fundamentals.
ruffle *v* **1** dishevel, disorder, rumple, tousle. **2** agitate, annoy, confuse, disquiet, disturb, fluster, harass, irritate, torment, trouble, upset, worry; (*Inf*) peeve, rattle, shake up.
rugged *adj* **1** broken, bumpy, craggy, difficult, irregular, jagged, ragged, rocky, rough, uneven. **2** furrowed, leathery, lined, strong-featured, weather-beaten, worn, wrinkled.
ruin *n* bankruptcy, collapse, crash, defeat, destruction, downfall, failure, fall, havoc, overthrow, the end, undoing, wreckage; (*Inf*) crackup.
ruin *v* bankrupt, break, bring down, bring to ruin, crush, defeat, demolish, destroy, devastate, lay in ruins, overturn, shatter, smash.
rule *n* **1** decree, guideline, law, order, regulation, ruling. **2** authority, command, control, direction, empire, government, influence, jurisdiction, leader-

The rugged skin of the hippopotamus is thick, smooth, hairless and leathery. It secretes a thick, oily pink sweat to keep the hide moist and shiny.

Three of Great Britain's best known royal rulers

Elizabeth I

Henry VIII

Victoria

ship, power, regime. **3** custom, habit, practice, procedure, routine. **4** course, formula, method, policy, procedure, way.
rule *v* **1** administer, command, control, direct, govern, guide, lead, manage, preside over, regulate, reign; (*Inf*) be number one. **2** decide, determine, establish, find, judge, lay down, pronounce, resolve, settle.
ruler *n* **1** commander, crowned head, emperor, empress, governor, head of state, king, leader, lord, monarch, prince, princess, queen, sovereign. **2** measure, rule, straight edge, yardstick.
ruling *n* decision, finding, judgment, resolution, verdict.
ruling *adj* **1** commanding, controlling, dominant, governing, leading, reigning, upper. **2** chief, current, dominant, main, predominant, pre-eminent, prevailing, prevalent, principle, supreme.
rumour *n* buzz, gossip, hearsay, news, story, talk, whisper, word.
run *v* **1** bolt, dash, gallop, hurry, jog, race, rush, scramble, scurry, speed, sprint; (*Inf*) leg it. **2** bolt, escape, flee, take flight. (*Inf*) beat it, leg it, scarper, skedaddle, take off. **3** go, operate. **4** administer, carry on, conduct, control, direct, head, lead, manage, mastermind, operate, oversee, regulate, supervise, take care of; (*Inf*) boss. **5** continue, extend, go, last, proceed, spout, steam. **6** dissolve, go soft, liquefy, melt, turn to liquid. **7** come undone, ladder, tear, unravel. **8** climb, creep, spread. **9** display, feature, print, publish. **10** be a candidate, challenge, compete, contend, put oneself up for, stand, take part. **11** bootleg, deal in, ship, smuggle, sneak, traffic in.
run *n* **1** dash, gallop, jog, race, rush, sprint, spurt. **2** drive, excursion, jaunt, journey, lift, outing, ride, round, trip; (*Inf*) joy ride, spin. **3** chain, course, cycle, passage, period, round, season, sequence, series, spell, streak, stretch, string. **4** ladder, rip, snag, tear. **5** coop, enclosure, pen. **6** **in the long run** at the end of the day, eventually, in the end, in the final analysis, in time, ultimately, when all is said and done. **7** **on the run** at liberty, escaping, fugitive, in flight, on the loose. **8** defeated, falling back, fleeing, in flight, in retreat, retreating, running away. **9** at speed, hastily, hurriedly, hurrying, in a hurry, in a rush, in haste.
runaway *n* deserter, escapee, fugitive, refugee, truant.
runaway *adj* **1** escaped, fleeing, fugitive, loose, out of control, uncontrolled, wild. **2** easily won, easy, effortless.
run away *v* abscond, bolt, clear out, decamp, escape, flee, make a run for it, run off, show a clean pair of heels, take flight, take off, take to one's heels; (*Inf*) beat it, cut and run, do a bunk, scarper, scram, skedaddle.
run-down *adj* **1** drained, exhausted, out of condition, tired, unhealthy, weak, worn-out; (*Inf*) under the weather. **2** broken-down, dilapidated,

dingy, ramshackle, shabby, tumbledown, worn-out.

run into *v* **1** bump into, collide with, crash into, dash against, hit, ram, strike. **2** be confronted by, bump into, chance upon, come across, come upon, encounter, meet with, run across.

running *adj* **1** constant, continuous, perpetual, unbroken. **2** flowing, moving, streaming; (*Inf*) on the trot. **3** administration, charge, conduct, control, coordination, direction, leadership, management, organization, regulation, superintendency, supervision. **4** functioning, maintenance, operation, performance, working. **5** competition, contest.

run-of-the-mill *adj* average, common, commonplace, fair, mediocre, modest, ordinary, tolerable, unexceptional.

run over *v* **1** hit, knock down, knock over, run down, strike. **2** overflow, spill over. **3** check, examine, go over, run through.

rupture *n* **1** breach, burst, crack, fissure, fracture, split, tear. **2** breach, break, rift, split; (*Inf*) bust-up, falling out.

rupture *v* **1** break, burst, crack, fracture, puncture, separate, sever, split, tear. **2** break off, disrupt, divide, split.

rural *adj* agricultural, rustic.

rush *v* accelerate, bolt, dart, hurry, run, scramble, scurry, shoot, speed, speed up, sprint, tear.

rush *n* charge, dash, dispatch, expedition, haste, hurry, race, scramble, speed, surge, swiftness, urgency.

rust *n* **1** corrosion, oxidation. **2** blight, mildew, mould, must, rot.

rust *v* oxidize.

rustic *adj* **1** countrified, pastoral, rural. **2** artless, homley. homely, plain, simple, unrefine. unsophistigate. **3** awkward, coarse, crude, rough, uncultured; (*Inf*) clodhopping.

rustic *n* boor, bumpkin, clod, clown, country boy, country cousin, countryman, country-woman, hillbilly, Hodge, peasant, son of the soil, yokel.

rustle *v* crackle, crepitate, crinkle, swish, whish, whisper, whoosh.

rustle *n* crackle, crepitation, crinkling, whisper.

rut *n* **1** furrow, gouge, groove, indentation, score, track, trough, wheelmark. **2** dead end, groove, habit, existence, pattern, routine.

ruthless *adj* adamant, callous, cruel, ferocious, fierce, hard-hearted, harsh, heartless, merciless, remorseless, savage, severe, stern, without pity.

Some metals oxidize badly on contact with air and water. Iron corrodes to form rust. The Golden Gate Bridge in San Francisco needs regular painting to prevent rust forming.

Ss

sabotage *v* damage, disable, disrupt, incapacitate, vandalize, wreck; (*Inf*) throw a spanner in the works.
sabotage *n* destruction, disruption, treachery, treason.
sack *v* **1** discharge, dismiss, give someone his cards, give someone his marching orders; (*Inf*) axe. **2** give someone his books, give someone the boot, give someone the elbow; (*Inf*) fire.
sad *adj* **1** blue, depressed, down, glum, grief-stricken, sombre, unhappy; (*Inf*) down in the dumps, down in the mouth. **2** dark, depressing, disastrous, dismal, heart-rending, moving, poignant, tragic, upsetting. **3** distressing, grave, miserable, regrettable, shabby, unfortunate.
safe *adj* **1** all right, out of danger, out of harm's way, protected, safe and sound, secure. **2** harmless, nontoxic, pure, unpolluted; (*Inf*) OK, okay. **3** cautious, reliable, sure, tried and true.
safe *n* coffer, deposit box, repository, safe-deposit box, strongbox, vault.
safeguard *v* defend, guard, look after, preserve, protect, shield, watch over.
safety *n* protection, refuge, sanctuary, security, shelter.
sail *v* **1** cast anchor, embark, get under way, put to sea, set sail, weigh anchor. **2** captain, cruise, go by water, navigate, pilot, skipper, steer, voyage. **3** drift, float, fly, guide, shoot, skim, soar, sweep, wing. **4 sail into** assault, attack, begin, get going, get to work on, set about; (*Inf*) tear into.
sailor *n* mariner, navigator, seafarer.
sake *n* account, advantage, behalf, benefit, consideration, gain, good, interest, profit, regard, respect, welfare, well being.
salary *n* earnings, income, pay, remuneration, wages.
sale *n* **1** auction, disposal, selling, transaction, vending. **2** buyers, consumers, customers, market, outlet, purchasers. **3 for sale** available, in stock, on sale, on the market.
sallow *adj* colourless, pale, pallid, pasty.
salute *v* **1** greet, welcome. **2** acknowledge, pay tribute to, present arms, recognize; (*Inf*) take one's hat off to.
salvage *v* recover, rescue, retrieve, save.
same *adj* alike, duplicate, equal, equivalent, identical, twin.
sample *n* example, illustration, model, pattern, specimen.
sample *v* experience, inspect, taste, test, try.
sample *adj* pilot, representative, specimen, test, trial.
sanction *n* **1** allowance, backing, confirmation, endorsement, ratification, stamp of approval. **2** ban, boycott, embargo, penalty; (*Inf*) OK, okay.
sanction *v* approve, back, endorse, lend one's name to, permit, support, vouch for.
sanity *n* **1** mental health, reason, stability. **2** common sense, sense, wisdom; (*Inf*) right mind.
sarcastic *adj* bitter, caustic,

Safety in an airship is of paramount importance. They are cigar-shaped balloons, filled with gas. Nowadays the gas used is helium, which cannot catch fire, unlike the hydrogen used in earlier airships. In the 1930s, the Germans developed airships called zeppelins, until the disastrous fire and tragic crash of the Hindenburg in 1937 which spelled the end of the airship as a practical and safe mode of transport.

cutting, cynical, derisive, mocking, sneering, taunting; (*Inf*) sarky.

satire *n* caricature, irony, parody, ridicule, sarcasm, wit; (*Inf*) send-up, spoof, takeoff.

satisfaction *n* **1** enjoyment, gratification, peace of mind, pleasure, well-being. **2** achievement, resolution, settlement. **3** compensation, damages, justice, recompense, restitution, vindication.

satisfactory *adj* acceptable, all right, fair, good enough, up to standard, up to the mark.

satisfy *v* **1** content, gratify, indulge, pacify, please. **2** be enough, do, fulfil, meet, qualify, suffice; (*Inf*) fit the bill. **3** assure, convince, persuade, reassure. **4** answer, comply with, fulfil, meet, pay off, settle. **5** compensate, make good, make reparation for, recompense, reward.

saturate *v* douse, drench, soak, steep, suffuse, waterlog, wet through.

saunter *v* amble, dally, linger, loiter, ramble, roam, rove, stroll, tarry, wander; (*Inf*) mosey.

saunter *n* amble, breather, stroll, walk.

savage *adj* **1** rough, rugged, wild. **2** brutal, cruel, ferocious, fierce, merciless, ruthless, vicious. **3** primitive, uncivilized, unspoilt.

savage *n* **1** barbarian, heathen, native, primitive. **2** barbarian, bear; (*Inf*) boor, beast, brute, fiend, monster.

savage *v* attack, lacerate, mangle, maul; (*Inf*) tear into.

save *v* **1** bail someone out, come to someone's rescue, free, rescue, set free. **2** economize, gather, hoard, put aside for a rainy day, put by, reserve, set aside, store; (*Inf*) keep up one's sleeve, tighten one's belt. **3** conserve, guard, keep safe, look after, preserve, protect, shield.

saving *n* bargain, discount, economy, reduction.

In Christianity, Jesus is regarded as the Saviour of men and the Son of God. With 12 disciples he undertook two missionary journeys through Galilee performing miracles, and preaching love, humility and charity. He was betrayed by Judas one of his disciples and was crucified. He is believed by Christians to have risen from the dead and ascended to Heaven after 40 days.

saviour *n* defender, friend in need, Good Samaritan, Jesus, knight in shining armour, protector, rescuer, salvation.

savour *n* **1** flavour, smell, tang, taste; **2** distinctive quality, excitement, flavour, spice, zest.

savoury *adj* **1** appetizing, delicious, mouthwatering, palatable, rich, spicy, tangy, tasty; (*Inf*) scrumptious. **2** decent, honest, reputable.

say *v* **1** announce, declare, remark, speak, state, utter, voice; (*Inf*) come out with. **2** disclose, divulge, give as one's opinion, make known, reply, respond, reveal, tell. **3** allege, claim, report, suggest. **4** deliver, do, orate, perform, read, recite, rehearse, repeat. **5** assume, guess, imagine, presume, suppose. **6** express, give the impression that, imply.

say *n* authority, influence, power, sway, weight; (*Inf*) clout.

saying *n* byword, proverb, slogan.

scale *n* **1** proportion, ratio. **2** degree, extent, range, scope; (*Inf*) pecking order.

scale *v* ascend, climb, mount, surmount.

scamper *v* dart, dash, fly, hurry, scoot, scurry, scuttle.

scan *v* check, examine, glance over, investigate, look through, run over, scour, search, skim, survey; (*Inf*) size up.

scandal *n* **1** crime, disgrace, offence. **2** disgrace, dishonour, shame, stigma. **3** abuse, dirt, gossip, rumours, skeleton in the cupboard, slander, talk, tattle; (*Inf*) dirty linen.

scanty *adj* bare, deficient, inadequate, narrow, restricted, scant, short, skimpy, slender, sparing, sparse, thin.

scar *n* blemish, injury, mark, wound.

scar *v* brand, disfigure, mark, traumatize.

scar *n* bluff, cliff, crag, precipice.

scarce *adj* few, few and far between, rare, uncommon, unusual, wanting.
scarcely *adv* **1** barely, hardly, only just. **2** definitely not, hardly, not at all, on no account, under no circumstances.
scarcity *n* deficiency, lack, paucity, poverty, rareness, shortage, undersupply, want.
scare *v* alarm, daunt, dismay, frighten, intimidate, shock, startle, terrorize; (*Inf*) give someone a turn, put the wind up someone.
scare *n* alarm, alert, fright, panic, shock, start, terror.
scathing *adj* brutal, critical, cutting, harsh, savage.
scatter *v* **1** shower, sow, spread, sprinkle. **2** disperse, disunite, separate.
scene *n* **1** drama, exhibition, pageant, picture, show, sight, spectacle. **2** area, locality, place, position, setting, situation, spot. **3** backdrop, location, set, setting. **4** act, division, episode, incident, part, stage. **5** commotion, confrontation, display of emotion, performance, row, tantrum, upset; (*Inf*) carry-on. **6** landscape, panorama, prospect, view, vista.
scenery *n* **1** landscape, terrain, view, vista. **2** backdrop, décor, flats, setting, stage set.
scent *n* **1** aroma, bouquet, fragrance, odour, perfume, smell. **2** track, trail.
scent *v* be on the track, detect, discern, get wind of, nose out, recognize, sense, smell, sniff.

Sharks scare and alarm us and a few species such as the white shark have been known to attack humans or even boats. However,while all sharks are meat eaters, 90% of all species of shark are not dangerous to humans at all.

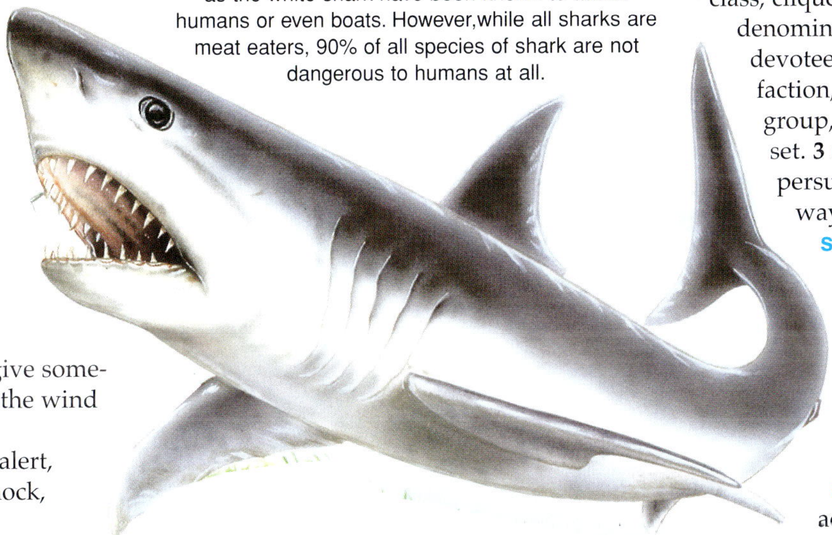

sceptical *adj* cynical, doubtful, dubious, hesitating, questioning, quizzical, scoffing, unbelieving, unconvinced.
schedule *n* agenda, calendar, catalogue, inventory, itinerary, list, list of appointments, plan, programme, timetable.
schedule *v* arrange, book, organize, plan, programme, slot, time.
scheme *n* **1** course of action, design, plan, project, proposal, strategy, tactics. **2** arrangement, blueprint, draft, layout, outline, pattern, schedule. **3** conspiracy, intrigue, plot, ploy, subterfuge; (*Inf*) game.
scheme *v* **1** contrive, design, devise, frame, imagine, lay plans, plan, project, work out. **2** collude, conspire, plot; (*Inf*) wheel and deal.
scholarship *n* **1** education, knowledge. **2** bursary, exhibition, fellowship.
school *n* **1** academy, college, department, discipline, faculty, institute. **2** circle, class, clique, denomination, devotees, disciples, faction, following, group, pupils, sect, set. **3** faith, outlook, persuasion,stamp, way of life.
school *v* coach, discipline, drill, educate, instruct, prepare, prime, train, tutor, verse.
scientific *adj* accurate, exact, precise, systematic.
scoff *v* belittle, laugh at, mock, poke fun at, ridicule, sneer, taunt; (*Inf*) knock.
scold *v* blame, lecture, nag, reprimand; (*Inf*) give someone a dressing-down, go on at, tell off, tick off.
scoop *n* **1** ladle, spoon. **2** coup, exclusive, exposé, inside story, revelation, sensation.
scoop *v* bail, excavate, gouge, hollow, ladle, scrape, shovel.
scope *n* area, capacity, compass, confines, extent, opportunity, range, reach, span, sphere.
scorch *v* blacken, blister, burn, char, parch, roast, sear, shrivel, singe, wither.

score *n* **1** grade, mark, outcome, points, result, total. **2** account, basis, cause, ground, grounds, reason. **3** grievance, grudge, injustice, wrong. **4** amount due, bill, charge, debt, tally, total.
score *v* **1** achieve, amass, gain, make, win; (*Inf*) chalk up, count, keep a tally of, record, register. **2** crosshatch, cut, deface, notch, scratch, slash. **3 score through** cross out, put a line through, strike out. **4** arrange, orchestrate, set. **5** impress, make an impact, make a point, put oneself across, triumph.
scorn *v* look down on, make fun of, scoff at, sneer at; (*Inf*) turn up one's nose at.
scornful *adj* defiant, insolent, jeering, mocking, sneering.
scoundrel *n* cheat, good-for-nothing, rascal, rogue, scamp, villain; (*Inf*) rotter, swine.
scour *v* **1** cleanse, polish, rub, scrub, wash. **2** beat, comb, forage, go over with a fine-tooth comb, hunt, look high and low, rake, ransack, search.
scramble *v* **1** clamber, climb, crawl, struggle. **2** jostle, push, rush, vie; (*Inf*) look snappy.
scramble *n* **1** climb, trek. **2** commotion, hustle, melee, race, rush, tussle; (*Inf*) free-for-all, hassle.
scrap *n* **1** atom, bit, bite, crumb, fragment, grain, iota, mite, morsel, particle, piece, portion, sliver, snippet, trace. **2** junk, off cuts, waste. **3** bits, leftovers, remains, scrapings.
scrap *v* abandon, break up, discard, dispense with, drop, get rid of, jettison, shed, throw on the scrapheap, toss out, write off; (*Inf*) ditch, junk, trash.
scrape *v* **1** graze, rub, scratch, scuff. **2** grate, grind, rasp, scratch, screech, set one's teeth on edge **3** clean, erase, rub, scrub, scour. **4 scrape together** collect, save, scrimp, skimp.
scratch *v* **1** claw, cut, damage, graze, lacerate, make a mark on, mark, rub, score, scrape. **2** annul, cancel, delete, eliminate, erase, pull out, stand down, strike off, withdraw.
scratch *n* blemish, claw, graze, laceration, mark, scrape.
scratch *adj* hastily prepared, impromptu, improvised, rough, rough-and-ready.
scream *v* **1** bawl, cry, shriek, squeal, yell. **2** clash, jar, shriek; (*Inf*) holler.
scream *n* wail, yell, yelp.
screen *v* **1** cloak, conceal, cover, hide, mask, shade, shut out. **2** defend, protect, safeguard, shelter, shield. **3** examine, filter, scan, sift, sort, vet. **4** broadcast, put on, show.
screen *n* **1** awning, canopy, cloak, concealment, cover, guard, hedge, mantle, shade, shelter, shield, shroud. **2** mesh, net, partition, room divider.
screw *v* tighten, turn, twist, work in.
scrub *v* **1** clean, cleanse, rub, scour. **2** abandon, abolish, call off, cancel, discontinue, drop, forget about, give up.
scuffle *v* clash, come to blows, fight, grapple, jostle, struggle, tussle.
scuffle *n* affray, brawl,

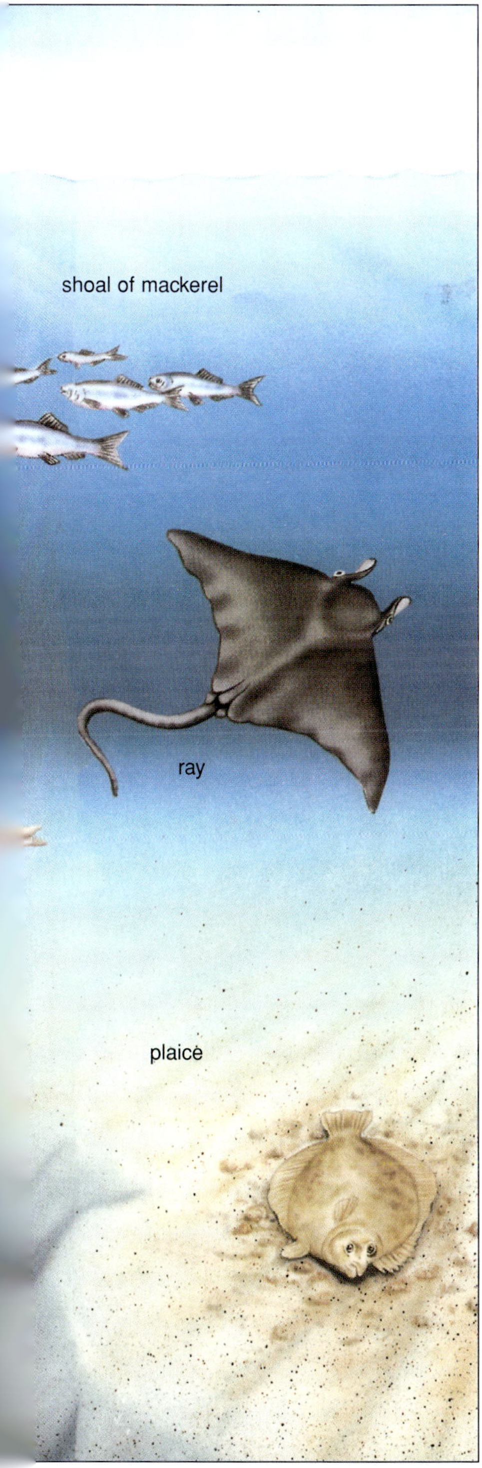

commotion, disturbance, fight, fray, rumpus, tussle; (*Inf*) scrap, set-to.

scurry *v* dash, hurry, scamper, scuttle, sprint.

sea *n* **1** main, ocean, the deep, the waves; (*Inf*) the briny, the drink. **2** abundance, expanse, mass, multitude, profusion, sheet, vast number.

sea *adj* aquatic, briny, marine, maritime, ocean, ocean-going, oceanic, saltwater, seagoing.

search *v* examine, inspect, investigate, probe, ransack, rifle through, sift, turn inside out, turn upside down; (*Inf*) frisk.

search *n* examination, hunt, pursuit, researches, scrutiny; (*Inf*) going-over, in search of, hunting for, in need of, looking for, making enquiries concerning, on the look out for, on the track of, seeking.

season *n* division, interval, juncture, occasion, opportunity, period, spell, term, time, time of year.

seat *n* **1** bench, chair, pew, settle, stall, stool, throne. **2** capital, centre, headquarters, heart, hub, location, place, site, situation, source, station. **3** base, bed, bottom, cause, footing, foundation, groundwork. **4** ancestral hall, house, mansion, residence. **5** chair, constituency, membership, place.

seat *v* **1** accommodate, cater for, contain, have room for, hold, sit, take. **2** deposit, fit, install, locate, place, set, settle, sit.

secluded *adj* cut off, isolated, lonely, off the beaten track, out-of-the-way, private, reclusive, remote, retired, sheltered, solitary, tucked away.

seclusion *n* privacy, solitude, withdrawal.

second-hand *adj* handed down, nearly new, used; (*Inf*) hand-me-downs.

second-hand *adv* at second-hand, indirectly; (*Inf*) on the grapevine.

second-rate *adj* cheap, inferior, low-quality, mediocre, poor, shoddy, substandard; (*Inf*) tacky.

secret *adj* **1** camouflaged, cloak-and-dagger, close, concealed, covert, disguised, furtive, hidden, under wraps; (*Inf*) closet, hush-hush. **2** clandestine, cryptic, mysterious. **3** out-of-the-way, private, secluded. **4** deep, discreet, sly, underhand.

secret *n* code, enigma, formula, key, mystery, recipe.

Sea life

It is likely that life on our planet began in the sea. As much more of the Earth is covered with water than with land, and the sea can be thousands of metres deep, there is simply more space for living things in the ocean. However the conditions that they experience there are not so varied, so there are fewer different species than there are on land. Well over 90% of the living things that thrive in the sea are found in the fairly shallow waters around the continents. However scientists have found that there is life even in the deepest oceans, although it is not easy to study wildlife in such remote areas.

secretive *adj* close, reserved, tight-lipped, uncommunicative, withdrawn; (*Inf*) cagey.
secretly *adv* behind closed doors, confidentially, covertly, furtively, on the sly, privately, surreptitiously; (*Inf*) on the q.t.
sect *n* denomination, faction, schism, school.
section *n* component, cross section, division, fraction, fragment, installment, part, passage, piece, portion, sample, segment, slice, subdivision.
secure *adj* **1** impregnable, protected, safe, sheltered. **2** fast, firm, fixed, solid, tight. **3** unharmed, unhurt, unscathed.
secure *v* **1** acquire, come by, gain, get, obtain, pick up; (*Inf*) land. **2** attach, bolt, chain, fasten, lash, lock, moor, padlock, tie up.
security *n* **1** asylum, immunity, protection, refuge, sanctuary. **2** defence, protection, safeguards, safety measures**. 3** confidence, conviction, sureness. **4** collateral, guarantee, insurance, pledge.
sedate *adj* calm, composed, cool, placid, proper, quiet, slow-moving, sober, solemn, staid, tranquil, unruffled.
sedative *adj* calming, relaxing, sleep-inducing, tranquillizing.
sedative *n* anodyne, calmative, downer, narcotic, opiate, sleeping pill, tranquillizer.
see *v* **1** glimpse, make out, note, notice, observe, recognize, regard, spot, view, witness; (*Inf*) get a load of. **2** appreciate, comprehend, grasp, realize, take in, understand; (*Inf*) catch on to, get the hang of. **3** determine, discover, find out, investigate, make enquiries. **4** ensure, guarantee, make sure. **5** decide, make up one's mind, reflect, think over. **6** consult, encounter, interview, meet, speak to, visit. **7** attend, escort, lead, show, usher, walk. **8** anticipate, foresee, imagine, picture, visualize.
seed *n* **1** egg, egg cell, embryo, germ, grain, kernel, ovule, ovum, spore. **2** beginning, germ, inkling, nucleus, source, start, suspicion.
seek *v* **1** follow, go in search of, hunt, look for, pursue, search for. **2** aim, aspire to, attempt, endeavour, strive, try. **3** ask, beg, invite, petition, request.
seem *v* appear, assume, give the impression, have the appearance of, look like, pretend, sound like.
seethe *v* **1** boil, bubble, churn, ferment, fizz, froth. **2** be livid, foam at the mouth, fume, rage, simmer. **3** swarm, teem; (*Inf*) get hot under the collar.
segment *n* bit, division, part, piece, portion, section, sector
select *v* choose, opt for, pick, prefer, single out, sort out.
select *adj* choice, excellent, first-class, first-rate, hand-picked, picked, preferable, prime, rare, recherché, selected, special, superior; (*Inf*) posh, topnotch.
selection *n* **1** choice, option, pick, preference. **2** anthology, assortment, choice, collection, line-up, medley, miscellany, potpourri, range, variety.
selective *adj* careful, discerning, discriminating, particular.
self-centred *adj* egotistic, inward looking, narcissistic, selfish, wrapped up in oneself.
self-confidence *n* composure, confidence, nerve, poise, self-assurance, self-reliance.
self-confident *adj* assured, confident, fearless, self-assured, sure of oneself.
self-conscious *adj* awkward, embarrassed, insecure, nervous, uncomfortable.
self-control *n* calmness, cool, coolness, self-restraint, strength of mind, willpower.
self-important *adj* assuming, proud, overbearing.
self-indulgence *n* excess, extravagance.
selfish *adj* greedy, mean, self-centred.

Segments of colour opposite each other in the colour wheel generally contrast, while colour segments next to each other tend to harmonize.

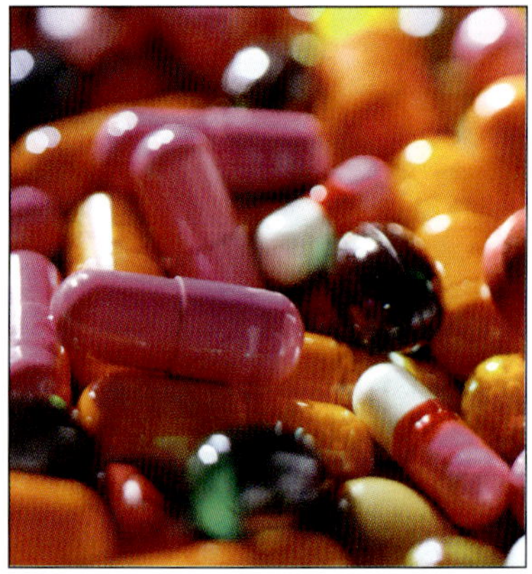

Sedatives in powder form are stored in capsules that dissolve in the stomach.

self-possessed *adj* confident, cool, poised, self-assured, sure of oneself, unruffled; (*Inf*) cool as a cucumber, together.
self-respect *n* dignity, faith in oneself, pride, self-esteem.
self-righteous *adj* complacent, hypocritical, smug, superior; (*Inf*) goody-goody.
sell *v* **1** barter, dispose of, exchange, put up for sale, trade. **2** be in the business of, deal in, handle, hawk, market, merchandise, peddle, retail, stock, trade in, traffic in, vend.
seller *n* agent, dealer, merchant, rep, representative, retailer, salesman, saleswoman, shopkeeper, tradesman, traveller, vendor.
send *v* **1** communicate, convey, direct, dispatch, forward, remit, transmit. **2** cast, deliver, fire, fling, hurl, let fly, propel, shoot.
senior *adj* elder, higher ranking, older, superior.
sensation *n* **1** awareness, feeling, impression, sense, tingle; (*Inf*) vibes. **2** agitation, commotion, excitement, furore, scandal, stir, surprise, thrill, wow; (*Inf*) crowd puller, hit.
sensational *adj* amazing, breathtaking, dramatic, exciting, spectacular, startling, thrilling.
sense *n* **1** faculty, feeling, sensation. **2** appreciation, atmosphere, aura, awareness, consciousness, feel, impression, intuition, perception, premonition, sentiment. **3** drift, gist, implication, meaning, message, significance. **4** common sense, intelligence, judgment, reason, sanity, sharpness, understanding, wisdom, wits; (*Inf*) brains, gumption.
sense *v* detect, feel, grasp, guess, notice, observe, pick up, realize, understand; (*Inf*) have a feeling in one's bones.
senseless *adj* **1** absurd, crazy, foolish, halfwitted, idiotic, irrational, ludicrous, mad, ridiculous, silly, stupid, unwise; (*Inf*) daft. **2** anaesthetized, cold, numb, stunned, unconscious, unfeeling.
sensible *adj* discreet, down-to-earth, far-sighted, intelligent, matter-of-fact, practical, realistic, sound, well-thought-out, wise.
sensitive *adj* **1** delicate, fine, keen, perceptive, precise, responsive. **2** delicate, easily upset, irritable, tender, touchy.
sentence *n* decision, decree, judgment, order, ruling, verdict.
sentence *v* condemn, pass judgment on, penalize.
sentimental *adj* emotional, nostalgic, romantic, tearful, tender, touching; (*Inf*) corny, sloppy, tear-jerking, weepy.
separate *v* **1** break off, come apart, come away, detach, disconnect, divide, sever, split. **2** isolate, segregate, single out. **3** break up, diverge, divorce, go different ways, part company, split up.
separate *adj* **1** detached, divided, divorced, isolated, unattached. **2** alone, apart, independent, single, solitary.
separately *adv* alone, apart, independently, individually, one at a time, one by one, personally, severally, singly.
separation *n* **1** break, division, gap. **2** break-up, divorce, parting, split.
series *n* chain, course, line, order, progression, relay, run, sequence, set, string.
serious *adj* **1** grave, humourless, long-faced, solemn, thoughtful. **2** deliberate,

Sending messages

The speed of sending messages around the world has increased beyond belief recently. A few hundred years ago, the fastest way a piece of news could travel was by people on horses. Messages sent overseas could only travel as fast as the fastest sailing ship and were at the mercy of the wind and weather. The breakthrough came with the invention of the electric telegraph and messages in Morse Code. Now images of written documents, sound recordings or televison pictures can be flashed around the globe in less than a second by means of satellites links and electronic communications via computers and fibreoptic telephone lines.

genuine, honest, resolute, sincere. **3** crucial, significant, urgent, worrying. **4** acute, alarming, dangerous, grave, severe.

serve *v* **1** assist, help, wait on, work for. **2** act, attend, do, fulfil, observe, perform. **3** be good enough, content, do duty as, function as, satisfy, suit; (*Inf*) fill the bill. **4** deliver, distribute, handle, present, provide, supply.

service *n* **1** advantage, assistance, benefit, help, supply, usefulness, utility. **2** check, maintenance, overhaul. **3** business, duty, office, work. **4** ceremony, function, rite, worship.

service *v* check, fine tune, go over, maintain, overhaul, repair, tune up.

session *n* conference, hearing, meeting, period, sitting, term; (*Inf*) get together.

set *v* **1** arrange, deposit, locate, position, settle. **2** fasten, fix. **3** adjust, correct, put right, rectify. **4** congeal, harden, stiffen, take shape. **5** allocate, decide, establish, identify, name. **6** ask, formulate, put forward, suggest, write.

set *n* **1** batch, bunch, collection, series. **2** scene, scenery, setting, stage set, stage setting.

set *adj* **1** agreed, arranged, definite, fixed, prearranged. **2** entrenched, firm, hard and fast, inflexible, rigid, strict.

set *n* **1** band, circle, class, clique, company, coterie, crowd, faction, gang, group, sect; (*Inf*) crew, outfit. **2** batch, collection, kit, outfit, series.

setback *n* bit of trouble, blow, check, defeat, disappointment, hitch, hold-up, stumbling block.

A relay is a race in which each member of a team covers a specified portion of the overall distance passing a baton between them in several changes.

set off *v* **1** depart, embark, leave, set out, start out. **2** detonate, explode, ignite, light, set in motion, trigger off.

setting *n* backdrop, context, frame, mounting, scene, scenery, set, site, surroundings.

settle *v* **1** colonize, occupy, set up home, stay. **2** land, rest, sit down. **3** calm down, sink, subside. **4** agree, choose, decide, fix. **5** conclude, deal with, reconcile, desolve. **6** pay.

settlement *n* **1** conclusion, resolution. **2** clearance, clearing, defrayal, discharge, liquidation, payment, satisfaction. **3** colony, community, hamlet, kibbutz, outpost, village.

settler *n* colonist, colonizer, frontiersmen, frontierswoman, immigrant, pioneer, planter.

set up *n* **1** arrange, begin, compose, establish, initiate, install, organize, prearrange. **2** assemble, build, construct, erect, put together, put up, raise.

server *v* **1** divide, part, separate, sunder. **2** detach, disconnect, disjoin, disunite.

several *adj* assorted, different, diverse, individual, some, sundry, various.

severe *adj* **1** austere, cruel, Draconian, harsh, rigid, strict, unrelenting. **2** cold, forbidding, grave, stern. **3** critical, dangerous, extreme, intense, violent. **4** plain, simple, Spartan, unfussy. **5** arduous, demanding, difficult, exacting, punishing, rigorous.

sew *v* baste, bind, embroider, hem, machine stitch, stitch, tack.

shade *n* **1** coolness, dimness, dusk, gloom, shadiness, shadow, shadows. **2** blind, canopy, cover, covering. **3** colour, hue, stain, tinge, tint, tone. **4** apparition, ghost, phantom, shadow, spectre, spirit.

shade *v* cast a shadow over, cloud, cover, darken, dim, hide, obscure, protect, screen, shield, shut out the light, veil.

shadow *n* **1** darkness, dimness,

dusk, gloom, shade. **2** hint, suggestion, suspicion, trace. **3** ghost, image, representation. **4** cloud, gloom, sadness. **5** cast a shadow over, darken, overhang, screen, shade, shield. **6** dog, follow, spy on, stalk; (*Inf*) tail.
shady *adj* **1** cool, dim, dark, leafy, shaded. **2** dubious, questionable, shifty, suspect, suspicious; (*Inf*) crooked, fishy.
shake *v* **1** bump, jquiver, rock, shudder, sway, totter, tremble, vibrate, wobble. **2** brandish, flourish, wave. **3** distress, frighten, intimidate, move, unnerve, upset; (*Inf*) rattle.
shake *n* agitation, convulsion, disturbance, quaking, shiver, shock, shudder, trembling, tremor, vibration.
shaky *adj* **1** faltering, insecure, precarious, rickety, tottering, unstable, unsteady, wobbly; (*Inf*) all of a quiver. **2** dubious, questionable, suspect, uncertain, undependable, unreliable, unsound, unsupported.
shallow *adj* empty, frivolous, simple, superficial, trivial.
shame *n* disgrace, embarrassment, guilt, humiliation, remorse, stigma.
shame *v* **1** disgrace, embarrass, humiliate, mortify, reproach, ridicule. **2** blot, debase, defile, degrade, discredit, dishonour, smear, stain.
shameful *adj* **1** atrocious, degrading, disgraceful, low, mean, outrageous, scandalous, wicked. **2** degrading, embarrassing, humiliating, mortifying, shaming.
shape *n* **1** configuration, cut, form, outline, profile, silhouette. **2** frame, model, mould, pattern. **3** appearance, aspect, likeness, semblance. **4** condition, fettle, health, state.
shape *v* carve, fashion, form, make, model, mould.
share *v* apportion, deal out, distribute, divide, dole out, go halves in, parcel out, partake, split; (*Inf*) go Dutch, go fifty-fifty.
share *n* allotment, allowance, contribution, division, due, lot, part, portion, quota, ration; (*Inf*) cut, whack.
sharp *adj* **1** jagged, knife-edged, pointed, razor-sharp, serrated, sharpened, spiky. **2** abrupt, extreme, hairpin, steep, sudden, unexpected. **3** bright, clever, perceptive, quick. **4** acute, alert, incisive, intelligent, quick, shrewd, smart. **5** acerbic, acid, barbed, biting, bitter, caustic, critical, cutting, harsh, sarcastic, scathing, unkind. **6** acid, acrid, bitter, caustic, sour, tart, vinegary. **7** clear high, penetrating, shrill.
shatter *v* break, burst, crack, destroy, disintegrate, explode, smash, split.
shave *v* **1** crop, cut off, mow, pare, slice, trim. **2** graze, skim, touch. **3** pare, plane, shear.
sheepish *adj* bashful, coy, guilty, shy, timid, timorous.
sheer *adj* **1** perpendicular, steep, vertical. **2** absolute, complete, downright, out-and-out, pure, total, utter. **3** fine, flimsy, see-through, transparent.
sheet *n* **1** folio, leaf, page. **2** pane, panel, plate. **3** skin, slab, stratum, surface, veneer. **4** area, blanket, coating, covering, expanse, film, layer, skin. **5** area, surface.
shell *n* **1** case, husk, pod. **2** chassis, framework, hull, skeleton, structure.
shell *v* **1** husk, shuck. **2** attack, barrage, blitz, bomb, bombard, open fire on, strafe, strike. **3 shell out** lay out, pay out, spend; (*Inf*) shell out.
shellfish *n* crustacean, mollusc.
shelter *v* cover, defend, guard, harbour, hide, protect, safeguard, seek refuge, shield, take

The shells and skeletons of millions of little creatures called polyps make up coral reefs. Polyps live in colonies begun by just one polyp that buds and produces new polyps. Each polyp builds a hard shell around itself and when it dies, the skeleton remains and the reef gets bigger. The Great Barrier Reef in Australia is so big it can be seen from space.

in, take shelter.
shelter *n* **1** barrier, cover, protection, retreat, roof over one's head, screen, shield. **2** asylum, haven, protection, refuge, safety, sanctuary.
sheltered *adj* hermetic, isolated, protected, quiet, reclusive, retired, screened, secluded, shaded, shielded, withdrawn.
shelve *v* defer, freeze, hold over, mothball, postpone, put aside, put off, put on ice, suspend.
shield *n* **1** buckler, escutcheon. **2** barrier, cover, defence, guard, protection, rampart, safeguard, screen, shelter.
shield *v* defend, guard, protect, safeguard, screen, shelter.
shimmer *v* gleam, glisten, twinkle.
shine *v* **1** beam, emit light, flash, glimmer, glisten, glow, radiate, shimmer, sparkle, twinkle. **2** be outstanding, do well, excel, stand out, star.
shipshape *adj* neat, orderly, tidy, trim, well-arranged.
shirk *v* avoid, dodge, evade, get out of, neglect, shun, sidestep, slack; (*Inf*) duck out of, skive.
shiver *v* **1** break, shatter, splinter. **2** quake, quiver, shake, shudder, tremble.
shiver *n* **1** bit, fragment, piece, slice, sliver, splinter. **2** shaking, shivering, shuddering, tremor.
shock *v* astound, horrify, offend, outrage, stun, stupefy, unsettle; (*Inf*) give someone a fright.

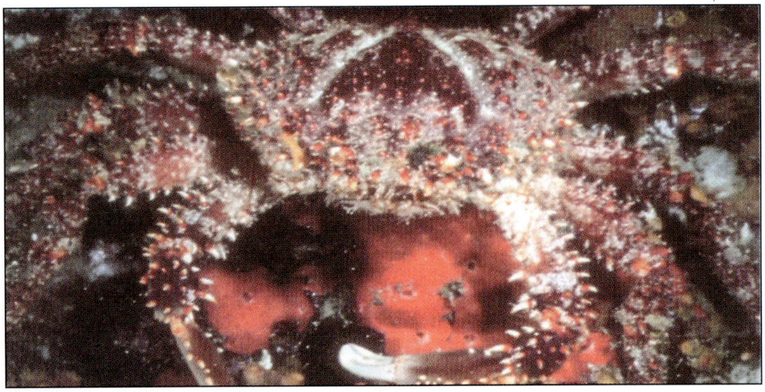

Shellfish are crustaceans. Some crustaceans such as crabs and lobsters have particularly hard outer casings. Shrimps and barnacles are also crustaceans. Centipedes, millipedes, spiders, insects and crustaceans are all arthropods.

shock *n* blow, bombshell, breakdown, collapse, distress, trauma, upset; (*Inf*) turn.
shocking *adj* appaling, atrocious, detestable, disgusting, ghastly, horrible, offensive, outrageous, scandalous.
shoot *v* **1** hit, kill, open fire; (*Inf*) blast. **2** plug, pumpfull of lead. **3** discharge, emit fire, fling, launch, project, propel. **4** bolt, charge, dart, hurtle, race, tear.
shoot *n* branch, bud, offshoot, sprig, sprout, twig.
shoot *v* bud, germinate, sprout.
shore *n* **1** beach, coast, foreshore, lakeside, sands, seaboard, seashore, waterside. **2** beam, brace, buttress, prop, stay, support.
shore *v* brace, buttress, prop, stay, support.
short *adj* **1** abridged, brief, concise, summary. **2** little, low, petite, small, squat, wee. **3** brief, fleeting, momentary, short-lived, short-term. **4** short of deficient, inadequate, insufficient, limited, low (on), meagre, scant, short-handed, slim, sparse, wanting.
shortage *n* deficiency, deficit, failure, scarcity, shortfall.
shortcoming *n* defect, flaw, imperfection, weak point.
shorten *v* abbreviate, abridge, curtail, cut, cut back, cut down, decrease, diminish, dock, lessen, prune, trim, truncate, turn up.
shot *n* **1** discharge, lob, pot shot, throw. **2** ball, bullet, projectile, slug. **3** marksman, shooter. **4** chance, effort, go, stab, try, turn; (*Inf*) attempt, crack. **5 have a shot** have a crack, have a go, stab, tackle, try, try one's luck; (*Inf*) have a bash. **6 like a shot** at once, immediately, like a flash, quickly, unhesitatingly.
shoulder *v* **1** accept, assume, bear, be responsible for, carry, take on. **2** elbow, jostle, press, push, shove, thrust.
shout *n* bellow, call, cry, roar, scream, yell.
shout *v* bawl, bay, bellow, call out, cry out, raise one's voice, roar, scream, yell.
shove *v* crowd, drive, elbow, impel, jostle, press, propel, push, shoulder, thrust.
show *v* **1** appear, disclose, display, divulge, exhibit, indicate, make known, reveal. **2** assert, demonstrate, explain, instruct, present, teach. **3** accompany, attend, conduct, escort, guide, lead.
show *n* **1** demonstrate, display, exhibition, exposition, sight,

view; (*Inf*) expo. **2** air, display, illusion, likeness, ostentation, parade, performance, pose, pretence, production; (*Inf*) gig. **3 run the show** enterprise, entertainment, organization, venture. **4 steal the show** be the main attraction, get all the attention.
showdown *n* clash, climax, confrontation, crisis, culmination, face-off, moment of truth, open conflict.
shower *n* barrage, deluge, fusillade, rain, stream, torrent.
shower *v* deluge, heap, inundate, lavish, load, overwhelm, pour, rain, spray, sprinkle.
show-off *n* **1** advertise, demonstrate, display, exhibit, flaunt, parade, spread out. **2** boast, brag, make a spectacle of oneself, swagger.
showy *adj* **1** dressy, flashy, gaudy, loud, smart. **2** grand, magnificent, ostentatious, pretentious, sumptuous.
shred *v* cut up, rip, tear up.
shred *n* bit, fragment, piece, rag, scrap, strip, tatter.
shrewd *adj* astute, calculating, crafty, cunning, intelligent, keen, perceptive, sharp, sly, wily; (*Inf*) fly.
shriek *v* scream, screech, squeal, yell, yelp.
shriek *n* cry, scream, screech, yell.
shrill *adj* acute, ear-piercing, high-pitched, piercing, sharp.
shrink *v* **1** contract, diminish, dwindle, lessen, narrow, shrivel, wither, wrinkle. **2** cringe, draw back, flinch, recoil, shy away, withdraw.
shut *v* bar, close, draw to, fasten, push to, seal, secure, slam.
shut out *v* bar, debar, exclude, keep out, lock out, ostracize.
shut up *v* **1** bottle up, box in, cage, confine, coop up, immure, imprison, incarcerate, intern, keep in. **2** fall silent, gag, hold one's tongue, hush, muzzle, silence; (*Inf*) be quiet, keep one's trap shut, pipe down.
shy *adj* bashful, coy, hesitant, nervous, reserved, timid, wary.
side *n* **1** border, boundary, edge, limit, margin, perimeter, rim, sector, verge. **2** aspect, face, surface, view. **3** angle, light, opinion, point of view, slant, stand, standpoint, viewpoint. **4** camp, cause, faction, party, sect, team. **5** airs, arrogance, pretentiousness; (*Inf*) snootiness.
sidetrack *v* deflect, distract, divert, lead off the subject.
siege *n* beleaguerment, blockade, investment.

Meteor showers are associated with comets. Comet material is spread out along its orbital path. At certain times the Earth passes through the orbial paths of some comets which allows larger than average amounts of particles to enter the Earth's atmosphere resulting in a high number of meteors.

sick *adj* **1** ill, nauseous, queasy; (*Inf*) green around the gills, throw up. **2** diseased, feeble, indisposed, unwell; (*Inf*) laid up, on the sick list, poorly, under the weather. **3** black, cruel, ghoulish, gruesome, macabre, morbid, perverted, sadistic.
sicken *v* **1** disgust, nauseate, revolt, shock. **2** become ill with, contract; (*Inf*) come down with; become bored with, feel jaded, tire, weary; (*Inf*) be fed up with.
sickly *adj* ailing, bilious, faint, feeble, in poor health, weak.
sift *v* **1** bolt, filter, pan, part, riddle, separate, sieve. **2** analyse, examine, go through, probe, scrutinize.
sight *n* **1** eyes, eyesight, vision. **2** appearance, field of vision, perception, view, visibility. **3** display, exhibition, pageant, scene, show, spectacle. **4** catch sight of, espy, glimpse, recognize, spot, view.
sight *v* distinguish, make out, observe, see, spot.
sign *n* **1** clue, hint, indication, mark, note, proof, signal, token. **2** notice, placard, warning.

These silhouettes are confusing to our brains. The picture can be seen as two faces looking at each other or a Grecian vase. But the two images cannot be seen at the same time.

3 badge, character, device, emblem, logo, mark, symbol. **4** omen, portent, presage, warning, writing on the wall.
sign *v* **1** autograph, endorse, initial, inscribe. **2** beckon, gesticulate, gesture, indicate, signal, wave.
signal *n* beacon, cue, flare, gesture, green light, indication, indicator, mark, sign, token; (*Inf*) go ahead.
signal *v* beckon, gesture, give a sign to, indicate, motion, nod, sign, wave.
silence *n* **1** calm, hush, lull, noiselessness, peace, stillness. **2** dumbness, muteness, reticence, speechlessness, uncommunicativeness.
silence *v* cut off, cut short, deaden, extinguish, gag, muffle, quell, quiet, quieten, stifle, still, strike dumb, subdue, suppress.
silent *adj* **1** hushed, mute, noiseless, quiet, still. **2** dumb, mute, speechless, uncommunicative, voiceless, wordless; (*Inf*) struck dumb. **3** implicit, implied, tacit, understood, unexpressed, unpronounced, unspoken
silhouette *n* form, outline, profile, shape.
silhouette *v* etch, outline, stand out.
silly *adj* **1** absurd, childish, foolhardy, idiotic, irresponsible, pointless, ridiculous, senseless, stupid, unwise; (*Inf*) dopy, dozy; **2** dazed, groggy, in a daze, muzzy, stunned, stupefied.
similar *adj* alike, comparable, corresponding, in agreement, much the same, resembling, uniform.
similarity *n* likeness, relation, resemblance, similitude.
simmer *v* boil, bubble, seethe, stew.
simple *adj* **1** easy, elementary, intelligible, lucid, manageable, plain, straightforward. **2** classic, natural, plain, spartan, unfussy. **3** elementary, pure, single. **4** childlike, green, innocent, naive, simplistic. **5** basic, direct, frank, honest, naked, plain, sincere, stark. **6** homely, lowly, modest, rustic. **7** dense, feeble, foolish, half-witted, moronic, shallow, slow, stupid; (*Inf*) dumb.
simplicity *n* **1** clarity, clearness, ease, straightforwardness. **2** clean lines, plainness.
sin *n* crime, misdeed, offence, wrongdoing.
sin *v* err, fall, fall from grace, go astray, lapse, offend, transgress.
since *conj* as, because, considering, seeing that.
sincere *adj* genuine, honest, straightforward, true.
sinful *adj* bad, evil, wrong.
sing *v* carol, chant, chirp, croon, pipe, trill, vocalize, warble, yodel.
singe *v* burn, scorch, sear.
single *adj* **1** individual, isolated, lone one, only, sole, solitary, unique. **2** umarried.
singular *adj* exceptional, extraordinary, odd, peculiar, strange, unusual.
sinister *adj* disturbing, evil, frightening, menacing, threatening, upsetting.
sink *n* basin.
sink *v* cave in, drown, fall, plunge, sag, scupper, scuttle, submerge, subside.
sip *v* sample, sup, taste.
sip *n* drop, swallow, taste, thimbleful.
sit *v* **1** perch, rest, settle, squat, take a seat, take the weight off one's feet. **2** assemble, convene, meet, officiate, preside.
site *n* ground, location, place, plot, position, setting, spot.
site *v* install, locate, place, position, set, situate.

This Devil of the Sins is used by the local population in Bali to ward off evil spirits and forgive their misdeeds, wrongdoings and transgressions.

situation *n* **1** environment, locality, location, place, position, setting, site. **2** circumstances, condition, plight, state of affairs.
size *n* amount, bigness, bulk, dimensions, extent, greatness, hugeness, immensity, largeness, magnitude, mass, measurements, proportions, range, vastness, volume.
size *v* categorize, classify, sort; size up appraise, assess, estimate, evaluate, gauge, judge, rate.
sketch *v* block out, delineate, depict, draft, draw, outline, paint, plot, portray, represent, rough out.
sketch *n* delineation, design, draft, drawing, outline, plan, skeleton.
sketchy *adj* incomplete, outline, rough, scrappy, vague.
skilful *adj* able, accomplished, adept, adroit, apt, clever, competent, dexterous, experienced, expert, handy, masterly, practised, professional, proficient, quick, ready, skilled, trained.
skill *n* ability, aptitude, art, competence, experience, knack, readiness, skillfulness, talent, technique.
skilled *adj* able, accomplished, experienced, expert, masterly, practised, professional, proficient, skillful, trained; (*Inf*) a dab hand at.
skim *v* **1** brush, glance, graze, touch lightly. **2** fly, glide, sail, whisk. **3** dip into, glance at, scan, skip, thumb over.
skin *n* casing, coating, crust, film, husk, peel, rind.
skinny *adj* emaciated, lean, thin; (*Inf*) skin and bone.
skip *v* **1** bob, bounce, caper, cavort, dance, flit, frisk, gambol, hop, prance, trip. **2** leave out, miss out, omit,
skirmish *n* battle, conflict, fracas, incident, tussle; (*Inf*) dust up, scrap, set-to.
skirmish *v* clash, collide, come to blows, tussle; (*Inf*) scrap.
skirt *v* border, edge, flank, lie alongside.

The skin of an alligator is thick with bony plates reminding us of dinosaurs. Alligators and crocodiles are more closely related to dinosaurs than any other living reptile.

slack *adj* **1** baggy, loose, relaxed. **2** careless, idle, lazy, neglectful, negligent; (*Inf*) asleep on the job. **3** inactive, quiet, slow, sluggish.
slacken (off) *v* decrease, ease off, let up, moderate, reduce, slow down, tire.
slam *v* bang, crash, dash, fling, hurl, smash, throw, thump.
slander *v* backbite, blacken someone's name, defame, libel, malign, smear, vilify.
slant *v* **1** bend, incline, lean, list, shelve, skew, slope, tilt. **2** angle, bias, colour, distort, twist, weight.
slant *n* **1** gradient, incline, pitch, slope, tilt. **2** angle, emphasis, leaning, one-sidedness, point of view, prejudice, viewpoint.
slanting *adj* angled, bent, diagonal, inclined, listing, oblique, sloping.
slap *n* bang, blow, cuff, punch, smack, spank; (*Inf*) belt, clip, clout, swipe, wallop.
slap *v* **1** bang, blow, cuff, punch, smack, spank; (*Inf*) belt, clip, clout, sock, swipe, wallop. **2** fling, hurl, plonk, slam, throw, toss. **3** daub, plaster, spread. **4** add, put on, tack on.
slapdash *adj* careless, clumsy, hasty, hurried, messy, slipshod, thrown-together, untidy; (*Inf*) sloppy.
slash *v* cut, gash, hack, lacerate, rend rip, score, slit.
slate *v* blame, censure, criticize, lambaste, pitch into, rail against, rebuke, scold, take to task; (*Inf*) haul over the coals, lay into, pan, rap someone's knuckles, roast, slam, tear someone off a strip.
slaughter *n* blood bath, bloodshed, butchery, carnage, extermination, holocaust, killing, liquidation, massacre, murder, slaying.
slaughter *v* butcher, destroy, do to death, exterminate, kill,

liquidate, massacre, murder, put to the sword, slay.
slave *v* labour, slog, sweat, toil, work one's fingers to the bone, work like a Trojan; (*Inf*) skivvy.
slay *v* kill, massacre, murder, put to death, slaughter.
sleek *adj* glossy, silky, soft, smooth, velvety, well-groomed.
sleep *v* catnap, doze, drowse, hibernate, slumber, snore, take a nap; (*Inf*) drop off, nod of, snooze, take forty winks.
sleepy *adj* **1** drowsy, lethargic. **2** dull, inactive, quiet, sleep-inducing, slow, slumberous, somnolent, tired, weary.
slender *adj* **1** lean, slim, svelte, willowy. **2** little, meagre, scanty, small. **3** faint, feeble, flimsy, fragile, poor, remote, slight, thin, weak.
slice *n* cut, helping, piece, portion, segment, share, sliver, wedge.
slice *v* carve, cut, divide, sever
slick *adj* **1** polished, smooth. **2** professional, sharp, skilful.
slide *v* coast, glide, skim, slither, toboggan, veer.
slim *adj* lean, narrow, slender, slight.
slim *v* diet, go on a diet, lose pounds, lose weight, reduce, shed weight, slenderize.
slip *v* **1** slide, skate, slide, slither. **2** fall, lose one's balance, stumble. **3** creep, hide, sneak, steal. **4** slip up blunder, err, go wrong, made a mistake, miscalculate, misjudge, mistake.
slip *n* error, failure, fault, mistake, oversight, slip of the tongue; (*Inf*) bloomer, slip-up.
slippery *adj* **1** greasy, icy, perilous, smooth, unsafe, unsteady; (*Inf*) skiddy, slippy. **2** cunning, devious, dishonest, evasive, shifty, tricky, two-faced, unpredictable.
slit *v* cut open, knife, lance, pierce, rip, slash, split open.
slit *n* cut, fissure, gash, incision, opening, rent, split, tear.
sliver *n* chip, fragment, scrap, shred, splinter.
slogan *n* catch-phrase, catch-word, jingle, logo, motto, rallying cry.
slope *v* drop away, fall, incline, lean, pitch, rise, slant, tilt.
slope *n* descent, gradient, inclination, incline, ramp, rise, scarp, slant, tilt.
sloppy *adj* sludgy, slushy, splashy, watery, wet; careless, clumsy, inattentive, messy, slip-shod, slovenly, unkempt, untidy, weak; (*Inf*) amateurish, hit-or-miss
slot *n* **1** aperture, channel, crack, groove, hole, notch, slit. **2** niche, opening, period, place, position, space, time, vacancy.
slow *adj* **1** cautious, gradual, leisurely, sluggish, snail-like, tortoise-like, unhurriedly. **2** backward, behindhand, delayed, late, tardy, unpunctual. **2** gradual, long-drawn-out, prolonged, protracted, time-consuming. **3** inactive, sleepy, sluggish; (*Inf*) dead-and-alive. **4** dense, dim, slow-witted, stupid, thick; (*Inf*) dopey, dumb.
sluggish *adj* dull, lethargic, listless, slow-moving.
slump *v* collapse, fall, plummet, plunge, sink; (*Inf*) go downhill.
slump *n* collapse, crash, down-turn, recession, trough.
slur *n* blot, discredit, disgrace, insult, smear, stain.
sly *adj* clever, conniving, covert, cunning, devious, scheming, shifty, underhand, wily.
smack *v* hit, slap, spank, strike.
small *adj* **1** little, mini, miniature, minute, petite, pocket-sized, teeny, tiny, wee; (*Inf*) pint-sized. **2** minor, slight, trifling, trivial. **3** limited, meagre, scanty. **4** humble, modest, small-scale. **5** grudging, mean, petty, selfish.
small-minded *adj* envious, grudging, narrow-minded, petty,

The slow-moving giant dome-shaped tortoise of the Galapagos Islands can live to a great age and grow to a considerable size.

The slope on this pursuit cycling track helps the riders create extra velocity and momentum by using the gradient.

ungenerous.
smart *adj* **1** astute, bright, clever, ingenious, intelligent, keen, neat, quick, ready, sharp, shrewd. **2** chic, elegant, stylish; (*Inf*) natty, trendy. **3** brisk, fast, quick.
smart *v* burn, hurt, pain, sting, throb, tingle.
smash *v* **1** break, disintegrate, shatter. **2** destroy, overthrow, ruin, wreck.
smear *v* **1** blur, coat, cover, daub, dirty, patch, plaster, rub on. **2** blacken, malign, slander.
smell *v* aroma, bouquet, fragrance, odour, perfume, scent.
smell *n* **1** get a whiff of, nose, scent, sniff. **2** reek, stink; (*Inf*) hum, niff, pong, stink to high heaven, whiff.
smooth *adj* even, flat, flush, horizontal, level, plain, plane, unwrinkled. **2** glossy, polished, shiny, silky, sleek, soft, velvety. **3** calm, peaceful, serene, tranquil. **4** mellow, mild, pleasant, soothing. **5** glib, slick, suave; (*Inf*) smarmy. **6** easy, effortless, fluent, steady.
smooth *v* **1** flatten, iron, level, plane, polish, press. **2** calm, ease, pave the way, soften.
smother *v* **1** choke, extinguish, snuff, stifle, strangle, suffocate. **2** conceal, hide, keep back, muffle, repress, stifle, suppress.
smug *adj* complacent, conceited, self-opinionated, superior.
smuggler *n* bootlegger, runner, trafficker.
snack *n* bite to eat, break, elevenses, light meal, nibble, refreshments, titbits.
snack *v* munch, nibble.
snap *v* **1** break, come apart, give way, separate. **2** bite at, catch, grip, nip, seize, snatch. **3** blow up, boil, fume, lash out at, snarl; (*Inf*) fly off the handle at, jump down someone's throat. **4** click, crackle, pop.
snap *adj* abrupt, immediate, instant, on-the-spot, sudden, unpremeditated.
snatch *v* clutch, gain, grab, grasp, grip, make off with, pluck, pull, rescue, seize, take, win, wrench, wrest.
snatch *n* bit, fragment, part, piece, smattering, snippet, spell.
sneak *v* **1** cower, lurk, pad, sidle, skulk, slink, slip, smuggle, spirit, steal. **2** inform on, tell tales.
sneak *n* informer, telltale; (*Inf*) grass on, tell on.
sneaking *adj* **1** hidden, private, secret. **2** intuitive, nagging, niggling, persistent, worrying.
sneer *v* curl one's lip, jeer, laugh, look down on, mock, ridicule, scorn, snigger; (*Inf*) turn one's nose up at.
sneer *n* jeer, ridicule, scorn.
sniff *v* breathe, inhale, smell, snuff, snuffle.
snigger *n* giggle, laugh, smirk, sneer, snicker, titter.
snip *v* clip, crop, cut, nick, nip off, notch, shave, trim.
snip *n* bit, fragment, piece, shred, snippet; (*Inf*) bargain, giveaway, good buy.
snobbish *adj* arrogant, patronizing, pretentious, superior; (*Inf*) high and mighty, snooty, stuck-up, toffee-nosed.
snooze *v* catnap, doze, drowse, nap; (*Inf*) drop off, kip, nod off.
snooze *n* catnap, doze, nap, siesta; (*Inf*) drop off, forty winks, kip, nod off.
snug *adj* comfortable, comfy, cosy, homely, sheltered, warm.
soak *v* bathe, damp, drench, immerse, marinate, penetrate, permeate, saturate, steep, wet.
soft *adj* **1** cushioned, elastic, spongy, squashy. **2** bendable, flexible, pliable, supple. **3** cosy, feathery, silky, smooth, velvety. **4** creamy, dim, faint, gentle, mellow, mild, pale, pastel, soft-toned. **5** compassionate, gentle, kind, sensitive, sympathetic.
soften *v* calm, cushion, ease,

lighten, relax, soothe, subdue.
soil *n* clay, dirt, dust, earth, ground, loam.
soil *v* contaminate, dirty, foul, pollute, stain, tarnish.
soldier *n* commando, fighter, GI, gunner, lancer, marine, mercenary, sapper, sentry, squaddy, trooper, warrior.
solemn *adj* **1** earnest, glum, grave, serious, thoughtful. **2** awe-inspiring, formal, grand, imposing, majestic, stately.
solid *adj* **1** compact, concrete, dense, firm, hard, rigid, stable, strong, sturdy, substantial, unweighty. **2** genuine, pure, real, reliable, tangible. **3** constant, decent, dependable, reliable, sensible, trusty, upstanding. **4** robust, sound, steady, sturdy, well made.
solidify *adj* cake, coagulate, congeal, harden, jell, set.
solution *n* **1** answer, explanation, key, resolution, result. **2** blend, compound, emulsion, mixture, solvent, suspension.
solve *v* answer, clarify, decipher, explain, interpret, work out.
sombre *adj* dark, drab, dull, gloomy, sad.
somebody *n* celebrity, dignitary, household name, public figure, star, superstar, VIP; (*Inf*) big noise, big shot, bigwig, celeb.
sometimes *adv* at times, every now and then, every so often, from time to time, now and then, occasionally, off and on, once in a while.
soon *adv* any minute now, in a minute, in a moment, in a short time, in the near future, shortly.
sore *adj* **1** angry, burning, chafed, hurting, inflamed, painful, raw, sensitive, smarting, tender. **2** annoying, distressing, grievous, harrowing, severe, sharp, troublesome. **3** acute, critical, desperate, dire, extreme, pressing, urgent. **4** angry, grieved, hurt, irritated, pained, resentful, stung, upset, vexed; (*Inf*) peeved.
sorrow *n* grief, regret, sadness.
sorrowful *n* anguish, distress, grief, heartache, misery, regret, sadness, unhappiness, woe.
sorrowful *v* agonize, be sad, grieve, mourn, weep.
sorry *adj* **1** apologetic, regretful, repentant. **2** distressed, grieved, sad, sorrowful. **3** compassionate, moved, sympathetic. **4** dismal, miserable, pitiful, shabby, vile.
sort *n* brand, breed, category, class, family, group, kind, make, order, quality, race, species, style, type, variety.
sort *v* arrange, assort, catalogue, classify, distribute, grade, group, order, rank, select.
sort out *v* **1** clear up, organize, put straight, resolve, tidy up. **2** choose, pick out, select, sift.
sound *n* din, noise, resonance, tone, voice. **3** idea, impression, look, tenor. **4** earshot, hearing, range.
sound *adj* **1** complete, entire. **2** fit, healthy, robust, sturdy. **3** fair, just, logical, rational, sensible, wise. **4** established, proven, recognized, reputable, safe, secure, stable. **5** deep, peaceful, undisturbed.
sound *v* fathom, plumb, probe.
sour *adj* **1** acid, bitter, pungent, sharp, tart. **2** cynical, grumpy, irritable.
space *n* **1** capacity, expanse, extension, room, scope, volume. **2** blank, distance, gap, interval, lacuna, omission. **3** duration, interval, period, time, while.
spacious *adj* ample, broad, capacious, comfortable, commodious, expansive, extensive, huge, large, roomy, sizeable, uncrowded, vast.

How is sound measured

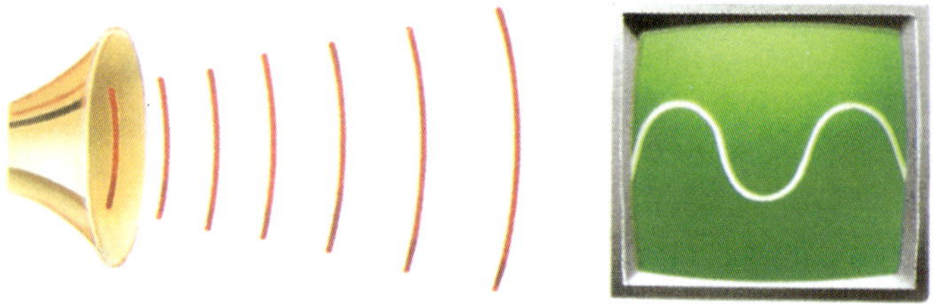

Sound travels as waves. The shape of the wave determines the kind of sound produced. The pitch of a sound depends on the frequency of the sound waves. The frequency of the sound is how many waves or vibrations the sound makes in one second measured in hertz (Hz). How loud the sound is depends on the magnitude or height of its waves. As sounds push air molecules together, air pressure rises. Between vibrations air pressure falls. It is this change in air pressure that can be shown as waves on a screen when sounds are made near a microphone.

span *n* **1** amount, distance, extent, length, reach, spread, stretch. **2** duration, period, spell.
span *v* arch across, bridge, cross, link, range over.
spank *v* **1** cuff, slap, smack; (*Inf*) belt, give someone a good hiding, tan, wallop, whack.
spare *adj* additional, extra, free, leftover, reserve, odd, over, surplus, unused, unwanted; (*Inf*) going begging.
spare *v* **1** do without, give, grant, let someone have, part with. **2** deal leniently with, have mercy on, pardon, release, save from; (*Inf*) go easy on, let off.
spark *n* flare, flash, flicker.
sparkle *v* **1** beam, flash, glint, glow, shimmer, shine, twinkle. **2** bubble, effervesce, fizz, fizzle.
sparkling *v* **1** brilliant, dazzling, flashing, glinting, glittering, shimmering, shining, twinkling. **2** aerated, bubbling, carbonated, effervescent, fizzy, foaming.
speak *v* **1** communicate, converse, express, pronounce, say, state, talk, tell, utter, voice. **2** address, argue, lecture, plead; (*Inf*) spiel.
speaker *n* lecturer, orator, public speaker, spokesman, spokesperson, spokeswoman.
special *adj* **1** distinguished, exceptional, extraordinary, momentous, significant, unique, unusual. **2** appropriate, certain, characteristic, distinctive, individual, particular, peculiar, precise, specialized, specific. **3** chief, main, major, particular, primary.
species *n* breed, category, class, collection, description, genus, group, kind, sort, type, variety.
specific *adj* **1** clear-out, definite, explicit, precise, unambiguous. **2** characteristic, distinguishing, peculiar, special.
specify *v* be specific about, cite, define, designate, itemize, mention, name, stipulate.
spectacular *adj* astonishing, breathtaking, daring, dazzling, dramatic, eye-catching, glorious, impressive, magnificent, sensational, splendid, striking; (*Inf*) fantastic, out of this world, stunning.
spectator *n* bystander, eye-witness, observer, onlooker, viewer, watcher, witness.
speech *n* **1** conversation, dialogue, discussion, talk. **2** address, lecture, oration.
speechless *adj* **1** dumb, inarticulate, mute, silent, tongue-tied. **2** amazed, astounded, dazed, dumbfounded, dumb-struck, shocked, thunderstruck.
speed *n* acceleration, haste, hurry, momentum, pace, quickness, rapidity, rush, swiftness, velocity.
speedy *adj* fast, fleet, fleet of foot, hasty, headlong, hurried, nimble, prompt, quick, rapid, swift, winged.
spell *v* **1** add up to, amount to, cause, result in. **2** clarify, detail, itemize, set out, stipulate.
spell *n* **1** bout, course, interval, patch, period, season, stint, stretch, term, time, tour of duty, turn. **2** abracadabra, bewitch, charm, sorcery, witchery.
spend *v* **1** disburse, lay out, pay out; (*Inf*) dish out, fork out, shell out, splash out. **2** consume, deplete, dispense, drain, empty, fritter away, squander, use up, waste; (*Inf*) blow the money.
sphere *n* **1** ball, circle, globe, orb. **2** capacity, compass, domain, field, function, province, range, realm, scope, territory, walk of life.
spherical *n* globe-shaped,

Sparks fly all around during an industrial welding process.

What is the DNA spiral?

The series of molecule chains known as DNA is formed in a spiral, making a shape known as a double helix. DNA is the name given to a chemical deoxyribonucleic acid. It contains the instructions for making and controlling each living thing. Inside the cell's nucleus, DNA forms chromosomes. Living things have different numbers of chromosomes. Human beings have 46 aranged in 23 pairs. Each of us has inherited one half of each chromosome from our father and the other half from our mother. The DNA structure was discovered in 1953 by James Watson and Francis Crick. The work of Rosalind Franklin another British scientist had helped them make the discovery.

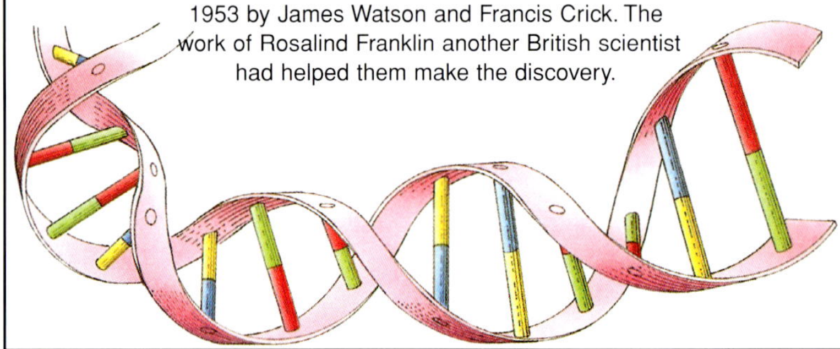

rotund, round.

spice *n* relish, savour, seasoning; colour, excitement, gusto, pep, piquancy, tang; (*Inf*) kick, zap, zip.

spike *n* barb, point, prong, spine.

spike *v* impale, spear, spit, stick.

spill *v* discharge, disgorge, overflow, overturn, scatter, shed, slope over, spill over, upset.

spin *v* **1** gyrate, pirouette, reel, revolve, rotate, turn, twirl, twist, wheel, whirl. **2** be giddy, be in a whirl.

spin *n* gyration, revolution, roll, twist, whirl.

spiral *adj* circular, cochlear, cochleate, coiled. corkscrew, helical, scrolled, twist, voluted, whorled, ending.

spiral *n* coil, corkscrew, helix, screw, twist, volute, whorl.

spirit *n* **1** air, breath, life, life force, soul. **2** character, essence, outlook, quality, temperament. **3** courage, energy, force, grit, life, mettle, resolution, sparkle, vigour, warmth, zest; (*Inf*) guts, spunk. **4** motivation, resolve, willpower. **5** atmosphere, feeling, humour, tone. **6** intention, meaning, purpose, sense, substance. **7** apparition, ghost, phantom, shadow, spectre, vision; (*Inf*) spook. **8** vindictive; (*Inf*) bitchy, catty.

splash *v* **1** shower, spatter, spray, spread, sprinkle, squirt, wet. **2** bathe, paddle, wade, wallow. **3** break, buffet, dash, plash, plop, wash. **4** flaunt, headline, plaster, publicize.

splendid *adj* **1** brilliant, grand, heroic, magnificent, outstanding, remarkable, superb, supreme. **2** dazzling, gorgeous, imposing, impressive, lavish, magnificent, ornate, sumptuous, superb. **3** excellent, first-class, glorious, marvellous, wonderful; (*Inf*) fab, fantastic, great, terrific. **4** bright, brilliant, glittering, glowing, lustrous, radiant.

splendour *n* brightness, brilliance, dazzle, display, glory, grandeur, lustre, pomp, show.

split *v* **1** branch, break, break up, burst, come apart, come undone, crack, fork, gape, go separate ways, open, part, pull apart, rip, slash, slit, snap. **2** allocate, allot, apportion, carve up, distribute, divide, dole out, share out, slice up; (*Inf*) divvy up.

split *n* **1** breach, crack, damage, division, fissure, gap, slash, slit, tear. **2** break-up, division, partition, rift, rupture.

split-up *n* break-up, divorce, go separate ways, part company, separate.

spoil *v* **1** blemish, damage, deface, destroy, disfigure, harm, impair, injure, mess up, ruin, upset, wreck. **2** baby, indulge, kill with kindness, molly-coddle, overindulge, pamper, spoon-feed. **3** curdle, decay, decompose, go bad, rot; (*Inf*) go off.

spoken *adj* by word of mouth, expressed, oral, phonetic, put into words, said, told, unwritten, uttered, verbal, voice, voiced.

sponsor *n* backer, godparent, guarantor, patron, promoter; (*Inf*) angel.

sponsor *v* back, finance, fund, guarantee, lend one's name to, patronize, promote, put up the money for, subsidize.

spontaneous *adj* impulsive, instinctive, natural, unforced.

sport *n* **1** amusement, entertainment, exercise, game, pastime, physical activity, play, recreation. **2** banter, fun, jest, joking, merriment, teasing; (*Inf*) kidding. **3** buffoon, butt, derision, fair game, game, laughing stock, mockery, plaything, ridicule.

sport *v* amuse oneself, cavort, entertain oneself, exhibit, gambol, have on show, romp, show off, wear.
spot *n* **1** blemish, blot, boil, flaw, mark, pimple, smudge, speck, speckle, stain, zit. **2** locality, location, place, point, position, scene, site, situation; difficulty, mess, plight, predicament, quandary, tight corner, trouble; (*Inf*) fix, hot water, jam. **3** bit, bite, morsel, smidgen. **4** little, splash.
spot *v* **1** catch sight of, detect, discern, identify, make out, observe, pick out, recognize, see, sight. **2** blot, dot, fleck, mark, mottle, soil, spatter, speckle, splodge, splotch, stain, sully, taint, tarnish.
spotted *adj* dappled, dotted, flecked, mottled, pied, polka-dot, pecked, speckled.
spout *v* discharge, emit, erupt, gush, jet, shoot, spray, spurt, squirt, stream, surge.
sprawl *v* flop, loll, lounge, ramble, slouch, slump, spread, straggle, trail.
spray *v* atomize, diffuse, scatter, shower, sprinkle.
spray *n* **1** drizzle, droplets, fine mist, moisture, spindrift, spoondrift. **2** aerosol, atomizer, sprinkler.
spread *v* **1** arrange, display, open out, unroll. **2** broaden, expand, extend, lengthen, mushroon, proliferate, widen. **3** apply, cover a surface with. **4** advertise, broadcast, circulate, make known, pass round, publicize, transmit.
spread *n* **1** advance, escalation, expansion, increase, proliferation, transmission. **2** extent, period, reach, span, stretch, sweep, term.
spring *v* **1** bounce, bound, hop, jump, leap, rebound, recoil, vault. **2 spring from** arise, be derived, be descended, come, derive, descend, emanate, emerge, grow, issue, originate, proceed, start, stem. **3 spring up** appear, come into being, develop, mushroom, shoot up.
spring *n* **1** bound, buck, hop, jump, leap, vault. **2** bounce, elasticity, flexibility, recoil, springiness; (*Inf*) give. **3** beginning, cause, fountain-head, origin, root, source, well, wellspring.
sprinkle *v* dredge, dust, pepper, powder, scatter, shower, spray, strew.
sprout *v* bud, develop, emerge, germinate, grow, shoot up, spring up.
spur *v* **1** animate, drive, goad, incite, press, prompt, prick. **2** impetus, incentive, motive, stimulus.
spy *n* double agent, foreign agent, mole, secret agent, secret service agent, undercover agent.

The spotted coat of the leopard is tawny yellow with black dappled spots.

During dry periods, a lawn sprinkler can be a useful tool to irrigate large areas of lawn and ensure that the grass survives the drought.

spy *v* catch sight of, descry, espy, glimpse, notice, observe, set eyes on, spot.
squabble *v* argue, bicker, brawl, clash, dispute, fight, have words, quarrel, row, wrangle.
squabble *n* argument, difference of opinion, disagreement, dispute, fight, row, spat, tiff; (*Inf*) barney, scrap, set-to.
squad *n* band, company, crew, force, gang, group, team, troop.
squalid *adj* broken-down, decayed, dirty, disgusting, filthy, foul, low, nasty, run-down, seedy, sleazy, slovenly, slummy, sordid, unclean.
squalor *n* decay, filth, foulness, meanness, sleaziness, slumminess, squalidness, wretchedness.
squander *v* consume, expend, fritter away, lavish, misuse, spend, spend like water, throw away, waste; (*Inf*) blow.
square *adj* **1** above board, decent, fair, fair and square, genuine, honest, just, straight, straightforward; (*Inf*) on the

level. **2** bourgeois, conservative, conventional, old-fashioned, out of date, straight, strait-laced; (*Inf*) behind the times.
square *n* **1** market square, quadrangle, town square, village square. **2** conservative, conventionalist, die-hard, old fogy, traditionalist; (*Inf*) fuddy-duddy, stick-in-the-mud.
squash *v* **1** compress, crumple, crush, distort, flatten, mash, pound, press, pulp, smash, stamp on, trample down. **2** crowd, pack, quash, squeeze.
squeeze *n* **1** clasp, embrace, handclasp, hold, hug. **2** congestion, crowd, crush, jam, press, squash.
stab *v* bayonet, cut, gore, injure, jab, knife, pierce, puncture, run through, spear, stick, thrust, transfix, wound.
stab *n* **1** gash, incision, injury, jab, puncture, thrust, wound. **2** ache, pang, spasm, throb, twinge. **3** attempt, endeavour, try, venture.
stable *adj* abiding, constant, deep-rooted, durable, enduring, established, fast, firm, fixed, immutable, invariable, lasting, permanent, reliable, secure, sound, steadfast, steady, strong, sturdy, sure, unalterable, unchangeable, unwavering, well-founded.
stack *n* **1** accumulation, collection, hoard, mound, mountain, pile, mass, stockpile, store. **2** abundance, amplitude; (*Inf*) bags, heaps, lots, oodles, tons. **3** hayrick, haystack.
stack *v* accumulate, amass, bank up, collect, heap up, load, pile up, stockpile, store.
staff *n* **1** employees, lecturers, officers, personnel, teachers, team, workers, workforce. **2** cane, pole, prop, rod, stave, wand.
stage *n* division, juncture, lap, leg, length, level, period, phase, point, step.
stage *v* **1** direct, perform, present, put on. **2** arrange, engineer, lay on, orchestrate, put together.
stagger *v* **1** falter, hesitate, lurch, reel, sway, teeter, totter, waver, wobble. **2** amaze, astonish, astound, confound, dumbfound, flabbergast, overwhelm, shock, stun, surprise, take someone's breath away, throw off balance; (*Inf*) bowl over, strike someone dumb. **3** alternate, overlap, step, zigzag.
stain *v* **1** blemish, blot, colour, dirty, discolour, dye, mark, soil, spot, tarnish, tinge. **2** blacken, contaminate, corrupt, disgrace, drag through the mud, taint.
stain *n* **1** blemish, blot, discolouration, dye, spot, tint. **2** blemish, blot, disgrace, dishonour, infamy, reproach, shame, slur, stigma.
stale *adj* decayed, dry, faded, flat, fusty, hard, insipid, musty, old, sour, stagnant, tasteless.
stamp *v* beat, crush, trample; engrave, fix, impress, imprint, inscribe, mark, mould, print.
stamp *n* **1** brand, cast, earmark, hallmark, imprint, mark, mould, signature. **2** breed, cast, character, cut, description, fashion, form, kind, sort, type.
stampede *n* charge, flight, rout, rush, scattering.
stamp out *v* crush, destroy, eliminate, eradicate, extinguish, extirpate, extinguish, extirpate, put down, put out, quell, quench, scotch, suppress.
stance *n* **1** bearing, carriage, posture. **2** attitude, position, stand, standpoint, viewpoint.
stand *v* **1** be erect, be upright, be vertical, rise. **2** erect, mount, place, position, put, rank, set.

Stampeding buffalo in the United States and Canada used to be a formidable sight. The species was drastically reduced in numbers due to excessive hunting which led to their near extinction. Today, buffalo occupy small, protected areas and conservationists estimate their numbers at approximately 200,000.

There are countless stars in space. Millions of stars form groups which are known as galaxies. The stars in a galaxy are held together by gravity. The Earth is a part of the Milky Way galaxy which is a spiral shape. There may be as many as 100 billion galaxies of stars in the universe and many of them are grouped together in clusters with huge areas of space between them.

3 belong, continue, exist, halt, hold, obtain, pause, remain, rest, stay, stop. **4** abide, allow, bear, cope with, endure, experience, handle, stomach, submit to, suffer, support, sustain, take, tolerate, undergo, weather, with stand; (*Inf*) put up with, wear.

stand *n* **1** halt, rest, standstill, stay, stopover. **2** attitude, determination, form, stand, opinion, position, stance, standpoint.

standard *n* average, benchmark, criterion, example, gauge, grade, guide, measure, model, norm, pattern, principle, rule, sample, specification, touchstone, type, yardstick.

standard *adj* accepted, average, basic, normal, popular, regular, set, staple, stock, typical, usual.

standardize *v* bring into line, mass-produce, stereotype.

stand out *v* attract attention, be highlighted, be prominent, catch the eye, project; (*Inf*) stare one in the face, stick out a mile.

star *n* **1** asteroid, planet, planetoid. **2** celebrity, dignitary, idol, lead, gruous, in disagreement, out of harmony, out of line, out of phase, pulling different ways. **3** leading lady, leading man, luminary, main attraction, name, principal, somebody, superstar, VIP; (*Inf*) celeb, draw.

star *adj* brilliant, celebrated, illustrious, leading, major, principal, prominent, talented, well-known.

stare *v* **1** ape, gaze, goggle, look, ogle. **2** be blatant, be obvious, be prominent, stand out.

start *v* **1** begin, commerce, depart, get on the road, get under way, leave, set off, set out; (*Inf*) go ahead, hit the road, pitch in. **2** activate, embark upon, engender, enter upon, get going, initiate, instigate, make a beginning, open, originate, set about, set in motion, start the ball rolling, take the first step, turn on; (*Inf*) kick off, take the plunge. **3** begin, create, establish, father, found, inaugurate, initiate, institute, introduce, launch, lay the foundations of, pioneer, set up. **4** blench, flinch, jerk, jump, recoil, shy, twitch.

start *n* **1** beginning, birth, commencement, dawn, first steps, foundation, inauguration, inception, initiation, inset, opening, outset; (*Inf*) kickoff; **2** advantage, edge, head start, lead. **3** convulsion, jar, jump, spasm, twitch.

startle *v* agitate, alarm, amaze, astonish, astound, frighten, make someone jump, scare, shock, surprise, take someone aback; (*Inf*) give someone a turn.

starving *adj* faint from lack of food, famished, hungering, hungry, ravenous, sharp-set, starved; (*Inf*) able to eat a horse.

state *v* assert, declare, explain, express, present, propound, put, report, say, specify, voice.

state *n* **1** case, category, circumstances, condition, mode, pass, plight, position, predicament, shape, situation, state of affairs. **2** attitude, frame of mind, mood, spirits. **3** ceremony, dignity, display, glory, grandeur, majesty, pomp, splendour, style.

state *n* commonwealth, country, federation, government, kingdom, land, nation, republic, territory.

statement *n* account, comment, communiqué, declaration, explanation, notice, proclamation, recital, relation, report, testimony.

station *n* **1** base, depot, headquarters, location, place, position, post, seat, situation.

The steep, world famous White Cliffs of Dover have been a British stronghold since ancient times. Dover was Julius Caesar's first point of attack in the Roman invasion of Britain in 55BC. It is an important port and links Britain to Europe via sea crossings and the Eurotunnel car and rail services to France.

2 appointment, business, calling, employment, grade, occupation, position, post, rank, situation, sphere, standing, status.

station *v* assign, establish, fix, garrison, install, locate, place, post, set, stand.

stationary *adj* at a standstill, fixed, inert, moored, motionless, parked, standing, static, stock-still, unmoving.

status *n* condition, consequence, degree, distinction, eminence, grade, position, prestige, rank, standing.

stay *v* **1** abide, continue, delay, establish oneself, halt, hover, linger, loiter, pause, put down roots, remain, reside, settle, sojourn, stand, stay put, stop, tarry, wait; (*Inf*) hang around. **2** adjourn, defer, discontinue, hold over, put off, suspend.

stay *n* holiday, stopover, visit.

steady *adj* **1** firm, fixed, stable, substantial. **2** balanced, calm, dependable, level-headed, reliable, sedate, sensible, serene, settled. **3** consistent, constant, continuous, even, nonstop, persistent, regular, rhythmic.

steady *v* balance, brace, secure, stabilize, support.

steal *v* **1** appropriate, be light-fingered, embezzle, filch, make off with, misappropriate, pilfer, pirate, poach, shoplift, take, thieve, walk off with; (*Inf*) lift, nick, pinch, swipe. **2** creep, slink, slip, sneak, tiptoe.

stealth *n* furtiveness, secrecy, slyness, sneakiness, stealthiness, surreptitiousness, unobtrusiveness.

stealthy *adj* clandestine, covert, furtive, secretive, skulking, sly, sneaking, underhand.

steep *adj* **1** abrupt, headlong, precipitous, sheer. **2** excessive, exhorbitant, extortionate, extreme, high, overpriced, stiff; (*Inf*) over the top, OTT. **2** uncalled-for, unreasonable.

steer *v* **1** control, direct, govern, guide, pilot. **2 steer clear of** avoid, evade, give a wide berth to, shun.

stem *n* axis, branch, peduncle, shoot, stalk, stock, trunk.

stem *v* ring to a standstill, check, contain, curb, dam, hold back, oppose, resist, restrain, stanch, stop, withstand.

step *n* **1** footfall, footprint, footstep, gait, impression, pace, print, stride, trace, track, walk. **2** act, action, deed, expedient, manoeuvre, means, measure, move, procedure, proceeding. **3 take steps** act, intervene, move in, prepare, take action, take measures, take the initiative. **4** advance, advancement, move, phase, point, process, progression, stage. **5** degree, level, rank, remove. **6** in step coinciding, conforming, in harmony in line. **7 out of step** erratic, in disagreement, out of harmony, out of line, out of phase, pulling different ways.

step *v* move, pace, tread, walk.

stereotype *n* formula, mould, pattern, perceived idea.

stereotype *v* categorize, dub, pigeonhole, standardize, take to be, typecast.

sterile *adj* **1** bare, barren, dry, empty, fruitless, unproductive, unprofitable, unprolific.

2 antiseptic, aseptic, disinfected, germ-free, sterilized.
stern *adj* austere, bitter, cruel, frowning, grim, hard, hard, inflexible, relentless, rigid, rigorous, serious, severe, steely, strict, unrelenting, unsparing, unyielding.
stick *v* **1** adhere, affix, attach, bind, bond, cement, cling, fasten, fix, fuse, glue, hold, hold on, join, paste, weld. **2** dig, gore, insert, jab, penetrate, pierce, pin, poke, prod, puncture, spear, stab. **3 stick out** bulge, extend, jut, protrude, show. **4** become immobilized, catch, clog, jam, lodge, snag, stop. **5** linger, persist, remain, stay. **6** defend, stand up for, support, take the part of side of, uphold.
stick *n* baton, birch, cane, pole, rod, staff, stake, twig, wand.
sticky *adj* **1** adhesive, clinging, gluey, glutinous, gummy, syrupy, tacky, tenacious, viscous; (*Inf*) gooey. **2** awkward, delicate, difficult, embarrassing, nasty, painful, tricky, unpleasant; (*Inf*) hairy.
stiff *adj* **1** brittle, firm, hard, hardened, inflexible, rigid, solid, solidified, taut, tense, tight. **2** artificial, cold, formal, prim, uneasy, unrelaxed, wooden. **3** arthritic, awkward, clumsy, crude, graceless, jerky, ungainly, ungraceful; (*Inf*) rheumaticky.
stiffen *v* brace, congeal, crystallize, harden, jell, reinforce, set, solidify, starch, tense, thicken. silence, smother, suppress.
still *adj* at rest, calm, hushed, inert, lifeless, motionless, peaceful, quiet, restful, serene, silent, smooth, stationary, tranquil, undisturbed, unruffled.
still *v* allay, alleviate, appease, calm, hush, lull, pacify, quiet, quieten, settle, silence, smooth, smooth over, soothe, subdue, tranquillize.
still *conj* but, however, nevertheless, notwithstanding, yet.
stimulate *v* animate, arouse, encourage, excite, fan, fire, foment, goad, impel, incite, inflame, instigate, prompt, provoke, quicken, rouse, spur, urge; (*Inf*) turn on.

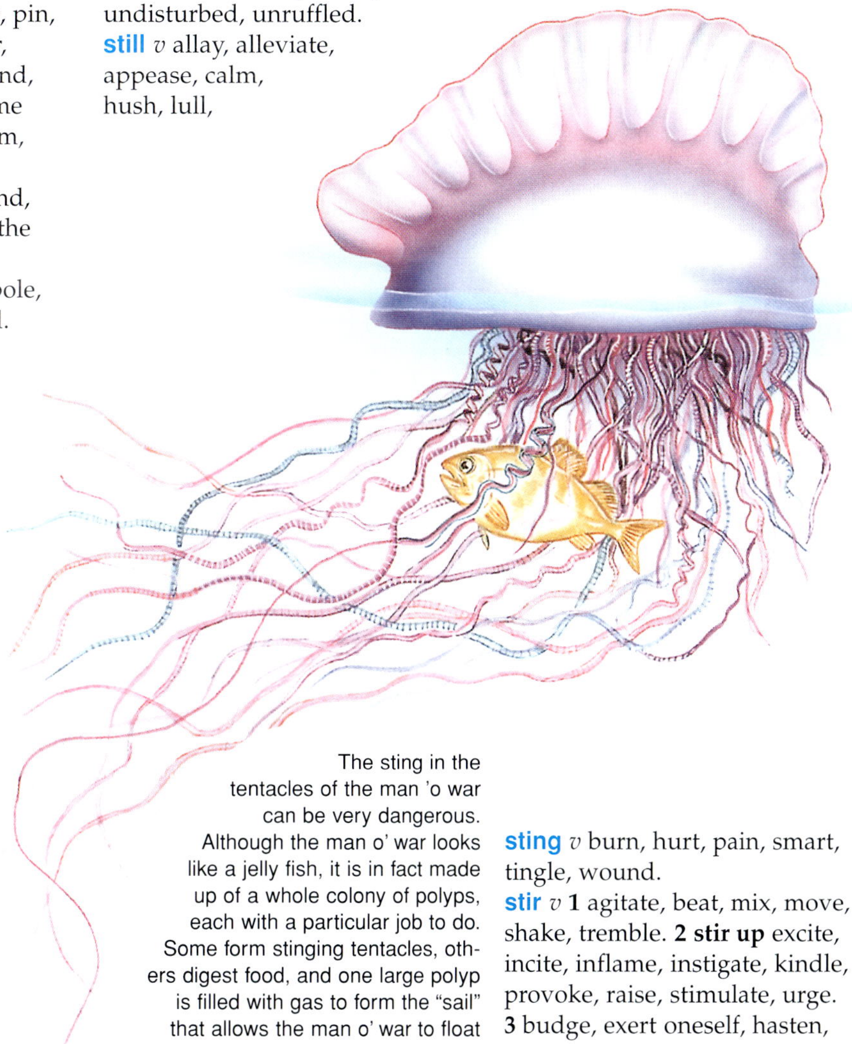

The sting in the tentacles of the man 'o war can be very dangerous. Although the man o' war looks like a jelly fish, it is in fact made up of a whole colony of polyps, each with a particular job to do. Some form stinging tentacles, others digest food, and one large polyp is filled with gas to form the "sail" that allows the man o' war to float and be blown by the wind

sting *v* burn, hurt, pain, smart, tingle, wound.
stir *v* **1** agitate, beat, mix, move, shake, tremble. **2 stir up** excite, incite, inflame, instigate, kindle, provoke, raise, stimulate, urge. **3** budge, exert oneself, hasten, make an effort, mill about,

move; (*Inf*) be up and about, get a move on, get moving, look lively, shake a leg.
stir *n* activity, agitation, bustle, commotion, disorder, disturbance, excitement, flurry, fuss, movement, to-do, uproar.
stomach *n* **1** abdomen, belly, paunch; (*Inf*) gut, insides, pot, spare tyre, tummy. **2** appetite, desire, inclination, mind, relish, taste.
stomach *v* abide, bear, endure, reconcile oneself to, submit to, suffer, swallow, take, tolerate; (*Inf*) put up with.
stoop *v* be round-shouldered, bend, bow, crouch, descend, hunch, incline, kneel, lean.
stop *v* **1** be over, break off, bring to a halt, bring to a standstill, cease, come to an end, conclude, cut short, end, finish, halt, leave off, pause, peter out, put an end to, quit, refrain, shutdown, stall, terminate; (*Inf*) call it a day, cut out, pack in. **2** arrest, bar, block, break, check, close, forestall, frustrate, hinder, hold back, impede, intercept, interrupt, obstruct, plug, prevent, rein in, repress, restrain, seal, silence, staunch, stem, suspend. **3** break one's journey, lodge, put up, rest, sojourn, stay, tarry.
stop *n* **1** cessation, conclusion, discontinuation, end, finish, halt, standstill break, rest, sojourn, stay, stopover, visit. **2** bar, block, break, check, control, hindrance, impediment, plug, stoppage. **3** depot, destination, halt, stage, station, termination, terminus.
store *v* hoard, keep in reserve, lay by, put aside, put by, put in storage, reserve, salt away, save, stock, stockpile; (*Inf*) stash.
store *n* **1** fund, hoard, plenty, quantity, reserve, reservoir, stockpile, supply, wealth. **2** chain store, department store, market, mart, outlet, shop, supermarket. **3** depository, storehouse, store-room, warehouse.
storm *n* **1** blast, blizzard, cyclone, gale, gust, hurricane, squall, tempest, tornado, whirl-wind. **2** anger, commotion, disturbance, furore, hubbub, outburst, roar, rumpus, turmoil.
storm *v* assail, assault, beset, charge, rush, take by storm.
storm *n* assault, attack, blitz, blitzkrieg, offensive, onset, onslaught, rush.
storm *v* **1** bluster, complain, fume, rage, rant, rave, scold, thunder. **2** flounce, fly, rush, stalk, stamp, stomp; (*Inf*) fly off the handle.
stormy *adj* blustery, boisterous, gusty, raging, rough, squally, turbulent, wild, windy.
story *n* **1** account, anecdote, chronicle, history, legend, record, relation, romance, tale, version, yarn. **2** article, feature, news item, report, scoop.
straight *adj* **1** direct, near, short. **2** aligned, horizontal, in line, level, perpendicular, plumb, right, smooth, square, true, upright, vertical. **3** accurate, decent, fair, honest, law-abiding, reliable, trustworthy. **4** arranged, in order, orderly, organized, ship shape, tidy. **5** continuous, non-stop, sustained, uninterrupted. **6** neat, undiluted, unmixed.
straight *adv* as the crow flies, at once, directly.

Red means 'stop' and green means 'go'. Everyone knows without thinking about it when they see a traffic light. Seeing the colour is much quicker than reading or hearing the word.

Storms occur due to changes in our atmosphere from heating and cooling. This produces the weather we experience on Earth.

straightaway *adv* directly, immediately, instantly, now, on the spot, right away, straight off, there and then, this instant, without any delay, without ore ado.
straightforward *adj* **1** above board, candid, direct, forthright, genuine, guileless, honest, open, sincere, truthful. **2** clear-cut, easy, elementary, routine, simple, uncomplicated, undemanding.
strain *v* **1** draw tight, extend, stretch, tauten, tighten. **2** drive, exert, injure, overexert, pull, push to the limit, sprain, tax, tear, twist, wrench. **3** make a supreme effort, strive, struggle. **4** filter, percolate, purify, riddle, screen, seep, separate, sieve, sift.
strain *n* **1** effort, exertion, force, injury, pull, sprain, struggle, tension, wrench. **2** anxiety, burden, pressure, stress.
strained *adj* artificial, awkward, constrained, difficult, embarrassed, false, forced, laboured, put on, self-conscious, stiff, tense, uneasy, unnatural, unrelaxed.
strand *n* fibre, filament, length, lock, rope, string, thread, tress, twist.
stranded *adj* aground, ashore, beached, cast away, grounded, marooned, wrecked.
strange *adj* astonishing, bizarre, curious, extraordinary, fantastic, marvellous, mystifying, peculiar, perplexing, weird. **2** alien, exotic, foreign, new, novel, unfamiliar, unknown, untried.
stranger *n* alien, foreigner, guest, incomer, new arrival, newcomer, outlander, unknown, visitor.
strangle *v* **1** asphyxiate, choke, garrotte, smother, strangulate, suffocate, throttle. **2** gag, inhibit, repress, stifle, suppress.
strap *n* bind, buckle, fasten, lash, secure, tie, truss.
strategy *n* approach, grand plan, manoeuvring, plan, policy, procedure, programme, scheme.
streak *n* **1** band, layer, line, slash, smear, strip, stripe, stroke, vein. **2** dash, element, strain, touch, trace, vein.
streak *v* dart, flash, fly, hurtle, speed, sprint, sweep, tear, whistle, zoom; (*Inf*) move like greased lightning, whiz.
stream *n* beck, brook, burn, course, creek, current, drift, flow, river, run, rush, surge, tide, torrent, tributary.
stream *v* cascade, course, emit, flood flow, glide, gush, issue, our, run, shed, spill, spout.
street *v* avenue, boulevard, lane, road, roadway, row, terrace, thoroughfare.
strength *n* **1** backbone, courage, fortitude, health, might, muscle, stamina, toughness. **2** energy, force, intensity, power, spirit, vigour. **3** anchor, mainstay, strong point, tower of strength.
strengthen *v* **1** fortify, invigorate, nourish, rejuvenate, restore, toughen. **2** bolster, brace, build up, buttress, enhance, establish, give a boost to, harden, heighten, increase, intensify, justify, reinforce, substantiate, support.
strenuous *adj* **1** arduous, demanding, exhausting, hard, taxing, tough going, up hill. **2** active, bold, determined, eager, earnest, energetic, persistent, resolute, spirited, strong, tireless, vigorous, zealous.
stress *n* **1** emphasis, force, importance, significance, urgency, weight. **2** anxiety, burden, nervous, tension, oppression, pressure, strain, tautness, tension, trauma, worry; (*Inf*) hassle. **3** accent, accentuation, beat, emphasis.
stress *v* accentuate, dwell on, emphasize, harp on, lay emphasis upon, point out, repeat, rub in, underline, underscore.
stretch *v* **1** cover, extend, put forth, reach, spread, unfold, unroll. **2** distend, expand, inflate,

lengthen, pull out of shape, strain, swell, tighten.
stretch *n* area, distance, expanse, extent, spread, sweep, tract.
strict *adj* **1** firm, harsh, severe, stern, stringent. **2** accurate, exact, meticulous, precise, true. **3** absolute, complete, perfect, total, utter.
strike *v* **1** beat, box, hammer, hit, pound, smack, smite, thump; (*Inf*) clobber, clout, lay a finger on, sock, wallop. **2** bump into, clash, collide with, hit, run into, smash into, touch. **3** drive, force, hit. **4** assault, attack, devastate, set upon. **5** achieve, arrive at, reach. **6** down tools, mutiny, revolt, walk out.
striking *adj* astonishing, dazzling, extraordinary, memorable, outstanding, stunning, wonderful; (*Inf*) great, smashing.
string *n* **1** cord, fibre, twine. **2** chain, file, line, procession, queue, row, sequence, series. 3 orchestra instruments (strings).
strip *v* **1** bare, dismantle, empty, loot, pillage, ransack, rob, spoil. **2** disrobe, uncover, undress.
strip *n* band, belt, bit, fillet, piece, ribbon, shred.
stroke *n* attack, collapse, fit, seizure, shock.
stroke *v* caress, fondle, pat, rub.
stroll *v* amble, ramble, saunter, stretch one's legs, take a turn, toddle, wander; (*Inf*) mosey.

Instruments of the Orchestra

Strings are one of the sections of an orchestra. Orchestras have different instruments that produce sounds in different ways, but all cause the air to vibrate in order to carry sound to listening ears.

stroll *n* breath of fresh air, constitutional, excursion, promenade, ramble, turn, walk.
strong *adj* **1** athletic, hardy, Herculean, powerful, robust, stout, strapping, sturdy, tough, virile. **2** aggressive, brave, courageous, determined, hard as nails, resolute, tenacious; (*Inf*) gutsy. **3** dedicated, eager, intense, keen, zealous. **4** clear-cut, compelling, convincing, distinct, overpowering, persuasive, telling, urgent. **5** Draconian, drastic, extreme, forceful, severe. **6** durable, hard-wearing, heavy-duty, reinforced, sturdy, substantial, well-armed, **7** biting, concentrated, highly-flavoured, hot, spicy, undiluted.
struggle *v* **1** exert oneself, labour, strain, strive, work like a Trojan. **2** battle, compete, fight, grapple, scuffle, wrestle.
struggle *n* **1** effort, exertion, grind, labour, long haul, scramble, toil, work. **2** battle, brush, clash, conflict, encounter, hostilities, skirmish, strife, tussle.
stubborn *adj* bull-headed, dogged, inflexible, intractable, obstinate, pig-headed, tenacious, unbending, wilful.
stuck *adj* **1** cemented, fastened, firm, fixed, glued, joined. **2** at a loss, baffled, beaten, stumped; (*Inf*) up against a brick wall.
student *n* apprentice, disciple,

learner, observer, pupil, scholar, undergraduate.

studied *adj* **1** calculated, conscious, deliberate, intentional. **2** planned, wilful.

studious *adj* academic, bookish, careful, diligent, eager, hard-working, intellectual, scholarly, serious, thoughtful.

study *v* **1** apply oneself to, learn, meditate, pore over, read, read up; (*Inf*) cram, mug up, swot. **2** analyse, deliberate, examine, investigate, look into, peruse, research, scrutinize, survey.

study *n* **1** academic work, book work, lessons, reading, research, school work; (*Inf*) cramming, swotting. **2** analysis, attention, contemplation, examination, inquiry, investigation, review, scrutiny, survey.

stuff *v* **1** compress, cram, crowd, fill, force, jam, load, pack, pad, push, ram, shove, squeeze, stow, wedge. **2** gobble, gorge, guzzle, overindulge; (*Inf*) make a pig of oneself.

stuff *n* **1** belongings, bits and pieces, effects, equipment, gear, kit, luggage, paraphernalia, possessions, things; (*Inf*) clobber. **2** cloth, fabric, material, raw material, textile. **3** essence, matter, pith, substance.

stupid *adj* **1** brainless, deficient, dense, dim, doltish, dull, foolish, gullible, half-witted, moronic, naive, obtuse, simple, simple-minded, slow, slow-witted, sluggish, stolid, thick, unintelligent, witless; (*Inf*) dopey, dozy, dumb, slow on the uptake. **2** daft, futile, idiotic, ill-advised, irresponsible, ludicrous, mindless, pointless, unintelligent; (*Inf*) half-baked. **3** dazed, groggy, in a daze, punch drunk, semi-conscious, senseless, stunned, stupefied.

stupidity *n* **1** brainlessness, dimness, lack of intelligence, naivety, simplicity; (*Inf*) dopiness, doziness, dumbness. **2** absurdity, folly, foolishness, futility, irresponsibility, ludicrousness, lunacy, madness, rashness, senselessness, silliness.

sturdy *adj* athletic, durable, firm, hardy, powerful, robust, solid, substantial, well-made.

How a submarine submerges and surfaces

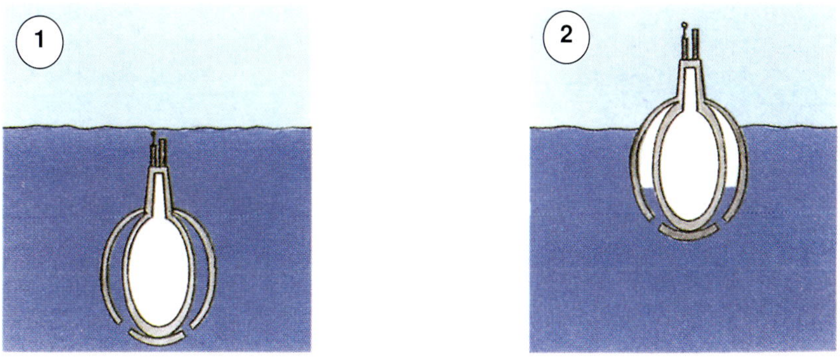

Submarines unlike ships are not always required to float! To make a submarine sink, or submerge, its density must be increased to be greater than that of the water. This is done by taking in water into ballast tanks attached to the submarine (1 above). To bring a submarine to the surface pumps force the water out of the tanks again (2). The submarine's density becomes less than that of water so it rises to the surface.

subjective *adj* biased, emotional, instinctive, intuitive, personal, prejudiced.

submerge *v* deluge, dip, drown, duck, engulf, flood, immerse, inundate, overflow, overwhelm, plummet, plunge, sink, swamp.

submission *n* **1** giving in, surrender. **2** resignation, submissiveness. **3** argument, proposal. **4** entry, handing in, presentation, submitting.

submit *v* **1** agree, comply, give in, resign oneself to, succumb, surrender, throw in the towel, toe the line, tolerate; (*Inf*) put up with. **2** commit, hand in, present, proffer, put forward, refer, table, tender.

subsidy *n* aidallowance, assistance, contribution, financial aid, grant, help, subvention, support.

substance *n* **1** body, element, fabric, material, stuff, texture. **2** essence, gist, main point, matter, meaning, subject, theme. **3** assets, estate, means, property, resources, wealth.

substantial *adj* ample, big, considerable, generous, goodly, important, large, significant, sizable, worthwhile; (*Inf*) tidy.

substantiate *v* confirm,

corroborate, prove, support, validate, verify.
substitute *v* change, commute, exchange, interchange, replace, switch; (*Inf*) swap.
substitute *n* agent, deputy, locum, relief, replacement, reserve, stand-by, stopgap, sub, surrogate, temporary; (*Inf*) temp.
substitute *adj* acting, additional, alternative, proxy, replacement, reserve, second, surrogate, temporary.
subtract *v* deduct, detract, diminish, remove, take away, take from, take off, withdraw.
suburbs *pl n* neighbourhood, outskirts, residential areas, suburbia.
succeed *v* **1** be successful, flourish, thrive, triumph, turn out well, work; (*Inf*) arrive, do all right for oneself, do the trick, get to the top, make it. **2** come next, follow, result.
success *n* **1** fame, favourable outcome, fortune, happiness, luck, prosperity, triumph. **2** best seller, big name, celebrity, market leader, sensation, star, VIP, winner; (*Inf*) hit, smash hit.
successful *adj* acknowledged, best-selling, booming, flourishing, lucky, lucrative, money-making, profitable, prosperous, rewarding, thriving, wealthy.
succulent *adj* juicy, luscious, lush, mellow, moist, mouth watering, rich.
sudden *adj* abrupt, hasty, impulsive, quick, rapid, rash, swift, unexpected, unforeseen.
suffer *v* **1** ache, agonize, be in pain, feel wretched, grieve, have bad time, hurt. **2** bear, experience, feel, go through, support, sustain, tolerate, undergo; (*Inf*) go through a lot, put up with. **3** be handicapped, be impaired, deteriorate, fall off.

Cacti are succulent plants and are modified to minimize water loss in the hot deserts where they live. Their fat, fleshy stems, store water so they can survive in times of little rain and are often covered with protective spikes.

suffering *n* affliction, agony, anguish, discomfort, distress, hardship, misery, ordeal, pain, torment, torture.
sufficient *adj* adequate, competent, enough, satisfactory.
suggest *v* **1** advise, advocate, move, propose, put forward, recommend. **2** hint, imply, indicate, insinuate, lead one to believe.
suggestion *n* **1** motion, plan, proposal, proposition, recommendation. **2** breathe, hint, indication, insinuation, suspicion, trace, whisper.
suit *v* **1** match, please, satisfy, tally. **2** accommodate, adapt, adjust, fashion, fit, modify, proportion, tailor.
suit *n* **1** action, case, lawsuit, proceeding, prosecution, trial. **2** clothing, costume, dress, outfit. **3** copy, emulate.
sulk *n* be in a huff, be put out, brood, pout; (*Inf*) take the hump. stifling, stuffy, sweltering.
sum *n* aggregate, amount, entirety, quantity, reckoning, score, sum total, tally, total.
summarize *v* abridge, condense, give the main points of, outline, précis, review, sum up.
summary *n* abstract, digest, extract, outline, précis, résumé, review, synopsis.
summit *n* apex, crown, crowning point, culmination, head, height, peak, pinnacle, top, zenith.
sunny *adj* **1** bright, brilliant, clear, fine, summery, sunlit, unclouded, without a cloud in the sky. **2** beaming, buoyant, cheerful, cheery, happy, joyful, light-hearted, optimistic, pleasant, smiling.

superior *adj* **1** better, grander, greater, preferred, unrivalled. **2** de luxe, distinguished, excellent, exceptional, exclusive, fine, first-class, first-rate, good quality, high-class, of the first order; (*Inf*) a cut above. **3** condescending, haughty, lofty, lordly, patronizing, pretentious, snobbish, supercilious; (*Inf*) stuck-up.
supernatural *adj* abnormal, dark, ghostly, hidden, miraculous, mysterious, mystic, occult, paranormal, phantom, psychic, spectral, supernatural, uncanny, unearthly, unnatural.
supply *v* afford, cater for, come up with, contribute, fill, furnish, give, grant, minister, produce, provide, replenish, satisfy, stock, store, victual, yield.
supply *n* **1** cache, fund, hoard, quantity, reserve, reservoir, source, stock, stockpile, store. **2** equipment, food, foodstuff, items, materials, necessities, provender, provisions, rations, stores.
support *v* **1** bear, bolster, brace, buttress, carry, hold, prop, reinforce, shore up, underpin. **2** to buoy up, finance, fund, keep, maintain, provide for, strengthen, subsidize, sustain, take care of. **3** advocate, assist, defend, help, promote, side with, stand up for. **4** endure, suffer, tolerate; (*Inf*) put up with.
support *n* **1** brace, foundation, lining, pillar, post, prop, underpinning. **2** assistance, backing, blessing, encouragement, friendship, help, moral support, protection, relief. **3** keep, livelihood, maintenance, subsistence, upkeep. **4** backbone, mainstay, supporter, tower of strength.

The surface of the Earth is composed of over 70% water. The Earth is the only planet in the Solar System that has water and which supports life. It has a constantly changing atmosphere which forces continous climatic change.

sure *adj* **1** assured, certain, clear, confident, definite, positive. **2** accurate, dependable, effective, precise, tried and tested, trustworthy. **3** assured, guaranteed, inescapable, inevitable.
surface *n* covering, exterior, façade, face, outside, plane, side, skin, top, veneer.
surface *v* appear, come to light, come up, emerge, materialize, rise, transpire.
surprise *v* **1** amaze, astonish, astound, bewilder, confuse, disconcert, stagger, stun, take aback. **2** burst in on, catch red-handed, discover, spring upon, startle; (*Inf*) bowl over, flabbergast.
surprise *n* **1** amazement, astonishment, bewilderment, incredulity, wonder. **2** bolt from the blue, bombshell, jolt, shock; (*Inf*) eye-opener, start.
surprising *adj* astonishing, astounding, extraordinary, incredible, marvellous, remarkable, staggering, startling, unexpected, wonderful.
survive *v* endure, exist, hold out, last, live on, outlive, pull through, remain alive; (*Inf*) keep body and soul together.

The Everglades National Park in the subtropical swamp region of South Florida was established to preserve the flora and fauna of the swamp.

suspect *v* **1** distrust, doubt, have one's doubts about, mistrust. **2** believe, conclude, consider, fancy, feel, guess, have a sneaking suspicion, hazard a guess, speculate, suppose. surmise, think probable; (*Inf*) smell a rat.

suspect *adj* doubtful, dubious, open to suspicion, questionable; (*Inf*) fishy.

suspicion *n* **1** distrust, doubt, lack of confidence, mistrust, wariness; (*Inf*) bad vibes, funny feeling, gut feeling. **2** conjecture, guess, hunch, idea, impression, notion. **3** glimmer, hint, shade, shadow, soupçon, strain, streak, suggestion, tinge, touch, trace.

swamp *n* bog, everglades, fen, marsh, mire, morass, moss, quagmire, slough.

swamp *v* capsize, drench, engulf, flood, inundate, overwhelm, sink, submerge, swallow up, upset, wash over, waterlog.

swear *v* **1** affirm, declare, give one's word, promise, state under oath, testify, warrant. **2** curse, turn the air blue.

sweat *n* **1** diaphoresis, perspiration. **2** anxiety, distress, panic, strain, worry; (*Inf*) agitation, flap. **3** chore, drudgery, effort, labour, toil.

sweat *v* **1** perspire. **2** agonize, fluster, fret, worry; (*Inf*) be in a lather, be in a stew, be in a tiz woz, be on pins and needles.

sweet *adj* **1** fragrant, honeyed, sugary, sweetened, syrupy. **2** affectionate, charming, delightful, gentle, kind, lovable, sweet-tempered, tender. **3** beloved, darling, dear, dearest, pet, treasured.

swelling *n* blister, bruise, bump, enlargement, inflammation, lump, puffiness.

swift *adj* abrupt, expeditious, express, fast, fleet, fleet-footed, flying, hurried, nimble, prompt, quick, rapid, ready, short, short-lived, speedy, sudden, winged; (*Inf*) nippy.

swing *v* **1** be suspended, dangle, hang, suspend. **2** fluctuate, oscillate, rock, sway, vary, veer.

swing *n* fluctuation, oscillation, stroke, sway, swaying, vibration.

switch *v* **1** change, change course, deflect, deviate, divert, exchange, rearrange, replace by, substitute, trade; (*Inf*) swap.

switch *n* about-turn, alteration, change, change of direction, exchange, shift, substitution.

symmetrical *adj* balanced, in proportion, proportional, regular, well-proportioned.

symmetry *n* agreement, balance, correspondence, evenness, form, harmony, order, proportion, regularity.

sympathy *n* **1** commiseration, compassion, condolences, pity, tenderness, understanding. **2** affinity, harmony, rapport, union, warmth.

symptom *n* expression, indication, mark, note, sign, token.

synthetic *adj* artificial, fake, man-made, manufactured, mock, pseudo, sham, simulated.

system *n* **1** arrangement, classification, combination, scheme, structure. **2** fixed order, method, practice, procedure, routine, technique, theory. **3** definite plan, logical process, method; (*Inf*) set-up.

systematic *adj* businesslike, efficient, methodical, orderly, organized, precise, standardized, systemized, well-ordered.

Tt

table *n* **1** bench, board, counter, slab, stand. **2** board, diet, food; (*Inf*) spread. **3** agenda, catalogue, chart, diagram, graph, index, plan, schedule.
table *v* propose, submit, suggest.
tact *n* diplomacy, discretion, skill, understanding.
tactful *adj* careful, considerate, delicate, diplomatic, discreet, perceptive, polished, polite, prudent, sensitive, subtle.
tactless *adj* insensitive, rude, thoughtless, undiplomatic, unfeeling, unkind, unsubtle.
tail *v* **1** keep under surveillance, shadow, stalk, track, trail. **2** decrease, drop off, dwindle, fade, fall away, peter out.
taint *v* blight, contaminate, corrupt, dirty, foul, infect, poison, pollute, soil, spoil.
take *v* **1** arrest, capture, carry off, catch, grasp, obtain, receive, secure, seize. **2** pocket, run off with, steal, walk off with; (*Inf*) filch, nick, pinch, swipe. **3** book, buy, engage, hire, lease, pay for, pick, reserve, select. **4** bear, endure, go through, stand, stomach, suffer, swallow, tolerate, withstand. **5** consume, drink, eat, swallow. **6** accept, adopt, undertake. **7** believe, presume, regard, understand. **8** bring, carry, cart, convey, ferry, fetch, haul, transport. **9** bring, escort, lead, usher. **10** deduct, eliminate, remove, subtract. **11** accept, contain, hold.
take in *v* **1** absorb, digest, grasp, understand. **2** comprise, contain, cover, encompass, include. **3** accommodate, admit, let in, receive. **4** cheat, deceive, dupe, fool, mislead, swindle, trick; (*Inf*) con, do, pull the wool over someone's eyes.
take-off *n* **1** departure, launch, lift off. **2** imitation, mocking, parody, satire; (*Inf*) send up.
take off *v* **1** drop, peel off, remove, strip off. **2** become airborne, leave the ground, lift off, take to the air. **3** depart, go, leave, set out, strike out; (*Inf*) hit the road, split.
take on *v* **1** employ, engage, enlist, enroll, hire, retain. **2** accept, agree to do, tackle, try, undertake. **3** compete against, face, fight, oppose.
tale *n* **1** account, legend, novel, report, romance, saga, short story. **2** fabrication, falsehood, fib, lie, rigmarole, rumour, untruth; (*Inf*) cock-and-bull story, tall story.
talented *adj* able, accomplished, artistic, brilliant, gifted, skilled, well-endowed.
talk *v* **1** communicate, converse, crack, gossip, natter, prattle, say, speak, utter; (*Inf*) gab, witter. **2** confer, hold discussions, negotiate. **3** give the game away, inform, reveal information; (*Inf*) grass.
talk *n* **1** address, dissertation, lecture, oration, sermon, speech. **2** chat, chit chat, conversation, crack, gossip, hearsay, natter, rumour, tittle-tattle; (*Inf*) gab, jaw, rap. **3** conference, dialogue, discussion, meeting, negotiation, seminar, symposium. **4** dialect, jargon, language, patois, slang, speech, words; (*Inf*) lingo.

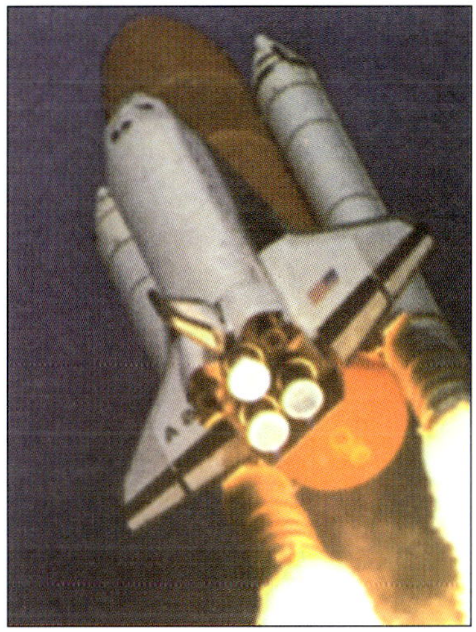

At take-off, the space shuttle has two huge rocket boosters. Jettisoned at a height of 43km (27 miles), they are refilled with fuel and reused when the shuttle returns to Earth.

tall *adj* **1** big, elevated, giant, high, lofty, soaring, towering. **2** demanding, difficult, exorbitant, hard, unreasonable, well-nigh impossible.
tally *n* count, mark, reckoning, record, running total, score, total.
tame *v* **1** break in, domesticate, gentle, house-train, pacify, train. **2** bridle, bring to heel, discipline, master, subdue, suppress.
tamper *v* **1** damage, interfere, intrude, meddle, mess about, monkey around, tinker. **2** bribe, corrupt, influence, manipulate, rig; (*Inf*) muck about, poke one's nose into, fix.
tang *n* **1** aftertaste, flavour, relish, savour, taste. **2** nip, sting.
tangle *n* **1** coil, confusion, jam, jungle, knot, mass, mat, mesh, snarl, twist, web. **2** complication, labyrinth, maze, mess, mix-up; (*Inf*) fix.

tangle *v* coil, confuse, entangle, interlace, interlock, intertwist, interweave, jam, kink, knot, mat, mesh, snarl, twist.
tangled *adj* **1** jumbled, knotted, matted, messy, scrambled, snarled, twisted. **2** complex, complicated, confused, convoluted, involved, knotty, messy, mixed-up.
tantrum *n* hysterics, outburst, storm, temper; (*Inf*) paddy.
tap *v* **1** beat, drum, knock, pat, rap, strike, touch. **2** bleed, drain, draw off, open, pierce, siphon off, unplug. **3** draw on, exploit, make use of, milk, mine, put to use, use, utilize.
tap *n* **1** beat, knock, light blow, pat, rap, touch. **2** faucet, spigot, spout, stopcock, valve. **3** bung, plug, spile, stopper.
tape *n* band, ribbon, strip.
tape *v* **1** bind, seal, secure, stick, wrap. **2** record, tape-record, video.
taper *v* come to a point, narrow.
target *n* **1** aim, ambition, bull's eye, end, goal, intention, mark, object, objective. **2** butt, quarry, scapegoat, victim.
tarnish *v* blacken, blemish, blot, darken, dim, discolour, drag through the mud, dull, rust, soil, spot, stain, sully, taint.
task *n* assignment, chore, duty, employment, job, mission, occupation, undertaking.
taste *n* **1** flavour, relish, savour, smack, tang. **2** bite, dash, drop, morsel, mouthful, sample, sip, soupçon, spoonful, titbit. **3** appetite, desire, fondness, inclination, partiality, preference. **4** appreciation, cultivation, elegance, refinement, style.
taste *v* **1** distinguish, perceive. **2** nibble, relish, sample, sip, test, **3** encounter, experience, feel, know, meet with, undergo.
tasteful *adj* artistic, beautiful, charming, cultured, delicate, elegant, exquisite, graceful, handsome, refined, stylish.
tasteless *adj* **1** bland, boring, uninteresting, watered-down. **2** cheap, rude, tactless, vulgar.
tasty *adj* appetizing, delectable, delicious, luscious, savoury; (*Inf*) scrumptious, yummy.
taunt *v* insult, jeer, mock, provoke, ridicule, sneer, tease, torment.
taut *adj* flexed, rigid, strained, stressed, stretched, tense, tight.
tax *n* **1** charge, contribution, customs, duty, excise, levy, rate, tariff, toll. **2** burden, demand, drain, load, pressure, strain, weight.
tax *v* **1** assess, charge, demand, extract, impose. **2** burden, drain, exhaust, put pressure on, strain, wear out. **3** blame, charge, impeach.
teach *v* coach, demonstrate, direct, educate, guide, inform, instruct, school, train, tutor.
teacher *n* coach, guide, guru, instructor, lecturer, master, professor, schoolmaster, schoolmistress, trainer, tutor.
team *n* band, body, bunch, company, crew, gang, group, line-up, set, side, squad, troupe.
team up *v* band together, cooperate, get together, join, link, unite, work together.
tear *v* **1** mutilate, pull apart, rip, rupture, scratch, shred, split. **2** bolt, dart, dash, fly, gallop, hurry, race, run, rush, shoot, speed, sprint, zoom; (*Inf*) belt. **3** grab, pluck, pull, rip, seize, snatch, wrench, wrest, yank.
tear *n* hole, laceration, rip, run, rupture, scratch, split.

The taste, texture and appearance of cooked food is usually different to that of the raw ingredients. This is due to new compounds being formed during the chemical reactions that take place when the ingredients are heated up.

A religious temple in Thailand with one of its many protective temple devils.

tease *v* annoy, pester, taunt, torment, worry; (*Inf*) aggravate, have on, kid, rib.
technique *n* **1** approach, manner, method, mode, style, system, way. **2** craftsmanship, delivery, performance, skill, touch; (*Inf*) know-how.
tedious *adj* annoying, boring, drab, dreary, laborious, lifeless, monotonous, uninteresting.
tedium *n* boredom, drabness, dullness, monotony, routine, tediousness, the doldrums.
teem *v* be crawling with, be full of, brim, burst at the seams, overflow, produce, swarm.
telepathy *n* mind-reading, sixth sense, thought transference.
telephone *n* handset, line, phone; (*Inf*) blower.
telephone *v* call, call up, dial, give someone a call, phone, put a call through to; (*Inf*) buzz, get on the blower, give someone a buzz, give someone a ring, give someone a tinkle, ring.
telescope *n* glass, spyglass.
telescope *v* concertina, crush.
tell *v* **1** announce, communicate, confess, disclose, divulge, inform, mention, notify, reveal, speak, state, utter. **2** authorize, command, direct, instruct, order, require, summon. **3** chronicle, depict, describe, give an account of, narrate, portray, recount, relate, report. **4** comprehend, discern, discover, make out, see, understand. **5** differentiate, discriminate, distinguish, identify. **6** count, have effect, have force, register, take its toll. **7** calculate, count, number, reckon, tally.
temper *n* **1** attitude, character, constitution, disposition, frame of mind, humour, mind, mood, nature, temperament, tenor, vein. **2** bad mood, rage, tantrum; (*Inf*) paddy. **3** anger, annoyance, heat, hot-headedness, ill-humour, irritation, passion, resentment. **4 loose one's temper** composure, coolness, self-control, tranquillity; (*Inf*) cool.
temper *v* moderate, restrain, soften, soothe, tone down; (*Inf*) soft pedal.
temperament *n* character, frame of mind, make-up, outlook, personality.
temperamental *adj* **1** emotional, erratic, excitable, explosive, fiery, highly strung, hot-headed, irritable, moody, sensitive, touchy, volatile. **2** erratic, unpredictable, unreliable.
temple *n* church, holy place, place of worship, sanctuary, shrine.
temporary *adj* brief, fleeting, here today and gone tomorrow, interim, passing, provisional, short-lived, transient.
tempt *v* **1** allure, appeal to, attract, coax, decoy, draw, entice, inveigle, invite, lead on, lure, make one's mouth water, seduce, tantalize, whet one's appetite, woo. **2** bait, dare, fly in the face of, provoke, risk, test.
temptation *n* appeal, attraction, draw, enticement, inducement, lure, pull, snare, tantalization; (*Inf*) come-on.
tempting *adj* alluring, appetizing, attractive, enticing, inviting, mouth-watering, seductive, tantalizing.
tend *v* **1** be inclined, be likely, have a tendency, lean, trend. **2** care for, control, feed, guard, handle, keep an eye on, look after, maintain, manage, nurse, see to, serve, take care of, wait on, watch over.
tendency *n* inclination, leaning, readiness, susceptibility.
tender *adj* **1** delicate, feeble, fragile, frail, soft, weak. **2** green, immature, raw, unripe, young; (*Inf*) wet behind the ears. **3** affectionate, caring, fond, gentle, kind, loving, warm, warm-hearted. **4** complicated, risky, sensitive, tricky. **5** aching, bruised, inflamed, painful, raw, sensitive, smarting, sore.
tender *v* bid, offer, present,

propose, suggest, volunteer.
tender *n* **1** bid, offer, proffer, proposal. **2** currency, money.
tenderness *n* **1** fragility, softness, vulnerability, weakness. **2** greenness, immaturity, newness, vulnerability, youth. **3** affection, care, compassion, fondness, kindness, love, sympathy, warmth. **4** aching, bruising, inflammation, pain, rawness, soreness.
tense *adj* **1** rigid, strained, stretched, taut, tight. **2** anxious, edgy, jumpy, keyed up, nervous, on edge, restless, strained, under pressure; (*Inf*) jittery, strung up, uptight, wound up. **3** exciting, nerve-wracking, stressful.
tension *n* **1** pressure, rigidity, stress, tautness, tightness. **2** anxiety, edginess, hostility, nervousness, restlessness, strain, suspense, unease; (*Inf*) the jitters.
tentative *adj* **1** indefinite, provisional. **2** cautious, doubtful, hesitant, timid, uncertain.
tepid *adj* **1** lukewarm, slightly warm. **2** apathetic, cool, half-hearted, indifferent, lukewarm, unenthusiastic.
term *v* call, denominate, designate, dub, entitle, label, name, style.
terminal *adj* **1** bounding, limiting. **2** final, ultimate.
terminal *n* **1** end, extremity. **2** bound, limit. **3** airport, depot, station, terminus.
terminate *v* abort, cease, close, conclude, discontinue, end, expire, finish, lapse, run out, stop, wind up.
terms *pl n* **1** language, manner of speaking, terminology. **2** conditions, particulars, specifications. **3** charges, fee, payment, price, rates.
terrible *adj* **1** bad, dangerous, extreme, serious. **2** appaling, dreadful, frightful, horrid, shocking, terrifying. **3** awful, bad, hideous, nasty, obnoxious, offensive, repulsive, revolting, unpleasant, vile; (*Inf*) dire, dreadful, duff, rotten.
terrific *adj* **1** awful, dreadful, extreme, fierce, gigantic, great, horrific, huge, intense, severe, terrible. **2** amazing, excellent, fine, magnificent, marvellous, outstanding, stupendous, superb, very good, wonderful; (*Inf*) ace, fabulous, fantastic, great, sensational, smashing, super.
terrify *v* alarm, appal, frighten, intimidate, make one's hair stand on end, petrify, scare, scare to death, shock, terrorize.
territory *n* area, country, district, domain, land, province, region, sector, state, terrain, tract, zone.
terror *n* alarm, anxiety, awe, dismay, dread, fright, horror, panic, shock.
terrorist *n* assassin, gunman, hijaker.
terrorize *v* **1** bully, intimidate, menace, threaten; (*Inf*) strong-arm. **2** dismay, frighten, horrify, intimidate, petrify, scare to death, shock, terrify.
test *v* analyse, assess, check, examine, investigate, try, try out, verify.
test *n* analysis, assessment, check, evaluation, examination, investigation, probation, trial.
texture *n* consistency, fabric, grain, quality, structure, surface, tissue, weave.
thaw *v* defrost, dissolve, melt, soften, unfreeze, warm.
theft *n* embezzlement, fraud, larceny, pilfering, purloining, robbery, stealing, swindling, thievery, thieving; (*Inf*) rip-off.
theme *n* **1** idea, subject, text, thesis, topic. **2** motif, idea. **3** composition, dissertation, essay, exercise, paper.
theory *n* **1** assumption,

Grand Central Terminal in New York City, is the world's largest and busiest transportation building occupying forty-nine acres and servicing over 426,000 commuters daily.

guess, hypothesis, presumption. **2** plan, proposal, scheme. **3** laws, principles, rules, science.
therapeutic *adj* beneficial, good, healing, remedial, restorative.
thick *adj* **1** broad, substantial, wide. **2** concentrated, dense, heavy. **3** abundant, brimming, bursting, chock-a-block, chock-full, packed, swarming, teeming. **4** brainless, dense, insensitive, slow, stupid; (*Inf*) dimwitted, dopey. **5** broad, distinct, marked, pronounced, strong. **6** close, devoted, familiar, friendly, on good terms; (*Inf*) chummy, matey, pally.
thief *n* bandit, burglar, cheat, crook, pick-pocket, robber, shoplifter, stealer; (*Inf*) mugger.
thin *adj* **1** fine, narrow, thread-like. **2** delicate, flimsy, gossamer, see-through, sheer, translucent. **3** bony, emaciated, skinny, slim, thin as a rake, under-weight. **4** deficient, meagre, skimpy. **5** diluted, runny, watery; (*Inf*) wishy-washy. **6** feeble, flimsy, lame, poor, shallow, superficial, unconvincing, weak.
thing *n* **1** article, fact, matter, object, part, portion. **2** event, incident, occurrence. **3** device, gadget, implement, instrument, machine, tool. **4** detail, feature, particular point. **5** belongings, bits and pieces, clothes, goods, luggage, possessions, stuff; (*Inf*) clobber, gear.
think *v* **1** believe, conclude, estimate, imagine, judge, reckon, suppose. **2** consider, have in mind, ponder, reflect, weigh up; (*Inf*) chew over. **3** recollect, remember. **4** anticipate, expect, plan for, presume.
thirst *n* **1** craving to drink, drought, dryness, thirstiness. **2** desire, eagerness, hunger, longing, lust, yearning.
thirsty *adj* arid, dehydrated, dry, parched.
thorny *adj* **1** barbed, bristly, prickly, sharp, spiky. **2** awkward, difficult, trying, worrying; (*Inf*) sticky.
thorough *prep* **1** complete, full, indepth, intensive, sweeping. **2** absolute, entire, perfect, pure, sheer, total, utter.
though *conj* although, despite the fact that, even if, while.
thought *n* **1** consideration, deliberation, reflection, regard. **2** belief, concept, conclusion, idea, notion, view. **3** attention, scrutiny, study. **4** aim, design, intention, object, plan, purpose. **5** anticipation, dream, expectation, hope, prospect. **6** anxiety, care, compassion, concern, kindness, regard, sympathy, thoughtfulness.
thoughtful *adj* **1** caring, helpful, kindly, unselfish. **2** pensive, reflective, studious, thinking, wistful.
thread *v* **1** ease, pass, string. **2** inch, push, squeeze, wind.
thread *n* **1** cord, fibre, filament, hair, line, strand, twist. **2** cotton, silk, twine, wool, yarn. **3** course, direction, drift, story-line, theme, thought.
threadbare *adj* frayed, old, seedy, shabby, tattered, worn.

Camels do not suffer from thirst as they are well adapted to dry desert conditions. They are able to close their nostrils to keep sand out, and their eyes are also protected by long eyelashes. The fat in their humps is a food store. Camels rarely sweat, so they can conserve water in their bodies more efficiently than humans.

The thrill of a motorcycle is provided by the power of its breath-taking acceleration.

threat *n* **1** menace, threatening, remark, warning. **2** foreboding, omen, warning.
threaten *v* **1** jeopardize, put at risk. **2** be imminent, be in the air. **3** browbeat, bully, make threats to, menace, pressurize, terrorize; (*Inf*) lean on.
thrill *n* **1** adventure, sensation, stimulation, tingle; (*Inf*) buzz, charge, kick. **2** flutter, quiver, shudder, throb, tremble, tremor.
thrill *v* **1** excite, stimulate, stir, tingle. **2** flutter, quake, quiver, shake, shudder, throb, tremble.
thrilling *adj* **1** exciting, gripping, hair-raising, rivetting, stirring. **2** quaking, shaking, shivering, trembling; (*Inf*) rip-roaring.
thrive *v* advance, bloom, do well, flourish, prosper, succeed.
throb *v* beat, palpitate, pound, pulsate, pulse, thump, vibrate.
throttle *v* **1** choke, strangle, strangulate. **2** control, inhibit, silence, stifle, suppress; (*Inf*) gag.
through *prep* **1** between, by, from one side to the other, in and out of, past. **2** as a result of, because of, by mean of, by virtue of, by way of, using, via, with the help of. **3** during, in, in the middle of, throughout.
through *adj* completed, done, ended, finished, terminated; (*Inf*) washed-up.
throughout *prep* all over, everywhere, from start to finish, right through, the whole time.
throw *v* fling, hurl, launch, pitch, propel, put, send, shy, sling, toss; (*Inf*) chuck, lob.
throw *n* cast, fling, heave, pitch, projection, put, shy, sling, toss; (*Inf*) lob.
throw away *adj* **1** cast off, discard, dispense with, dispose of, get rid of, jettison, reject, scrap, throw out; (*Inf*) ditch, dump. **2** fail to exploit, fritter away, lose, make poor use of, squander, waste; (*Inf*) blow.
throw off *v* **1** abandon, cast off, discard, drop, shake off. **2** elude, escape from, evade, get away from, give someone the slip. **3** leave behind, lose, outdistance, outrun, shake off. **4** confuse, disturb, unsettle, upset.
thrust *v* **1** butt, drive, elbow one's way in, force, impel, jam, plunge, poke, press, prod, propel, push, ram, shove, urge. **2** jab, lunge, pierce, stab, stick.
thrust *n* **1** drive, lunge, poke, shove, stab. **2** impetus, momen-tum, propulsive force.
thud *n/v* clonk, clunk, crash, knock, smack, thump, wallop.
thug *n* assassin, bandit, gang-ster, hooligan, killer, mugger, murderer, robber, villain; (*Inf*) bovver boy, heavy, hit-man.
thump *n* bang, blow, clout; (*Inf*) clunk, crash, knock, rap, smack, thud, thwack, wallop, whack.
thump *v* bang, batter, beat, belabour, crash, hit, knock, pound, rap, smack, strike, thrash, throb, thud, thwack, whack; (*Inf*) belt, clout, wallop.
thunder *n* boom, booming, cracking, crash, detonation, explosion, pealing, rumble.
thunder *v* blast, boom, clap, crack, crash, detonate, explode, peal, resound, reverberate, roar, rumble.
thunderstruck *adj* astonished, astounded, dazed, speechless, open-mouthed, petrified, rooted to the spot, shocked, staggered, struck dumb, stunned, taken aback; (*Inf*) bowled over, flabber-gasted, floored, knocked for six.
ticket *n* **1** certificate, coupon, pass, slip, token, voucher. **2** card, docket, label, marker, sticker, tab, tag.
tickle *v* amuse, delight, divert, enliven, gladden, gratify, please, rejoice, titillate.
ticklish *adj* **1** precarious, risky, uncertain, unstable, unsteady. **2** critical, delicate, difficult, nice.
tide *n* **1** course, current, ebb, flow, stream, tidal flow. **2** course, direction, drift, run, trend.
tidy *adj* businesslike, clean, methodical, neat, orderly, ship-shape, spick-and-span, spruce,

trim, well-groomed, well-kept.
tie *v* **1** attach, fasten, join, knot, lash, link, moor, secure, tether. **2** bind, confine, hinder, limit, restrict. **3** be even, be neck and neck, draw, equal, match.
tier *n* bank, layer, level, line, order, rank, row, series, storey.
tight *adj* **1** close, close-fitting, cramped, firm, narrow, rigid, secure, taut. **2** hermetic, sealed, sound, watertight. **3** mean, miserly, stingy. **4** close, evenly-balanced, near, well-matched. **5** drunk, intoxicated, inebriated, tipsy; (*Inf*) half-cut, pickled, plastered, smashed, sozzled, tiddly, under the influence.
tighten *v* close, constrict, cramp, fasten, fix, narrow, secure, squeeze, stretch, tense.
tilt *n* angle, incline, list, pitch, slant, slope.
timber *n* beams, boards, forest, logs, planks, trees, wood.
time *n* **1** age, chronology, date, duration, era, generation, period, season, term. **2** day, life span, lifetime. **3** heyday, hour, peak. **4** beat, tempo. **5 in time** early, in good time, on schedule, on time. **6** by and by, eventually, one day, someday, sooner or later.
time *v* clock, count, measure, regulate, schedule, set.
timely *adj* at the right time, convenient, suitable, well-timed.
timetable *n* diary, list, schedule.
timid *adj* apprehensive, fearful, nervous, retiring, shy.

What are time zones?

As the Earth spins, different parts of it face the Sun. Therefore, it cannot be the same time all over the world at the same moment. When it is the middle of the night in one country, it is dawn in another part of the world. To keep expressions of time consistent in every part of the world, the Earth is divided into 24 time zones, each one exactly one hour apart.

The first clocks were based on the Sun, using shadow movements to read time from a marked area of earth or stone. Later time measurement was based on actions that happened at a fixed rate such as grains of sand.

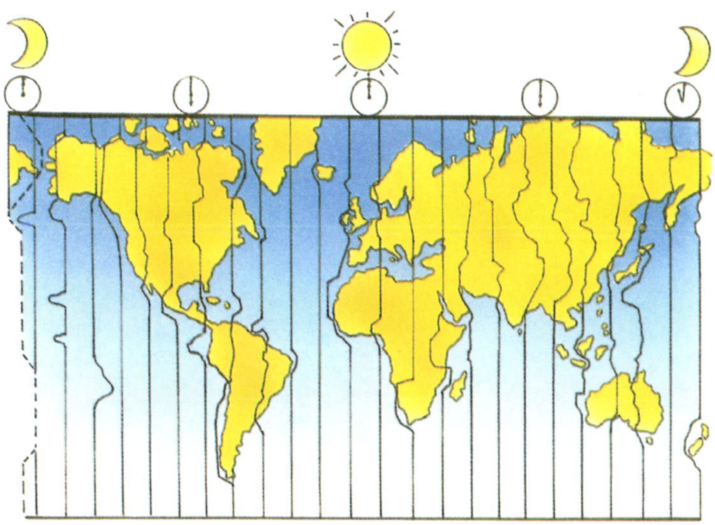

tint *n* **1** cast, colour, hue, shade, tone. **2** dye, rinse, stain, tincture, tinge, wash.
tint *v* **1** colour, dye, rinse, stain, tincture, tinge. **2** affect, taint.
tiny *adj* little, microscopic, mini, miniature, minute, petite, slight, small, wee; (*Inf*) pint-sized.
tip *n* apex, cap, crown, end, extremity, head, peak, point, summit, top.
tip *v* **1** incline, lean, list, over-turn, slant, spill, tilt, topple over, upend, upset. **2** ditch, dump, empty, pour out, unload. **3** reward. **4** tap, touch. **5** cap, crown, top.
tip *n* **1** dump, refuse heap, rub-bish heap. **2** gift, gratuity. **3** apex, crown, peak, point, summit, top. **4** cap, cover, end, extremity, point. **5 tip-off** clue, forecast, hint, information, inside infor-mation, pointer, suggestion, warning, word, word of advice.
tire *v* **1** drain, droop, enervate, exhaust, fail, fatigue, flag, jade, sink, wear down, wear out, weary; (*Inf*) take it out of you, whack. **2** annoy, bore, harass, irk, irritate, weary.
title *n* **1** caption, heading, inscription, label, legend, name, style. **2** denomination, name, nickname, term; (*Inf*) handle. **3** championship, crown, laurels. **4** claim, entitlement, ownership, prerogative, privilege, right.
toast *v* **1** brown, grill. **2** honour, pledge, propose, salute.
toast *n* **1** compliment, drink, pledge, salute. **2** favourite, pet.
together *adv* **1** as one, closely, hand in hand, in unison, jointly, shoulder to shoulder, side by side. **2** all at once, at the same time, simultaneously. **3** one after

the other, successively.
toil *n* application, donkey-work, drudgery, effort, exertion, hard work, industry, labour pains, slog, sweat; (*Inf*) elbow grease, graft.
toil *v* labour, push oneself, slave, struggle, work like a Trojan, work one's fingers to the bone; (*Inf*) graft, grind, sweat.
toilet *n* **1** grooming, washing. **2** bathroom, closet, convenience, ladies' room, latrine, lavatory, mens' room, outhouse, powder room, urinal, washroom, water closet, WC.
tolerable *adj* **1** acceptable, bearable. **2** adequate, all right, average, fair, fair to middling, mediocre, middling, passable, run-of-the-mill; (*Inf*) not bad, OK, so-so.
tolerance *n* **1** broad-mindedness, patience, permissiveness, sympathy. **2** endurance, resilience, stamina, staying power, toughness. **3** fluctuation play, swing, variation.
tolerant *adj* **1** patient, sympathetic, understanding. **2** easy-going, free and easy, indulgent, lenient, soft.
tolerate *v* allow, bear, endure, permit, sanction, stand, stomach, suffer, swallow, turn a blind eye to, undergo; (*Inf*) put up with.
tomb *n* burial, chamber, catacomb, crypt, grave, mausoleum, sepulchre, vault.
tombstone *n* gravestone, headstone, memorial, monument.
tone *n* **1** accent, emphasis, pitch, stress, volume. **2** air, approach, aspect, attitude, character, drift, effect, feel, frame, grain, manner, mood, note, quality, spirit, style, temper, tenor, vein. **3** cast, colour, hue, shade, tinge, tint.
tone *v* blend, go well with, harmonize, match, suit.
tongue *n* **1** dialect, language, talk; (*Inf*) lingo. **2** speech, verbal expression, voice.
tonic *n* boost, refresher, stimulant; (*Inf*) bracer, pick-me-up, shot in the arm.
too *adv* **1** as well, besides, in addition, likewise. **2** excessively, extremely, unduly, very.
tool *n* **1** device, gadget, implement, instrument, machine, utensil. **2** agency, agent, intermediary, medium, vehicle, wherewithal.
top *n* **1** apex, crest, crown, head, high point, peak, pinnacle, summit, vertex. **2** cap, cork, cover, lid, stopper. **3** first place, head, highest rank, lead. **4** a bit too far, over the limit, over the top, too much, uncalled-for.
top *adj* best, chief, elite, finest, first, greatest, highest, leading, prime, superior, topmost, upper, uppermost; (*Inf*) crack.
top *v* **1** beat, best, better, eclipse, exceed, excel, go beyond, outdo, outshine, outstrip, surpass. **2** decorate, cover, garnish.
torment *v* **1** agonize, crucify, distress, pain, torture. **2** annoy, bother, harass, irritate, pester, provoke, tease, worry; (*Inf*) devil.
torn *n* **1** anguish, misery, pain, suffering, torture. **2** bother, irritation, nuisance, trouble, worry; (*Inf*) pain in the neck.
tornado *n* cyclone, hurricane, storm, typhoon; (*Inf*) twister.
torrent *n* cascade, deluge, down pour, flood, flow, gush, outburst, rush, spate, stream, tide.
torture *v* afflict, agonize, pain, persecute, torment.
toss *v* **1** fling, hurl, sling, throw. **2** jiggle, joggle, jolt, rock, roll,

The top of Ayers Rock is 330m (1100ft) high. It is the world's largest monolith in the Northern Territory of Australia and has a base circumference of 9km (5.6 miles).

The Eiffel Tower in Paris (designed by Alexandre Gustave Eiffel) was erected for the 1889 Paris Exposition. It was originally built to a height of 300m (984ft), but it was raised further in 1959 to 321m (1052ft).

shake, thrash, tumble, wriggle, writhe; (*Inf*) chuck, lob.

total *n* aggregate, all, entirety, full amount, sum, whole.

total *adj* absolute, complete, comprehensive, full, outright, sheer, whole.

total *v* add up, amount to, sum up, tot up.

touch *n* **1** feel, physical contact. **2** brush, caress, pat, stroke, tap. **3** bit, dash, drop, hint, pinch, small amount, speck, spot, taste, tinge, trace. **4** characteristic, method, style, technique, trade-mark, way. **5** ability, flair, knack, skill.

touch *v* **1** brush, fondle, handle, pat, stroke. **2** border, converge, meet. **3** affect, disturb, have an effect on, influence; (*Inf*) get to. **4** compare with, equal, match, rival; (*Inf*) hold a candle to.

touching *adj* heartbreaking, moving, poignant, sad.

tough *adj* **1** durable, resilient, rigid, rugged, solid, strong. **2** fit, hardy, sturdy. **3** inflexible, strict, stubborn; (*Inf*) hard-nosed. **4** arduous, difficult, puzzling.

tough *n* brute, bully, hooligan, ruffian, thug; (*Inf*) roughneck.

tour *n* **1** excursion, journey, outing, trip. **2** circuit, course, round.

tour *v* explore, go on the road, holiday in, journey, sightsee, travel round, visit.

tourist *n* globetrotter, holidaymaker, sightseer, traveller, tripper, voyager.

tow *v* drag, draw, haul, lug, pull, trail, trawl, tug.

towards *prep* **1** en route for, in the direction of, on the road to, on the way to, to. **2** about, with regard to. **3** almost, close to, just before, nearly, not quite.

tower *n* belfry, castle, column, fort, fortress, keep, skyscraper, steeple, turret.

tower *v* dominate, overlook, surpass, top.

toy *n* doll, game, plaything.

trace *n* **1** evidence, indication, mark, record, remnant, sign. **2** bit, dash, drop, tinge, touch.

trace *v* **1** detect, discover, find, hunt down, pursue, search for, seek, track. **2** copy, draw, mark out, outline, record, sketch.

track *n* **1** footprint, mark, path, scent, trail. **2** course, flight path, line, orbit, path, trajectory, way. **3** line, permanent way. **4 keep track of** follow, keep an eye on, monitor, oversee. **5 lose track of** lose, lose sight of, misplace.

track *v* chase, follow, hunt down, pursue, stalk, trace, trail.

tracks *pl n* footprints, impressions, imprints, tyremarks, tyreprints, wheelmarks.

trade *n* **1** barter, buying and selling, commerce. **2** calling, job, line of work, profession, skill. **3** deal, exchange, interchange, swap. **4** clientele, customers, market, patrons, public.

trade *v* **1** bargain, barter, deal, peddle. **2** barter, exchange, swap, switch.

traffic *n* **1** freight, passengers, transport, vehicles. **2** barter, buying and selling, commerce, communication, dealing, trade.

tragic *adj* appalling, awful, catastrophic, disastrous, fatal, heart breaking, shocking, unfortunate.

trail *v* **1** dangle, hang down, haul, pull, tow. **2** chase, follow,

Traffic in New York featuring one of the famous yellow taxis.

Night-time illuminated freeway transport in Los Angeles, California.

hunt, pursue, shadow, stalk, tail, trace, track. **3** bring up the rear, dawdle, fall behind, follow, hang back, straggle; (*Inf*) traipse.
trail *n* **1** footprints, marks, path, scent, track. **2** beaten track, footpath, route, track, way.
train *v* **1** coach, discipline, drill, educate, guide, instruct, school, teach, tutor. **2** aim, direct, focus, line up, point.
train *n* **1** chain, order, progression, sequence, series. **2** caravan, column, convoy, file, procession.
training *n* **1** coaching, discipline, education, instruction, tuition. **2** body building, exercise, practice, working-out.
traitor *n* back-stabber, betrayer, defector, deserter, informer, Judas, turncoat; (*Inf*) snake-in-the-grass, two-timer.
tramp *v* **1** hike, march, ramble, roam, slog, trek, walk. **2** march, plod, stamp, trudge. **3** heavily; (*Inf*) traipse. **4** crush, stamp, tread, walk over.
tramp *n* **1** down-and-out, drifter, vagrant; (*Inf*) hobo. **2** hike, march, ramble, slog, trek.
trample *v* **1** crush, flatten, squash, stamp, walk over. **2** hurt.
trance *n* daze, hypnotic state.
tranquil *adj* at peace, calm, cool, peaceful, placid, quiet, restful, sedate, serene, untroubled.
transcribe *v* **1** copy out, note, reproduce, rewrite, take down, write out. **2** interpret, translate. **3** record, tape, tape-record.
transfer *v* carry, change, hand over, pass on, relocate, remove, shift, transport, turn over.
transform *v* change, convert, remodel, renew.
translate *v* **1** convert, decipher, decode, interpret, transcribe. **2** explain, make clear, simplify, spell out. **3** alter, change, transform.
translation *n* **1** interpretation, transcription. **2** explanation, simplification. **3** alteration, change, conversion. **4** move, removal.
transmission *n* **1** sending, spread, transfer, transport. **2** air, broadcast, programme, show.
transmit *n* **1** bear, carry, convey, dispatch, forward, pass on, send. **2** broadcast, put on the air, radio, relay, send out.
transparent *adj* **1** clear, see-through, sheer, translucent. **2** evident, obvious, plain, understandable, visible. **3** candid direct, frank, open, plain-spoken, straightforward.
transport *v* bear, bring, carry, convey, fetch, haul, move, ship.
transport *n* **1** vehicle. **2** carriage, removal, shipping.
transpose *v* alter, change, move rearrange, reorder, shift, switch, transfer; (*Inf*) swap.
trap *v* **1** catch, corner, entrap, snare, take. **2** ambush, deceive, dupe, trick.
travel *v* cross, go, journey, proceed, progress, roam, rove, take a trip, tour, traverse, trek, voyage, walk, wander.
tread *v* **1** hike, march, pace, plod, stamp, step, stride, tramp, trudge, walk. **2** crush underfoot, squash, trample. **3** bear down, crush, oppress, quell, repress, ride roughshod over, subdue, subjugate, suppress.
tread *n* step, stride, walk.
treasure *n* **1** cash, fortune, gold, jewels, money, riches, valuables. **2** darling, gem, jewel, pearl, precious, pride and joy.
treasure *v* adore, cherish, love, revere, value, worship.
treasury *n* **1** bank, cache, hoard, repository, store, storehouse, vault. **2** assets, capital, coffers,

exchequer, finances, funds, money, resources, revenues.
treat *n* **1** banquet, celebration, entertainment, feast, gift, party, refreshment. **2** delight, enjoyment, fun, gratification, joy, pleasure, satisfaction, surprise, thrill.
treat *v* **1** behave towards, deal with, manage, use. **2** attend to, care for, nurse. **3** buy for, give, pay for, provide, wine and dine; (*Inf*) stand.
treatment *n* cure, medication, remedy, surgery, therapy.
tremble *v* quake, quiver, shake in one's shoes, shiver, shudder, vibrate, wobble.
tremendous *adj* **1** appalling, colossal, dreadful, immense, mammoth, stupendous, terrible, terrific, vast; (*Inf*) whopping. **2** amazing, extraordinary, great, incredible, wonderful; (*Inf*) ace, fabulous, fantastic, super, terrific.
tremor *n* agitation, quivering, shaking, trembling, vibration.
trial *n* **1** audition, probation, test, test-run; (*Inf*) dry run. **2** contest, hearing, judicial, examination, litigation, tribunal. **3** attempt, effort, endeavour, go, stab, try, venture; (*Inf*) crack, shot, whack. **4** distress, grief, hardship, pain, suffering, trouble, unhappiness. **5** bother, irritation, nuisance, pest; (*Inf*) hassle, pain in the neck, plague.
trial *adj* experimental, pilot, provisional, testing.
tribe *n* blood, caste, clan, class, division, dynasty, ethnic group, family, people, race, stock.
tribute *n* **1** accolade, honour, praise, respect. **2** applaud, celebrate, pay homage to.
trick *n* **1** deception, fraud, hoax, ploy, swindle; (*Inf*) con. **2** antic, caper, joke, practical joke, prank, stunt. **3** art, command, craft, device, expertise, gift, knack, secret, skill, technique; (*Inf*) hang, know-how.
trick *v* cheat, deceive, defraud, dupe, fool, hoax, mislead, pull the wool over some-one's eyes, swindle; (*Inf*) bamboozle, con, take in.
trickle *v* crawl, creep, dribble, drip, drop, exude, ooze, percolate, run, seep, stream.
tricky *adj* complicated, delicate, difficult, problematic, thorny, touch-and-go; (*Inf*) sticky.
trim *adj* **1** compact, neat, nice, orderly, smart, spick-and-span, spruce, tidy, well-groomed, well turned-out. **2** fit, shapely, sleek, slender, slim, streamlined, svelte, willowy; (*Inf*) natty.
trim *v* barber, clip, crop, curtail, **1** cut, dock, pare, prune, shave, shear. **2** decorate, embroider. **3** adjust, arrange, balance, distribute, order, prepare, settle.
trio *n* threesome, triad, trilogy, triple, triplet.
trip *n* errand, excursion, journey, outing, tour, travel, voyage.
trip *v* fall, lose one's balance, slip, stagger, stumble,totter, tumble; (*Inf*) slip up.
triple *adj* threefold, three times as much, three-way, tripartite.
triumph *n* **1** elation, happiness, joy. **2** accomplishment, success, victory; (*Inf*) hit, smash-hit, walkover.
triumphant *adj* jubilant, proud, successful, victorious, winning.
trouble *n* **1** agitation, distress, grief, heartache, misfortune, pain, sorrow, suffering, torment,

During the triumphant Apollo 11 mission, on July 20, 1969, Neil Armstrong stepped out of a small, awkward-looking spaceship called the 'Eagle' and became the first human to set foot on the surface of the Moon. As millions of people on Earth watched that first 'small step' into a future of space exploration on television, the lunar landing became a part of mankind's collective history.

If both dogs tug with equal force, the shirt will not move. It will be in equilibrium. If the forces on it are too strong, the fabric will tear apart.

worry; (*Inf*) hassle. **2** agitation, commotion, disturbance, unrest; (*Inf*) bother. **3** complaint, disease, illness. **4** concern, mess, predicament, problem; (*Inf*) hot water, pickle, scrape.
trouble *v* **1** afflict, annoy, bother, disturb, fret, pester, plague, torment. **2** be concerned, put out. **3** exert oneself.
true *adj* **1** accurate, authentic, correct, exact, genuine, precise, pure, real, valid. **2** dedicated, devoted, honest, loyal, pure, reliable, sincere, trusty. **3** correct, exact, on target, perfect, precise, proper, unerring; (*Inf*) spot-on.
true *adv* **1** honestly, rightly, truthfully. **2** accurate, correctly, on target, precisely, properly.
trunk *n* **1** bole, stalk, stem, stock. **2** body, torso. **3** proboscis, snout. **4** bin, box, case, chest, coffer, crate, kist, locker.
trust *n* **1** confidence, faith, hope, reliance. **2** duty, obligation, responsibility. **3** care, charge, custody, protection, safekeeping.
trust *v* **1** assume, believe, expect, presume, suppose. **2** bank on, depend on, rely upon. **3** confide, entrust, give, sign over.
truth *n* **1** accuracy, precision, reality, validity. **2** dedication, devotion, fidelity. **3** fact, law.
truthful *adj* candid, frank, reliable, sincere, trustworthy.
try *v* **1** attempt, do one's best, have a go. **2** make an attempt, strive, struggle. **3** check out, evaluate, examine, sample, taste. **4** annoy, irritate, tax, trouble, upset, vex, weary. **5** adjudicate, examine, hear.
try *n* attempt, effort, shot, stab, whack; (*Inf*) crack, whack.
trying *adj* **1** difficult, hard. **2** deplorable, dire, distressing, hard, painful, severe.
try out *v* check out, evaluate, inspect, put into practice, put to the test, sample, taste, test.
tug *v* drag, haul, heave, jerk, lug, pull, tow, wrench, yank.
tumble *v* drop, fall, lose one's footing, pitch, plummet, roll, stumble, topple, toss, trip up.
tunnel *n* burrow, passage, shaft, subway, underpass.
tunnel *v* burrow, excavate, mine, scoop out.
turbulent *adj* **1** agitated, choppy, rough, unsettled. **2** riotous, rowdy, unruly, violent, wild.
turf *n* **1** clod, divot, grass, green, lawn, sod. **2** horse-racing, racing. **3** race-courses.
turn *v* **1** circle, pivot, revolve, rotate, spin, swivel, twist, whirl. **2** change course, go back, move, return, reverse, swerve, switch, veer, wheel. **3** arc, go round, negotiate, pass. **4** adapt, alter, convert, fit, mould, shape, transform. **5** change one's mind, change sides, defect, desert, influence, persuade, talk into; (*Inf*) bring round. **6** **turn tail** bolt, flee, run away, run off.
turn *n* **1** bend, curve, pivot, spin, twist. **2** change of course, change of direction, curve, deviation, shift. **3** chance, go, opportunity, stint, try; (*Inf*) crack, shot. **4** flair, gift, knack, talent. **5** bend, twist, **6** one after another.
turning-point *n* change, critical moment, crossroads, decisive moment, moment of truth.
turn up *v* **1** appear, arrive, attend; (*Inf*) show up. **2** appear, become known, come to light, dig up, disclose, discover, expose, find, pop up, reveal, transpire, unearth; (*Inf*) crop up.
twist *v* **1** coil, corkscrew, curl, encircle, intertwine, screw, spin, swivel, twine, weave, wind, wrap, wreathe, wring. **2** contort, distort, screw up. **3** sprain, turn, wrench. **4** alter, change, distort, misrepresent.
twist *n* **1** coil, curl, spin, swivel, twine, wind. **2** braid, coil, hank, roll. **3** change, revelation, slant, surprise, turn. **4** arc, bend, curve, meander, zigzag. **5** defect, flaw. **6** pull, sprain, turn, wrench. **7** fault, peculiarity, quirk, trait. **8** confusion, entanglement, kink, mess, mix-up, snarl, tangle.
type *n* **1** breed, category, class, group, order, species, variety. **2** case, characters, face, font, print, printing. **3** essence, example, model, original, pattern, prototype, specimen.

Uu

ugly *adj* **1** unattractive, unsightly; (*Inf*) not much to look at. **2** disgusting, hideous, horrid, offensive, repulsive, revolting. **3** dangerous, ominous, sinister, threatening. **4** bad-tempered, nasty, spiteful.
ultimate *adj* **1** decisive, end, eventual, extreme, final, furthest, last, terminal. **2** maximum, supreme, utmost.
umpire *n* adjudicator, arbiter, arbitrator, judge, moderator, referee; (*Inf*) ref.
unanimous *adj* agreed, at one, common, harmonious, of one mind, united.
unarmed *adj* defenceless, exposed, helpless, open to attack, unprotected.
unassuming *adj* humble, meek, modest, quiet, reserved, retiring, simple, unpretentious.
unauthorized *adj* illegal, prohibited, unlawful, unlicensed, unofficial.
unbalanced *adj* **1** asymmetrical, lopsided, unequal, uneven. **2** crazy, disturbed, eccentric, irrational, unstable.
unbearable *adj* intolerable, unacceptable; (*Inf*) too much.
unbelievable *adj* astonishing, intolerable.
uncertain *adj* **1** doubtful, risky, unpredictable; (*Inf*) iffy. **2** dubious, unclear, unsure, up in the air, vague.
uncomfortable *adj* **1** awkward, cramped, ill-fitting, irritating, painful. **2** awkward, confused, distressed, ill at ease, out of place, self-conscious, uneasy.
uncommon *adj* **1** curious, novel, odd, peculiar, queer, rare, scarce, strange, unusual. **2** distinctive, exceptional, extraordinary, notable, noteworthy, outstanding, rare.
unconscious *adj* **1** comatose, senseless; (*Inf*) blacked out. **2** ignorant, oblivious, unaware. **3** accidental, unintentional.
uncover *v* **1** bare, show, unwrap. **2** disclose, expose, reveal.
undercover *adj* covert, hidden, secret; (*Inf*) hush-hush.
undergo *v* bear, endure, go through, withstand.
undergrowth *n* bracken, brambles, briars, brush, scrub.
underhand *adj* deceitful, devious, dishonest, secretive, sly; (*Inf*) crooked.
underlying *n* **1** concealed, hidden, lurking. **2** essential, fundamental, primary.
underprivileged *adj* deprived, impoverished, needy, poor.
understand *v* **1** appreciate, comprehend, grasp, know, make out, realize, see; (*Inf*) catch on, cotton on, get the hang of, twig. **2** assume, believe, gather, learn, presume, suppose.
understudy *n* double, fill-in, replacement, reserve, stand-in, substitute.
undertake *v* **1** agree, promise, take upon oneself. **2** attempt, embark on, set about, tackle, try.
undo *v* **1** loosen, open, unfasten, untie, unwrap. **2** cancel, wipe out. **3** destroy, ruin, wreck.
unearth *v* **1** dig up, excavate, exhume. **2** bring to light, come across, discover, expose, find, reveal, turn up, uncover.
uneasy *adj* **1** agitated, anxious, apprehensive, edgy, ill at ease, nervous, perturbed, restless, troubled, uncomfortable, unsettled, upset, worried; (*Inf*) jittery. **2** awkward, precarious, shaky, strained, tense, uncomfortable, unstable.
unemployed *adj* jobless, out of work, redundant, workless; (*Inf*) on the dole, resting.
uneven *adj* **1** bumpy, rough. **2** irregular, variable. **3** lopsided, not parallel, odd, unbalanced. **4** one-sided, unequal, unfair.
unexpected *adj* abrupt, out of the blue, sudden, unforeseen.
unfair *adj* biased, one-sided,

The traditional use of cut peat for use a fuel in Ireland is in decline as conservationists try to provide alternative fuels to protect the peatbogs from further excavation.

unjust, unreasonable.
unfaithful *adj* **1** disloyal, false, treacherous.
unfamiliar *adj* curious, different, novel, strange, unusual.
unfasten *v* loosen, uncouple, undo, unlace, unlock, untie.
unforeseen *adj* accidental, out of the blue, surprising, unexpected, unpredicted.
unfounded *adj* groundless, unjustified, unproven, without basis, without foundation.
ungrateful *adj* impolite, selfish, thankless, unappreciative.
unhappy *adj* **1** blue, dejected, depressed, dispirited, down, long-faced, miserable, sad. **2** cursed, ill-fated, unfortunate, unlucky. **3** ill-advised, ill-timed, inappropriate, unsuitable.
unidentified *adj* anonymous, nameless, unknown.
uniform *n* costume, dress, habit, outfit, regalia, suit.
uniform *adj* **1** consistent, even, regular, smooth. **2** alike, equal, identical, like, same, similar.
unimportant *adj* immaterial, insignificant, irrelevant, minor, of no consequence, trivial.
uninhabited *adj* abandoned, deserted, desolate, unoccupied, unpopulated.
unique *adj* **1** lone, single, solitary. **2** unrivalled, without equal.
universal *adj* all-embracing, general, total, unlimited, whole, widespread, worldwide.
unkind *adj* cruel, harsh, mean, nasty, spiteful.
unlawful *adj* against the law, banned, illegal, out-lawed, prohibited.
unlikely *adj* **1** doubtful, remote, unimaginable. **2** incredible, unbelievable, unconvincing.
unload *v* discharge, empty, off-load, relieve, unpack.
unmistakable *adj* certain, distinct, evident, obvious, plain, positive, sure.
unnecessary *adj* non-essential, redundant, surplus to requirements, uncalled-for, useless.
unoccupied *adj* empty, uninhabited, vacant.
unofficial *adj* informal, personal, private, unauthorized, unconfirmed, wildcat.
unorthodox *adj* abnormal, unconventional, unusual.
unpopular *adj* disliked, rejected, shunned, undesirable, unloved, unwanted, unwelcome.
unprecedented *adj* abnormal, exceptional, extraordinary, new, novel, original, remarkable, singular, unexampled, unheard-of, unparalleled, unrivalled, unusual.
unpredictable *adj* erratic, fickle, random, unreliable, unstable, variable; (*Inf*) iffy.
unreasonable *adj* absurd, excessive, extortionate, unacceptable; (*Inf*) steep.
unrelated *adj* **1** different, dissimilar, not related, unconnected, unlike. **2** inappropriate, irrelevant, unassociated.
unreliable *adj* **1** disreputable, untrustworthy. **2** deceptive, delusive, fake, false, implausible inaccurate, mistaken, uncertain, unconvincing, unsound.
unrest *n* **1** agitation, discontent, dissatisfaction, protest, rebellion, strife, tumult. **2** agitation, anxiety, disquiet, distress, restlessness, uneasiness, worry.
unsafe *adj* dangerous, perilous, precarious, risky, threatening, treacherous, uncertain, unreliable, unsound, unstable.
unseen *adj* concealed, hidden, invisible, lurking, unnoticed, unobserved, unobtrusive, unperceived, veiled.
unsightly *adj* hideous, horrible, offensive, repulsive, ugly, unpleasant, unprepossessing; (*Inf*) revolting.
unsound *adj* **1** ailing, defective, delicate, frail, ill, unbalanced,

During the Roman Empire, the soldiers wore uniforms with distinctive plumed helmets and carried spears and decorated shields.

unhealthy, unstable, unwell. **2** faulty, flawed, weak.
unstable *adj* **1** infirm, insecure, precarious, unbalanced, unsafe, unsteady. **2** changeable, erratic, fickle, unsteady, variable, weak.
unsuitable *adj* improper, inappropriate, incompatible, out of character, out of place, unacceptable, unsuited.
unsure *adj* **1** insecure, lacking in confidence. **2** doubtful, dubious, hesitant, mistrustful, sceptical, suspicious, undecided.
untidy *adj* bedraggled, chaotic, cluttered, disorderly, jumbled, littered, messy, shambolic; (*Inf*) higgledy-piggledy, sloppy.
untie *v* free, loosen, release, undo, unfasten, unknot, unlace.
untrained *adj* amateur, green, inexperienced, unqualified.
untrustworthy *adj* devious, dishonest, disloyal, unreliable; (*Inf*) fly-by-night.
unusual *adj* abnormal, bizarre, curious, different, exceptional, extraordinary, phenomenal, rare, remarkable, singular, strange, surprising, uncommon, unfamiliar.
unveil *v* bare, bring to light, disclose, divulge, expose, lay bare, lay open, make known, make public, reveal, uncover.
unwelcome *adj* **1** excluded, unacceptable, undesirable, unwanted. **2** disagreeable, displeasing, distasteful, undesirable, unpleasant.
unwell *adj* **1** ailing, ill, off colour, out of sorts, sick, unhealthy; (*Inf*) poorly, under the weather.
unwind *v* **1** disentangle, slacken, uncoil, unravel, unroll, untwist. **2** calm down, let oneself go, loosen up, quieten down, relax, sit back, slow, down, take a break, wind down; (*Inf*) take it easy.
unwrap *v* open, unfold.
upheaval *n* disruption, disturbance, eruption, revolution, turmoil.
uphill *adj* **1** ascending, climbing, mounting, rising. **2** difficult, exhausting, gruelling, hard, punishing, strenuous, taxing, tough, wearisome.
uphold *v* endorse, justify, maintain, promote, support.
upkeep *n* **1** maintenance, preservation, repair, support. **2** expenses, operating costs, outlay, overheads, running costs.
upper *adj* **1** higher, top, topmost. **2** elevated, eminent, greater, important, superior.
upright *adj* **1** erect, perpendicular, straight, vertical. **2** above board, conscientious, principled, trustworthy, virtuous.
uproar *n* brawl, commotion, confusion, furore, mayhem, noise, pandemonium, racket, riot; (*Inf*) ruckus, ruction.
uproot *v* eradicate, root out.
upset *v* **1** capsize, knock over, overturn, tip over, topple over. **2** change, disturb, mess up, turn topsy-turvy. **3** bother, dismay, distress, disturb, trouble. **4** conquer, defeat, overcome, win against the odds.
upside down *adj* **1** bottom up, inverted, on its head, overturned, upturned, wrong side up. **2** chaotic, disordered, in chaos, in disarray, jumbled, muddled, topsy-turvy; (*Inf*) at sixes and sevens, higgledy-piggledy.
urban *adj* city, citified, civic, inner-city, metropolitan, municipal, town.
urge *v* **1** appeal to, beg, implore, plead. **2** advise, advocate, champion, insist on, push for, recommend, support. **3** egg on, encourage, force, incite,

Expeditions to the North and South Poles are both mentally and physically punishing for participants as the extremes of climate take their toll in the remote surroundings.

induce, press, propel, push, spur, stimulate.
urge *n* compulsion, desire, drive, fancy, impulse, itch, longing, wish, yearning; (*Inf*) yen.
urgency *n* gravity, hurry, importance, need, pressure, seriousness, stress.
urgent *adj* **1** critical, crucial, important, instant, pressing, top-priority. **2** intense, persistent.
usable *adj* available, ready for use, serviceable, valid, working.
use *v* **1** apply, employ, make use of, operate, put to use, utilize. **2** handle, manipulate, take advantage of, treat. **3** consume, exhaust, expend, run through, spend, waste.

Specially designed electrically powered wheelchairs are of great benefit to disabled people, enabling them to move about at the same speed as pedestrians.

use *n* **1** application, operation, service, wear and tear. **2** benefit, help, service, usefulness, value, worth; (*Inf*) mileage. **3** custom, habit, practice, usage, way, wont
used *adj* cast-off, nearly new, not new, second-hand, shopsoiled, worn; (*Inf*) hand-me-down.
useful *adj* beneficial, helpful, of help, of use, practical, profitable, valuable, worthwhile.
useless *adj* **1** futile, hopeless, of no use, pointless, worthless. **2** no good, stupid, weak.
use up *v* absorb, consume, exhaust, finish, squander, swallow up, waste.
usher *n* attendant, doorkeeper, escort, guide, usherette.
usher *v* conduct, direct, escort, guide, lead, pilot, show in, show out, steer.
usual *adj* common, customary, everyday, familiar, general, normal, regular, routine, standard, stock, typical.
usually *adv* as a rule, by and large, commonly, generally, in the main, mainly, mostly, most often, normally, on the whole, ordinarily, regularly, routinely.
utility *n* benefit, convenience, practicality, profit, service, usefulness.
utilize *v* employ, exploit, make use of, put to use, use.
utmost *adj* **1** chief, greatest, highest, maximum, supreme. **2** extreme, farthest, final, last, most distant, remotest.
utmost *n* best, greatest, hardest, highest, most.
utter *v* **1** express, put into words, say, speak, verbalize, vocalize, voice. **2** declare, divulge, make known, proclaim, publish, reveal, state.
utter *adj* absolute, complete, entire, sheer, total.
utterance *n* disclosure, speech.
utterly *adv* absolutely, entirely, fully, thoroughly, totally, to the core, wholly.

Vv

vacancy *n* **1** job, opportunity, position, post, situation. **2** lack of interest.
vacant *adj* **1** available, empty, free, idle, not in use, to let, unfilled, unoccupied. **2** absent-minded, blank, dreaming, expressionless, thoughtless.
vacate *v* **1** abandon, evacuate. relinquish, surrender. **2** abolish, cancel, invalidate, quash.
vague *adj* blurred, doubtful, hazy, ill-defined, indefinite, indistinct, obscure, uncertain.
vain *adj* **1** arrogant, conceited, proud, self-important; (*Inf*) big-headed, stuck-up. **2** abortive, futile, hollow, idle, pointless, senseless, unimportant, useless.
valiant *adj* brave, courageous, fearless, heroic, intrepid.
valid *adj* authentic, genuine, lawful, legal, legally binding, legitimate, official.
valley *n* coomb, coom, dale, dell, depression, dingle, glen, hollow, strath, vale.
valour *n* boldness, bravery, courage, daring, gallantry, heroism, prowess, spirit.
valuable *adj* **1** costly, dear, expensive, high-priced, precious. **2** beneficial, important, prized, profitable, treasured, useful, valued, worthwhile, worthy.
value *n* **1** cost, equivalent, market price, monetary worth, rate. **2** advantage, benefit, help, importance, merit, significance. **3** code of behaviour, ethics, standards, principles.
value *v* **1** account, appraise, assess, compute, evaluate, put a price on, survey. **2** appreciate, cherish, esteem, hold dear, hold in high esteem, prize, regard highly, respect, set store by, treasure.
vanish *v* become invisible, die out, disappear, evaporate, exit, fade away, melt away.
vanity *n* **1** arrogance, conceit, pretension, pride, self-conceit; (*Inf*) big-headedness, showing off. **2** emptiness, futility, use-lessness, worthlessness.
vanquish *v* **1** conquer, defeat, outwit, overpower, overthrow. **2** crush, foil, master.
vapour *n* breath, fumes, haze, mist, smoke, steam.
variable *adj* changeable, fickle, flexible, fluctuating, shifting, unstable, wavering.
variation *n* alteration, change, departure, deviation, difference, discrepancy, diversity, innovation, variety.
varied *adj* assorted, different, diverse, miscellaneous, mixed, sundry, various.
variety *n* **1** change, difference, variation. **2** array, assortment, collection, cross section, medley, miscellany, mixture, range. **3** brand, breed, category, class, kind, make, order, sort, species, strain, type.
various *adj* assorted, different, diverse, varied.
varnish *v* adorn, decorate, embellish, gild, glaze, gloss, japan, lacquer, polish, shellac.
vary *v* alter, change, depart, differ, disagree, diverge, diversify, fluctuate, intermix, modify, transform.
vast *adj* astronomical, colossal, enormous, gigantic, huge, immense, mammoth, massive; (*Inf*) ginormous, mega.
vault *v* **1** bound, clear, hurdle, jump, leap, spring. **2** arch, bend, bow, curve, span.
vault *n* **1** arch, ceiling, roof, span. **2** catacomb, cellar, crypt, mausoleum, tomb. **3** depository, repository, strongroom.
veer *v* be deflected, change course, change direction, sheer, shift, swerve, turn.
vendetta *n* bad blood, blood feud, feud, quarrel.
veneer *n* appearance, façade, front, guise, mask, pretence.
vengeance *n* reprisal, retaliation, retribution, revenge, settling of scores.
venom *n* **1** bane, poison, toxin. **2** acidity, bitterness, grudge,

Pottery can be decorated in a variety of ways. They can be dipped in a glaze, made of tiny fragments of glass in a liquid, and fired for a second time. The pots can also be decorated after glazing, with transfers or hand-painted designs and fired for a third time to fix the design.

hate, malice, spite, spitefulness.
venomous *adj* **1** deadly, poisonous, toxic. **2** caustic, malicious, malignant, mischievous, noxious, spiteful.
vent *n* aperture, duct, hole, opening, orifice, outlet, split.
vent *v* air, come out with, discharge, emit, empty, express, give expression to, pour out, release, utter, voice.
ventilate *v* air, bring out into the open, broadcast, debate, discuss, examine, make known, scrutinize, sift, talk about.
venture *n* adventure, chance, enterprise, fling, gamble, hazard, jeopardy, project, risk, speculation, undertaking.
verdict *n* conclusion, decision, finding, judgment, opinion, sentence.
verge *n* border, boundary, brim, brink, edge, extreme, limit, lip, margin, roadside, threshold.
verify *v* attest, attest to, authenticate, bear out, check, confirm, corroborate, prove, substantiate, support, validate.
versatile *adj* adaptable, adjustable, all-purpose, all-round, flexible, functional, handy, variable.
version *n* account, adaptation, interpretation, portrayal, side.
vertical *adj* erect, on end, perpendicular, upright.
vertigo *n* dizziness, giddiness, lightheadedness.
very *adv* absolutely, extremely, truly, wonderfully; (*Inf*) awfully, jolly, terribly.
vessel *n* **1** barque, boat, craft, ship. **2** container, pot, receptacle, utensil.
vet *v* appraise, check, examine, investigate, review, scrutinize; (*Inf*) give someone the once over, size up.
veteran *n* master, old hand, old stager, old-timer, past master, past mistress, trouper, warhorse; (*Inf*) pro.
veto *v* ban, forbid, prohibit, refuse permission, turn down; (*Inf*) kill, put the kibosh on.
veto *n* ban, embargo, interdict, non-consent, prohibition.
vex *v* **1** annoy, bother, distress, harass, irritate, offend, pester, provoke, torment, trouble, upset, worry; (*Inf*) aggravate, bug, needle, peeve.
vibrate *v* fluctuate, oscillate, pulsate, pulse, quiver, resonate, reverberate, shake, shiver, sway, swing, tremble; (*Inf*) judder.

Quartz crystals are made of silicon and oxygen. When an electric current is passed through them, they vibrate at a regular rate. They can be used in clocks and watches to give very accurate timing.

vibration *n* oscillation, pulse, quiver, reverberation, shaking, throb, tremor; (*Inf*) juddering.
vice *n* corruption, evil, sin, wickedness.
vicinity *n* nearness, proximity, locality, neighbourhood.
vicious *adj* **1** abandoned, bad, corrupt, cruel, dangerous, ferocious, savage, violent. **2** wicked, worthless, wrong. **3** mean, spiteful, vindictive; (*Inf*) bitchy.
victim *n* **1** casualty, fatality, martyr, sacrifice, scapegoat. **2** dupe, easy prey, sitting target; (*Inf*) fall guy, sitting duck, sucker.
victim *n* **1** casualty, fatality, scapegoat. **2** dupe, easy prey, sitting target; (*Inf*) fall guy, patsy, sitting duck, sucker.
victor *n* champion, conquering hero, conqueror, prizewinner, vanquisher, winner; (*Inf*) champ, number one, top dog.
victorious *adj* champion, first, successful, triumphant, winning.
victory *n* conquest, success, superiority, the prize, triumph.
view *n* **1** aspect, landscape, outlook, panorama, scene, vista. **2** attitude, belief, opinion, point of view, way of thinking.
view *v* **1** examine, explore, gaze at, inspect, observe, regard, scan, watch, witness. **2** consideration, look on, regard, think about.
vigilant *adj* alert, attentive, cautious, on one's guard, on the lookout, sleepless; (*Inf*) keep one's eyes peeled.
vigour *n* energy, forcefulness, gusto, health, liveliness, power, zip; (*Inf*) oomph, punch, snap.
vile *adj* **1** despicable, evil, mean, shocking, vulgar, wicked, worthless, wretched.

What is a vintage car?

The term 'vintage car', refers to cars constructed after 1904 and before 1930. The car pictured above is an Austin 7 'Chummy' Tourer, built in 1923.

2 disgusting, foul, horrid, nasty, offensive, revolting, sickening.
villain *n* criminal, rogue, scoundrel.
vindicate *v* acquit, clear, defend, excuse, exonerate.
vintage *n* collection, crop, era, generation, harvest, origin, year.
vintage *adj* choice, classic, prime, rare, ripe, select, superior.
violate *v* **1** break, contravene, infringe.
violence *n* bloodshed, cruelty, fighting, frenzy, terrorism; (*Inf*) strong-arm tactics.
violent *adj* **1** brutal, cruel, murderous, raging, savage, strong, vicious, wild. **2** blustery, boisterous, gale force, powerful, raging, tempestuous, turbulent.
virtue *n* **1** decency, goodness, honesty, justice, morality. **2** advantage, asset, attribute, credit, good quality, strength.
visible *adj* apparent, clear, evident, in view, noticeable, obvious, plain, unmistakable.
vision *n* **1** eyes, eyesight, sight, view. **2** daydream, dream, fantasy, mental picture, pipe dream. **3** apparition, ghost, hallucination, illusion, mirage.
visit *v* be the guest of, call in, go to see, pay a call on, stay at, stay with, stop by; (*Inf*) drop in on, pop in, take in.
visit *n* call, stay, stop.
visualize *v* envisage, imagine, picture, see in the mind's eye.
vital *adj* **1** essential, fundamental, imperative. **2** critical, crucial, decisive, important, key, urgent. **3** dynamic, energetic, lively, spirited, vibrant, vivacious.
vitality *n* energy, exuberance, liveliness, sparkle, stamina, strength, vivacity; (*Inf*) go, vim.
vivid *adj* **1** bright, brilliant, clear, colourful, glowing, intense, rich. **2** distinct, dramatic, graphic, memorable, powerful, realistic, strong, true to life.
vocation *n* business, calling, career, employment, job, mission, office, post, profession, pursuit, role, trade.
vogue *n* **1** custom, fashion, style, trend. **2** acceptance, popularity, usage; (*Inf*) the thing.
volatile *adj* changeable, erratic, explosive, unstable, variable; (*Inf*) up and down.
volume *n* **1** amount, capacity, quantity, total. **2** book, publication. **3** loudness.
voluntary *adj* free, optional, unpaid, volunteer.
vomit *v* be sick, bring up, regurgitate, retch, spew up; (*Inf*) puke, throw up.
vote *n* ballot, election, franchise, poll, referendum, right to vote, show of hands, suffrage.
vote *v* ballot, cast one's vote, elect, go to the polls, opt, return.
vow *v* affirm, dedicate, devote, pledge, promise, swear.
vow *n* oath, pledge, promise.
voyage *n* crossing, cruise, journey, passage, travels, trip.
vulgar *adj* coarse, common, crude, dirty, gross, impolite, nasty, rude, tasteless.
vulnerable *adj* accessible, open to attack, susceptible, tender, thin-skinned, unprotected, weak.

Ww

wade *v* **1** ford, paddle, splash, walk through. **2** wade into attack, go for, launch oneself at, set about, tackle; (*Inf*) get stuck in, tear into.
wage *n* allowance, earnings, fee, pay, renumeration, reward.
wager *n* bet, flutter, gamble, pledge, punt, stake, venture.
wait *v* bide one's time, delay, hang fire, hold back, linger, mark time, pause, remain, rest, stand by, stay; (*Inf*) hold on.
wait *n* delay, hold-up, interval, pause, rest, stay.
wake *v* **1** awaken, come to, get up, rouse, stir. **2** activate, arouse, excite, fire, galvanize, kindle, stimulate, stir up.
wake *n* aftermath, backwash, path, trail.
walk *v* amble, go on foot, hike, march, move, ramble, saunter, stride, stroll, tramp, trek, trudge.
wall *n* **1** divider,, partition, screen. **2** barricade, fortification. **3** barrier, block, fence, hedge, obstacle, obstruction.
wallow *v* **1** lie, roll about, splash around, tumble. **2** flounder, lurch, stagger, stumble, wade. **3** bask, delight, glory, indulge oneself, luxuriate, relish, revel.
wand *n* baton, rod, sprig, stick.
wander *v* **1** drift, meander, ramble, straggle, stroll; (*Inf*) mooch around, traipse. **2** depart, deviate, diverge, get lost, swerve, veer. **3** babble, ramble, rave, talk nonsense.
wane *v* decline, decrease, die out, diminish, dwindle, ebb, fade away, subside, taper off, weaken, wind down, wither.
want *v* **1** covet, crave, desire, long for, need, pine for, wish, yearn for; (*Inf*) have a yen for. **2** be deficient in, be short of, be without, call for, demand, lack, miss, need, require.
want *n* **1** craving, desire, fancy, hunger, longing, need, thirst, wish; (*Inf*) yen. **2** lack, scarcity, shortage. **3** destitution, need, neediness, poverty.
war *n* armed conflict, battle, bloodshed, combat, conflict, contest, hostility, warfare.
war *v* battle, campaign against, carry on hostilities, clash, combat, conduct a war, contend, contest, fight, make war, strive, struggle, take up arms, wage war.
ward *n* **1** area, district, division, precinct, quarter, zone. **2** charge, dependant, minor, protégé, pupil. **3** care, custody, guardianship, protection, safekeeping.

Pearl Harbor, seen of one of the worst disasters of World War II, where 360 Japanese bombers attacked the US Navy prior to declaring war with America. Over 2,400 men died and more than 1,100 were injured in the attack on December 7, 1941.

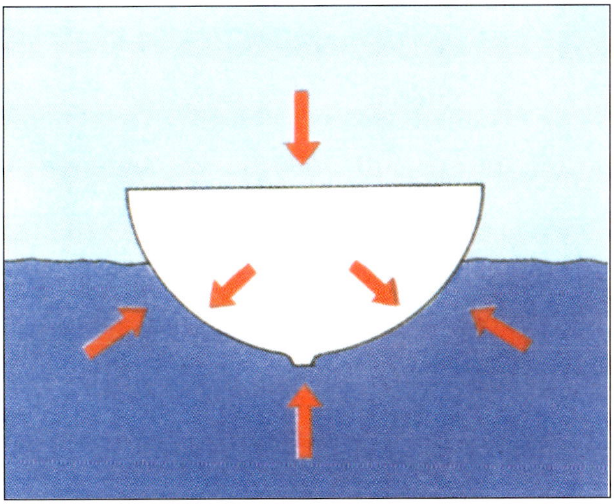

How do ships float in water?

Ships float in water because their overall density is less than that of the water that supports them. The water displaced (pushed aside) by the hull of the ship pushes back upwards with a force called upthrust or buoyancy. If this is equal to or greater than the force of gravity pulling the ship's mass downwards, the vessel will float.

wardrobe *n* **1** closet, clothes cupboard, clothes-press. **2** clothes, outfit.
warehouse *n* depository, depot, stockroom, store, storehouse.
warfare *n* armed conflict, armed struggle, battle, clash of arms, combat, conflict, fighting, hostilities, strategy, struggle, war.
warily *adv* cautiously, with care; (*Inf*) cagily.
warm *adj* **1** balmy, lukewarm, sunny, tepid. **2** friendly, happy, hospitable, loving, pleasant. **3** enthusiastic, excited, intense, keen, lively, passionate, spirited, stormy, vigorous.
warm *v* **1** heat, melt, thaw. **2** excite, interest, put some life into, rouse, stimulate; (*Inf*) get going, turn on.
warn *v* advise, forewarn, inform, notify, tip off.
warrant *n* assurance, guarantee, license, permission, permit, pledge, sanction.
warrant *v* **1** assure, certify, declare, guarantee, stand behind, vouch for. **2** approve, authorize, commission, demand, justify, permit, require, sanction.
warrior *n* champion, fighter, fighting man, soldier.
wary *adj* alert, attentive, careful, cautious, chary, circumspect, distrustful, guarded, heedful, mistrustful, observant, on one's guard, on the lookout, prudent, suspicious, vigilant, watchful, wide-awake; (*Inf*) cagey, leery.
wash *v* **1** bathe, clean, launder, moisten, rinse, scrub, shampoo, shower, wet. **2** carry off, move, sweep away, wash off. **3** be convincing, be plausible, hold up, stand up; (*Inf*) stick. **4** accept no responsibility for, give up on, have nothing to do with, leave to one's own devices.
wash *n* **1** ablution, bath, cleaning, laundering, rinse, shampoo, shower. **2** ebb and flow, roll, surge, sweep, swell, wave.
waste *v* **1** fritter away, lavish, misuse, squander, throw away; (*Inf*) blow. **2** consume, corrode, crumble, decay, decline, deplete, disable, drain, dwindle, eat away, fade, perish, sink, wither. **3** devastate, lay waste, pillage, ruin, spoil, wreak havoc upon.
waste *n* **1** extravagance, loss, lost opportunity, squandering. **2** destruction, devastation, havoc, ravage, ruin. **3** debris, dregs, leftovers, litter, refuse, rubbish, scrap, trash. **4** desert, solitude, void, wasteland, wild, wilderness.
waste *adj* **1** leftover, superfluous, unwanted. **2** bare, barren, desolate, dismal, dreary, empty, uninhabited, unproductive, wild.
wasteful *adj* extravagant, lavish, uneconomical.
watch *v* **1** gaze at, look, look at, observe, pay attention, peer at, see, stare at, view. **2** attend, be on the alert, be vigilant, be wary, be watchful, keep an eye open; (*Inf*) look out, take heed, wait. **3** guard, keep, look after, mind, protect, take care of, tend.
watch *n* **1** chronometer, clock, pocket watch, timepiece, wristwatch. **2** alertness, attention, eye, inspection, lookout, notice, observation, surveillance, vigil, vigilance, watchfulness.
watchful *adj* alert, attentive, guarded, on one's guard, on the lookout, suspicious, vigilant, wary, wide awake.
water *v* **1** dampen, drench, flood, hose, irrigate, moisten, soak, spray, sprinkle. **2** add water to, dilute, put water in, thin, water down, weaken.
waterfall *n* cascade, cataract, chute, fall.

watertight *adj* **1** sound, waterproof. **2** airtight, firm, foolproof.
watery *adj* **1** aqueous, damp, fluid, humid, liquid, marshy, moist, soggy, squelchy, wet. **2** diluted, flavourless, runny, tasteless, thin, washy, watered-down, waterish, weak; (*Inf*) wishy-washy.
wave *v* **1** flap, flourish, flutter, move to and fro, oscillate, ripple, shake, stir, sway, swing, wag, waver, wild. **2** beckon, direct, gesture, indicate, signal.
wave *n* **1** breaker, ridge, ripple, roller, surf, swell. **2** current, drift, flood, movement, outbreak, rash, rush, stream, surge, tendency, trend.
waver *v* **1** hesitate, swither; (*Inf*) blow hot and cold, shillyshally. **2** flicker, fluctuate, quiver, shake, sway, tremble, wobble.
way *n* **1** approach, method, mode, system, technique. **2** direction, path, road, route. **3** elbowroom, opening, room, space. **4** distance, journey, length, stretch, trail. **5** custom, manner, practice, style. **6** aspect, detail, feature, particular, point, respect, sense. **7 by the way** in passing. **8 give way** collapse, fall to pieces, subside. **9** back down, concede, withdraw. **10 under way** begun, in progress, moving, started; (*Inf*) on the go.
weak *adj* **1** delicate, fragile, frail, infirm, unsteady, wasted. **2** cowardly, indecisive, infirm, powerless, soft, spineless; (*Inf*) weak-kneed. **3** dull, faint, low, muffled, poor, quiet, slight, soft. **4** deficient, inadequate, lacking, poor, substandard, understrength. **5** pathetic, shallow, unsatisfactory. **6** defenceless, exposed, helpless, vulnerable, wide open. **7** diluted, runny, tasteless, thin, understrength, watery; (*Inf*) wishy-washy.
weaken *v* **1** decline, diminish, dwindle, fade. **2** adulterate, cut, debase, dilute, thin, thin out, water down.
weakness *n* **1** defect, fault, flaw, imperfection.
wealth *n* **1** affluence, fortune, money, prosperity, riches. **2** abundance, mass, plenty, profusion, store.
wealthy *adj* affluent, prosperous, rich, well-off, well-to-do; (*Inf*) filthy rich, in the money, loaded, made of money, quids in, rolling in it, stinking rich, well-heeled.
wear *v* **1** be dressed in, dress in, have on, put on, sport. **2** display, exhibit, fly, show. **3** become thin, fray, rub, use, wash away, waste. **4** be durable, last, stand up.
wear off *v* decrease, diminish, disappear, dwindle, ebb, fade, lose effect, lose strength, peter

Spiders belong to the class of arachnids, not insects. They are meat-eaters and weave a web in order to catch food, which can include other spiders.

A whirlpool is a rotary oceanic current, produced by the interaction of the rising and falling tides and has a central downdraft of swirling water called a vortex.

out, subside, wane, weaken.
wear out *v* **1** drain, exhaust, fray, use up, wear through. **2** fatigue, sap, tire, weary; *(Inf)* fag out, frazzle.
weary *adj* **1** drained, exhausted, flagging, jaded, tired, worn out; *(Inf)* all in, dead on one's feet, dead beat, dog tired, done in, whacked. **2** arduous, taxing, tiresome, tiring, wearing.
weather *n* **1** climate, conditions. **2 under the weather** ill, off-colour, out of sorts; *(Inf)* poorly, seedy, sick.
weather *v* **1** expose, season, toughen. **2** endure, get through, suffer, survive, withstand; *(Inf)* stick it out.
weave *v* **1** braid, interlace, intertwine, knit, plait, twist. **2** build, construct, create, fabricate, make up, put together. **3** crisscross, move in and out, weave one's way, wind, zigzag.
web *Inf* **1** cobweb, spider's web. **2** complex, knot, network, tangle, webbing.
weight *n* **1** burden, gravity, heaviness, load, mass. **2** ballast, heavy object, load, mass. **3** load, pressure, strain. **4** importance, influence, power, significance; *(Inf)* clout.
weird *adj* bizarre, odd, strange, supernatural; *(Inf)* creepy, far-out, spooky.
welcome *adj* acceptable, pleasing, wanted.
welcome *n* acceptance, greeting, reception, salutation.
welcome *v* accept gladly, greet, meet, offer hospitality to, receive, with open arms, roll out the red carpet for, usher in.
welfare *n* benefit, happiness, health, prosperity, wellbeing.
well *adv* expertly, proficiently, skillfully.
well *adj* able-bodied, fit, in good health, robust, strong,
well *n* **1** fountain, pool, source, spring, waterhole. **2** bore, hole, pit, shaft.
well-known *adj* famous, noted, popular, widely known.
well-off *adj* comfortable, flourishing, fortunate, lucky, successful, thriving.
wet *adj* **1** damp, humid, moist, soaking, waterlogged. **2** clammy, drizzling, humid, misty, pouring, raining, showery, teeming.
wet *n* condensation, damp, dampness, humidity, liquid, moisture, water, wetness.
wet *v* dampen, dip, drench, humidify, irrigate, moisten, saturate, soak, splash, sprinkle, steep, water.
wharf *v* dock, jetty, landing stage, pier, quay.
wheel *n* circle, pivot, revolution, roll, rotation, spin, turn.
wheeze *v* breathe roughly, catch one's breath, cough, gasp, hiss, rasp, whistle.
wheeze *n* idea, plan, scheme, stunt, trick.
whereabouts *n* location, position, site, situation.
whiff *n* aroma, blast, hint, puff, scent, smell, sniff.
whiff *v* breathe, inhale, puff, smell, smoke, sniff, waft.
whirl *v* **1** circle, gyrate, pirouette, pivot, revolve, roll, rotate, spin, swirl, turn, twirl, twist, wheel. **2** feel dizzy, reel, spin.
whirlpool *n* vortex.
whirlwind *n* tornado, waterspout; *(Inf)* dust devil.
whirlwind *adj* hasty, headlong, impetuous, impulsive, lightning, quick, rapid, rash, short, speedy, swift.
whisper *v* **1** breathe, murmur, say softly, utter under the breath. **2** gossip, hint, murmur,

spread rumours. **3** hiss, sigh.
white *adj* **1** ashen, bloodless, grey, pale, pasty. **2** grey, silver, snowy. **3** clean, immaculate, pure, spotless, unblemished.
whitewash *n* camouflage, cover-up, deception.
whole *adj* **1** complete, entire, full, total, uncut. **2** flawless, in one piece, intact, mint, perfect, undamaged. **3** able-bodied, fit, healthy, in good health, robust, strong, well.
whole *n* **1** all, everything, lot, sum total, the entire amount, total. **2** entirety, totality.
wholehearted *adj* committed, dedicated, determined, devoted, enthusiastic, genuine, sincere, true, unreserved.
wicked *adj* **1** bad, corrupt, scandalous, vile. **2** mischievous, naughty, roguish. **3** difficult, distressing, offensive, trying, unpleasant.
wide *adj* **1** ample, broad, comprehensive, expansive, far-reaching, general, immense, inclusive, large, sweeping, vast. **2** distant, off target, remote. **3** distended, expanded, fully open, outstretched. **4** ample, baggy, loose, roomy, spacious.
widespread *adj* broad, extensive, far-reaching, general, universal.
width *n* breadth, diameter, extent, girth, measure, range, reach, scope, span, thickness, wideness.

wield *v* **1** brandish, employ, handle, swing, use. **2** apply, command, control, exert, have, hold, manage, possess, utilize.
wild *adj* **1** feral, untamed. **2** free, native, natural. **3** desolate, uncultivated, unpopulated. **4** barbaric, ferocious, fierce, savage. **5** boisterous, chaotic, disorderly, rowdy, turbulent, unruly, wayward. **6** berserk, crazed, delirious, demented, excited, frenzied, hysterical, irrational, mad, raving.

Wind farm

A wind farm is a cluster of wind turbines (up to several hundred) erected in areas where there is a nearly steady prevalent wind. These propeller-type units are able to extract only a proportion of the kinetic energy. Their ability to produce electricity is controlled by the changeable patterns of the Earth's weather and the presence of strong winds.

wilderness *n* desert, jungle, waste, wasteland, wild.
will *n* **1** choice, decision, option. **2** last wishes, testament. **3** decree, desire, fancy, preference, wish. **4** aim, intention, resolve. **5** attitude, feeling.
willing *adj* agreeable, content, eager, enthusiastic, happy, in favour, in the mood, pleased, ready; (*Inf*) game.
will-power *n* determination, drive, grit, resolution, resolve, self-discipline, single-mindedness.
win *n* conquest, success, triumph, victory.
wind *n* **1** air-current, blast, breeze, draught, gust. **2** hot air, humbug, talk, verbalizing; (*Inf*) gab. **3** breath, puff. **4** about to happen, approaching, close at hand, coming, imminent, impending, in the offing, near, on the way; (*Inf*) on the cards.
wind *v* **1** coil, curl, spiral, turn around, twine, twist. **2** bend, curve, meander, ramble, snake, turn, zigzag.
windfall *n* bonanza, jackpot, stroke of luck.
wind up *v* close down, conclude, end, finish, terminate, wrap up; (*Inf*) tie up the loose ends.
windy *adj* blowy, blustery, breezy, gusty, squally, stormy, wild, windswept.
winner *n* champion, conquering hero, conqueror, first, master, vanquisher, victor; (*Inf*) champ.

wintry *adj* **1** chilly, cold, frosty, frozen, icy, snowy. **2** bleak, cheerless, cold, desolate, dismal.
wipe out *v* annihilate, blot out, destroy, eradicate, exterminate, massacre, obliterate.
wire *n* cable, flex, lead.
wise *adj* clever, intelligent, perceptive, well-informed.
wit *n* **1** fun, humour. **2** brains, common sense, intellect, reason, sense, wisdom.
withdraw *n* **1** draw back, pull out, remove, take away. **2** depart, drop out, fall back, go, leave, pull back, retire, retreat; (*Inf*) make oneself scarce.
wither *v* decay, decline, fade, perish, shrivel, wilt.
witness *n* **1** bystander, eye-witness, observer, onlooker, spectator, viewer. **2** testifier. **3** give evidence, give testimony, testify. **4** bear out, be proof of, confirm, corroborate, prove, show, vouch for.
witty *adj* amusing, brilliant, clever, droll, funny.
wonder *n* **1** amazement, awe, fascination, surprise. **2** curiosity, marvel, miracle, phenomenon, prodigy, sight, spectacle.
wonder *v* **1** doubt, inquire, puzzle, question, speculate. **2** be amazed, be astonished, marvel, stare; (*Inf*) be flabbergasted, boggle, gawk.
wood *n* **1** logs, planks, timber. **2** forest, woods.
wooden *adj* **1** awkward, clumsy. rigid, stiff. **2** empty, lifeless. **3** dense, slow, stupid, thick.
woolly *adj* **1** fleecy, shaggy. **2** blurred, clouded, confused, foggy, fuzzy, hazy, indistinct, muddled, vague.
word *n* **1** chat, discussion, talk, tête-à-tête; (*Inf*) chit-chat, confab, pow-wow. **2** comment, declaration, expression, remark. **3** name, term. **4** account, advice, bulletin, communication, communiqué, dispatch, message, news, report; (*Inf*) gen, low-down. **5** command, green light, order, signal. **6** go-ahead, oath, promise, solemn oath, solemn word, undertaking, word of honour; (*Inf*) green light. **7** command, decree, edict, mandate, will. **8** countersign, password, slogan, watchword.
word *v* couch, express, phrase, put, say, state, utter.
words *pl n* **1** lyrics, text. **2** angry exchange, argument, bickering, disagreement, dispute, quarrel, row; (*Inf*) barney, falling out, run-in, set-to, squabble.
work *n* **1** drudgery, exertion, industry, labour, slog, sweat, toil; (*Inf*) elbow grease, grind. **2** business, calling, craft, duty, employment, job, livelihood, occupation, office, profession, piursuit, trade. **3** assignment, chore, commission, duty, stint, task, undertaking. **4** achievement, composition, creation, handiwork, performance, piece, production. **5** art, craft, skill, workmanship. **6 out of work** idle, jobless. out of a job, unemployed; (*Inf*) on the dole.
work *v* **1** drudge, exert oneself, labour, slave, slog away, sweat, toil. **2** be employed, be in work, earn a living, have a job. **3** direct, manage, operate, use, wield. **4** cultivate, dig, farm, till.
worker *n* craftsman, employee, hand, labourer, tradesman, wage earner, working man, working woman, workman.
working *n* **1** action, functioning, manner, method. **2** excavations, mine, pit, quarry, shaft.
working *adj* **1** active, employed, in a job, in work, labouring. **2** functioning, going, operative, running. **3** effective, practical,

Athletes often use videotape during their work-outs to study their overall performance, particularly in fast-moving sports. They are able to check for errors and so improve their technique.

useful, viable.

work out *v* **1** accomplish, achieve, attain, win. **2** calculate, clear up, figure out, find out, puzzle out, solve. **3** arrange, construct, contrive, develop, devise, elaborate, evolve, form, formulate, plan, put together. **4** be effective, flourish, go as planned, go well, prosper, prove satisfactory, succeed. **5** add up to, come to, reach, reach a total of.

work-out *n* **1** drill, physical exercise, training. **2** aerobics, exercises, gymnastics. **3** training session.

works *pl n* **1** factory, mill, plant, shop, workshop. **2** productions, writings. **3** mechanism, moving parts, workings; (*Inf*) guts, innards, insides.

workshop *n* factory, mill, plant, shop, studio, workroom, works.

work up *v* agitate, animate, arouse, excite, incite, inflame, instigate, move, rouse, spur, stir up; (*Inf*) wind up.

world *n* **1** earth, mundane, physical, terrestrial. **2** grasping, greedy, materialistic, selfish. **3** blasé, experienced, knowing, sophisticated, worldly-wise.

worldwide *adj* global, international, universal.

worn *adj* **1** frayed, ragged, shabby, tattered, tatty, threadbare. **2** exhausted, jaded, spent, tired, wearied, weary, worn-out; (*Inf*) played-out.

worried *adj* afraid, anxious, apprehansive, concerned, distracted, distressed, disturbed, fearful, fretful, ill at ease, nervous, on edge, perturbed, tense, uneasy, upset.

worry *v* agonize, annoy, badger, bother, disturb, disturb, irritate, make anxious, perturb, pester, plague, tantalize, tease, torment; (*Inf*) hassle.

worry *n* annoyance, care, irritation, pest, plague, problem, trouble.

worsen *v* damage, decay, decline, degenerate, deteriorate, get worse, go from bad to worse, take a turn for the worse; (*Inf*) go downhill.

worship *v* adore honour, idolize, love, praise, respect, revere.

worst *v* beat, best, conquer, rush, defeat, gain the advantage over, get the better of, master, overcome, overpower, overthrow, subdue.

worth *n* **1** benefit, goodness, help, importance, merit, quality, virtue. **2** cost, price, rate, value.

worthless *n* futile, ineffectual, miserable, pointless, poor, trashy, trifling, useless, wretched.

worthwhile *adj* beneficial, good, helpful, useful, valuable.

Germany received worldwide condemnation during the blitz of London in World War II.

St Paul's Cathedral avoided serious damage despite the bombing of buildings all around it.

Wrestling is a body contact sport, where the object is to force your opponent to touch the ground with some part of his body other than his feet; usually forcing down on his back and holding him there for a minimum length of time.

worthy *adj* commendable, creditable, decent, dependable, deserving, excellent, good, honest, reliable, respectable, valuable, virtuous, worthwhile.
worthy *n* dignitary, luminary, notable; (*Inf*) big shot, big wig.
wound *n* **1** cut, gash, harm, hurt, injury, laceration. **2** distress, grief, pain, pang, sense of loss, shock, slight, torment, torture, trauma.
wound *v* **1** cut, damage, hurt, injure, irritate, lacerate, pierce, slash, wing. **2** annoy, distress, hurt the feelings of, offend, pain, shock, sting, traumatize.
wrangle *v* altercate, argue, bicker, brawl, contend, disagree, dispute, fight, quarrel, row, scrap, squabble; (*Inf*) fall-out.
wrangle *n* altercation, angry exchange, bickering, clash, contest, controversy, dispute, quarrel, row, squabble, tiff; (*Inf*) argy-bargy, barney, falling out, set-to, slanging match.
wrap *v* absorb, bind, cover, encase, enclose, envelop, fold, package, roll up, shroud, swathe, wind.
wrapper *n* case, cover, envelope, jacket, packaging, paper, sheath, sleeve, wrapping.
wrath *n* anger, exasperation, fury, indignaiton, irritation, passion, rage, resentment, temper.
wreath *n* band, coronet, crown, festoon, garland, loop, ring.
wreck *v* **1** adorn, break, dash to pieces, demolish, destroy, devastate, mar, play havoc with, ravage, ruin, shatter, smash, spoil. **2** founder, go aground, run onto the rocks, shipwreck, strand.
wreck *n* derelict, hulk, shipwreck, sunken vessel.
wreckage *n* debris, fragments, hulk, pieces, remains, rubble, ruin, wreck.
wrench *v* **1** force, jerk, pull, rip, tear, tug, twist, wring, yank. **2** ache, blow, distort, pain, rick, sprain, strain.
wrench *n* **1** jerk, pull, rip, tug, twist. **2** ache, blow, pain, pang, shock, upheaval, uprooting.
wrest *v* **1** force, pull, strain, twist, wrench, wring.
wrestle *v* battle, combat, fight, grapple, scuffle, struggle, tussle.
wretch *n* outcast, rascal, rogue, ruffian, scoundrel, swine, villain; (*Inf*) rat, rotter.
wretched *adj* **1** brokenhearted, dejected, depressed, distressed, miserable, pathetic, unhappy, worthless. **2** deplorable, inferior, miserable, poor.
wriggle *v* **1** jerk, jiggle, squirm, twist and turn, wag, wiggle,

worm, writhe. **2** crawl, slink, snake, twist and turn, worm, zigzag **3** crawl, dodge, extricate oneself, manoeuvre, sneak, talk one's way out, worm.

wring *v* **1** extort, extract, force, screw, squeeze, twist, wrench. **2** distress, hurt, lacerate, pain, pierce, rack, rend, stab, tear at, wound.

wrinkle *n* corrugation, crease, crinkle, crow's feet, crumple, fold, furrow, gather, line, pucker, ruck, rumple.

writ *n* court order, decree, document, summons.

write *v* commit to paper, compose, copy, correspond, create, dash off, draft, draw up, inscribe, jot down, list, put down in black and white, put in writing, record, scribble, set down, take down, tell, transcribe; (*Inf*) drop a line.

write-off *n* **1** annual, cancel, cross out, disregard, forget about, give up for lost, score out, shelve, wipe out. **2** crash, damage beyond repair, demolish, destroy, smash up, wreck; (*Inf*) total.

writer *n* author, biographer, novelist, poet, reporter, scriptwriter, wordsmith.

writhe *v* contort, distort, jerk, squirm, struggle, thrash, thrsh, toss, twist, wiggle, wriggle.

writing *n* **1** calligraphy, hand-writing, print, scrawl, scribble. **2** book, composition, document, letter, opus, publication, work.

wrong *adj* **1** false, faulty, inaccurate, incorrect, in error, mistaken, off target, out, untrue, wide of the mark; (*Inf*) off-beam. **2** bad, criminal, crooked, dishonest, evil, felonious, illegal, illicit, immoral, unethical, unfair, unjust, unlawful, wicked. **3** funny, improper, incorrect, unacceptable, unfitting, unhappy, unsuitable. **4** defective, faulty, not working, out of commission, out of order. **5** opposite, reverse.

wrong *adv* **1** amiss, askew, inaccurately, incorrectly, mistakenly, wrongly. **2 go wrong** come to nothing, fail, fall through, miscarry, misfire; (*Inf*) come to grief, flop. **3** err, go astray, make a mistake; (*Inf*) boob, slip up. **4** break down, cease to function, fail, malfunction, misfire; (*Inf*) conk out, go kaput, go on the blink, go phut. **5** fall from grace, go astray, lapse, sin; (*Inf*) go off the straight and narrow.

wrong *n* abuse, crime, error, evil deed, dishonesty, grievance, immorality, injustice, misdeed, offense, sin, trespass, unfairness, wickedness.

wrong *v* abuse, cheat, discredit, dishonour, harm, hurt, ill-treat, ill-use, impose upon, injure, malign, mistreat.

wrongdoer *n* criminal, culprit, delinquent, felon, law breaker, offender, sinner, villain.

wrongful *adj* balmeworthy, criminal, dishonest, evil, illegal, illegitimate, illicit, immoral, improper, unethical, unjust, unlawful, wicked.

wry *adj* **1** askew, awry, contorted, crooked, deformed, distorted, lopsided, off the level, twisted, uneven, warped. **2** droll, dry, humorous, ironic, mocking, sarcastic, sardonic, witty.

Calligraphy derives its name from the Greek words *kallos* (beauty) and *graphe* (writing) and means literally 'beautiful handwriting'. The example above was written in Latin between 974–986 c. AD and contains writing in gold, black and red inks.

Xx

Yy

Zz

xerox *v* copy, duplicate, photocopy, reproduce.
X-rays *n* image, radiogram, radiograph.
xylograph *n* cut, woodcut, wood engraving.

X-ray equipment is not just used for taking images of the inside of the human body. Images are also taken for security purposes at airports and customs points of items such as suitcases and hand luggage.

yank *v* jerk, pull, tug, wrench.
yap *v* bark, cry, yelp.
yard *n* compound, courtyard, enclosure, garden.
yardstick *n* guideline, measure, model, pattern, scale, standard.
yarn *n* **1** fibre, strand, thread. **2** story, tale; (*Inf*) cock-and-bull story, tall story.
yearly *adj* annual, every year, once a year.
yearn *v* crave, desire, fancy, long, want, wish for.
yell *v* bawl, cry out, howl, roar, scream, screech, shout, shriek, squeal, whoop; (*Inf*) holler.
yell *n* cry, howl, scream, screech, shout, shriek, squeal, whoop; (*Inf*) holler.
yelp *v* bark, howl, yap.
yes *adv* all right, certainly, sure.
yield *n* crop, harvest, income, produce, profit, return, takings.
yield *v* **1** bear, provide, supply. **2** bring in, earn, fetch, generate. **3** abandon, give in, give way, submit, surrender; (*Inf*) cave in, throw in the towel.
young *adj* **1** adolescent, infant, junior, juvenile. **2** fledgling.
young *n* **1** family. **2** babies, little ones.
youngster *n* boy, cub, girl, teenager, youth; (*Inf*) kid, pup.
youth *n* **1** adolescence, boyhood. **2** adolescent, boy, lad, teenager, young man, youngster; (*Inf*) kid.

Young kittens display typical curiosity about their surroundings.

zany *adj* comical, crazy, funny.
zeal *n* enthusiasm, passion.
zenith *n* apex, climax, crowning point, pinnacle, summit, top, vertex.
zero *n* **1** naught, nil, nothing, nought; (*Inf*) zilch. **2** lowest point, nadir, rock bottom.
zest *n* appetite, enjoyment, enthusiasm, relish, vigour, zeal; (*Inf*) oomph. **3** flavour, relish, savour, smack, spice, tang, taste; (*Inf*) kick.
zip *n* eagerness, life, liveliness, pep.
zip *v* dash, fly, hasten, hurry, rush, scurry, shoot, speed, tear; (*Inf*) hare, whiz, zoom.
zodiac *n* signs of: aquarius, pisces, aries, taurus, gemini, cancer, leo, virgo, libra, scorpio, sagittarius, capricorn.
zone *n* area, belt, district, province, region, section, sector, sphere
zoom *v* buzz, fly; dash, hurry, pelt, race.